Three Boys Missing

Three Boys Missing

The Tragedy That Exposed The Pedophilia Underworld

James A. Jack

HPH Publishing
Chicago, IL

First edition: October 9, 2006

Copyright © 1998 James A. Jack

Cover Illustration by Dave Mikulskis and Ania Kitka

Publisher's Cataloging-in-Publication Data

Jack, James A.
  Three Boys Missing : the tragedy that exposed the pedophilia underworld/ James A. Jack.
    p. cm.
    Includes index.
    ISBN 0-9776281-4-0
    ISBN 13 9780977628148

1. Murder Illinois Chicago Case studies. 2. Children Crimes Against Illinois Chicago case studies. 3. Cold Case (Criminal Investigation) Illinois Chicago Case Studies. 4. Child Molestation I. Title.

HV6534. C4 J12 2006
364.152/30977311--dc22
2006929299

HPH Publishing,
333 West North Avenue
Suite 289
Chicago, IL 60610

Printed in Canada

*This book
is dedicated to the
men and women of the
Chicago Police Department
who worked tiredlessly to solve the
Schuessler-Peterson murders
and to
John and Anton Schuessler
and Robert Peterson*

May you rest in peace

Contents

Three Boys Missing

The Crime

Sunday
October 16, 1955
11:05 p.m.

My partner and I were at the end of our shift. We drove along Milwaukee Avenue, a street that cuts across Chicago in a northwest direction from just beyond downtown to the city limits.

It was raining, and as a result, there wasn't much traffic. Most of the businesses in the area were closed for the day. Though it was quiet, especially on days like this, Frank Czech and I liked working this shift. We could get around the District without much trouble and it was easy to find suspects and witnesses home on Sunday night.

For the past few hours, we ran down leads on new cases and were now headed back to the station. The rain came down hard, and I had trouble seeing much farther than one or two car lengths ahead of me. I slowed the car down to barely a crawl.

"Let 'em know we're going back to the station, Frank. Nothing's going on out here."

I leaned toward the steering wheel and stared through the windshield as heavy sheets of rain smeared against the glass. Frank was gazing out the passenger's side window and chewing slowly on the end of an El Producto cigar clenched in his mouth.

We traveled north, passing scores of small retail businesses, which lined the street. We cruised past the Sears Department Store, a currency exchange, clothing stores, and corner taverns. Bright blue neon signs advertising "Pabst Blue Ribbon" and "Blatz Beer" spread soft halos of light around the small windows of the neighborhood bars. The marquee of the Portage Theater had been dark for over an hour, and the only other places still open were a couple of bowling alleys not far from the movie theater.

As our car drove by Schuleman Lanes, I noticed a few brave "kegglers" dash out of the building's front entrance to meet their rides at the curb. The other bowlers waited inside, keeping out of the rain.

Frank turned his head away from the window, reached for the handset and brought the black metal microphone close to his face. He squeezed the "SEND" button.

"Yeah…this is 19. We're coming back. Got anything for us?" He released the button with a quick snap. The sharp, high-pitched hiss that shot out of the speaker filled the car with the sound of static. It stopped after a second, and we heard a familiar voice. It was the desk sergeant, Sgt. Petz.

"Okay, come on in. Not much going on here, either."

We could barely hear above the static and clacking of the wiper blades sweeping across the windshield.

Frank looked over at me, as I focused my attention on the dimly lit taillights of the pick-up truck ahead. Sheets of rain continued to slap down on the hood of the car.

"Hey, Frank," I said, "weather like this usually keeps the bad guys at home."

"Don't say that. Now we'll get a 'domestic call,' Jim. Then you can spend an hour with the happy couple, trying to calm them down right after you drop me off." Frank had already put in fifteen years with the Department and believed in what some people might say is superstition. Most cops call it experience.

"What's the matter? Don't you like police work?" I said sarcastically, knowing he'd laugh at my wisecrack.

Soon, we reached the intersection of Milwaukee Avenue and Gale Street. I made a soft left turn and drove past the Masonic Temple, past the front entrance of the District station, and made a quick right onto the side street next to a gray stone building. I eased the car into one of the parking spaces and cut the engine.

The rain had let up and became a soft drizzle as we quickly moved into the station.

The 33rd District of the Chicago Police Department was known as the Gale Street Station. People often referred to police stations by the name of the street on which they were located. Like the Maxwell Street, Shakespeare Avenue, and Foster Avenue stations, each District's daily activities and calls for assistance reflected the demographics of the community.

Gale Street was in a middle-class neighborhood of Chicago named Jefferson Park. An area of single-family homes with carefully hedged lawns and tree-lined streets, it was a community where many of the city's police and fire department employees lived. City employees were required to live within its limits. Those who could afford it lived in Jefferson Park.

It had a reputation for having the lowest crime rate in the city, occasional burglaries, some stolen autos, problems with juvenile delinquents, but very few homicides. The station was built in the 1930s, and its exterior was a combination of Roman governmental architecture and Depression era utility.

Not quite a full two stories in height, its light gray stone exterior made it look like a fortress. The front entrance had heavy, brown double doors that opened into a small foyer. A flight of six marble stairs led up to another set of doors. Just beyond was the front desk, which ran the length of the reception area, and off to the right was the Commander's Office.

A uniformed police sergeant was stationed behind the desk at all times, taking phone calls, logging them in, and greeting every person entering the station. Tonight, Sgt. Petz was on duty.

The reception area also served as the assembly room, where each shift was briefed and where individual assignments were given. At the far end of the reception area was a door that opened into a long, narrow hallway. On the right side were three small offices used by detectives. On the left side was the barred door of the station's lock-up, which had holding cells for prisoners awaiting interrogation or transfer to police headquarters.

Frank and I walked up the stairs and strode into the reception area. At the desk was a man in his thirties. His face was tense, his clothes were wet, and his gaze was fixed. He held a crumpled paper cup in his hand.

Petz looked up quickly in our direction and caught my attention. He gave a quick nod then reached for the telephone and began dialing while asking the man questions.

I stopped before reaching the hallway door and turned to look again at the man. Just then, Petz glanced up and saw me looking in his direction.

"Hey, Jim. Would you speak with this gentleman? I have to make a few phone calls to some movie theaters." Petz began to dial the phone again.

"Go ahead and start the reports, Frank. I'll be back there in minute," I said over my shoulder as I walked away.

The man was wearing a short, dark jacket with large, white, diamond-shaped designs on its front. It was zipped to the top. His shoes, pants, and the collar of his shirt were all wet. Obviously, he had been out in the rain for some time.

"I'm Detective James Jack," I said. I didn't offer to shake the man's hand. Every gesture, look, and word I spoke in a situation like that was deliberate and had a purpose.

"I'm Malcolm Peterson," the man responded as he shivered from the cold rain.

"My wife called at about 10:00 tonight. The officer on the phone—I think it was Sgt. Petz—told her that if she didn't hear from my son I should come to the station."

At the mention of his name, Petz looked at me, nodded in agreement, then began to flip through the phone book again.

I looked over at the clock on the wall. It was 11:15 p.m. Peterson caught my eyes and turned to look as well. He let out a barely audible sigh.

"I couldn't stay home and wait any longer. I needed to do something…make a report or talk to somebody. My son never does this. Stay out late, I mean. My wife and I are really worried. Please, can you help us?" As he spoke, he tightened his grip on the cup, his jaws narrowed, and his eyes looked tense.

"Let's go to my office." I pointed across the reception room. "Can I get you more water?"

Noticing the crumpled cup, he nodded.

I walked to the water cooler, filled it, then motioned in the direction of my office.

We walked through the door and down the hallway, passing several offices. The first office belonged to Detective Sergeant George Murphy, the supervisor of detectives. Being the supervisor, he usually didn't work the weekend shift, so tonight his office was empty. The remaining offices were used by the detectives. My partner and I sat in the last of the three offices.

As we walked through the hall, short, sharp clacking noises filled the space. Frank sat punching the keys of an Underwood typewriter using both index fingers. Our desks, only two feet apart, were covered with loose papers, file folders, telephones, and ashtrays filled with unfiltered cigarette and cigar butts.

"Mr. Peterson, this is my partner Detective Frank Czech."

Frank looked up from the burglary report sandwiched between two black rollers. His unlit El Producto cigar was still clenched between his teeth. He gestured with a quick nod then began to punch the keys again.

"Have a seat," I said, pointing to the chair and moving a pile of brown manila folders from one side of the desk to the other. I took off my overcoat, hung it on the coat rack, and sat down at my desk.

I pulled a pad from the drawer and took a pen from my suit pocket.

"Now, let's start at the beginning. What's your boy's name?"

"Robert."

"How old is he?"

"He's 13," Peterson replied, again beginning to crumple the paper cup in his hand.

I wrote the name and age on the note pad, put my pen down, and sat back in my chair to look at Mr. Peterson.

"When did you last see Robert?"

"About 3:30 this afternoon. He left with John Schuessler, a classmate, and John's younger brother, Anton. They live a few blocks away." He paused and looked straight at me. "Can you help us? We're really worried. This has never happened before."

I pushed my chair back a few inches and pulled out a form with the words "Missing Persons Report-CPD Form 867" across the top in heavy, black letters.

"This is just routine, Mr. Peterson. We fill this out whenever somebody's reported missing. Could you give me your address?"

I wrote down the information and completed the form, being careful to include the date and time of Mr. Peterson's arrival at the station, as well as the time of the initial phone call. After signing my name at the bottom, I put my pen down and started to ask a few more questions.

"What were you talking to Sgt. Petz about when I walked in?"

"The boys went downtown to a movie, a Walt Disney movie. When they didn't come home, my wife and I started to worry. My wife thought maybe the boys spent all their money and were walking home. Then Dorothy, my wife, she got a call from Mrs. Schuessler, the mother of Robert's friends. Dorothy said Mrs. Schuessler sounded like a nervous wreck. I told her I would drive over, pick up Mr. Schuessler, and go look for the boys.

"We looked in all the hamburger places on Milwaukee Avenue. Since it was raining out, I thought maybe they stopped until the rain let up. We even drove downtown, but the theater was closed…the one that had the Disney movie, the Loop Theater." Mr. Peterson stopped talking. The paper cup was now completely crumpled. He was still trembling, from the rain and the fear that began to betray his emotions.

"Have you heard from any of Robert's other friends?" I asked. "Do you know if anyone else went with them to the movie?"

The clacking of the typewriter stopped. Frank looked in our direction and waited for the answer.

"We called everybody we know. No one's seen them since this afternoon. My wife's really worried. And Mr. and Mrs. Schuessler… they're sick about this. When I dropped Mr. Schuessler off, he looked like he was going to have a heart attack. I thought it would be better if I came here by myself." He crumpled the paper cup into a ball and held it tightly in his hand.

"What were the boys wearing?" I kept my voice calm and tried to keep Mr. Peterson focused on facts and specific information that could help us.

"Robert had on a White Sox jacket, with the emblem on it. I can't remember what...oh, wait. The boys—the Schuessler brothers—they both had on Cubs jackets.

"Is there anything else we can do right now, detective." He glanced at the clock on the wall. It was approaching 11:30 p.m.

I began to feel personally involved in the interview. This guy was really worried. He didn't seem like a lot of the parents who reported their kids missing. Very often, after a kid had been out all night, the parents would finally come into the station the next day and make out a report. Most of the time the parents would find out that the kid had stayed overnight with a friend. Things usually turned out all right.

Police officers know that if a kid had a background of trouble, his parents sometimes got used to it. They'd been through it before. Some parents even had a bad attitude when they finally reported their son or daughter missing, like it was the police department's job to know where the kid was or why he hadn't come home.

Peterson hadn't waited all night to do something. He called the station, went out looking for the kids with the other father, and drove all the way downtown and back. Now here he was at the police station, so nervous and tense that he had unknowingly destroyed two paper cups.

He was polite and seemed almost apologetic about having to inconvenience us with his concerns. We could see the worry on his face, how tense he was during the interview, and hear the sincerity in his voice.

I pushed my chair back and stood up.

"Mr. Peterson, my partner and I are going to tour the area up and down Milwaukee Avenue. We'll check out a few more restaurants and bus stops. We'll see what we can do tonight. It was raining pretty heavily out there, and they might have ducked into a place that's open late, or even gone into an apartment building entrance to wait until it stops."

As I tried to reassure Mr. Peterson, I calculated the distance to downtown, the time it would take to walk, the approximate time the movie might have ended, and the chances the boys were walking home.

I also calculated the chances these boys had ever been home this late before, at least without calling their parents. No, I thought, these boys weren't the type to worry their parents. Now I started to wonder where they could be. But I kept that thought to myself.

Frank edged to my desk. He leaned over, picked up the note pad, and looked over the information.

"My partner is right. We were just out there. The boys are probably just waiting for the rain to let up." Frank and I had been partners long enough to read each other's minds on things like this. He was backing me up.

Going to the coat rack, he pulled his coat from the hook then grabbed the one next to it and tossed it to me.

It was 11:30 p.m., and our shift was almost over. But we knew going out to look for the boys was what we should do.

"Mr. Peterson, is there anything else you can think of right now?" I asked as we reached the hallway leading to the front of the station.

"No, I told you everything I know. I'm going to call home and tell my wife that you'll be looking for them and have her call the Schuesslers. I'm going to stay out a while longer and keep looking."

I nodded to indicate that I understood. "If you hear something, call Sgt. Petz at the front desk. I'll tell the detectives and the uniformed officers on the next shift to keep an eye out as well."

When we reached the front desk, Petz was still making phone calls.

"Any luck?"

He shook his head. "Most of the movie theaters are closed. The ones I got through to didn't remember seeing any young kids that fit their description."

"Petz, Mr. Peterson needs to use your phone for a minute. He's going to call his wife. We'll be in Car 19 looking for them. Let us know if anything comes up."

I'm still haunted by the frantic look on Mr. Peterson's face. He pleaded for help in finding his son and his friends. Yet even as his voice betrayed his fear and his body trembled, he thanked us.

As we left, he reached across the desk for the telephone and slowly began to make his call home.

Frank and I walked down the flight of stairs leading from the reception room to the front doors of the police station. It had begun to rain again, so we dashed from the entrance to the car. Frank got behind the wheel as I flipped on the police radio.

"Frank, let's drive north and start near the boys' homes. Then we can work our way south down Milwaukee Avenue and criss-cross the side streets." I reached down and grabbed the radio mike, hit the metal "SEND" button, and informed the dispatcher that we were in Car 19 and taking an hour beyond our shift to check on a missing person's report.

Frank left the station heading northbound on Milwaukee Avenue. After driving for about a block, he brought the car to a stop under the viaduct for the Chicago and Northwestern train tracks. He switched on the searchlight, then slowly, he turned it to his left, then his right.

The bright beam of the searchlight flooded the southbound lanes of Milwaukee Avenue, moved up the sidewalk, and against the wall of the underpass. It swept across the street in front of the car and lit up the sidewalk to our right.

"Never know," he said after he was sure that no one was standing under the viaduct. "They could be right under our noses."

He turned off the searchlight and drove slowly under the viaduct while continuing to look left and right. Satisfied nothing was there, he continued north.

We drove past bus stops and apartment buildings, slowing down to ensure we could make out figures in the dark. Nothing. The car's tires hissed as we drove through lakes of water accumulating on the side streets. Nothing came over the radio.

Finally, I called the station to see if any information had been received. Again nothing.

We returned at 12:30 a.m. and informed the detectives and uniformed officers on the next shift about the missing boys. I gave them the paperwork and descriptions, instructed them to place the information on the police Teletype, and told them to periodically check with the front desk in case news about them came in.

As I drove home, I thought about what Mr. Peterson reported to Frank and me only a few hours earlier. Thoughtfully, I began to put what little information we had through my own deductive processes.

Three boys were missing. They had gone downtown to a movie and were expected to return home that evening, at the latest by 8:00 p.m. No one reported hearing from or seeing them since they left the Peterson home at 3:30 Sunday afternoon. It was unusual for these boys to be late getting home. They hadn't called their parents to tell them they would be late. They had a total of four dollars among them for bus fare and admission to the movie. Maybe they had bought some popcorn and candy.

It was about five miles from downtown Chicago to their homes: a three- or four-hour walk, minimum, in good weather. Stops to keep out of the rain. No money to call home or take the bus.

Okay, I thought, it was still possible they were coming home.

But I knew that it just didn't click, didn't fit with what I had observed of Mr. Peterson. He seemed like a good father. It was probably the only time in his life the poor guy had been inside a police station. From what Mr. Peterson told Frank and me, these boys had no reports of prior involvement with the police. Never ran away from home, no trouble in school. Mr. Peterson was genuinely worried about these boys. So was I.

Monday
October 17, 1955
9:15 a.m.

I looked at the time and shook my head. By this time of the day I was usually showered, dressed, and eating breakfast while reading the morning paper. But I hadn't been able to sleep. I couldn't stop thinking about my interview with Mr. Peterson the night before. Too many things just didn't add up.

As I got up from the bed, I held the receiver of the phone tightly against my ear, while pulling back the bedroom curtains. There weren't many cars parked on the street at this time of the day, and the only person I saw was the mailman walking toward my neighbor's house.

"Murph, this is Jim. Frank and I wrote up a "Missing Persons" on three boys last night, and we drove around after our shift looking for them. I put the paperwork on your desk before we signed out. Did you get to look at it?"

"Jim, I know all about it. I read your report. We put out a message on the Teletype at about 12:30 this morning."

I spoke loudly into the phone to compensate for the noise at Murphy's end of the line. "No news, then?"

"No, Jim. I told all of my guys to keep a lookout and gave them the descriptions. I also had the uniform officers pick up the same information this morning before they hit the streets."

"Sarge, I don't like this."

"Neither do I, Jim. Listen, could you come in early today. I'll call Frank and get him down here, too. I want to talk to you guys about this."

"Sure, Murph. No problem. Soon as I can, I'll be right there."

I couldn't recall a case since being assigned to the District where a young kid didn't turn up after he was reported missing. Older teenagers sometimes left town and headed someplace like California. Or had gotten arrested someplace and a few days later the district got an inquiry from a sheriff in Wisconsin about a kid they were holding up there.

But three kids? Young kids who weren't even out of grade school? It didn't feel right to me. Something was wrong. I kept trying to think of all the reasons why I shouldn't feel that way, but the gnawing in my stomach wouldn't subside no matter how much I tried to find a reasonable explanation.

I got dressed and headed out the back door toward the garage. It was warm for October, but I still wore a gray suit with matching tie under my heavy wool coat that I always put on by force of habit. My partner Frank and I were known around the Department as the "dapper duo," always wearing well-pressed suits, sharp ties, and gray fedoras whenever we hit the streets.

I got to the station at 10:05 a.m.—two hours into the day shift. Sgt. Nelson was covering the front desk. I walked past him and toward the detectives' offices at the back of the station. As soon as I entered the hallway, I heard voices coming from my office.

I walked in and saw that in addition to Murphy and Frank, Detectives Fred Koeppe and Frank Schulze were also present. They had been held over from the midnight shift. Right next to them, seated at Frank's desk, was Captain Russell Corcoran, Commander of the 33rd Police District. Their presence confirmed what I had been feeling for the past eleven hours. The Captain didn't come into our office just to have coffee.

"Morning, Jim. I'm glad you and Czech could come in early." Captain Corcoran looked up from the desk and waived the Missing Person's File. "I know there's not much to go on yet, but the Commissioner called me first thing this morning. I tried to tell him we're on top of this and that these kids will probably turn up after spending the night at the bus station or something. But he must have gotten a call from somebody, maybe the Alderman or the Ward Committeeman out here. He wants us to pull out all the stops and find these kids now."

He went on to say that Commissioner Timothy O'Connor had told the Captain that he would make additional manpower and resources available if the District needed it.

Murphy walked toward the file cabinet at the far end of the detectives' office. He leaned his back against it and crossed his arms. As the "bull dick" in charge of all of the detectives assigned to the 33rd District, he had been with the Department longer than anybody in the room, including the Captain. Like the Captain, he was tough but fair, meticulous and demanding. Every detective who worked with these men respected them and knew that they never asked any detective under their command to do anything they hadn't done themselves.

"We started the search this morning at seven o'clock." Murphy said. "As he just told you, Captain Corcoran has been put in charge of the search. Everyone in the District will join in, including the uniformed officers. The area will be divided into two parts. Today's search will be concentrated from Foster Avenue to the city limits up north, and from Cicero Avenue to the western limits of the city. This includes the forest preserves north of Foster Avenue all the way up to and including Caldwell Woods. If we don't find the boys, we'll expand the search tomorrow and cover the southern half of the District from Foster Avenue to Belmont. The Captain wants the officers in the traffic division to check every vacant lot, every vacant building, basement and garage in the area. That's it for now."

Murphy opened the door to the detectives' office and motioned for Frank and me to go out into the hall. As we walked behind Sgt. Murphy and headed into the hallway, I glanced at the map of Chicago showing the various police districts. The 33rd District was the second largest, comprising twenty-three square miles and a population of over 160,000 people. That's a lot of doorbells, I thought to myself.

We walked down the hallway and out the door leading to the main assembly room and the front of the station. As we approached the Captain's office, we could see Mr. Peterson. He was holding a worn, gray hat in his hand and nervously turning its brim as he spoke to the man standing next to him.

"Jim, Frank…this is Mr. Anton Schuessler, Sr." Murphy said as we reached the two men. "Mr. Schuessler is the father of Anton and John Schuessler. You both know Mr. Peterson from last night."

We each shook hands first with Mr. Schuessler, then with Mr. Peterson. Mr. Schuessler looked past us and noticed the uniform officers and detectives walking up to the desk and taking sheets of paper. They were Missing Person bulletins containing the information I had taken from Mr. Peterson the night before.

Mr. Schuessler turned to us, and in an almost inaudible voice said, "We know you officers are doing everything you can. Mr. Peterson and I were out looking for the boys. Right before he came in and talked to you, we drove all over. My wife is worried sick about our sons. They're all good boys. We don't know what to do."

Sgt. Murphy spoke up, directing his response to Frank and me.

"Mr. Peterson and Mr. Schuessler came in this morning to talk with Captain Corcoran. The Captain told them that we're doing a complete search of the neighborhood and that if they hear anything from the boys, they are to call the District immediately. I told Sgt. Nelson that if they call, he is to contact you right away. If you're out in your car, he'll get the dispatcher to reach you. In the meantime, see if you can arrange to talk to the families at their homes sometime today. I think it would be better to interview them and the mothers at home, not here at the station."

"Sure, Sarge. We'll be spending some time here this morning getting the other detectives up to speed on what's been going on." I looked at the two men. They appeared to have been up all night.

"When would it be all right for my partner, and I to come out and speak with you and your families?" I asked.

Mr. Peterson's hands stopped turning his brim, and he quickly answered, "Any time would be fine, Detective. I know my wife would feel a lot better if she had the chance to talk with you about this."

"The sooner the better," Mr. Schuessler said.

"Okay, how about if Detective Czech and I stop at your home first, Mr. Peterson? Say about 1:30 this afternoon? If it's all right with you, Mr. Schuessler, we'll be at your home right after that—about 2:30?"

Both men nodded. Anton Schuessler, Sr. was almost in tears as his voice rose nervously, and he looked directly at me.

"None of us has gotten any sleep...we've been up all night. Mr. Peterson and his wife, me and my wife...we've been calling everybody. We don't know what else to do."

"Mr. Schuessler, we're doing everything possible to find the boys. I'm sure we'll find them soon."

I tried to sound confident, but later regretted telling Mr. Schuessler I was sure about anything. It was just so damned unusual to have three kids out all night without anyone having seen or heard from them.

"Thanks, Detective. We know you're all doing what you can," Mr. Peterson said in a soft voice. He turned and placed his right hand on Mr. Schuessler's shoulder.

"We better go home for now," he said, looking into Mr. Schuessler's darkened face. We could barely hear his voice over the noise of officers passing us on their way out of the station. We watched as the fathers waited patiently for a group of policemen to pass them. Then they walked slowly down the flight of marble steps and out the double doors.

1:30 p.m.

Frank was at the wheel of our gray, unmarked Ford as we drove north on Milwaukee Avenue. It took only a few minutes to reach the intersection of Milwaukee and Central Avenues. It's very busy, with other main roads intersecting from many directions, and leaving a tiny "island." in the midst of traffic just south of where the Peterson family lived.

Before leaving the station, Frank and I spoke with the traffic officers involved in the search. We briefed the detectives on the day shift as well as the detectives assigned to the case from other Districts.

Nothing had been heard about the boys. Follow-up calls to all the downtown theaters were made, but it was as if they had vanished into thin air.

"What do you think, Frank?"

"I think it looks bad." Frank kept his eyes on the bus just in front of us. He reached into the ashtray for the remains of the unlit La Corona cigar he had been chewing on since noon and made half of it disappear into the side of his mouth.

"These kids don't have any history with us. I checked with the Youth Division this morning. Nothing. They don't even have any station adjustments." Frank's cigar hardly moved as he spoke, teeth clenched just enough to keep it from getting in the way of his speech.

Station adjustments were a way of handling cases involving juveniles without the need to call in the State's Attorney or refer the matter to court. If a kid was picked up for shoplifting or some other minor offense, the desk sergeant or the reporting officer referred the youth to the juvenile officer. The case was evaluated, the parents were called, and if the kid didn't have much of a history, he was turned over to the custody of his parents with a harsh warning to stay out of trouble.

After a few station adjustments, the juvenile officer had to decide whether to refer the case to juvenile court. It was a practical and usually efficient way to keep tabs on the kids: it gives a break to the kids who did the stupid things kids sometimes do and builds a rap sheet on the ones who would become real problems.

Nobody at the District knew these kids, their parents or families. That's what bothered us.

Frank waited for the bus in front to pull out into traffic, then slowly turned the car onto Farragut. The Peterson home was on the south side of the street. It was a two-story Dutch-style home on a quiet, tree-lined street next to a large apartment building. Most of the homes in this area were single-family. Many were Chicago bungalows, all with neatly trimmed front lawns and a one or two-car garage in the back.

Neighbors were standing in front of their homes, and a few were on the sidewalk in front of the Peterson home, when we arrived. Some people didn't appear to live in the neighborhood. Reporters were also there. You could easily spot them in their well-worn suits and hats. They were asking questions and talking to the people gathered on the sidewalk.

"Jesus, reporters. These guys get around fast," Frank muttered.

"Better let me talk to them, Frank." I knew how he felt about reporters.

"Look, why don't you guys wait in your cars," I said as we walked to the front door. "We don't have anything for you yet. When we do, we'll let you know."

Still, the reporter from the Chicago Tribune approached me. "You're Detective James Jack, right?"

"Yeah, that's right. Now would you and your associates here please let us do our work?" The reporter followed us as we walked along the sidewalk and up to the front porch of the Peterson house. Frank had walked past me, and the reporter, and was already walking up the stairs to the front door.

Frank stopped at the top of the stairs and threw a mean look at the reporter. He began to walk down the steps again, but stopped. "Ring the bell Frank," I said. "He was just leaving."

The reporter glanced past me and saw Frank glaring at him. He took two steps back, turned and walked toward the street to a black Buick parked just behind our police car. He opened the door, stopped for a second, looked back at us, then got in and slammed the door.

As I made my way to the top of the porch, the door opened slowly, and I recognized Mr. Peterson.

We identified ourselves again, and he asked us to come inside. He quietly shut the door, looked out the small window, and motioned for us to enter the living room of their home.

"The neighbors know the boys are missing. I must have called every friend Robert knows, plus the neighbors to see if they had seen him. Word travels pretty fast in this area. But I didn't know the newspaper people would be here."

Frank took the cigar from his mouth and asked Mr. Peterson if the reporters had been bothering him.

"No, not really. I haven't been answering the door unless I know who it is."

"Well, just let us know if they start ringing your doorbell or calling you on the phone." The gruffness in Frank's voice, plus the dark scowl on his face, left no doubt about his personal opinion of the press.

We followed Mr. Peterson as he walked into the living room and toward his wife, who sat on a worn and faded couch.

"Dorothy, these are the detectives I spoke with last night. This is Detective James Jack and Detective Frank Czech. They came in on their own time this morning to help look for the boys."

We stepped forward to shake Mrs. Peterson's hand as she got up from the couch. I reached her first and noticed the firmness of her grip. It was as if she didn't want to let go of my hand.

"It's a pleasure, Mrs. Peterson. Sorry we have to trouble you at this time. Detective Czech and I aren't the only ones working to find the boys this morning. The entire District has been notified to keep an eye out, and we're beginning a house-to-house search." I stepped to one side as Frank extended his hand to greet Mrs. Peterson.

"It's no bother, Detective, if it will bring my son back."

Both Mr. and Mrs. Peterson looked emotionally spent. Their eyes were blood-shot and Mrs. Peterson was still crying. She was an attractive woman, in her middle thirties, with fine features and light skin. Her face and eyes were swollen and darkened by the tension and anxiety she had experienced in the past sixteen hours. She pointed to the two upholstered chairs across from the couch and asked us to sit down.

This is never easy, I thought to myself. Every time Frank and I had to question a family member, especially a parent, about a missing child, or about a person who had been killed in an accident, or shot by some jerk in a hold-up, I noticed that my stomach would tense up and everything inside me seemed to freeze.

I knew I wasn't supposed to get emotionally involved, but I always reacted in the same way in these situations. I believed that "emotionally involved" didn't mean you had to be some kind of robot and not have feelings for a fellow human being's tragedies. In order to help control my personal reactions, I found that if I just thought about being someplace else or that someone else was talking instead of me, that seemed to help.

Focus on the job you have to do, I told myself over and over again. Like you're in the ring, I thought.

I had been a boxer, had even coached the boxing team at one of the Catholic high schools in the years before joining the Department. I always told my fighters, "You feel the punches, but don't let the other guy know it."

The other thing I told "my boys" before they put the gloves on was simple. Get ready for that punch, but back away from it when you see it coming and move back with it when it hits. It softens the blow. Keep thinking about what you have to do next. It keeps you focused and you don't feel the pain. That was the secret.

I suddenly realized that Mrs. Peterson was saying something as I looked around the living room, evaluating everything from the furniture to the pictures on the walls in order to get some idea of who these people were and how they lived.

"Would either of you like some coffee?" Mrs. Peterson asked.

I quickly responded, "No thanks. We won't be long. We just want to get some information about Robert and the Schuessler boys. How long have you and your family lived in this area, Mr. Peterson?"

Mr. Peterson told us that he and his family had lived on this block for the past twelve years, and had moved from another home just three blocks away on Foster Avenue. He was a carpenter with a construction company and had recently begun a new job about six months ago. He stated that Robert was the oldest of their four children. Barbara Ann was seven; Susan was five; and Tommy was the youngest. He was only three.

He said that Robert attended Farnsworth School since the first grade and that he had become good friends with the Schuessler boy during the past year. They were both very interested in sports and played football after school. On Saturdays, he would play football or basketball or baseball, depending on the season. He worked around the house a little bit and since he was the oldest he cut the grass and raked the leaves.

"When does Robert usually come home from school?" I began to narrow the questions to activities after school and Robert's interests outside of school.

"You know, I really can't say. Since I'm at work, Dorothy is home when the kids come home from school." He turned to his wife, who had been staring across the living room at the trees outside the front windows. She startled a bit at the mention of her name then looked in our direction.

"The kids usually get home at about 3:30 in the afternoon, right after school. Robert comes home nearly every day at that time. Sometimes he comes home a little later, but that's because he stays after school to play sports. He just stays after school and plays football. Then he comes home for dinner." Her voice began to soften and trail off. Soon, she began to cry. Mr. Peterson walked over, put his hand on her shoulder and gently touched her arm.

"Come on, Dorothy. It'll be fine. They'll find the boys soon. You'll see."

"I see you're a bowler, Mr. Peterson. Is Robert a bowler?" I purposely kept the question in the present tense and pointed to the trophies on the wall.

"Yes, he is," Mr. Peterson said. "Robert and I go bowling twice a week, if we can, every Tuesday, and sometimes on Friday. I bowl two nights a week, and he comes with me most of the time."

"While Robert was with you at these bowling alleys, did you ever notice him making an acquaintance with somebody you didn't know. What I mean is, did you see him talking to any adults, any grown-ups other than kids his own age?"

"No, I didn't. He likes to talk to the fellows I bowl with and people in the alley that I know. Sometimes he brings one of his friends with him. In fact, just last week, last Friday night, he brought Johnny Schuessler along with us when we went bowling."

Frank got up from his seat, walked toward the front windows and looked out at the small crowd of people still on the sidewalk. He noticed that neighbors were also gathering across the street and looking at the Peterson house. The reporters were still in their cars.

I kept asking the necessary questions, but continued in an almost friendly and conversational tone.

"What bowling alleys do you bowl at?"

"Well, on Tuesday nights the Bower Lanes. That's around 6800 on Broadway. And on Friday nights, I bowl at Faetz & Nielsen at Ridge and Clark."

"Are those leagues that you're bowling in, Mr. Peterson?"

"Yes, they are."

Continuing the questioning about bowling alleys, I tried to match up what I knew about these places with the possibility that the boys had gone bowling and not to the movies. I knew that the bowling alleys were hangouts for a lot of different kinds of people, older men in leagues and young kids who were in gangs that hung out there. I also knew some strange characters hung around bowling alleys. I had gotten to know some of them after arresting them for things like burglary, disorderly conduct, and worse. I kept that to myself.

"Have you or Robert ever been to the Jefferson Park bowling alley?"

"The one over at Giddings and Milwaukee where you go down the stairs and into a small bowling alley? Yes, we've been there."

"If Robert went there, would the owners recognize him?"

"Yes. He's met them before. The owner is Jack Sanpayo."

"Did Robert ever go bowling alone, without you?"

"Yes, he's gone on Saturday afternoons. Sometimes he would go to the Mayfair Lanes, or Natoma Lanes in Niles."

"Did Robert or any of the boys he bowls with ever tell you that he was accosted by someone in the bowling alley?"

Mr. Peterson's body suddenly stiffened. He looked puzzled in response to the question then looked over at his wife.

"Robert never told me anything about anybody ever bothering him. If that ever happened, I think he would have told me or his mother."

"Mr. Peterson, I hope you and Mrs. Peterson understand that I have to ask these questions. They may seem strange, but you'll have to believe that I'm asking them for a reason. I'm not suggesting anything about Robert, but I need to know about his interests and where and how he spent his time." I wanted the Petersons to realize that this kind of question wasn't easy to ask.

"I understand, Detective. Please, just ask anything you want to know."

"Does Robert belong to any scout organization or any clubs?"

"Yes, he's a Boy Scout and also a member of the YMCA. He went to camp about five or six years ago for about two weeks. We asked him if he wanted to go back, but he said no. He didn't give us any reason, just that he didn't like it and that he would rather stay home and play with the neighborhood kids. You know, football or baseball."

"Do you let your children stay out after dark, Mrs. Peterson?"

"No, we have a rule in this house that you have to be in when the streetlights go on, especially in the summertime."

"How long has Robert known the Schuessler boys?"

"Well, I don't know, but I guess he knew them since they moved into the neighborhood and ever since the Schuessler boy was in the same classroom as Robert. I would say they were pretty close pals for the last year. Little Tony, I had never seen him before, but I had seen Bobby with Johnny a lot of times. In fact, they've gone downtown together once or twice to a show. Bobby has been going downtown alone for about a year."

"The Schuessler boy has gone downtown with Robert in the

past?"

"That's right."

"Do the Schuesslers know that their son John has gone downtown on prior occasions with your boy?"

"I don't know. I don't think so. Mrs. Schuessler sounded pretty upset when my wife told her that the boys went downtown yesterday."

"When you referred a while ago to little Tony, are you referring to little Anton Schuessler? Is that what his friends call him?"

"Yes, that's his nickname. I guess everybody calls him Tony, but his real name is Anton."

"Has Robert ever been out late with either one of the Schuessler boys?"

"No."

Frank looked at his watch and returned to join the Petersons and me. As he sat down and settled into one of the comfortable chairs, he glanced over and caught my attention. He then looked down at his right hand and moved the band on his watch, slightly turning it around on his wrist.

I understood the gesture and decided that some of these questions could be asked later on. But I still needed to know about Sunday, when the boys were last seen.

"Mr. Peterson, can you tell me what happened from the time you and Robert got up yesterday morning, that is, Sunday morning?"

"Well, we got up and we kept Robert home from church yesterday. The reason was that I was working on my garage, and I needed some help with the boards. I thought Robert could hold them for me. So we kept him home from Church. He goes to Jefferson Park Lutheran Church. He worked in the back yard until about 1:00 or 1:30 p.m. and then we came in to eat."

"Do you recall what you had for lunch yesterday? I know this might sound strange, but it really is important that we know as much as we can about the boys before they left for the movies."

"We understand. We had fried chicken and mashed potatoes. Robert wouldn't eat anything but the chicken and the potatoes as far as I can remember. He could have had some sliced tomatoes, but I don't remember if he ate them.

"After lunch, we sat down for a little while, maybe for about ten or fifteen minutes, and we listened to the Cardinals and New York football game. Then the two Schuessler boys rode over to our house. One rode Bobby's bike and the other boy rode his own bike. They called for John and went into the house."

"Why did one of the Schuessler boys ride Bobby's bike back home?"

"Well, on Saturday, Bobby went bowling with them and rode his bike to their home. They took the bus to the Natoma Bowling Alley in Niles and when they came back, Bobby walked home from the Schuessler's. He forgot his bike and when he got home at about 5:30 that evening he called up and told Johnny 'I forgot my bike' and would he please take care of it and put it in a safe place and the next time he comes over would he bring the bike back.

"I believe that's one of the reasons why the Schuessler boys came over. They drove Bobby's bike back home. Bobby mentioned to me that he was going to go to the show and the Schuessler boys were going to go with him. Bobby also asked me—he didn't know what show he should go see—so I recall sitting down and we looked at the paper. We saw that "The African Lion" was playing at the Loop Theater.' He thought that would be a good movie to see."

"Did they mention anything about the possibility of going to the Gateway, the Portage, the Congress, or the Irving theaters. Ones that are in the neighborhood?"

"Maybe. I think they'd already seen those pictures," Mr. Peterson said.

"Did you call the Loop Theater?"

Suddenly, a voice abruptly stopped my questioning. Mrs. Peterson was still staring quietly out the front windows. Surprised by the unexpected interruption, we turned and looked at her.

"Yes, my husband called the Loop, and they told him that the price would be fifty cents and that the movie would take about an hour and forty-five minutes," she said.

"He kissed his father good-bye. He kissed me and his brother and his sisters good-bye. That's what we do in this house. Then he went with the Schuessler brothers. I looked down the street, and he was walking with the two Schuessler boys. Bobby was in the middle. That was the last time I saw him." Her soft sob was now an anguished wail.

Mr. Peterson tried to calm her, to reassure her that the boys would be found. She apologized for being so emotional; but we understood. It was obvious that she couldn't help it.

We learned that the boys left for the movies at about 3:15 or 3:30 p.m. and that Mr. Peterson had given Robert $1.50. He overheard the Schuessler boys telling Robert that they each had $1.25. Robert didn't have a billfold or wallet with him, but he did have a student pass and a handkerchief. He was wearing a pink flannel shirt flaked with black and blue jeans. The jeans were worn, had a flannel lining, and may have had a patch ironed over one of the knees. He wore a beaded moccasin-type belt with no buckle, just a plain catch.

Mr. Peterson went on to say that he and his wife first became alarmed at about 7:30 or 8:00 p.m. Sunday evening. He said he told his wife that maybe the boys stayed to see the movie twice. They both had made all kinds of excuses for the kids being out late, saying that maybe they would be home at 9:00 p.m. Mrs. Peterson seemed to remember the boys saying something like that.

Mr. Peterson continued to say that about 9:00 p.m. Mrs. Schuessler had called the Petersons. She apologized for calling so late, but had explained that she couldn't find their phone number. If the boys came to the Peterson's, they were not to ride their bike home at that late hour. Mr. Peterson explained that his wife had told Mrs. Schuessler that Mr. Peterson would drive the brothers home in his car. Mrs. Schuessler called a second time while the fathers were out looking for the boys.

Mr. Peterson stated that after dropping off Mr. Schuessler, he went home and called some bowling alleys to see if the boys had been there.

"I called the 20th Century Bowling alley because they stay open 22 or 23 hours a day, and I just thought maybe the boys went there because of the late hour. I also called the Natoma Bowling Alley in Niles. Nobody answered. Finally, I was so exhausted, and there was nobody else to call, I just laid down for a while. It must have been about 3:30 or 4:00 in the morning. Then I went to the station a little after 8:30 this morning with Mr. Schuessler.

"When I was talking to Sgt. Murphy and Captain Corcoran this morning, they asked about whether Bobby had school today. Then it suddenly dawned on me—maybe someone should check at the school. I drove over there and spoke with the principal to see if maybe Bobby was in school. But the principal, Mr. Thornton, said Bobby and the Schuessler boys weren't at school today."

As he recounted his conversation with the school principal, Mr. Peterson turned to look at his wife, suddenly realizing that perhaps he shouldn't have told her of his visit to the boys' school. When he had learned that the boys weren't at school, it only made him more anxious and concerned about where they could be. However improbable it would have been for Bobby, Tony, and John to have gone to school that morning without coming home or even calling, their absence from school added to the already frantic concern for their safety.

Frank got up and walked slowly to the living room windows again. He parted the thin, white curtains at the side of the windows and looked out. Turning to us, he asked, "Mr. Peterson, did Bobby ever play hooky from school?"

The neighbors outside continued to look at the house, and the reporters continued to talk with each other in their cars with the front and back passenger doors open as more of their colleagues joined them.

Mrs. Peterson responded before her husband had a chance to answer.

"Yes, Bobby skipped school a few times last year when he was in the 7th grade, maybe for a couple of weeks. We talked with the teachers at school, and with Bobby. We got it all straightened out."

I looked at my partner staring out the living room windows. Frank looked back at me, and his expression said I should continue the questioning.

"He didn't go to school for two weeks?" trying to control the surprise in my voice.

"He would go to school one day and stay home maybe the next day." The matter-of-fact tone in Peterson's voice indicated that Mr. Peterson didn't think this was unusual for a 7th grader.

"Did you ever ask Bobby if anyone else played hooky with him or where he spent the time when he was playing hooky?"

"Well, I know he stayed in the garage once and hid in the basement another time. He said he just sat there. At the time, I thought it might have had something to do with his grades. You know, if he didn't get good grades, he would kind of brood about it. But his report cards were excellent at the time. Like I said, we talked with his teachers at the time and they said he wasn't doing his homework there for a while. But we got it taken care of and that was it."

I thought about what Mr. Peterson had said for a moment then decided not to pursue it further.

"Well, I think that's all we need for now Mr. and Mrs. Peterson." I got up and walked toward Frank who was already at the front door.

I stopped before reaching the door and turned to Mr. Peterson, who was following close behind. "By the way, is there any reason that you know of why Robert would stay away from home?"

Peterson looked over his shoulder at his wife, who had eased herself up from the couch and was walking toward us.

"No," he replied. "None."

"Thanks again. Detective Czech and I can be reached at the station. If either of you think of anything else, here's our direct line. If we're not at the station, the desk sergeant will know where to reach us." I reached into my coat pocket and took out a small white card with blue lettering.

I handed it to Mrs. Peterson who thanked us. Her face was wet with tears, but she had managed to calm down. Mr. Peterson put his arm around his wife, thanked us again for our help, and closed the door as we walked down the front steps of their home.

Moving toward the car, we waved off reporters who rushed towards us. "We got nothing for you right now. And do everybody a favor. Don't bother these people, okay?"

The sidewalks and streets were still wet from the heavy rainfall the night before, and the weather had changed from unseasonably warm to a sharp autumn chill. We strode quickly across the small front lawn, which was strewn with wet, rust-colored leaves.

Frank got behind the wheel and waited for me to get in.

"What do you think, Frank?" I pushed back into my seat as Frank punched the accelerator and wheeled away from the curb. He turned his head slowly, took the cigar from his mouth and said, "I think I need another cigar. This one's shot."

2:15 p.m.

The Schuessler's lived only a few blocks away. Frank made a u-turn and drove one block west to Central Avenue, made a right turn and headed north toward Bryn Mawr Avenue, where he turned left and then right onto Mango.

He pulled the car into a parking space in front of a small, light yellow brick home. Once again, we were confronted with news reporters. There were only one or two them, not as many as at the Peterson home, but more than enough for Frank's liking.

"I told you Jim, they're starting to come out of the woodwork."

"Relax, Frank. At this point, they know as much as we do, so there's nothing to say."

Before we were able to get out of the car, two men approached the vehicle. One of them had a small notebook in his hand. The smaller man had a large, box-like camera hanging from his right hand.

"Are you from the 33rd District?" Asked the one with the camera as Frank opened the driver's door.

"Yeah, and if you don't watch out, you'll get pinched for loitering."

"Let's go Frank," I said across the hood of the car as we started towards the Schuessler home.

By the time Frank reached the front door of the bungalow, the door opened and a distraught man in his early forties stood in the doorway. He appeared to be on the verge of collapsing, his face was pale and drawn, with beads of sweat on his forehead.

We introduced ourselves as detectives assigned to the case, and reminded Mr. Schuessler that we had briefly been introduced to him that morning at the Station.

Mr. Schuessler responded politely. "Yes, now I remember you. Thank you for coming. You know, it has been terrible since last night. My wife and I are so worried about the boys." Although I had met Mr. Schuessler briefly that morning, it had been by way of a cursory introduction. Now I saw that the man was about five feet, eight inches in height, a bit overweight, and had dark hair, which he drew across his head to minimize his receding hairline. He had a broad face, a long, thin nose and thin lips. He held an unfiltered cigarette in his hand, which was about to burn his fingers.

We were led into the living room, and Mr. Schuessler introduced his wife, Eleanor. She was seated in a green stuffed chair; pillows were propped up behind her back and she looked as distraught and tense as her husband. The dark circles under her eyes and her pale complexion were evidence that she had gotten little sleep the night before. Her thick dark hair was unkempt and swept up from her high forehead. It reminded me of a lion's mane tussled and windblown.

"I'm sorry we have to come into your home at this time, Mrs. Schuessler." I wasn't sure she had heard me. I paused for a moment, and when she did not respond I said, "Mrs. Schuessler, I'm Detective James Jack and this is Detective Frank Czech. We're here to ask you a few questions about John and Anton."

Eleanor Schuessler stared past us, gazing at the front door. The living room was dark. The curtains were drawn and the lamps in the living room had not been turned on.

Mrs. Schuessler suddenly twisted her head in our direction.

"The boys are all we have. All we live for. We bought this house for them. Oh God, please help us." She began to cry and as she did, her body convulsed and shuddered uncontrollably.

Mr. Schuessler leaned over and put both hands on his wife's shoulders. He stroked her head and hair, as she tried to regain her composure.

I spoke softly to both of them. "We just have a few questions. It'll help us if you could talk to us for a few minutes."

Frank went to the front of the living room and looked out the window. He moved to his right and pulled the cord next to the heavy white drapes of the bay windows, causing them to whisk between him.

I continued the discussion with the Schuesslers, asking them to reconstruct their activities with the boys the day before, what they wore when they left, and where they planned to go.

"We didn't know they were going downtown. They were not allowed to go downtown by themselves. They said they were going to go to Bobby Peterson's house. We found out from Mr. Peterson last night that the boys said they were going to a movie. They never went downtown alone." Mrs. Schuessler suddenly became energized as she spoke.

She told the detectives that she and her husband had become worried about the boys not being home when it was almost 9:00 p.m., and they hadn't heard from them. How she tried to contact the Petersons, but didn't know their number. That she finally reached them and had Mr. Peterson come over and pick up her husband and they both went out in the rain to look for the boys. Suddenly, her voice became louder as she recounted how she learned they had gone downtown. DOWNTOWN! She said it as if the mere idea of boys their age going to the Loop on Sunday afternoon was the most outrageous and unthinkable thing anyone could imagine.

Frank looked over at me from across the room and raised his eyebrows. I looked back at him and shook my head. Earlier that afternoon, Mr. Peterson had mentioned to us that on at least one prior occasion, John Schuessler had gone downtown with Bobby Peterson. This information could be important, but how important we didn't know just yet. But clearly, now was not the time to press the parents on it.

"Mr. and Mrs. Schuessler, we want to thank you for your help. I know it's hard to remember everything, but just bear with us for a few minutes." I continued to speak in a soft but firm tone of voice. "How long have you been living at this address?"

Mr. Schuessler answered. "About five years. We had a home on the 2700 block of North Mozart. The boys went to...." His voice trailed off, and he looked at his wife for help in remembering where they had gone to school before they had moved.

"They went to Brentano School. Then after we moved here, they transferred to Farnsworth." She was quick to finish his sentence.

I went on to ask if the boys had ever mentioned anything about being in trouble or being stopped by any adult, or if they had ever been accosted by anyone at anytime. Had they ever been followed home or had anyone tried to offer them a ride in a car?

Mrs. Schuessler sharply interrupted the detective when her husband silently shook his head to each of his questions.

"I can tell you more about the boys than he can. He works long hours. The only time he spends with them is on Sundays, his day off." I could hear the sharpness in her voice before she seemed to regain her composure and lower the tone of her voice. I couldn't tell if it was the panic she was feeling because her boys were missing or frustration with her husband and his nonverbal responses to our questions.

She quickly responded "no," she never saw the boys acknowledge a greeting from someone they didn't know; they knew everyone the boys knew; they went bowling a lot on Sundays with their father.

At the mention of bowling and bowling alleys, I asked Mr. Schuessler where he and the boys bowled and if the boys had ever been approached by anyone in a bowling alley that they didn't know?

No, Mr. Schuessler said. The boys never told him of any problems with anyone, at school or when they went bowling. They were good kids. He told the detectives the boys helped him hang a clothesline in the basement on Sunday. They were aware that he hadn't been feeling well and wanted to help. Then they had eaten dinner around 1:30 in the afternoon. They had chicken noodle soup. Then some time around 2:15 p.m. one of the boys had called Bobby Peterson and after a short conversation; they asked if they could go to the Peterson home. I made a mental note of the discrepancy concerning the time Mr. Schuessler believed one of the boys had called Bobby Peterson and the information received from Mr. Peterson a short time earlier.

I thanked the Schuesslers and made a point of telling them that if they think or hear of anything else to please call the station.

As we walked to the front door, I turned and asked one more

question.

"Is there any reason why John and Anton would stay away from home or of anyone who would want to harm them?"

Mrs. Schuessler was firm in her answer. "Absolutely not. They are good students. They are well liked and are active and normal boys. They are my whole life. Please help us find our boys." Tears streamed down her cheeks.

I told her that everything possible was being done to help find the boys and that they would be notified immediately if any new information was received.

Mr. Schuessler thanked us and walked us to the front door. "Please let us know something," he said as he looked out at the people gathered in front of his home. "Anything."

My partner and I walked quickly down the narrow walk and through the growing crowd of neighbors and reporters. Frank directed one of his meanest scowls at the group of people in front of him, which discouraged them from asking any questions. Many of the reporters had already retreated to their cars, ready to follow us to our next stop.

Once inside the squad car, Frank gunned the engine and sped off down Mango. He looked into the rear-view mirror and noticed two cars following them. Reporters.

"Frank, what do you say we hit the Farnsworth School over on Linder Avenue before we go back and check in? Murphy wants things checked out with the teachers and principal, and the school is on the way back to the station. Besides, now might be a good time since school's almost out and we can talk to them before they go home."

The car spun around a corner and headed in the direction of Farnsworth School. Frank gripped the steering wheel tightly and said, "Great. Let's lose these jerks before we get there, though. I still need some cigars." He swung a quick left, then a right and sped into an alley and out onto Bryn Mawr Avenue. He ran the red light and turned right on Milwaukee Avenue.

"If they blow that light, we got 'em one way or the other," he said confidently as he checked the outside mirror. "Either we lose them or

we'll run 'em in for interfering with police business." He looked into
the rear view mirror again. No reporters.

2:45 p.m.

The Farnsworth Elementary School was located not far from
the homes of the missing boys. It was a two story, red brick building
typical of the school buildings erected in the 1920s and '30s to
accommodate the growing population of the northwest side of the
city. A large schoolyard was next to the main building. We parked as
close to the main entrance as possible.

A few students were leaving the building as we walked up
the stone steps and through the entrance. Frank felt that most city
schools looked and even smelled alike. The floors were gleaming and
reflected the yellow light from the hanging fixtures every twenty feet
down a hall that seemed two blocks long. He had said the distinctive
smell was due to the oiled sawdust that the janitors used when
sweeping the floors. It left a slight sheen on the dark linoleum tiles
and smelled musty.

Students were walking in the halls, but most were still in their
classrooms. I knew the location of the principal's office from previous
visits to the school. Nothing serious. But occasionally, I had to check
on the few young boys who had gotten into more mischief than any
real trouble in the neighborhood.

Juvenile delinquency was not a problem at Farnsworth School.
Most of these kids were from middle class or working class families
and discipline was, at the time, still a family concern. But every school
seemed to have a group of kids who got into trouble on occasion, and
the Juvenile Officers at the 33rd District had a file on most of them.

We walked into the principal's office at the far end of the hallway
and identified ourselves as police detectives to the woman behind a
counter. She was speaking to two small children when we walked
into the office. Frank asked to speak with Mr. D. W. Thornton, the
principal of Farnsworth School.

"I know why you're here," said the woman. She appeared very
nervous and her voice shook as she spoke. "I'll call him right now."
Directing her attention to the children at the counter, she told them

to go back to their classrooms and come back after the three o'clock bell had rung, officially marking the end of the school day.

She took a few steps back from the counter and turned toward a desk cluttered with books, papers, and files. She pressed a button on a small intercom, bent over slightly to bring herself closer to the speaker and said, "Mr. Thornton, there are some gentlemen here to see you. They say it's urgent."

Before we heard any response, a middle-aged man in a dark gray suit emerged from a door directly behind the woman who was still bent over the intercom.

"Good afternoon, officers," the man said as he stepped around the counter and extended his hand, first to me then to Frank. "I assume you know why we're here," I said to him.

"Yes, I do," the man said. "Would you please come into my office? We'll be able to talk privately without being disturbed."

Frank made the guy out to be in his early fifties, neatly dressed and pleasant. From what we learned at the District, Thornton was a fairly decent guy for a principal. He had been at Farnsworth for a number of years and didn't live too far from the school.

The office was neatly furnished with a standard Board of Education desk, chairs and a bookcase. Diplomas and certificates hung on the wall behind the desk, and a few school trophies were on bookshelves just under the framed certificates.

Frank and I sat facing the principal, across a desk devoid of any papers, files, or clutter. A notepad, a pen and pencil, a small intercom, and a standard black telephone were the only items on the his desk.

"Mr. Thornton," I began, "as you may know, Robert Peterson, and John and Anton Schuessler have been reported missing by their parents. They haven't been home nor have they been seen since yesterday afternoon, and no one's heard from the boys. We were wondering if you could supply us with some information about them."

"Certainly. You probably know that Mr. Peterson stopped in to see me late this morning. He wondered if the boys had been to school. He told me that they hadn't been home since yesterday afternoon. Of course, I became alarmed at hearing of this, and I asked their teachers immediately if the boys had been at school. Perhaps you would like to have their teachers speak with you."

I told him that would be fine. Mr. Thornton reached for the intercom and pressed the small button on top of the speaker. "Miss Johnston, would you please get Mrs. Jonas and Miss Schwachten to come to my office?" He didn't wait for any reply, but moments later we could hear the door to the hall open and the sound of children's voices rise up and then disappear. Then we heard the outer door of the principal's office close as Miss Johnston left to find the two teachers.

"They are all good standing boys, "Mr. Thornton continued. "They serve as helpers for their teachers. The Peterson boy, in fact, is in charge of our movie projector. Robert Peterson and John Schuessler are in the eighth grade and Anton Schuessler is in the sixth grade. They are reliable youngsters. They've never been truant; never get into any trouble. It's just a shame that they're missing. I hope there's something we can do to help."

Mr. Thornton rose from his chair and walked to a row of black filing cabinets, which were standing against a wall to the left of where we were seated. He pulled out the third drawer of the first cabinet, and ran his right index finger along the row of files inside the drawer. After pulling first one, then two, then three slim file folders out, he returned to his chair and placed the files on his desk and moved them toward us.

"As you can see, these boys were no trouble. In fact, Robert and John have perfect attendance records for this semester. After speaking with Mr. Peterson this morning, I pulled their files and looked through them. You'll see for yourselves they are good students, have good grades."

Frank reached over and took one file, then gave the other to me. The files were thin and contained attendance records, notes from the teachers concerning their progress, and each file had four by eight inch report cards with grades for each year the boys were in school at Farnsworth. The Schuessler boys' files also contained transfer paperwork and report cards from the Brentano School.

The report cards had just been issued last Thursday, October 13, 1955 and all three boys had received good grades, very good attendance records, and no reports of infractions of school rules. Frank noticed that Anton Schuessler had two half-day absences on September 12 and October 10. But each absence had a note from Mrs. Schuessler explaining that Anton had an earache and a headache, respectively, on those two days.

I heard the hallway door open again, the muffled voices of children in the halls, and the sound of the door closing again. The door to Mr. Thornton's office opened seconds later and three women stood in the doorway.

"Please, come in. Thank you Mrs. Johnston. If you would, please make sure that we're not disturbed for a while." The tallest of the three women turned and closed the door behind her.

"Officers, this is Mrs. Cecelia Schwachten and Mrs. Bernice Jonas. Mrs. Jonas is Anton's sixth grade teacher, and Mrs. Schwachten is Robert and John's eighth grade teacher. Ladies, this is—I'm sorry—Detective James Jack and Detective Frank Czech from the Gale Street Station. They're here to speak with us about the boys and ask us some questions which will help find them."

Frank and I stood up and shook hands with the teachers, thanking them for their time. We motioned for the teachers to please take a seat in the chairs we had been seated in. We stood off to the side of Mr. Thornton's desk, holding the boys' files in our hands.

Mrs. Schwachten took her seat and stared first at the ceiling, then down at the floor. She appeared to be in her early fifties, was thin, well dressed and had fine features. Her wavy hair was dark brown, with a few strands of gray at the temples. She wore black-rimmed glasses and had her arms folded in front of her, her fingers clenched tightly into her arms. Frank said later she was probably tough as nails with these kids.

"The doors of Farnsworth School opened thirty years ago. I'm the only original teacher here," Mrs. Schwachten said to no one in particular. "Robert Peterson and John Schuessler are in my eighth grade class. They sit in the fifth and sixth seats of the front row." She continued to shift her glance from the ceiling to the floor, not looking at Mr. Thornton or us as she spoke. It was apparent that she was trying to control her emotions.

"The school never had a boy in any trouble where he might have to go to a juvenile home. Not in my thirty years here. We did have some girls many years ago that went to some juvenile home, but not any boys.

"Robert is a good boy and a good student. He is very quiet. Both he and John Schuessler are well liked. They don't have any discipline problems."

I asked the teacher about the parents' interest in the children, were they involved with their children's school activities and school.

Mrs. Schwachten stated that she had forty-three children in her class and every parent was involved in the school's Parent Teacher Association. "We get wonderful cooperation from the parents," she said.

Mrs. Bernice Jonas, Anton's teacher, was visibly moved as she re-iterated the same praise for the boys. She, too, was concerned about the boys. Anton was well liked, a nice boy. He plays football with other boys at recess and after school. He goes to Boy Scout meetings and was a good student.

At this point, Mr. Thornton interrupted the conversation.

"Excuse me, but now that you mention the Boy Scouts, a classmate of Robert and John brought a message from Mrs. Schuessler today asking if the school might help in looking for her sons and the Peterson boy."

Frank looked at me and asked the principal, "When did that happen?"

"Well, this morning. Robin Schroeder is in the eighth grade with Robert and John. He's also in the Boy Scouts. I thought that might be a good idea. I called their Scout leaders this morning as well as some Girl Scout leaders. I also called the Forest Rangers. I thought that all of us could get a search going if the boys aren't back today."

I put the school file down on the desk and looked over at Mr. Thornton. "Who did you speak with?"

"I called Glen Nolte, he's a personal friend of mine and he's the Scout leader of Troop 962. That's the troop Anton belongs to. You know, most of the boys in the school are active in Scouting, and we have boys in ten different Scout Troops. I also mimeographed notes to the parents of about 200 of the youngsters from fifth grade through eighth asking the parents' permission to let the kids meet after school tomorrow and join in a search in the Forest Preserve and along the river. The Rangers and Scout Leaders can lead the search. I was planning on giving out the mimeographs today before the students leave."

Frank and I were both startled by the efforts Mr. Thornton had made in just a short time. We were also concerned that a civilian was orchestrating a search involving school children, their parents, and even the Forest Rangers without clearance from the police force.

"We appreciate your efforts, Mr. Thornton," I said, trying to sound grateful. But the truth of the matter was this could cause a big problem for the search effort. "Maybe you should hold off on that until we get further information. You know, we have an awful lot of officers out there looking for the boys. We'll let you know tomorrow morning if that's necessary. We don't want to cause any unnecessary alarm."

Thornton continued as if he hadn't heard one word that I said.

"When Mr. Peterson spoke with me this morning, I knew that this was serious. These boys never stayed out late before, they never caused problems in school. We thought the North Branch of the Chicago River in the forest preserve might be a good place to start. You know, about a year ago a grade school pupil was molested by a high school boy near the river not far from the school."

This information was news to Frank and me: we hadn't heard of the case, even though it was something that apparently had occurred in our District.

"Mr. Thornton, maybe you could check with the Board of Education and see if they have any objections to your plans about a search tomorrow. If you could also check with their lawyers about it and have them call us, I'm sure we'll be able to work something out."

I knew that the reference to the Board of Education would at least temporarily slow up whatever search plans Mr. Thornton would have. Back then getting the Board to agree to purchase a box of chalk was a problem, not to mention putting 200 kids in the forest preserve. By the time the bureaucrats down at the Board of Education figured out who could give the okay, the boys would be back home.

Mrs. Jonas, who had been quietly listening as we discussed the need for a search, suddenly interrupted the conversation.

"A few of the students in my class told me this afternoon that they had seen one or two men a few weeks ago trying to attract the students' attention near the school."

I looked at her and wondered how many stories were circulating among the students. I asked if the incident had reported this to the police or their parents. She said she didn't know but would provide us with the names of the students.

I thanked the teachers and Principal Thornton for their assistance and asked them to contact either me or Frank should they obtain any other information they believed could be useful in locating the boys.

As we left the principal's office, the hallway was beginning to fill with younger students on their way home. The fifth, sixth, seventh and eighth grade classes would let out in a few minutes and soon the halls would be filled with kids talking about the missing boys and wondering where they could be.

Frank and I reached the exit and walked out across the schoolyard to our car. I noticed that many parents were at the school to pick up their children and walk home with them. Some were standing in small groups with their children, talking to each other. This was unusual for this particular school, where most kids could easily walk down the quiet, tree-lined residential streets to their homes a few blocks away.

"Word spreads fast around here, Frank. Let me take a minute and talk to some of these kids." I walked over to the first group of older children and their parents, introduced myself and showed them my badge. As I did, a few other parents moved closer to the group I had approached.

I asked the students if they knew the boys, when was the last time they had seen them, did they know where the boys usually went after school. None of the children had seen them since school that Friday. Some parents asked what was being done to find the boys, and I assured them all that everything possible was being done to locate the boys. I was sure, I told them, that they would be found. If anyone heard from them or from anyone who saw them on Sunday, please call the 33rd District I said.

Frank had gone to the car and waited for me to finish speaking with the parents. He turned on the police radio, picked up the mike and pressed the send button on the handset.

"This is Detective Czech. Put me through to Sgt. Murphy." He released the send button and listened to the static spit out from the small speaker as he waited for Murphy's voice. He looked out to where I stood in the schoolyard talking to the small gathering of parents and their children. Soon I backed away from the crowd and headed to the car.

"Frank, this is Murphy. What do you guys have?"

"Sarge, we're at the school. We talked to the principal and the kids' teachers. The principal was getting a couple hundred kids ready for a search party in the forest preserve tomorrow."

"What? Jesus, did you guys tell him to hold off? What's he doing?" Murphy's voice could be heard well above the buzz and crackle of static coming over the radio. It wasn't difficult to imagine his face getting redder by the second at the thought of a Scout Leader and 200 school kids tramping through the forest preserve.

"Don't worry, Sarge. We told him he better check with the Board of Education before he does anything. We also told him to talk to us first, too. He's pretty organized, though."

"I want you guys back here right away. Things are moving pretty fast." Murphy's voice had dropped a few decibels.

"Okay, Sarge. Jim and I just finished interviewing some parents here at the school. We'll be there in a few minutes."

Frank popped the button on the mike and set it into its cradle on the radio. He unwrapped a fresh cigar. Licking the end, just behind the gold and red wrapper, he stuck it into his mouth.

After starting the engine, he honked the horn. I hurried my pace toward the car, opened the passenger door and got in. Before I had a chance to close the door, Frank had hit the accelerator and the car was moving.

"Murphy wants us back at the station. Did you get any new information?"

"Nothing. Just a lot of parents worried sick about their kids disappearing. Goofy rumors about how maybe the boys ran away from home."

Frank grumbled as he drove the car to Gale Street.

"You know, Frank, unless these boys show up later this afternoon or tonight, I got to believe there's some foul play here."

I thought, what kind of foul play? Good kids, good families. The teachers and principal didn't have a bad word to say about them. Neither did their classmates. My mind raced to the possibilities these boys were still alive. I didn't want to consider anything else.

We got to the station and went immediately to Sgt. Murphy's office. It looked like the Maxwell Street Market on Sunday morning. Papers were piled on his desk, files scattered all over the floor, phone messages blowing off the desk and onto his chair. Murphy was combing through a filing cabinet as we walked in, and without glancing up, barked, "Sit down guys. What do you have for me?"

I looked around the room for a place to sit and found none. All the chairs had files on them; bound reports, notebooks, and mugshot books stacked on one another.

"A lot of broken hearts and distress, Sarge. Besides that, nothing's new. But the principal and one of the teachers at Farnsworth gave us a couple of incidents—one in the last few weeks—where one or two guys hanging around the school were trying to get some kids over to talk to them. Another one about a year ago where a grade school kid was molested by some high school kid."

We could see that Murphy's face was red. Either he had just bawled out someone or he was getting heat from downtown on the case. The condition of the office indicated that the latter was more than likely the case.

"Right now, guys, I want a full report in chronological order on my desk as soon as possible. This is going to be a big one. I want every minute and movement of this case recorded in your notes and reports. I'm going to start coordinating this investigation right now."

That explained Murphy's outburst on the car radio. He was to run the investigation himself now, and was not going to have Boy Scouts wandering around in the Forest Preserve unless he was the one supervising the operation.

Murphy called over his shoulder again in our direction as he continued to search the file drawers. "Frank, I want you guys to start looking at these reports here on this chair."

He pointed to the chair closest to him, piled with well-thumbed case folders. "Those are the closed files on the most recent child molester cases in the District. There are also reports of exhibitionists and "Peeping Toms" in there. We've got nothing from the officers out on the street on the boys. Nobody's seen them. After you go through those files and get the names of the suspects, find out if any of those creeps are back on the street. You can interview them later.

"But first, I want you to check on two stolen vehicles reported over the Teletype. They were stolen around Lawrence and Milwaukee Sunday night. I also want you to interview the CTA bus drivers that worked the Milwaukee Avenue route Sunday night."

Frank and I split the files between us and began to jot down the names of the suspects in each case, along with their last known address. If the address was Statesville or Joliet Prison, we noted that as well and kept those names separate from the others.

While we were going through the files, the phone beneath the pile of papers on Murphy's desk rang constantly. No one answered it, since Murphy had told the desk sergeant not to put any calls through until after 6:00 p.m. He instructed the sergeant to take messages, and if any were from Police Headquarters, he should come in to Murphy's office and let him know. If any calls came from the Peterson or Schuessler families, he was to get Frank or me immediately.

5:00 p.m.

I looked at my watch after letting the last file folder fall to the pile on the floor and looked over to where Sgt. Murphy was standing in front of the file cabinet. "I could go for something to eat. Come on, Sarge. We better eat now because this is going to be a long night."

Murphy looked at me, his face still red and small beads of sweat appeared on his forehead and upper lip.

"You guys have been working all day. Are you gonna work this shift, too?"

Frank and I looked at each other, then at Murphy.

"You better believe it, Sarge," Frank answered.

Murphy seemed pleased to hear that but expected as much. He occasionally gave us some ribbing. "You don't look like detectives," he once told us. "You dress too good."

Although both Frank and I had the reputation of being among the best-dressed detectives in the Department, we didn't wear expensive or flashy clothes. On a detective's salary you couldn't have a big wardrobe. But we always wore suits that were pressed, immaculate shirts and ties, and clean overcoats. Most other detectives weren't as careful about their appearance.

We left Murphy's office and walked north on Gale Street to Milwaukee Avenue, then walked a short distance to the Gale Street Inn. It was a neighborhood place with good food where a lot of the guys from the station would go for something decent to eat and to have a drink or two after their shift.

After eating, Frank and I told Murphy we were going to check out the bus depot and talk to some of the drivers who might have seen the boys Sunday night.

"Fine, but before you go, let me give you some information on those stolen vehicles." Murphy pulled out the notebook from his inside pocket and gave us the license plate and description of the vehicles, one a 1955 green Ford station wagon and the other a black Chevy station wagon.

I wrote the information down on my notepad and told Murphy we would be back at the station later that evening. We walked out of the station, got into our Ford and drove to the CTA depot on Elston Avenue, just south of Milwaukee Avenue and only a few blocks north of the Schuessler home.

6:25 p.m.

The Chicago Transit Authority (CTA) depot at Milwaukee and Elston Avenues was one of several located throughout the city. The depot on Elston Avenue was the starting point for several bus lines, including the bus line that ran down Milwaukee Avenue from the northernmost edge of the city to the center of the Loop, ending at State and Madison Streets.

Milwaukee Avenue, as it cut across the city, passed through several distinct neighborhoods: Scandinavian, German, Polish, and Hispanic. It was a barometer of the socio-economic progress of several different ethnic groups. As they struggled up the economic ladder of success, they moved progressively north to the tree-lined streets of the Mayfair, Portage Park, Jefferson Park, and Forest Glen communities.

We pulled into the depot lot off Elston Avenue and parked our car near the dispatch building. We located the depot supervisor and inquired about the schedule of the Milwaukee Avenue bus and who would have been on duty between the hours of 2:00 p.m. and midnight on Sunday, October 16.

The supervisor took out the scheduling book for every bus line departing from the depot and scanned the pages indicating the names of the drivers, their route number, bus number and schedule for each day of the week. As he scanned the pages, he informed us that the Milwaukee Avenue bus running from Milwaukee and Central Avenues, where the boys would have boarded for the ride downtown, ran on a fifty-four minute running time. Buses ran six minutes apart until 4:30 p.m. then seven minutes apart until 8:00 p.m. From eight to midnight, they ran eight minutes apart.

He gave us the names of the bus drivers who would have been driving the route between 2:00 p.m. and midnight. Because of their scheduling for the week, some of the drivers were on duty and some had the day off.

I wrote each name down in my notebook, along with the times each driver left the depot. Each name would have to be checked out with the CTA main office downtown and a request for the addresses of each driver would have to be made. Then each driver would have to be interviewed about any recollection they might have concerning three boys traveling on the Milwaukee Avenue bus.

Frank looked over my shoulder at the list of names written in the small, spiral bound book.

"That's a lot of people to interview. They probably live all over the city. Are any of these guys coming in to the depot tonight? Maybe we can knock a few of these names off this list before we call the CTA."

The supervisor nodded in agreement. "You can probably interview four or five of these drivers tonight as they come in, if you want to wait."

We agreed that might be easier. So we waited as each Milwaukee Avenue bus came into the depot and approached the drivers, along with the depot supervisor, and asked if he had seen three boys traveling together on Sunday afternoon or Sunday evening. After interviewing three bus drivers who weren't of any assistance, we were returning to the depot office when a man in his mid-forties approached us dressed in a crisply pressed CTA uniform.

"Are you the detectives who are asking about the three missing boys?"

I replied, "Yes. I'm Detective James Jack and this is Detective Frank Czech. We're asking the drivers of the Milwaukee Avenue route if they saw those kids yesterday afternoon or last night. You know anything about them?"

"I was just starting my first run and one of the guys told me you were asking questions about some boys. My name is Bruno Mancarini, and I was driving that route last night between 8:00 and 9:00 p.m. I think I saw those kids."

I felt like we were just dealt a royal flush. Even though I was initially skeptical about witness statements received at the very beginning of any investigation, I felt optimistic about this. It was the first break we had gotten so far. Someone had seen the kids after they left the Peterson home Sunday night.

I took out my notebook and asked the supervisor if it was all right to use his office for a few minutes.

"What about my route? I'm on Elston Avenue tonight and the 4332 bus is ready to go out. I'm substituting for Jim Czeplewski."

The supervisor responded that he could get someone else to take the 4332 bus and Mancarini could take the next one out after his interview was complete.

We entered the dispatch office and took seats next to a large, gray metal desk. After we were seated and I had my notebook and pen out, the bus driver proceeded to tell us about what he saw.

"I live over on the 5400 block of Linder Avenue. So it's pretty easy for me to get here if they need somebody, and I want to put in some overtime. I don't usually take the Elston route, but they called me from downtown and said get right over here 'cause they were short one driver. I usually have Mondays and Tuesdays off. I work the weekend, so they give us two days off in a row."

Mancarini went on to tell us that he'd been employed by the CTA for the past fourteen years. He wasn't that familiar with the Milwaukee route and hadn't driven the route very often in the past. Due to difficulties with the bus at the beginning of the run, his supervisor had ordered him to proceed only as far as Central Avenue, instead of advancing farther north to Devon Avenue at the city limits.

He recalled that the sign giving the destination of the bus, located above the windshield, had been changed to indicate that Central Street was as far as it would go that evening.

"Like I said, I was on the Milwaukee route last night. The weather was pretty bad, so I was running a little late on my schedule. Hardly anyone was on the bus, maybe about five or six people. You know, Sunday night and everything. Not many people are on the bus at that time of the night.

"Anyway, at about Berteau Avenue, these three young kids get on the bus."

"Okay, three boys? About how old were they?" I interrupted him and took control of the interview.

"I'd say they were about twelve or thirteen years old. One of them could have been younger. He was smaller than the other two."

"Did you notice how they were dressed? What kind of clothes were they wearing?"

The driver paused for a second, looked down at the floor of the office then up to the ceiling, trying to remember.

"Gee, I don't know. They weren't sloppy. You know, just casual clothes, I guess. Blue jeans, maybe. Whatever these young kids wear."

"Were they alone or was someone with them?"

"They got on alone. Like I said, there weren't many people on the bus last night."

"Are you sure you saw three boys get on the bus together?"

"Yes. The reason I remember them is they showed their student I.D. cards and all three paid the ten cents fare. I kind of kidded around with one of them, because he looked so young. That's one of the reasons I remember there were three of them."

I reached into the left inside pocket of my suit coat and took out three small black and white photographs. I put them on top of the desk, one-by-one, and lined them up in a row. The fathers had given us the pictures, indicating they had been taken in the past year. Each one was a formal portrait picture, similar to those taken by school photographers for a yearbook.

"Are these the three boys you saw last night on your bus?"

Without any hesitation, Bruno Mancarini said, "Yes, that's them."

Hearing the confidence in the man's response, I was certain we had someone who would add a significant piece to the puzzle. I controlled my excitement about the driver's identification and continued to question him.

"Did you hear them talk about anything? Did they say anything to you when they got on the bus?"

"Well, just what I told you before. You know, they showed their I.D.s, and I joked with the smaller one about how old he was."

"Now about what time was this that they got on the bus?" I was double-checking the information out of habit. I was convinced the driver saw the boys, but wanted to be sure of the accuracy of the his recollection.

"Well, I was almost to the end of the route. So it was probably close to 9:00 p.m."

"And they got on near Irving Park Avenue?"

"Yes. I think it was the second stop after Irving Park, one or two stops after Irving Park. Like I said, it wasn't too busy last night." His answer was less confident about the exact location where the boys boarded the bus. I thought it was because the driver was not that familiar with the route. It was something Frank and I would have to check out by driving down there ourselves.

"Do you remember if you heard them talk about where they had been or where they were going?" I went back to my original line of questioning.

"No. Just that right before they got off the bus I heard the tallest boy yell out to the other two 'there's the bowling alley.'"

"What bowling alley? Where was the bus when he said that?"

"It must have been a few minutes after they got on the bus. We were just getting to Lawrence Avenue. I heard the boy yell out like that, kind of like he was excited and I looked up in my rear view mirror-the one that lets me look back at the passengers in the bus. I saw him looking out the window. Then they got off at Lawrence Avenue."

Both Frank and I knew there was only one bowling alley close to that location. It was a small one in the basement of a building on Giddings Avenue with about ten lanes. I continued with the interview, but casually looked in Frank's direction when the bus driver described the location of the bus when the boy saw the bowling alley.

"Where were they sitting when the boys said that?"

"I remember they were on the right side of the bus, we were going north so I guess he saw something on the east side of Milwaukee Avenue, just south of Lawrence. They got off at Lawrence Avenue. They were the only ones to get off at that stop. The other thing was, they didn't get any transfers when they got on and didn't get one when they got off the bus."

I knew immediately what that meant. The boys had intended to get off the bus at Central, near the Peterson home, when they first got on. Had they intended to get off and then re-board the bus, they probably would have requested a transfer slip allowing them to re-board without paying another fare. Did they see someone they knew or were they going to meet someone at the bowling alley? I stored that information and continued to question the driver.

"Did you see where the boys went after they got off the bus?"

"No, I didn't. I had a green light at Lawrence Avenue, so I was paying attention to getting through the intersection after they got off, and I closed the door."

After showing Bruno Mancarini the list of names of other bus drivers on the Milwaukee Avenue route, which I had taken down in the notebook, I asked Mancarini if he knew any of the drivers. Mancarini said he knew most of them and would ask if they had seen the boys. We planned to formally request that the CTA provide the names and addresses of each driver in the entire depot, not just the drivers of the Milwaukee Avenue route. Nothing would be left to chance, even though finding Mancarini on our first visit to the bus depot was a welcomed bit of luck.

We thanked Mr. Mancarini, and asked the depot supervisor for the name of the person whom they should contact at the CTA to get the list of drivers. We also asked that he tell every one of the bus drivers to contact either Frank or me at the station immediately if they had seen the boys or knew of anyone who said they saw them.

We returned to our car and drove back to the station. This was big news and it needed to be reported to Sgt. Murphy at once. We also planned to give the information to the news reporters waiting at the station as soon as it was cleared with Captain Corcoran. It was an opportunity to provide the reporters with some critical news on the case. More importantly, it was an opportunity to get the assistance of the media in locating the five or six passengers identified by Mancarini as being on the Milwaukee Avenue bus with the boys.

9:05 p.m.

After reporting what we had learned to Sgt. Murphy, we needed to confirm the locations where the bus driver had said the boys boarded and left the Milwaukee Avenue bus.

Overnight the number of detectives assigned to the case increased dramatically. Squads from two other Districts had been instructed to help in the investigation, and the number of uniformed officers on each shift increased to twice the usual number.

The descriptions of the boys had been sent out over the Department Teletype System to all Chicago Police Districts, with instructions to notify the 33rd District should anyone report they had seen the boys.

Murphy showed Frank and me a copy of the late afternoon edition of the Chicago Tribune. It was a short news article, only three paragraphs long. It described the boys, their addresses, ages, and the fact that they had been missing since Sunday evening.

I took the article with us as Frank and I left the Station. Frank drove south on Milwaukee Avenue to Lawrence Avenue, where the boys had reportedly gotten off the bus. He drove past Lawrence Avenue, proceeding slowly as we passed a bank, a bakery, and small neighborhood stores.

As we approached the first cross street on Milwaukee Avenue, Frank turned left and headed down Giddings Avenue.

One block from the intersection was a small, lighted sign hanging off the building on the north side of the street, and dark letters identified it as the "Jefferson Park Recreation Alleys."

We parked our car on the south side of Giddings Avenue and walked across the street to the building entrance. We walked down a flight of stairs and into a dimly lit, smoke-filled area with ten lanes, a bar, and a pool table.

Jack Sanpayo and his brother John Mandes owned the bowling alley. Frank knew them from the police leagues. They weren't at the alley when we arrived, so we identified ourselves to the manager and other employees and asked if they had seen three boys in the bowling alley on Sunday afternoon or evening. Each employee was shown the boys' pictures, but everyone stated that they had not seen them. One employee, however, stated that he knew the Peterson boy, and that Mr. Peterson often bowled at the lanes.

I asked the manager to contact the owners and have them call the District so that an interview could be arranged.

After leaving the bowling alley, we drove south on Milwaukee Avenue to Irving Park Road. By looking at the bus stop signs on the east side of Milwaukee Avenue, we concluded that the second stop after Irving Park was Montrose Avenue, not Berteau, as bus driver Mancarini had thought. This focused our attention on a specific location where the boys may have been before they boarded the bus.

We drove back to the District and reported to Sgt. Murphy what was learned from our interviews at the Jefferson Park Recreation

Alleys. In addition, we told Murphy we believed the boys boarded the Milwaukee Avenue bus at Montrose Avenue, just a few minutes south of Lawrence Avenue.

Murphy was seated at one of the extra desks that had been placed in the detectives' room to accommodate the additional men assigned to the case. He looked up from the small mound of files and phone messages littering the desk.

"Good work. When the owners of the bowling alley call in, you guys do the follow-up. I know you've been running with the case pretty hard since this morning, but you've gotten the best leads so far and you know this case better than anyone."

I understood how things went on these cases, and staying on it was fine by me. I told Sgt. Murphy that our reports and the most recent results from the investigation would be on his desk first thing in the morning.

Murphy nodded and said, "Thanks. Both of you have brought us the best news so far. By the way, while you were out on the street, I got a call from the Schuessler family. A relative called Mrs. Schuessler and said that friends of the relative's son reported that they had seen the boys in a bowling alley Sunday night. Mrs. Schuessler asked if you would go over to her house to get the names and addresses. I know it's almost 10:00 p.m., but she said to come over at anytime."

I walked over to my desk, picked up the original missing persons sheet I had filled out on Sunday evening, then checked my notebook for the phone number of the Schuessler residence. I dialed the number, and Mr. Schuessler answered the phone. His voice was noticeably weak and strained. Mr. Schuessler told me it was no problem to visit the home at this hour. In the background, I could hear the voices of several people and the sound of a woman crying.

10:10 p.m.

I drove the car this time. Speeding off from the lot next to the station, I drove north, turned right onto Central Avenue and then to Bryn Mawr, then right to Mango and approached the Schuessler home. There were several reporters waiting in their cars and milling around on the sidewalk.

Frank rang the doorbell and a woman in her thirties answered the door. We identified ourselves and were shown into the living room.

Mrs. Schuessler was seated on a green couch, her eyes darkened and swollen from crying. Though surrounded by relatives and friends, she was clearly inconsolable.

We approached her and were met by Mr. Schuessler who told the relatives and friends, "These are the two detectives who are helping us find our boys."

The small group of people quietly greeted us, but refrained from asking any questions.

"How are you doing, detectives?" asked Mrs. Schuessler, making every effort to be gracious even under such trying circumstances. "Are you getting anywhere on the case? I want my boys back so bad."

Frank looked down at his hands, which held his gray fedora, and nervously spun the rim of his hat. He was rarely at a loss for words, but now he couldn't seem to say anything.

I decided to step in. "We're doing everything we can, Mrs. Schuessler, which is why we're here. We're trying to collect any kind of information we can. The officers in the District have been working around the clock and we're just going to try as hard as we can."

The woman who had answered the door introduced herself as the relative who had called Mrs. Schuessler earlier in the evening.

"My son's friends were at my home Sunday night. They said that they saw the boys that night at a bowling alley. I didn't think much about it at the time. Then when the boys were missing, and I heard about it, I remembered what they had told me. I thought it was important, so I called Eleanor tonight. The neighbors have already been here, and they told Eleanor that their son saw the boys. That's when she called you."

The boy's name was Ernest Niewiadomski, age 17, and he lived in the 5700 block of Major Avenue, just around the corner from the Schuessler home. We thanked the woman and Mrs. Schuessler, and before leaving, politely reminded everyone to contact the station should they hear anything else about the boys.

As Frank and I left the Schuessler home, three reporters ran up to us. "Any new clues, detectives? Any suspects?" they asked. I stopped and looked at them, getting impatient with having to answer the same questions over and over again.

"We just told you what we found out while we were back at the station. Check with Detective Sgt. Murphy if you didn't get it." I was referring to the interview with the bus driver, Bruno Mancarini, and the request that any passengers on the Milwaukee Avenue bus who may have seen the boys call the District.

Some of the reporters looked at each other, wondering what scoop they had missed. One or two had been at the station when the news was given out, and they began to tell the reporters who hadn't been there of the latest results of the investigation.

I was satisfied that we could leave in the confusion of the moment and not be followed by the reporters. Still, we purposely drove four blocks out of our way then doubled back to the Niewiadomski address, just in case the reporters followed us.

We arrived at the address Mrs. Schuessler and her relative had given us and were met at the door by Mr. and Mrs. Niewiadomski. I introduced us as detectives from the 33rd District investigating the disappearance of the Schuessler brothers and Robert Peterson.

The couple was cordial and invited us into their home. They knew the purpose of the visit and called their son to join us in the living room

My first question was to the young man's parents, asking if they were giving us permission to question their son.

"Yes, it's okay. We're all trying to help find the boys," Mrs. Niewiadomski said nervously as she looked over at her husband. He nodded in agreement.

I started the interview by asking questions concerning the boy's background and learned that Ernest was 17 years old and a student at Gordon Technical High School. He knew the Schuessler boys because they were neighbors, and said that the Schuessler home was about five houses down from his, on the next street over. He knew the brothers very well and played baseball with them. Every so often, they would need extra players, and they would let the younger kids play. That's how he knew the younger of the Schuessler brothers,

Tony.

"We played every day in the summer. Even in the winter when the weather was good. We let the little kids play to fill in. Sometimes we let them play right field or something. Just to let everybody play. That's how I got to know them. We became real good friends." Ernest was a little nervous as he spoke, but we determined that it was probably because this was his first experience talking with the police.

"Now Ernest, tell us in your own words what took place Sunday night, last night." I was trying to calm the boy down a little, but without being condescending.

"Well, my two sisters, Leona and Delphine, and me went to the Monte-Cristo Bowling Alley on Montrose Avenue about 7:15 last night. We were standing around watching people bowl and..."

"How old are your sisters, Ernest?" I interrupted the boy and took out my notebook to jot down the information.

"Leona's 20 years old and Delphine is 10 years old."

"Okay, go ahead, you were watching people bowl at the Monte-Cristo on Montrose."

"I ran into the Schuessler brothers and their friend Bobby Peterson. The Schuesslers, Bobby and I talked a little bit, and they told me they were at a movie, and they got to the bowling alley on the bus."

"Did they tell you what movie they saw or where they saw it?"

"Yes. They said they had seen a Disney movie, the 'African Lion,' and they said they saw it downtown. I asked them if they wanted to bowl and one of them said 'Not unless you pay for it.' I told them that my sister was paying for me so I didn't have any money. "

"What else do you remember talking with them about?"

"Not much. Bobby and Tony went to the washroom. They were in there for a few minutes, and then they came out and met up with John Schuessler and said 'Let's go, John.' Then they left."

"Do you know where they went?"

"No, I don't."

"Do you know what they were wearing last night?"

"Yeah, John and Tony were wearing Cubs jackets and Bobby was wearing a White Sox jacket."

"Do you know what time it was, approximately, when you were talking to them and at about what time they left?"

"They probably left about twenty minutes after I got there, maybe around 8:00 p.m."

"Ernest, what was the next thing you did after you found out the boys were missing?"

"Well, I heard that they were missing, and I told my mother that we had seen them last night at the bowling alley. She said we should go see Mrs. Schuessler to tell her what we saw—me and my sisters. That maybe we could help a little."

"What happened when you got to the Schuessler home?"

"Well, we told Mrs. Schuessler that we had seen the boys and that there was another boy with them and not to worry because there was safety in numbers. There were three of them, and they probably just went someplace."

We thanked Ernest and his parents, gave them our card and asked that they call either Frank or me, if they remembered anything else about the boys.

10:55 p.m.

I drove the squad away from the curb of the Niewiadomski residence, and headed south. There was a lot of information flooding my mind.

"Frank, we still have some time left tonight. Why don't we take a fast run over to the Drake Bowling Alley over on Montrose and talk to somebody there before we check out the Monte-Cristo Bowl?"

"What for?" Frank leaned forward to turn up the volume on the car's police radio. "The kid said they were at the Monte-Cristo. That's where he says he saw the boys."

I looked over at Frank then glanced back at the road ahead. Traffic was light at this time of the night. Most people were home in bed after working an 8-hour day, but not the detectives working on this case. Our shifts were beginning to stretch into 14-hour days.

"I figure the Monte-Cristo is going to be a key point in the investigation, and we'll have to meet with Murphy and the Captain before we go in there to investigate. These kids were probably at two bowling alleys that night, maybe a third one. The Drake Bowl is close enough for them to walk to. Maybe they went there after stopping at the Monte-Cristo and before they got on the bus to head north. We'll have to check on it anyway, so why not do it now? We might get lucky."

"Sounds good to me." Frank unwrapped another cigar, licked the end and popped it into his mouth.

We arrived at the corner of Drake and Montrose Avenues and parked the car directly in front of the entrance to the bowling alley. League play was just about over and men were coming out of the doors in twos and threes with their bowling bags held firmly in one hand. They wore jackets with league names like "Ten Pins" and "Chicago Strikers" embroidered on the back.

Frank and I walked through the double doors, and introduced ourselves to the man at the main desk. His name was Walter Lungren, and he was the manager of the Drake Bowling Alley.

We showed him the pictures of the boys and asked if he had ever seen them. He replied that he recognized them and that they had been there last night about 8:00 p.m. and wanted to bowl, but left because the bowling leagues occupied all of the available lanes. He said the boys then walked away from the counter, and he never saw them again.

"Do you know if they stayed at the bowling alley after you spoke with them?" I began to get impatient. There was something about this guy that wasn't right. The uncaring way he responded bothered me.

"No, I don't."

"Do you know if they had any conversations or did you see them talking to anybody in the bowling alley?" I pressed on, trying to put a finger on what it was that I didn't like about the man.

"No, I didn't. I was paying attention to the league play and other bowlers coming up and getting shoes and things like that."

I showed him the pictures again, and the man stated positively that these were the boys that he talked to earlier in the evening on Sunday.

At that point, I turned to Frank and said, "Let's go." I stopped halfway to the door, turned in the direction of the manager and said,

"By the way, thanks. You were very helpful."

After we were out of the building, I stopped and said, "Frank, let's check with Murphy. I was right. This guy puts the kids here at about 8:00 last night. If Murphy says it's okay, we can go over to the Monte-Cristo and double check all the information we've got so far. We'll have a pretty good idea of where the kids were and what time they were there."

Frank shrugged his shoulders. It was after 11:00 p.m., and we were into the 15th hour of our shift. "Why not? My dinner's already cold."

I got on the car radio and told Sgt. Murphy about the information we had put together so far. I also told Murphy that we wanted to visit the Monte-Cristo, but knew that it was going to be an important point of the investigation, and we needed his okay first.

"Seeing as I already have you on the line, Sarge, what do you think? Should we go over there and see if all this stuff checks out with what the Niewiadomski kid already told us?"

"All right, you guys take a ride over there. Don't do too much. Get all the information you can and see if they can identify the boys as being in there."

"Okay, Sarge. We'll see you later."

I started to place the mike back on its cradle but stopped suddenly before hanging up. Murphy's voice was barking back at me.

"No, you won't. I'm going home. I'll see you guys tomorrow morning. We're gonna have a meeting somewhere around 10:00 a.m., and we're gonna put all this information together and discuss what we're going to do from that point on. So far, you guys are hitting bull's eyes."

"Night, Sarge. Talk to you later." I put the mike back on its cradle and smiled a little. Murphy didn't give out compliments like that very often.

I drove the car down the street, a few blocks east of the Drake Bowling Alley, and pulled up to the curb. The Monte-Cristo was an old, two-story building with the lanes on the second floor. As we stood at the bottom steps of the building, a few men passed us who had just navigated the steep flight of more than twenty stairs.

As I struggled up what felt like a straight vertical incline, I thought to myself, Jesus, those guys carry 15-pound balls up these damned stairs and then go bowling? By the time you get up the stairs, who the hell would want to bowl?

After reaching the top of the stairs, we looked around the lanes and saw that league play was just about over. The scorekeepers' tables were littered with empty Budweiser bottles and the ashtrays stuffed with cigarette and cigar butts. The place was supposed to be air-conditioned, but a thick cloud of smoke hung over the lanes, and the place was as warm as a hothouse in July.

I approached the counter as Frank took a look around and observed the last few frames being bowled by a league wearing "Arnie's Polka Palace" in hot pink letters on the backs of their bowling shirts.

The alley manager, Edward C. Davis, greeted me and carefully looked at the Chicago Police Department Detective's badge I held up to his face.

"Did you work here last night?" I asked the man.

"Yeah. I only work a few days a week. I'm getting too old for this. I work nights, mainly. Not feeling too well."

I showed him the pictures of the boys.

"Yeah. I remember seeing them in here. They were in here twice last night."

"Twice?" The surprise jumped out of my throat before I knew it.

"Yeah. Once about 3:15 p.m. yesterday afternoon."

I called Frank. "Frank, come here a minute." He stopped watching Arnie's team and walked over to the counter.

"The boys were in here before they went to the movies."

Frank's eyebrows arched.

The manager continued. "They were in here again about 7:00 p.m. I remember the first time they were in here they asked me how much it cost to bowl. I told them the price was forty-three cents a lane, plus shoe rental of fifteen cents. They told me that was too much for them, and they left. When they came back the second time later last night, the alleys were crowded with the leagues so they couldn't bowl anyway."

I asked the manager if he saw the boys leave.

"No, I didn't."

"Did you see the boys standing around the alleys watching the bowlers or talking to anybody else in the bowling alley?"

The man thought about it for a second. "I did see them talking to some other boy, and I think there were some girls around, but I don't know if they were friends. I know I saw them talking to a boy on the second visit."

We thanked the manager and asked if he would be willing to come into the District sometime later and give a written statement. He said he would be happy to, just that he would need a day or two notice so somebody else could cover for him at work.

As we walked carefully down the flight of stairs, I wondered if anyone had ever fallen down them with a 15-pound ball. I couldn't remember any emergency calls from this alley, at least, not on my shift.

Frank drove us back to the District. I turned the car's interior light on. It wasn't very bright, but I wanted to go over some of my notes.

"We have to complain about getting brighter lights in here, Frank."

"Shit, Jim, that's like trying to separate salt from sugar with a pair of boxing gloves."

"Well, I think we've got something pretty solid here. Number one, the Peterson and Schuessler boys were at the bowling alley—the Monte Cristo—at 7:15 p.m., talking to Ernest, their neighbor. That's a positive I.D.

"Number two, Niewiadomski said the boys told him they went to the movies. He even mentioned the movie that was playing at the Loop Theater."

Frank looked over at me. "And the boys also told the Niewiadomski kid they traveled by bus."

"Right. So we assume that they went downtown and spent money on the bus."

"Sounds right." Frank sped up a little bit, but kept it under the speed limit.

Tuesday
October 18, 1955
12:45 a.m.

Frank and I arrived at the station just after the midnight shift was starting and most of the officers were preparing to leave for their tours of duty. Most of them stopped in our office and wanted to know if we had any news about the boys.

"No one's heard anything about them yet," was my response. I knew how fast word could get around the District and the last thing I wanted was the entire District to know about the latest interviews before the Captain had a chance to review our reports.

I deflected any other questions by asking if the officers had photos and descriptions of the clothing worn by the boys. They responded by holding the flyers up and waiving them in the air like an old-time card cheer at a football game.

Frank and I sat down at our desks and knocked out the reports so Sgt. Murphy could have them first thing in the morning. When we left, we placed the reports on the top of the pile of papers and files steadily growing in height on Murphy's desk along with a note that read "See you at 10:00 a.m."

We left exhausted yet satisfied with our progress. We knew the boys had been at the bowling alleys, now all we had to do was fill in the missing pieces from the time the boys left for the movies, and more importantly, where they were now.

On the way home, I went over the details of the interviews and statements taken from the witnesses that night. Everything seemed to fit. If we could just find these kids, I could go back to a somewhat normal life. Maybe even get some sleep.

I rolled down the driver's side window of my 1953 Chevy to let in some fresh air. It was cold outside and a blast of frigid night air rushed into the car. That was just what I needed to help keep me awake during the drive home.

I thought about Frank and myself and hoped that we could handle the pressure this case was starting to give us. Frank was much older than I was, but when it came to police work he just kept going.

He was as dedicated as they come. And as tough as any two guys I knew in the Department. I was lucky to have Frank as my partner. But I still wished he would stop sucking on those damned cigars.

I turned on the car radio and tuned in on the police calls. Most of the detectives had a special frequency channel installed in their personal vehicles to pick up calls. You never knew when you could help out another officer.

On this particular night, however, I was listening for any word about the boys. There were some conversations about a burglary, another missing person-a young woman who had been reported missing by her husband but nothing about those kids.

At home, I set my alarm for 8:30 a.m. Usually, I didn't need an alarm clock because I wake up at about the same time every day. But I was tired from working the 16-hour shift, and I didn't want to oversleep.

9:30 a.m.

I got up just before the alarm went off and was shaved, showered, and out the door in less than thirty minutes. I drove directly to the District station, keeping the car radio tuned to the police frequency still hoping to hear anything new about the case.

It was a bright, sunny autumn day and the temperature was nearing sixty degrees. I really enjoy days like that one. Everything smells fresh and looks clean. I remember thinking to myself it would be great if the day brought some good news to match the beautiful fall weather.

I pulled into the station, and the parking area looked like the lots next to Wrigley Field. There wasn't an open space in sight. I could tell by the number of unmarked cars that the detective detail had been increased dramatically. The crowd outside was also getting out of hand, as the number of reporters assigned to case seemed to increase proportionally to the police effort. After parking nearly two blocks away, I decided to use the back entrance to avoid the crowd on Gale Street.

I stopped and stared at the dozens of media trucks and crews scurrying around the area carrying cameras, electrical cables, microphones, and lights. In this moment of hesitation, a group of reporters spotted me before I could make it into the building.

"Are you going to go out and search new areas today? Do you have any leads?" I knew they needed answers to those questions, but it wasn't my job to provide them. "Refer any questions to Detective Sgt. Murphy and Captain Corcoran," I yelled. With that, I strong-armed my way into the building.

The narrow hallway was so packed with uniformed officers and detectives that you could hardly move. I edged my way down the hallway to reach the door leading to the reception area. That room too was crowded with officers and detectives from other Districts. I could also see officials from Police Headquarters and the Mayor's Office. It was obvious that the case was heating up and the powers that be wanted answers just as the reporters did.

As I made my way through the crowded room to the front desk, I caught the attention of the desk sergeant who pointed in the direction of the double doors leading to the front of the station.

Sgt. Murphy was standing at the front entrance talking to several teams of detectives and supervisors. He was doing his best to be heard over the noise of scores of conversations taking place in the reception area. Murphy saw me coming over and motioned to me to join the group.

The detectives and supervisors were introducing themselves. I recognized most of them and Frank had worked with them in one-way or another on several other high profile cases.

"Glad to see you, Jim," Murphy said. He shook my hand and introduced me to the other detectives.

"This is Detective James Jack, one of my guys here at the District. He and Detective Frank Czech were the first ones on this case. They took the "Missing Persons" report Sunday night from the father of one of the boys. They've logged a lot of hours on this case."

I acknowledged the other men as Murphy continued talking.

"Sorry to cut this short, guys," Murphy said, "but I've got to get up front and start the briefing. We'll have a meeting in Captain Corcoran's office after the briefing so you can get our assignments and go over what we'll be doing today."

Murphy made his way through the crowd and reached a small podium at the front of the reception room used to give daily briefings to the uniformed officers by the Watch Commander.

"Attention, men. Attention," Murphy called out to us. He waited a few seconds as our conversations trailed off and the room became quiet.

"For those of you who have been assigned to this District for the purpose of locating the three missing boys, my name is Detective Sergeant Murphy. I hope you've all gotten to know each other's names because we'll all be working together on this one.

"This is the second day of the boys' disappearance. The search for the boys is still in progress. Captain Corcoran of this District is in charge, and he will direct the mass search. We have fifty patrolmen and detectives going house-to-house in search of the area surrounding Giddings and Milwaukee Avenues. That was the area where the boys were last seen Sunday night. The men who are conducting the search right now are working in two-man teams. They're interviewing and questioning all residents in that particular area. They're covering individual homes, apartments, passageways, basements, rooftops, garbage cans, alleys, vacant lots and attics.

"You all have the descriptions of the boys and what they were wearing when they left the Peterson home Sunday afternoon. You'll be briefed throughout the day on the search teams, the routes for the reports which you will be generating, and the times for these general briefings which will continue on for the duration of this search."

Just then Captain Corcoran entered and signaled Sgt. Murphy to continue the briefing. When Murphy finished, Captain Corcoran walked to the front of the reception area and Murphy introduced him to the men. Corcoran thanked Murphy; then addressed us. The room had been very quiet during Murphy's briefing, but now you could hear a pin drop. It was dead silence.

"Men, Detective Sergeant Murphy has provided you with all the information we have so far. I'll be brief. I want to impress upon you that as time passes in this case, the chances for a good outcome diminish significantly. The more efficient we are the better our chances are of finding these boys. Good luck, men. Now let's hit the street."

As soon as Captain Corcoran finished, Murphy called out to the detectives under his command. "Jack, Czech, Koeppe, and Schulze! Go to the Captain's office," he shouted over the noise of men leaving the room. The detectives and uniformed officers filed through the double doors at the back of the reception area, walked down the flight of marble stairs, and out the front doors of the station. Scores of reporters and a crowd of civilians eager for any word about the missing boys awaited them.

When our team arrived at Captain Corcoran office, he was on the phone. He waived to us to come in. Everyone took a seat, except Detective Koeppe who had to get a chair from the Captain's reception room.

He was over six feet tall and weighed 310 pounds, the standard wooden chairs in the Captain's office wouldn't support him.

After finishing his telephone conversation, Captain Corcoran carefully put the receiver back on its cradle and then turned to us.

"That was the Commissioner. He's personally following our progress on this case, and we have his okay to get as much assistance on it as we need. Now, what have we got so far?"

Corcoran wanted to know the status of the investigation and the results of the interviews conducted by Frank and me the day before. Murphy got up and handed the Captain the reports that we completed before going off duty last night.

A map of the 33rd District, dividing its twenty-three square miles into separate beat areas, hung on the wall of the Captain's office. Using the map and a list of assigned officers and detectives, Captain Corcoran and Murphy expanded the search area. Using the intersection of Lawrence and Milwaukee Avenues, where the boys were last seen, as the center point, the search area was expanded by drawing concentric circles around the area. The circles were marked off in one-mile increments until the last circle touched the boundaries of Cook County.

Each area was assigned as supervising detectives and sergeants routinely arrived at the Captain's office to be given their specific assignment. Reporting schedules were developed, with instructions that written reports be delivered to the Captain's office every two hours. Extra telephone lines were installed at the station, as was additional radio equipment to facilitate communication between the men in the search area and the District Commander's Office. The planning continued through the morning and into the early afternoon.

"Lou, I asked you to hold all the calls," the Captain shouted as he responded to the buzz coming through the intercom system.

A man's voice responded quietly, but firmly.

"Captain, you need to take this call."

1:15 p.m.

Captain Corcoran reached for the phone on the upper right side of his desk. He turned to us and said, "It's probably the Commissioner. I just got off the phone with him before you guys came in here. I told him we're out there all over the District, but he's getting heat from the Mayor's Office to get something new on this."

Corcoran seemed relaxed and leaned back in his chair as he acknowledged the caller. But then suddenly, he stood up and screamed, "Oh no!" His face turned pale, and he used the edge of his desk to keep steady. For a moment, I thought he might collapse. His sudden exclamation surprised all of us. He was usually calm, composed and didn't reveal much of himself, particularly in front of his men. But as he listened to the caller, his eyes began to tear and his voice trembled. "Yeah…I know…we'll be there." Slowly, he placed the receiver down and moved the phone back to the corner of his desk. With sadness in his eyes, he looked at us all somberly.

"Men, we've got a triple homicide." He sighed and sat down into his chair. His disappointment at the news was obvious. "The naked bodies of three boys have been found in a parking lot in Robinson's Woods."

The room was completely silent. We were stunned. As police officers, we felt we knew the worst that people can do to each other. Clearly, we were wrong.

My eyes began to blur, as tears rolled down my face. And like everyone else in the room, I sat motionlessly in my chair. Finally, I looked at Frank. He too was crying. In fact, there was not a dry-eye in the room.

Corcoran's eyes narrowed, and his jaws became clenched.

Suddenly, his eyes focused on Murphy, and he jumped to his feet. "I want you out there as fast as your ass can get you there," he barked. He leaned down and pressed the intercom button to his secretary.

"Get in here, NOW!"

Reacting to the command, we all began to rush towards the door. "You guys better control things out there, he said. "The Forest Rangers found the bodies, and God knows who else is there by now." He grabbed the phone and began dialing, then took a dark brown file from the top of his desk and pulled out the photographs of the boys.

Murphy nodded to the Captain, then turned to Frank and me, and said. "Jim, Frank…you go with me. Do you know where Robinson's Woods is?"

I shot back, "Sure do, Sarge."

"Good. Koeppe, Schulze you stay here with the Captain. Keep your phone lines open. We'll stay in contact with you by radio and let you know what's going on. Make sure the Captain is informed immediately about what we report."

The three of us dashed out the back door and ran to the squad car. I got behind the wheel with Frank in the front seat while Sgt. Murphy climbed into the back seat.

As the doors of the squad car closed, I hit the siren. As the lights began to flash, four reporters came running towards the car.

"What do we do about those guys?" I asked.

"Fuck 'em. Run 'em over," Frank growled. "They got no business on police property anyway."

I hit the accelerator and wheeled the car out of lot before the reporters could stop us. We sped through traffic, weaving around slower moving vehicles making our way past the city limits and out towards Robinson's Woods. Soon we had a small convoy of police cars following us. Murphy could see them from the back seat.

Every officer and detective with his radio on had gotten the news by now.

Lawrence Avenue was the main route to Robinson's Woods and

to Chicago's second airport. It was located outside the city limits, but still under the city's jurisdiction and considered city property. Whenever problems at the airport required police attention, the 33rd District was assigned to handle it. Department regulations required responding officers to use the most direct route, Lawrence Avenue, to reach the airport. Officers from the District often referred to the area surrounding it as "Shitsville." It was mainly an industrial area, with few homes and surrounded by the Forest Preserve District.

As we raced down Lawrence Avenue, I conducted a mental checklist. It was automatic, something I did before arriving at a crime scene: do I have everything I need before we get there? What about back up?

I glanced into the squad car's rear view mirror. A line of marked and unmarked squad cars continued to trail us, trying to keep up pace as we sped west. Well, I thought, there's plenty of back up.

When we arrived at the scene, cars from the Police Department, Cook County Sheriff's Police, Forest Preserve Rangers, and even the Coroner's Office already lined the road.

The only parking spot available was at the top of the bridge that spanned the Des Plaines River. Somehow, I managed to squeeze the squad between two Forest Ranger vehicles, and the three of us walked from there to the entrance of the woods.

As we walked up the driveway and into the small parking lot, we could see a crowd of about twenty-five officers 200 feet from the entrance, at the edge of the asphalt lot. Without saying a word, we carefully walked along the parking pavement to avoid stepping onto the grassy area next to the lot. We were trained to avoid damaging possible evidence, like footprints, and so we took precautions to approach the scene with care.

I yelled out to one of the uniformed officers. "Is there a marked route we can take to the scene?" The officer turned and motioned with his right arm to a spot a few feet away from the crowd of police officers. "Over here. This way."

A small path from the edge of the parking lot led up a small rise overlooking a ditch running parallel to the parking lot. We carefully walked up the small incline and to the ditch.

I had never seen anything so gruesome. Here, in the middle of a picnic area, lay the naked and brutalized bodies of the boys. One body was face down, with a twig clutched in one hand. He was stretched across the other two bodies, which faced the sky. The head of one of the bodies was coated with dried blood.

My hands began to shake, and my stomach churned. Though I fought hard to hold back the tears, it just wasn't possible. Soon, I staggered to the edge of the road and vomited. I couldn't begin to imagine what sort of animal could do such a thing.

I took a moment to collect myself. Images of the terrified and distraught mothers and fathers flashed in my head. The bodies would have to be positively identified. How on earth were the boys' parents going to get through this? For that matter, how would any of us get through this?

By the time I had walked back to reach Frank and Murphy, Coroner Walter McCarron, his chief investigator, Harry Glos, and Deputy Coroner Joseph Tigerman had begun checking the bodies. Being careful not to disturb the scene, they took notes of the location of the bodies, their position relative to the driveway, and made brief sketches.

Murphy suddenly broke the silence and asked the Coroner, "Are we tentatively identifying the victims from their description?"

Coroner McCarron turned to Murphy and replied, "Yes, that's what we're going to do right now until we get some positive identification from the parents."

I knew the reason for Murphy's question. We couldn't establish positive identification because there was no clothing. Although a description of the boys had been given, and we knew what they were wearing when they were last seen, in those days, physical evidence such as clothing was the primary means of positive identification. Shrewdly, the killer or killers had stripped the boys' clothing. This, unfortunately, meant positive identification from a family member or someone who personally knew the boys was required.

A small crowd of on-lookers and reporters began to arrive. It wasn't clear to me who was directing the larger group of officers, and the number of people coming into the forest preserve parking lot began to increase. I soon became annoyed by the apparent disorganization.

"Hey, Murphy," I asked, "Who's in charge here?"

"Right now, Sheriff Joseph Lohman of the Sheriff's Department is."

I quickly responded, "This should be considered a crime scene. There should be police personnel only. And look at those guys near the bodies. For Christ's sake, they're walking all over the place. If there were any footprints near those bodies before those guys got here, you can forget about it now. Let's get horses in here to block off the area, starting with the entrance to the parking lot. If access isn't controlled, we'll have half the city in here."

Murphy nodded in agreement. "You're right, Jim," he said. "Get that set up immediately. Put uniformed officers at the entrance, and I'll let Sheriff Lohman know what we're doing."

Frank and I walked quickly to the parking lot entrance. As we passed uniformed Sheriff's officers and Forest Rangers, we asked for their assistance in controlling the area.

"The Sheriff wants this area controlled," Frank said. "Don't let anyone without a badge or I.D. past the entrance."

"Frank, I'll get the Rangers and Sheriffs to clear the civilians and reporters out of here."

Though this was clearly a time when the numerous law enforcement agencies of the city involved at the scene needed to come together, each was operating as if it had sole jurisdiction over the area. Unfortunately, this practice has continued for more than forty years and still impacts the effectiveness of solving missing children cases to this day.

The Forest Rangers claimed that since the bodies were found in the Forest Preserve, they had the authority to lead the investigation. Similarly, the State's Attorneys Office, Coroner's Office, and Chicago Police Departments all believed that their offices should direct the scene.

Choosing to ignore the politics, Frank and I focused on what needed to be done, and at times took our authority beyond its limits. We saw something needed to be done and we just did it. Like telling an idiot with a camera, taking pictures of the scene and walking all over the place, to get the hell out of there before we arrested him. Or physically taking a few reporters who had crept around the control point back to the driveway entrance and handing them over to the Sheriff's deputies with orders to arrest them if they got past them again. As Frank noted, at times it was a zoo. But we had a job to do and nothing was going to stop us from doing it. Perhaps we were taking it personally. That's because it was personal.

Some time around 2:00 p.m., Captain Corcoran arrived with Detectives Koeppe, Schulze and James Lanners. They were briefed immediately. Murphy also informed the Captain that a positive identification of the bodies was needed.

"One thing though," Murphy interrupted. "Coroner McCarron said initially that the identification could be made by the boys' descriptions. But he's changed his mind and now wants a positive I.D. Only, he doesn't want the parents here at the scene. He thinks it'll be too much for them."

Captain Corcoran paused for a moment.

"Koeppe, you and Schulze go and locate a family member of the boys or a neighbor who can identify them. Get them over here as fast as possible. Murphy, you and I need to speak with McCarron."

Koeppe and Schulze radioed back to the station that they needed assistance locating individuals, other than the parents, who could positively identify the bodies. They were told that the parents and some neighbors had already called the station. Everyone wanted to know what the latest news was on the boys.

"Good," said Koeppe, "let's ask if the neighbors can help us on this, at least for now. Maybe we can get a positive I.D. for all three boys. Schulze and I will pick them up. Do us a favor, though, and let this Mrs. Kolk and Lieutenant O'Donohue know we're going to stop by. But don't mention anything about having them do the identification. Schulze and I will ask them when we get there. If anyone wants us, we'll be in our car and then back here at the scene. And don't let anyone know about this. I don't want to meet a bunch of curious civilians or reporters when we pick them up."

When Koeppe and Schulze arrived at Lt. O'Donohue's, who was a member of the Chicago Fire Department, they were relieved to find that there were no on-lookers.

After identifying themselves, they asked the lieutenant if he would help identify the boys' bodies. He, of course, agreed. When they approached Mrs. Kolk, she hesitated at first then seemed comforted by the fact that Lt. O'Donohue told her not to worry.

Koeppe and Schulze drove back to Robinson's Woods, with Kolk and O'Donohue in the back seat. No one spoke as they neared the entrance to the forest preserve parking lot. By this time, the Sheriff's deputies and Forest Rangers had directed most of the civilian traffic off the street and cleared the way for them to enter.

Captain Corcoran was speaking with the Coroner as Koeppe approached the group. A photographer from the Coroner's office was still taking pictures. The huge flash bulb on his box camera emitted a loud "click" and flash of light each time he hit the shutter button.

Koeppe got Corcoran's attention as he walked closer to the group. "Here they are now, Coroner." He said as he waived Koeppe over.

"Captain, we've got two neighbors of the Schuessler boys. One of them is a lieutenant with the Chicago Fire Department. He's the one who will probably make the identification. The other neighbor is Mrs. Marion Kolk. I don't think she's up to doing this, but on our way here she seemed to be okay"

"Can the lieutenant identify all three of the boys?"

"I don't think so, Captain. He doesn't know the Peterson boy."

"Okay. Bring him over anyway and we'll at least I.D. the Schuessler boys. If it's positive, we'll be almost 100 percent on the Peterson boy." Captain Corcoran turned toward Coroner McCarron to see if that was agreeable. The Coroner nodded back.

"I didn't want the parents out here. It's too much," McCarron said.

Koeppe walked back to the squad car where Schulze, Mrs. Kolk, Lt. O'Donohue were waiting with me.

"Lieutenant," Koeppe said, "the Coroner and Captain Corcoran would like you to formally identify the bodies. Mrs. Kolk, if you don't mind, you can wait here with Detective Jack." Instinctively, Koeppe knew she wouldn't be up to viewing the scene, so he gave her a way out.

None of this was easy for anyone. Everyone knew that and no one wanted to make it harder than it already was. Still, as we sat together in the car, Mrs. Kolk began to cry. "I'm sorry… I just can't… they were the two best boys in the neighborhood," she sobbed.

"It's alright, Mrs. Kolk," I said to her. "Just stay here with me."

Detective Koeppe led O'Donohue to where Captain Corcoran and Coroner McCarron were standing and introduced him.

They all walked toward the edge of the parking lot and toward the ditch. Lt. O'Donohue, dressed casually in a baseball jacket, walked next to Detective Schulze and the Coroner as they approached the bodies of the boys.

As they neared the scene, O'Donohue suddenly stopped. He raised his right arm and pointed with his index finger to the body closest to him.

"That's John Schuessler," he said. Then pointing in the opposite direction, he said "And that's Anton Schuessler." His face became contorted, his lips tightened against his teeth. He quickly turned away from the bodies and looked at Captain Corcoran.

"This has got to be the work of some madman," he said. "I've never seen anything like this."

Captain Corcoran put his hand on O'Donohue's shoulder and walked him toward the parking lot and away from the bodies.

"Thanks, Lieutenant. It's rough on all of us. We appreciate you coming out, and I'm sure the families are grateful that you spared them from seeing this. Detective Koeppe will drive you and Mrs. Kolk back to your homes."

Lt. O'Donohue shook the Captain's hand and said he was glad he could help. He walked slowly back to the squad car where I waited with Mrs. Kolk. He paused momentarily, sadly looked back at the scene, then turned and got into front seat of the car. I can only imagine what was going through his mind.

Frank and I still needed to complete our investigation of the scene. A crime reporter from the Sun-Times, Art Petacque, joined us. Together we jotted down observations and sometimes even compared notes. He was one of the few reporters allowed in the area.

"One: dried blood on boys' faces and heads. Bodies thrown in ditch; after rain storm blood should have washed away.

"Two: no footprints immediately next to bodies; maybe the bodies were thrown from a truck or car.

"Three: smudges on hands, back, soles of feet appear to be grease. Killed someplace else? Garage, machine shop, or dirty building?"

I was still taking notes and creating possible theories when Coroner McCarron approached Murphy and me.

"Sgt. Murphy, we're finished with our investigation here, and we'll be taking the bodies to the city morgue using vehicles from the Ochler Funeral Home in Des Plaines. Do you need more time? We can hold off until your detectives are through."

"That's okay, Coroner McCarron. We've got what we need. I know we all want to have results from your office as soon as possible."

Just then Frank walked up. "Excuse me Coroner McCarron. Jim, can I see you a minute?"

McCarron nodded and walked toward his chief investigator and deputy, who were preparing to direct the men from the Coroner's Office in the removal of the bodies. A black van pulled up next to the scene and two men emerged from the double doors at the back, each carrying a dark brown canvas stretcher and body bag.

"Jim, we haven't interviewed the guy who found the bodies," Frank said. "Has anyone identified him?"

"Yeah. He's over there." I pointed to the middle of the parking lot, where a small crowd of reporters had gathered around a man in his mid-fifties. He nervously turned from one reporter to another and attempted to respond to each one as they peppered him with questions.

We quickly crossed the parking lot to reach him, working our way to the center of the crowd. We identified ourselves as detectives.

"Excuse us, gentlemen. Sir, we're detectives with the 33rd District and we need to ask you a few questions." I was courteous to the reporters, but couldn't resist taking a small parting shot as we walked the man to an isolated area of the parking lot.

"My name is Victor Livingston," the man said softly. He was

still visibly shaken but as we asked him questions, he did his best to explain what had happened.

"Mr. Livingston, what do you do?" I asked.

"I'm a liquor salesman with Capital Wine and Liquors. I sell beer and liquor to the taverns, bars, and restaurants in this area."

"Okay, so why were you in the forest preserve this afternoon?"

"Well, the weather was perfect, and I had had a great sales day, nearly 30 percent higher than normal.

"For most of the morning, I'd been at Heuer's Restaurant and Bar. The owner, Red Heuer, has bought from me for the past five months, and we spent some time talking after he placed his liquor order.

"By the time we finished, it was past noon, and I started to get hungry.

"I bring my lunch with me on my route and eat it between stops, usually in my car while parked in a customer's lot. Today, the weather was so great I wanted to take advantage of it. I decided to find a place to eat in the forest preserve.

"I knew I was close to Robinson's Woods, so I decided to come here.

"On the right side of River Road, about a half-mile down, I saw the entrance to "Che-Che-Pin-Qua" Forest Preserves. That's the original Indian name of Robinson's Woods.

"I backed into one of the parking spaces on the east side of the parking lot and was the only car here.

"I reached for my lunch bag on the rear passenger's seat. When I did, I noticed something outside, behind the trunk of my car. It looked like a pile of something, but I didn't know what. I had to strain to see it, but when I did, I realized immediately that it was a body.

"I didn't get out of my car to see it. All I could think of was that I had to find someone, so I rushed back to Heuer's Restaurant.

"I told them I needed a phone and that we had to call the police.

"I explained what I had seen, and Don Gudeman, the owner of Mello-Rust Farm, had Red call the Forest Rangers. He said that he knew one of the Rangers.

"We waited in Don's car for the Forest Ranger to arrive. His name is Roger Byrne and he seemed to know Don and Red. Shortly after he arrived, we went to the forest preserve together. He asked us to stay in the car while he checked things out.

"Ranger Byrne walked to the edge of the pavement of the parking lot. He looked into the ditch and came running back to the car.

"I asked him if he had seen the body. He said it's not one body. It's three bodies. Three boys."

3:45 p.m

"Don't look now, Sarge, but we've got more company coming." I pointed to the parking lot entrance. Illinois Bell Telephone Company had dispatched two mobile units to the scene. The closest telephone was approximately one-half mile away (the one Mr. Livingston had used to call the Forest Rangers). The two mobile units pulled alongside the ditch where the bodies lie. Once the mobile units were set up, the police departments and other government agencies (and probably reporters) could maintain direct communications with their offices.

A man in a Cook County Forest Ranger uniform approached Frank, Sergeant Murphy, and me as we watched the Bell Telephone workmen set up their lines. He introduced himself as Captain Conway, and told us that one of his rangers had just arrived at the scene.

"I thought you might want to interview him. His name is Peter Carlino, and he was working the night shift last night. This is his beat." Conway called out to the man walking behind him.

"Carlino, come over here a minute. This is Detective Jim Jack, Detective Frank Czech, and Detective Sgt. Murphy from the 33rd District."

The man joined our group of detectives, shook hands with us and said, "Call me Pete."

I was the last to shake Pete's hand and started to question him before he broke off the handshake.

"Pete, could you tell us what kind of area this is?"

"Well, the good news is, this area is used by birdwatchers and persons out to see the fall colors."

I looked at Carlino, then looked at Frank and smiled. I already knew this guy was a jerk and a liar.

"Great, that's not the news I wanted to hear. That's the good news? How about the bad news? I hear this is a hang-out for perverts."

I guess you could say that," Carlino answered. I could tell Carlino got the message by the change in his response to the question. Still, I continued to push.

"Some reports have come across our desks through the months that Robinson's Woods is flooded with degenerates. Even the owners of riding stables have made complaints that there have been numerous attempts to molest riders on the trails."

"I guess you could say that," Carlino repeated. I started to get impatient.

"So you're telling me that there <u>are</u> degenerates and mopes in the forest preserves that hide out and try and grab people?

"Listen, Detective, there are a lot of remote sections in the Preserves here with a lot of underbrush. It goes on for miles. We can't be every place at once."

Captain Conway interrupted the conversation in an attempt to tone down the heated exchange and to provide useful information.

"The Forest Preserve Rangers drive in their vehicles and patrol the parking lots and the areas that service the roads outside. We also have mounted Rangers, and they try to get back into the secluded parts of the woods."

"Have you made any arrests, Captain?" I realized I was pressing too hard, so I toned my voice down a bit. The Captain sensed my frustration with Ranger Carlino's casual attitude. Maybe the guy hadn't seen the bodies, hadn't seen what the rest of us had seen.

"Yes, some."

"Would the reports be available to us if we drove over to your office? I would only want to get names, addresses, and dates."

"Detective, I would be happy to give you any information you want."

I directed my attention back to Ranger Carlino. "Pete, how many times a day do you patrol this lot?"

"It's visited hourly by Forest Preserve Rangers until about 2:00 in the morning.

"That's a.m.?"

"Yes." Ranger Carlino stiffened a bit, his responses more clipped and formal. "I personally checked this area out myself yesterday."

"Could you tell me, would that be Sunday night/Monday morning or Monday night/Tuesday morning?"

"Both nights before 2:00 a.m. I found no automobiles here, and I drove off."

"Do you lock up with a chain link?"

"No, I don't."

"So anyone can drive in even after two o'clock, is that right?"

"Yes."

Carlino went on to state that if the bodies had been in the ditch at the time he made his scheduled tour, he probably would not have seen them because the ditch is below the level of the lot itself. He speculated that the bodies would not have been in the range of his headlights because of the ditch being so low.

Captain Conway added that he had originally received the call from Livingston and had sent Ranger John Byrne to the scene. Byrne met Livingston at Heuer's Restaurant and then went to the scene. At that point, they discovered there were three bodies, not one.

"So you see, even Mr. Livingston's view of the ditch was obscured. He originally reported seeing only one body. When the Ranger drove out, got out of his vehicle and checked, that's when he saw all three bodies."

"Listen, Captain, I appreciate your help. Pete, thanks for your help, too. We'll pick up those addresses in the next day or two." The Rangers shook our hands again and walked back across the parking lot.

I scanned the area once more. Robert Randall, one of the crime lab experts, was making some plaster casts of all the tire marks found on the roadway and the ditches near where the bodies had been. He and John Bell would later take the casts to the Chicago Crime Lab for examination. I had known Bell and Randall from previous cases and knew they were meticulous and professional. If any evidence was there, they'd find it.

The Forest Rangers had found articles of clothing in their search of the area, including a pair of blue shorts and a pair of green shorts wrapped in a white bath towel. Frank and I didn't think the clothing was related to the crime, since it appeared that the shorts were too big be worn by any of the boys. But, they were sent to the Crime Lab anyway, along with the other clothing found near the scene.

By the time we'd returned from our interviews, Coroner McCarron was preparing to leave to continue his investigation at the morgue. I approached him and began to ask about what they had observed at the scene.

"Doc, before you leave can you give us something tangible to work on? How about the blood on the head of the Peterson boy? Could you give us some idea of what caused it? How about an estimated time of death? Frank and I noticed that the boys looked to have been beaten pretty badly. And we also noticed that some kind of tape was used on their nose and mouths. How about something to help us out?"

McCarron looked at me and shook his head. "Sorry, Detective. I would give you answers if I could, but I would rather not elaborate until a post-mortem is completed. The most important thing now is to find the clothing these boys were wearing and possibly the place of the slayings. That would be the most important thing you could do right now."

5:00 p.m.

The bright sunlight was fading through the brown and gold leaves of the forest. As we approached our car, a large group of reporters surrounded us.

"What have you got, detectives? Any idea who might have done this? What about the families?" The questions were repetitive, shooting from all sides.

Frank was the first to respond.

"We can't tell you guys anything. The Coroner hasn't completed his investigation and neither have we. Don't worry. You'll be the first to know." He forced a smile, jumped into the front seat of the car, turned on the ignition, and quickly pulled out of the parking space.

As we sped down Lawrence Avenue, we talked about what we had seen. We speculated on the significance of where the boys were found, why there had been no clothing found at the scene, and about the smudges of grease on the soles of their feet.

Murphy listened to our theories as he sat in the back seat.

"You guys did an excellent job at the scene," he said. "Don't forget to keep a running account of your observations, your interviews, and activities. We're going to need them to assist the other detectives coming in on the case. They'll be cold and won't know anything except what you've got documented in your notes.

"This is going to be the biggest case we've ever worked on, and we'll be under a lot of pressure to solve this thing quickly. Just remember, we can't jump to any conclusions until we've got facts to support them."

We were three blocks shy of the District when we saw the crowd. What had been a few dozen people earlier in the day had now grown to a few hundred people, filling the sidewalks, the street, blocking all the entrances to the Station.

"Shit," Frank remarked. "There must be 200 reporters out there. Roll up your windows, guys." He turned on the siren to get their attention. Then slowly cruised past the on-lookers as they opened a path for the squad car then swarmed around it like locusts.

"Any clues? Did you get the killers?" We could hear the questions shouted over and over, hands patting the car and faces peering into the windows.

"This really pisses me off." Frank was trying to control the steering wheel, while at the same time being careful not to run over anyone as he edged the car slowly toward the entrance bay. It seemed like minutes passed before we were able to clear the crowd and enter the side entrance.

5:55 p.m.

We ran up the back stairs and into Murphy's office. In the short time since we were gone, his desk had been piled with mounds of papers, messages, and files. The phone messages were from police headquarters, the Mayor's Office, and from what looked like hundreds of civilian tipsters offering to help in the investigation. Frank and I walked into our office and found similar mountains of messages and notes piled on our desks as well.

Murphy arrived a few minutes later, grinning sheepishly at the sight. Frank looked up, and said, "And every possible lead will have to be checked out, right?"

"That's right," Murphy replied. "Every fuckin' one of them."

"Murph, can I get authorization to send out a special bulletin?" I asked. "Can you authorize it in Captain Corcoran's name? It's a bulletin on the clothing worn by the boys when they were last seen."

"Sure, Jim. I'll okay it."

The bulletin I wrote out was entered and dated:

"6:17 p.m., October 18, 1955. #206-B: Victims in the above photos wearing the described clothing were last seen alive at 9:00 p.m. Sunday night, October 16, 1955 in the vicinity of Lawrence and Milwaukee Avenues. Any information relative to the above subjects should be forwarded at once to Chief of Detectives John T. O'Malley, Chicago Police Department, 1121 S. State Street, Chicago, Illinois by order of Timothy O'Connor, Commissioner of Police."

I had already sent out pictures of the boys along with a description of the clothing worn by each boy under each photograph.

In addition, a police artist, Detective Adolph Valanis, had compiled sketches of the boys showing how they were dressed when they disappeared. The drawings were printed in pamphlet form and handed out in the South Edgebrook area where the boys lived and in other areas where the boys may have been seen.

The District also issued an appeal through the press to five passengers on board the Northbound Milwaukee Avenue bus on the night of Sunday, October 16, 1955 from which the boys alighted. Potential witnesses were instructed to contact the 33rd District should they have any information.

Just as I was completing the last of the bulletins, I heard Sergeant Murphy call out from the hallway. "Jim, let me see you a minute." I got up and met him in the hallway.

"I want you and Frank to contact the Peterson and Schuessler families."

"Sarge, you've got to be kidding. Haven't they been through enough today?"

"Yes, they have. But, we need their help, and we can't wait. I want you to search the boys' effects, their bedrooms, their books, everything. See if they got any threatening notes, anything that can help us on this. Then get your asses back here because we have other things that's got to be checked out right away."

"Murph, do you know what those homes are going to be like right now?"

"Yes, I know," he responded softly. "But it's got to be done."

We drove to the Schuessler home on Mango Avenue. Once again, hordes of reporters and neighbors gathered outside.

"Why the hell don't they leave these people alone? Don't they have a fuckin' heart?" Frank was screaming. He was clearly annoyed and made no effort to hide it. Stone-faced, we walked up the sidewalk to the little bungalow and rang the doorbell.

A man answered the door, and we introduced ourselves. The man introduced himself as John Holtz, the father of Mrs. Schuessler.

"Have you got some news? Is that why you're here?"

"No, I wish we did, sir. We want to get permission from Mr. and Mrs. Schuessler to check the boys' effects. But first my partner and I want to express our deepest condolences and sorrow over the deaths of their boys."

Mr. Holtz could not hold his tears. He opened the door and led us into the living room of the home. There Mrs. Schuessler sat on a tiny green couch, with a blanket tucked around her legs. Relatives and neighbors were making every effort to console her.

Mr. Holtz introduced us. Though we had just visited the house the day before, Mrs. Schuessler seemed to have no recollection of this. Though we tried to be sensitive to her grief, she suddenly fainted.

The family's physician, Dr. Leonard Goldberg quickly rushed to her aid. After a short time, he revived her and gave her a sedative.

The house was charged with tension and grief as relatives sobbed around us. You could see the hurt in their eyes and bewilderment on their faces. This tragedy was incomprehensible for them and our presence only heightened their anguish. We motioned to get Mr. Holtz's attention in an attempt to complete our business.

However, as I caught his eye and began to move toward him, Mr. Holtz brushed past us and ran to the front door.

Mr. Schuessler and his brother-in-law were standing in the doorway. Dazed, the father could barely walk. His brother-in-law held him up as best he could. On seeing them enter the house, Mr. Holtz had rushed to help him.

Mr. Schuessler, Mr. Holtz and Mr. Schuessler's brother-in-law slowly crossed the room. When they reached the tiny green couch, Mr. Schuessler fell to his knees and began to cry. "Mother.... Mother...our boys...."

Though I tried to be strong and remain detached, I could feel tears swelling in my eyes. I turned to Frank and in hushed tones said, "We've got to get the hell out of here. Get permission from Holtz to search the house and let's go."

Frank moved closer to Mr. Holtz and quietly asked to speak with him.

"Mr. Holtz," Frank began. "Mr. Holtz, please. I know this is a terrible time for the family, but it's very important that my partner and I search the boys' room. We need to get back to the station and keep working on finding the people who did this."

When we returned from the boys' rooms, friends and relatives still surrounded their parents, and I knew it would be best to leave, without disturbing them.

"Please let Mr. and Mrs. Schuessler know that we're doing our best to find the person or persons who did this. Thanks again for your help, Mr. Holtz. Please call us for any reason."

Mr. Holtz nodded, took my card with the station phone number on it and showed us to the door. Of course, the reporters hadn't moved, and we didn't bother to respond to their questions.

As we got into our squad car, I turned to Frank and said "You know, we have to go through this all over again at the Peterson home. I don't know if I can be as polite to these newshounds when we get there."

Frank nodded. "Who says we have to be polite. They're just in the way, and they're not helping the families any by hanging around their homes like vultures. Trouble is, we can't run them in or knock 'em in the head for loitering or trespassing, as much as I'd like to. Otherwise, you and I are going to be writing traffic tickets on the Indiana border—if we're lucky."

I nodded and looked out the passenger window as we drove towards the Peterson home. The neighborhood still had some empty lots here. But being on the edge of the city limits, it wouldn't be long before homes or three-flats would be built to accommodate the newer residents moving slowly outward from the older neighborhoods.

We arrived at the Peterson home, and just as we had expected, were immediately surrounded by newspaper reporters, radio newsmen, and television crews gathered on the front sidewalk of the home. The questions started before we had a chance to get out of the car.

"Any news on the triple murders?"

"Any suspects yet?"

Frank and I walked quickly across the street, onto the small front lawn of the Peterson home and past the reporters. As we strode up the walkway to the front steps, we noticed that Mr. Peterson had already begun to open the door.

He didn't speak to us. He didn't need to. The anguish in his face said all we needed to know, but we had a job to do, so I started the conversation.

"Mr. Peterson, we're sorry for needing to disturb you and your wife, but we came over to check out Robert's personal effects. With your permission, of course." I let Frank go in first, then followed quickly behind him.

"We hate to do this to you. I know this is a difficult time for you and your wife." I continued into the entryway as Mr. Peterson closed the door behind us. From the foyer leading to the living room, we could hear children crying and the soft hum of a woman's wailing.

Mr. Peterson's expression grew noticeably pained as the sounds in the room consumed us. I never felt so uncomfortable or helpless in my life. Frank quickly found words of condolence.

"On behalf of the Department, we would like to express our deepest condolences and sorrow over the loss of your son. Every detective and police officer in the District has been called in to help us on this, Mr. Peterson. And we're getting more assistance every hour from Districts all across the city and county."

Mr. Peterson looked up, his eyes were watery and his face lacked color. We knew he would cry at any moment.

"My wife is in our bedroom with our family doctor. If she was up to it, I would let you talk to her, but she can't talk to anyone right now."

"We understand, Mr. Peterson. My partner and I just want to look at Robert's room and some of his personal effects. It might help us. We sincerely hate to bother you at a time like this, but it's very important that we work as fast as we can now to try and find the persons responsible for this."

"Robert's room is this way," he said in a half-whisper.

He led us up a flight of carpeted stairs to Robert's bedroom on the second floor.

According to Mr. Peterson, it was just as he had left it on Sunday afternoon. The bed was neatly made, no clothes were strewn about, and I was struck by the orderliness of the room. Frank and I checked Robert's dresser, and his closet, looked through his books and magazines. Typical kid, I thought to myself. There was Boy Scout clothing in the closet and a pocketknife in one of the drawers next to the baseball cards.

After the search was complete, we thanked Mr. Peterson as he brought us back downstairs and to the front door. He somberly looked at Frank and me for a moment, then turned and stared out at the crowd in front of his home. "You know, I went to the police station Sunday night to get help locating our boy. Only you and Detective Czech seemed interested. But now, take a look. Everybody's interested. I went to the television station this morning, and they wanted me to broadcast a description of the boys this evening. Now it's too late. They're gone."

There wasn't anything we could have said to ease his pain. As he would later say, Robert was not just his son; they were best friends. Our throats dry, and hearts heavy, any attempt to find words failed us. Our parting glances signaled to Mr. Peterson that we understood. Silently, Frank and I moved closer to the door.

Mr. Peterson opened it slowly, taking a moment to survey the crowd.

"Thanks for your help, detectives. Please find the people who did this to Robert and his friends."

Frank and I nodded and walked briskly down the steps, past the crowd of neighbors and reporters, and across the street to our car. No one asked us anything this time. The crowd was silent. Mr. Peterson stood in the doorway, his face ashen, with tears streaming down his cheeks. He waited until we had gotten into our car before slowly closing the door.

8:32 p.m.

As we walked into Sgt. Murphy's office, Koeppe, Schulze and O'Neil poured over notes, files, and messages still piled high on his desk.

Murphy looked up and said, "Good, you made it back just in time. Captain Corcoran just laid out plans for us. He has been in contact with Commissioner O'Connor, who promised the Captain that the Department will make available the required manpower we need on this case. Even though the boys were found outside the city, we're going to work with other authorities on this." Just then, Captain Corcoran appeared in the doorway.

"Men, this is going to be a tough one for us. We've got to get the killer or killers of those boys as soon as possible. Murphy, did you give them a summary of what's going to take place as of now?"

"No, Captain. Frank and Jim just got here, and I just started to brief them."

"Okay, then I'll tell you. First, all you guys will be working out of this unit under Sergeant Murphy and under my command. Tomorrow morning, a meeting will be held here in the assembly area at 7:00 a.m. sharp. That's 7:00 a.m SHARP!" He looked around the room at each of us, making sure that we understood him. He paused for a few seconds before continuing.

"Everybody else who was notified will be here, so there will be a large assembly of other detectives from all over the city here. I want you guys to be here early so we can show a little diplomacy and be 100 percent prepared with the latest information we have. Coroner McCarron or a representative will discuss the post-mortem autopsy at that time, at least, a prelim.

"Second, a special investigating unit will be set up to coordinate the efforts of the county, the state and the city authorities. One will be at Central Police Headquarters at 11th and State. The second one will be here at Jefferson Park Station where most of the fieldwork is going on.

"In charge of the unit will be Lt. Patrick J. Deeley, who is now acting Captain at Racine Police District. I think you all know him, and some of you have worked with him in the past. He will have his headquarters at the Central Building. I will be in charge at this office. Most of the records and reports will remain at Police Central but will be available between Police Central and our unit here. Most of the men will be called to some sort of meeting in the crime lab this week to review any and all evidence about this case which has been discovered up to this point. The unit working out of Jefferson Park, that's this unit, will have about sixty of the top detective investigators in the Chicago Police Department working out of here, who will also be deputized, within a week, by Coroner McCarron. This will give us more latitude and jurisdiction in our investigations if we need to make an arrest in the county or outside the City of Chicago.

"We'll also have 250 men from the traffic division. Their chief objective will be to find the clothing and the place where the boys were slain. I'll be directing the mass search. The men from traffic division will make a house-to-house search of the whole north half of the twenty-three square mile Jefferson Park District. They'll also be searching vacant lots and sheds, basements, and garages.

"The Commissioner wants a hand-picked squad of twenty men to help the county and forest preserve authorities in combing the area for possible murder weapons used on the victims. They'll probably be men from this Division. I'm going to send you guys scouring this area since you know it and have worked it. You're my ace detectives on this one. Also, Murphy will keep a map on his office wall for that purpose. The other officers will be searching the South Edgebrook area. Be prepared.

"All of the police officers will be distributing drawings of the boys showing how they were dressed when they disappeared. The sketch from Sgt. Valanis will be printed in sort of a pamphlet form, and they'll be handed out to each person the officers talk to in the South Edgebrook area where the boys lived and also where they went to school.

"I also want somebody from this unit to attend the inquest, the wakes, and the funerals of the boys. You never can tell. It's happened before in these cases, maybe the sick people who did this might turn up to see what they did. I also want the person in here from the bowling alley. Was it the maintenance guy? The guy who spoke to the boys Sunday night from the Monte-Cristo Bowling Alley. What was his name, Jim?"

"George Dillon, Captain."

"That's the guy."

"But Captain, this guy's really flaky."

"That's what Murphy said about him and why I want him in here as soon as possible. Then maybe we'll concentrate on the theory that some of the other police agencies were indicating that the boys were the victims of teenage gangs. That's the speculation right now."

I hesitated a moment. I didn't want to interrupt the Captain, but because of the nature of the case and the fact that I had been on it from the moment Mr. Peterson had walked into the station Sunday night to report the boys missing, I felt he would understand.

"Captain, I don't buy that too much. Not at this point. There are a lot of other theories that Sgt. Murphy, Frank, and I have been going over."

"I know, Jim. Murphy's been letting me know what you and the other guys have been thinking about."

I pressed on. "If it was up to me, the first thing I would do is round up every known sex offender and moron in the city."

It wasn't unusual for the men under his command to make such direct suggestions about the direction of an investigation. Captain Corcoran's style was not as dictatorial as some other District Commanders. He knew his men were on the street, day in, and day out, and he always listened.

"We're going to do that, too, Jim. Those are some of the things that are going to be discussed tomorrow. Now I want you all to go home and get a little sleep. You've been up day and night on this case, and today was pretty rough. Be back here at 7:00 a.m., fresh and ready."

The Investigation

Wednesday
October 19, 1955
6:30 a.m.

The sun had just crept up over the buildings and trees lining Gale Street as I arrived at the 33rd District. Not many neighbors had stirred from their homes to gather in front of the station, but dozens of media reporters were milling around. Some had been there since midnight, replacing colleagues who had gone home after covering the story the previous day. A few looked as if they hadn't gone home.

Traffic was blocked off on either side of the station house one block in either direction. Barricades were set up, manned by uniformed officers who allowed only authorized personnel to pass through. I parked two blocks from the station across from a nearby park. As I approached the building, uniformed officers waved me in.

Although it was not yet 7:00 a.m. the assembly area was packed with detectives and uniformed police officers. A thick cloud of smoke hung in the area continuously being fed by the cigars, cigarettes, and pipes nearly every officer and detective seemed to be smoking.

As I made my way through the crowd, I met detectives from other units and Districts who had been assigned to the case. Frank had worked with many of them on other cases, and they were all competent, seasoned detectives. As we waited for Captain Corcoran to arrive, we discussed the murders. It seemed that everyone had a theory about the case. None of the detectives I spoke with believed it was the result of some teenage gang. All of them thought their first task should be to pick up every known sex offender in the area. Great minds think alike, I thought to myself.

The room suddenly grew quiet and everyone turned towards the front of the assembly room. Captain Corcoran approached the podium to address the men. The room was filled with nearly three times the number of men who would normally stand awaiting their orders for the day.

Corcoran walked quickly toward the front of the assembly hall, turned toward the men assembled before him, while grasping the sides of the podium. He paused for a moment and looked at the faces of the officers and detectives. The only sound was the whirring of two floor fans in the back of the room.

"Good morning, gentlemen. My name is Captain Russell Corcoran. I'm Commander of the 33rd District. We're facing one of the most vicious slayings in Chicago's history. The brutal beating and strangulation of three young grade school boys—Robert Peterson, age thirteen, and the Schuessler brothers John, age thirteen, and Anton, eleven, whose bodies were found yesterday at approximately 12:15 p.m. in Robinson's Woods just outside the city near Lawrence and Dee Roads.

"I've been in contact with Commissioner Timothy O'Connor, and he has given me permission to detail twenty of my best men to cooperate with the county. The boys had been missing since Sunday, October 16, at about 8:55 p.m. and were last seen in the vicinity of Lawrence and Milwaukee Avenues.

"At this point, I'll let Detective James Jack fill you in on what we have discovered so far in our investigation. He and Detective Frank Czech have been working on this case from the very beginning. He'll give you a timetable of the victims' last hours. Coroner McCarron will be here shortly to brief you on the results of the autopsy conducted by the chief pathologist, Dr. Jerry Kearns. So if you have notebooks or pads, pull them out and if you don't get everything, see Jim or Frank after the briefing, and I'm sure they'll be able to give you everything that you need."

Captain Corcoran moved away from the podium and motioned for me to come to forward and address the men.

"Thanks, Captain. Good morning, men. I'm going to give you the timetable as briefly as possible. If you have any questions, just let me know."

I started from the time Frank and I returned to the District Sunday night and first interviewed Mr. Peterson. I recounted how the boys had gone downtown to a movie and never returned home. A neighborhood friend, Ernest Niewiadomski, and his two sisters at the Monte Cristo Lanes saw them at 7:00 p.m., Sunday night.

I then recounted how Victor Livingston had discovered the boys' bodies in Robinson's Woods. As I described the crime scene, my voice began to tighten. Conscious of being overcome with sadness, I looked away and coughed to clear my throat. Although I knew the other men sensed my discomfort, I took a deep breath and continued.

"That's where we are up to now. We do have other information, which we'll disseminate after the meeting. Let me turn things back over to Captain Corcoran so he can fill you in on the units that will be in charge of this investigation."

I stepped aside, and the Captain took over. He restated what he had told Sgt. Murphy and his own detectives the night before. He outlined the two command units, one downtown and one at this District.

"I will request that every man working out of this unit keep a chronological list and report on the investigator's activity for each day he is on assignment." Corcoran looked up and saw Coroner McCarron enter at the far end of the room.

"I see that Coroner McCarron has just arrived, and I know we're all anxious to hear what he has to say. If you have any questions, see Detectives Jack and Czech after this meeting."

The sea of faces turned to the back of the room. Quiet conversations began among the officers then stopped suddenly as a pudgy, middle-aged man walked to the side of the assembly room while taking off a heavy gray overcoat.

Coroner McCarron walked hurriedly to the front of the assembly room, making his way along the edge of the crowded room where officers and detectives stood against the wall. As he made his way, they backed up, allowing him a narrow space to reach the podium.

McCarron greeted Captain Corcoran and shook his hand. He held out his coat to one of the uniformed officers standing closest to him. The officer grabbed it and put it over his arm. McCarron turned and faced the officers in front of him.

"Good morning men. We have to get through this as fast as we can so we can hit the streets. First, you're going to be hearing this for a long time. This is one of the most brutal and vicious murders I've ever investigated. It's going to have the greatest search force ever assembled for a manhunt to find the killer or killers of the boys. I don't know where to start, but when I do, please don't interrupt. Take notes, and when I'm finished, I'll try to answer your questions. Just be patient and we'll get through this. It's not going to be pretty, but it has to be done.

"First, I want to say that our Chief Pathologist, Dr. Jerry Kearns, reported to me this morning. Dr. Kearns worked from yesterday afternoon when the bodies were found, all night last night with his associates, and I'm really grateful that he stayed until the examination was completed.

"He reported to me after the autopsies were done and indicated that the deaths of all three boys were the result of strangulation. There was no evidence of sexual assault. But sex is not eliminated entirely as a cause for the crime.

"The time of death was estimated at some time between 9:00 p.m. and midnight, October 16. The victims had been dead 36 to 40 hours before their bodies were found on October 18, at 12:15 p.m. This is only a preliminary examination. I wanted to have something for you men today and all the units that are working on this so that you have something to work on.

"The boys died of asphyxiation by suffocation and violence had been applied to their necks—this is concerning all three of the boys. The bodies bore abrasions and welts. Welts on the face could have been caused by being slapped or punched.

"The boy, Robert Peterson, received the worst treatment. The husky little boy was 5 feet 2 inches tall. He was hit repeatedly over the head, causing ten deep cuts, which reached the skull. All three boys received blows on the backs of their heads, causing internal hemorrhage. They were killed before discoloration could take place. Peterson was either hit with a tire tool, a jack handle, or perhaps the butt of a gun or a gun itself. But these injuries were not sufficient to kill him.

"At this time we believe that the Peterson boy was strangled with a necktie, cord, belt or something similar. The only obvious fact is that the Peterson boy fought for his life. The head injuries show that.

"The bodies of the two brothers, Anton and John Schuessler, indicate that they were choked. Fingernail marks on their necks indicate that they had been strangled by hand. Their bodies bore other wounds. Both Schuesslers had taken an awful lot of blows, also on the forehead, the eyes and elsewhere as if they were being punched with a fist, just like a boxing match.

"Anton Schuessler's body had been pounded heavily. His chest and stomach, as if someone was kicking him in the chest while lying down or kicking him in the stomach while lying down.

"The older Schuessler boy, John, apparently died from a blow on his Adam's apple with the edge of a hand, similar to a judo blow. His right eye was swollen and the skin around the right eye and his face had been beaten and battered. The right side of his face was bruised, probably the result of a punch or kick. Once again, they were beaten very badly. They were just manhandled.

"The evidence from the examination of the bruises shows a terrific struggle. Their noses and mouths had been taped. Also, their wrists were bound together in front of them. But the tape was removed when the bodies were dumped in Robinson's Woods. This tape was a type used by physicians. Dr. Kearns was unable to determine the exact width of the tape. He stated that the tape was applied after the boys were unconscious or dead.

"We found grease spots and smudges of grease on all three of the youths: elbows, heels and soles of the feet. This is considered a significant clue for the crime lab because Dr. Kearns interpreted this as indicating the killer or killers may have stripped the boys. With the grease smudges, the boys could have picked them up by walking around the floor of a machine shop, or the dirty floor of a garage.

"He also stated in his report that they were a little puzzled by the waffle-like impressions on the backs of the bodies. Dr. Kearns stated that apparently they were made by some kind of matting, perhaps a doormat or car mat or even springs. His theory is that the boys may have been made to lay on a bare bedspring or a matted rug. This would cause the waffle-like impressions.

"The Chicago Crime Lab also took scrapings from underneath the fingernails of the young Peterson boy in the belief that he may have struggled in a close combat with his killer or killers. The evidence also discounted the chance that the boys had been drugged. Even the fist of the eleven-year old Anton Schuessler was bruised. A person in a drugged state would not put up that kind of fight.

"Dr. Kearns' analysis of the contents of the boys' stomachs did not appear to provide any clues. His report stated that the Peterson boy died 'several hours after he had eaten his last meal.' The stomach showed traces of liquid, in other words practically empty.

"The stomachs of the Schuessler boys, John and Anton, showed remnants of tomato skins, noodles or macaroni, and vegetables. Dr. Walter Camp at the University of Illinois Department of Toxicology is analyzing the vital tissues.

"The killer or killers who perpetrated this crime knew what they were doing. They were careful to remove the adhesive tape used to gag them, since it may have shown fingerprints. As of yet, the tape has not been found.

"Dr. Kearns' report indicated that the examination disclosed that there was no evidence of sexual molestation, although I have spoken with Dr. Harry R. Hoffman, an associate of the Cook County Behavior Clinic. Dr. Hoffman's opinion is that the person 'who could commit such an act as this is one to whom the act itself is a gratification of sexual urges.'

"I myself have considered the possibility that these boys fell into the hands of a large group of older boys and were manhandled. Something may have gone wrong to frighten the gang, and the members killed the boys to make sure that they couldn't be identified."

"Men, at this point we don't have a single tangible clue. Our main objective is to sort out the slaying. We need to find the missing clothing of the victims and the adhesive tape used on their mouths and wrists. Especially, we need to determine the location of the slayings. Without these clues, it is going to be difficult to put this together. Therefore, let's concentrate on finding those pieces of evidence if we can. I'll take a few questions now. I don't want to take up too much time here since we have a lot of work to do, so just a few questions."

Every hand in the assembly room went up. It looked like an auction.

"Was this a complete autopsy, a thorough examination of the outside of the bodies and internal organs?"

McCarron was quick to answer. "Yes, it was. However we're still going over some tissue examinations. By tomorrow, we'll have the final results of Dr. Kearns' report."

"Is there much evidence found at the scene?"

"No, not much. As I stated earlier, the boys were found nude. Our prime area of investigation right now is to find the clothing and adhesive tape in the area where the boys were killed. We know they weren't killed in that area, they were brought there."

"Were there any footprints or tire marks found?"

"Yes, there were. Footprints, no. It was raining, and the way the boys were found dumped into the ditch, we felt that the person or persons drove up with the back end of a truck or a car and threw the bodies right out like cattle. This prevented them from coming onto the grass or muddy part of the ditch area. As far as tire tracks, the crime lab took several plaster imprints of the tires. They will be studied."

I raised my voice and interrupted, without raising my hand. Standing right next to the Coroner, the abruptness of my question got McCarron's immediate attention.

"So there is no trace evidence that we could use from the scene?" Trace evidence is any material or mark that could be used as direct or collateral evidence. It could be very visible evidence, such as bloody clothing. Or it could be evidence detected by using very complex scientific and analytical techniques: blood types, fingerprints, hair, dust and the like. It could also include things found in or on the body, such as drugs, semen, foreign objects, and imprints. Trace evidence links a suspect to the scene, and a victim to a certain location before the crime.

"That's right. No weapons were found at the scene or in the immediate area, so as of now we couldn't look for anything such as fingerprints. The wounds on the head were the only visible wounds and those were on the Peterson boy. And we do have a pattern, size and shape of the weapon. That's why I told you earlier that it was possibly a jack handle or a butt of a gun."

"Coroner, how about this being the work of sadists? Is that a strong theory?"

"Very much so. I know a lot of you have worked on cases involving sadism, someone who gets satisfaction from inflicting physical harm on others. I think we all need to remember how brutally these boys were beaten. I ask you all to have an open mind in this. Your theories may be just as good as the next guy's, or my theory, or Dr. Kearns' theory. We're looking for clues here, and that is the prime objective right now. So it could be teenage hoodlum groups, some homosexual degenerate, some sadist or whatever. The thing is, three innocent boys were slaughtered, killed and dumped in a ditch like sacks of potatoes."

Captain Corcoran deliberately approached the podium.

"Thank you Coroner McCarron. I think all of us have a thousand questions, but we need to get out there and help find the answers. Men, if you have any questions about this briefing, see Detective Jack or Detective Frank. Coroner McCarron will be briefing us again in a day or two after the conclusion of the tests and autopsy. Right now he's got to get to the County Morgue for the inquest which is set for 10:00 a.m. this morning."

The uniformed officer holding the Coroner's overcoat edged his way toward the podium and held it out to him.

"Thanks, officer," he said as he quickly grabbed it, put it on, and then turned to Captain Corcoran.

"Captain, you have a lot of good men here. Looking out into the crowd, I recognized a lot of officers and detectives I've worked cases with. It's not going to be easy, but I'm sure we'll find the killer of these boys."

"Thanks for your help, Coroner. I'll be at the inquest with two of my detectives. See you in a couple of hours."

The assembly room emptied quickly as the officers and detectives made their way to their cars or to the reception area to meet with their supervisors and get their assignments for the day. The thin cloud of gray smoke hanging beneath the ceiling began to dissipate as the floor fans whirred, releasing a soft hum as they did. Soon, that would be the only sound left in the room.

10:00 a.m.

Cook County Morgue is located on the west side of the city, down the street from Cook County Hospital. The original hospital building took up an entire city block and had been constructed with the intention of serving the needs of all the citizens of the county. Like most county hospitals, however, its grand plans had been scaled down considerably. Throughout the years, it has mainly served those who are poor or who had the misfortune of being injured within its "catchment" area, brought there by police, fire department ambulance or whatever available transportation could get them there.

Just down the street is the county morgue: the last stop for citizens who died on the street and whose bodies were not immediately claimed by relatives. For victims of crimes or suspected foul play, their bodies were subjected to minute scrutiny and study in order to determine the cause of death and to help identify and capture the perpetrators.

The scene in front of the morgue building was identical to that at the Gale Street station. Scores of reporters and civilians being held back by uniformed police officers as small numbers of police and local governmental officials were led through the crowd and into the gray stone building.

Frank and I remained at the station to go through the hundreds of messages left by citizens who called in response to the news of the boys' deaths. It was the first real chance we had to return calls and check out "every fuckin' lead" as Sgt. Murphy had said.

Captain Corcoran and Detectives Schulze and Koeppe went to the morgue for the inquest.

Most inquests were not conducted at the county morgue. They were held at funeral parlors in the area where the death occurred. Because they were usually routine, lower-level officials from the coroner's office performed these examinations into the probable cause of death. Many positions within the Coroner's Office, including the Chief Coroner, were filled by appointment. Medical training was not required, and the coroners were neither pathologists nor medical doctors.

The "blue-ribbon" jury, as they were called, required no qualifications either. In routine deaths, they were simply private citizens organized on the spur of the moment. But, this wasn't the usual inquest.

This case had its own unique set of circumstances, including the fact that the world was watching. Reporters from every major newspaper, radio, and television station across the country were present. Even some foreign correspondents had been sent to Chicago to attend the inquest and report on the murder of the boys.

According to Koeppe, the inquest was held in a large room that reminded him of the courtrooms he had been in as a traffic officer. By the time they arrived, the rows of benches were already filled; over 100 people were assembled. At the front of the room was a judge's bench, with seats on each side for the court reporter and witnesses. Off to the left and closer to the Coroner's bench was a jury box with six somber-looking men. The atmosphere was tense, and people in the room spoke in lowered tones. A deputy began the proceedings.

"Quiet, please. This is an inquest into the deaths of Robert Peterson, Anton Schuessler, and John Schuessler, Numbers 67, 68 and 69 respectively, of October 1955. I will call the roll of jurors, who will please answer to their names.

"J. Gruss?"

"Here."

"Charles Ross?"

"Here."

"J. Korinek?"

"Here"

"W. Cashman?"

"Here."

"J. Ahrens?"

"Here"

"T. Geeghan?"

"Here."

"Let the record reflect that the original jury is present, having been duly qualified and sworn in over the bodies of the deceased herein."

"Are there any legal representatives present?"

No one responded. The deputy became more specific.

"Is there a representative of the State's Attorneys Office present?"

Again, there was no response.

The deputy called out, "Let the record so show. Is there a representative of the Sheriff's Office present?"

A voice shouted out, "Yes, sir."

"Your names gentlemen?"

"Klein. Albert Klein."

The deputy raised his voice from across the room. "Who else is with you?"

"Deputy Kilkus."

"Representatives of the Sheriff's Office?"

"Yes, sir, " Klein responded.

"Is there someone of the Forest Ranger's present?" No response.

Coroner McCarron interjected. "Is Chief Dan Conway here or Deputy Donnelley?"

No response was heard.

"Thirty Third District represented here?"

"Yes, sir."

"Your name, Captain?"

"Russell Corcoran."

"And who else is with you?"

"Detective Frank Schulze and Detective Fred Koeppe, all of the 33rd District."

The Deputy Coroner duly took note and continued his witness list.

"Are there any others, City Police Officials, Chicago Police?"

A tall man sitting in the second row, just in front of the Coroner's Deputy stood up.

"You are with what division officer?"

"I'm Detective Lt. James McMahon, Chief of Homicide Division."

There was a flurry of movement from both sides of the room as photographers rushed to the middle of the room and began taking pictures of Lt. McMahon. Coroner McCarron pounded his gavel several times as he shouted, "Gentlemen, please sit down."

As the cameramen went back to their places, a few spent flashbulbs hit the floor. The buzz of whispering voices swelled up and then receded as Deputy Coroner Harry Glos began to move the process along. He turned to address the two grieving fathers huddled together on a small wooden bench.

"Mr. Peterson, will you step forward, please."

Mr. Peterson rose from his seat beside Lt. McMahon and walked slowly to the witness stand beside the Coroner's bench.

Coroner McCarron addressed the witness.

"You understand, sir, this is a procedure we have to go through, and I am going to make it as easy as I can for you. Just raise your right hand and be sworn."

Mr. Peterson slowly raised his right hand, listened to the Deputy, affirmed that his testimony was to be the truth, and put his hand down to his lap.

Coroner McCarron spoke in a soft, quiet voice.

"What is your name?"

"Malcolm Peterson."

"And your home address?"

"5519 West Farragut."

"Robert Peterson is your son who is now deceased?"

"Yes, sir."

"When was the last time you saw your son alive?"

"Just about three o'clock Sunday afternoon."

"That would be October 16, 1955, three o'clock in the afternoon?"

"Yes, sir."

"Did he say where he was going—what he was going to do?"

"Yes."

"Will you tell the jury?"

Mr. Peterson answered quietly.

"We knew he was going to a show."

"You knew he was going to a movie?"

"Yes, with the Schuessler boys, they came over to our house."

"Yes?"

"We had been working on the garage that morning, he and I."

"You and your son??"

"Yes, he was in the house listening to the Cardinal football game, and he just went away."

Throughout the inquest, Mr. Peterson's voice faded as he spoke. Most of his testimony was barely audible. His eyes were filled with tears, and he coughed softly. Koeppe said it was a painful ordeal to watch. Throughout the hearing, he just kept wishing it would be over.

"Three boys went to the show, you knew they were going downtown, to the Loop?"

"Not to the Loop, to a theater."

"Now, we are getting into Sunday evening, when they didn't come home."

"Yes."

"You and your wife became very much worried?"

"Yes, sir."

"Who did you call, and what did you do?"

"Well…" said Mr. Peterson after a long hesitation, "we called the police. I don't know when, between ten and eleven o'clock Sunday night, and they told me if the boys were not home at midnight, we should come down and give them a description."

"Yes?"

"Which we did. I went, gave them a description, before that, we got the idea that maybe the boys had gone to the show, eaten up all their money, and were walking home.

"Mr. Schuessler and I took a ride down Milwaukee Avenue to the Loop. We drove our car down Milwaukee, looked in all the hamburger joints and bus stations on our way downtown. We went down to the Loop Theater, which was closing, and then we got the idea they went across the street to the State and Lake Theater. We went over there, just as they were letting out."

"Yes?"

"We told the manager our predicament, he was very cooperative. Went all through the show, completely. The boys were not to be found. We took Elston Avenue home, and I went to the 33rd District Station to tell them what we had found, nothing."

"Yes."

"I got there, and the sergeant behind the desk was a very accommodating fellow. He called up the Clark Theater, and they searched the lobby and the auditorium. No boys. Then he called up the Woods Theater. Same thing.

"I then suggested we call several bowling alleys, the boys like that. We called bowling alleys, which we should have done sooner. We called them to ask if they had seen them.

"We called the 20th Century bowling alley. They said: 'No boys here.' Then, we called the Natoma. It was closed. This was about three to three thirty a.m. I talked to Mr. Schuessler at home, and that's about all I can say."

"Did you call the police by means of telephone?"

"The first time, yes."

"At what time was that?"

"The time element, I am not sure. I'd say from about ten to eleven at night. Between ten and eleven o'clock at night."

"You said your boys were missing?

"Yes."

"They asked you to come into the station, and you went into the station of your own volition?"

"Sure, they told me to come down at midnight if the boys were not at home, so I went down at midnight."

"It was not at nine-thirty?"

"Went down to the police?" asked Mr. Peterson.

"When you first made the telephone call." McCarron replied.

"No, sir, from ten and eleven."

"Do you know of any boy or boys, or gangs…? I don't mean to use this word. I don't want to call it…teenagers, gangs, cliques, or group of boys or of men…. in this vicinity, or any other vicinity, that your boy had ever…had ever complained to you about such boys or groups at any time that wanted to beat him up. Or do anything of that sort?"

"No, sir." Mr. Peterson said.

"Sir?"

"No, sir," came the reply.

"Your boy never registered any such complaint?"

"No, sir. Robert was a good boy. He was a home boy, sir."

McCarron continued this line of questioning for a considerable period of time without result. This was one of McCarron's theories so he tried to get as much information on this subject from the father as he could.

"I just remember that at the police station this morning, at three o'clock, there is the time element again, about which I am not sure, that it was maybe one year, or two years ago. A boy in school had brought a knife, or a gun, or something. My boy told us about this. They had trouble with that boy in school. Where he is now, I don't know, I couldn't say."

The Coroner turned his attention back to Mr. Peterson.

"What school?"

"At the Farnsworth."

"What grade was that boy in?"

"I don't know."

"This was a year ago?"

"The time element now, I am not sure; either one or two years. Time passes so rapidly."

McCarron continued with his questioning, but Mr. Peterson really didn't have any answers. Eventually, he decided to move on. He cleared his throat and asked one last question.

"Of course, you have seen the body of your son, downstairs here at the morgue, and identified it as his body?"

"Yes," Mr. Peterson said softly.

The day before the inquest, Mr. Peterson, his wife Dorothy, and his cousin, Bert Peterson, had gone down to the morgue to identify Robert's body.

Mrs. Peterson wanted to go with her husband into the room, but he refused to let her go. He didn't want her to see their son that way.

As he came out of the room weeping, "He was a very good boy," he told the detectives who were with him: "We were buddies, real buddies." They recall that he reached out for his wife, grabbed her, and hugged her as he sobbed uncontrollably asking the question all parents do, "How could it have happened to my boy?"

His wife pleaded with him. "I want to see him. Please, take me to see my boy." Mr. Peterson told her. "Honey, I don't want you to see him. You won't be able to recognize him if you see him."

According to Koeppe, Deputy Coroner Kiedro stepped in and abruptly ended the questioning.

"Let the record show that the corpus delicti has been duly established, in the case of Robert Peterson."

It was clear that nothing more needed to be said.

"You are excused. Thank you, sir," concluded Coroner McCarron.

As Mr. Peterson walked back to his bench, there was no movement at all among the scores of officers, public officials, and witnesses. No one made a sound. The floor fans in the back of the inquiry room hummed, and a few muffled voices could be heard in the hallway outside. He buried his face in his hands and cried softly.

To Koeppe, it seemed as if no one was quite sure what to do next. Coroner McCarron looked at Mr. Peterson. As he continued to sob, McCarron looked away. Awkwardly, he turned to his Chief Deputy, Harry Glos, to get some response as to what to do next. Deputy Coroner Kiedro, once again, took center stage, "Will Anton Schuessler step forward, please."

Mr. Schuessler was seated in the second row of benches, next to Lt. McMahon. He appeared to be somewhere else. His eyes darted from one side of the room to the other as if he were lost and trying to figure out where he was.

Lt. McMahon gently tapped the man's side, but he merely looked at the lieutenant quizzically, with tears in his eyes.

"Mr. Schuessler, you need to go up to the witness stand," McMahon whispered.

Schuessler nodded his head. He stood up and walked carefully toward the front of the room.

Once he had reached the witness stand, the Coroner leaned over and said, "I am very sorry for your trouble; just raise your right hand and be sworn."

Mr. Schuessler raised his right hand and swore to tell the truth, the whole truth.

"What is your name, sir?"

"Anton John Schuessler." A German accent was noticeable as he carefully pronounced his name for the court reporter.

"And your address?"

"5711 North Mango."

"I won't go over everything as I did with Mr. Peterson. You heard his testimony?"

"Yes, sir," Schuessler responded.

"You are the father of the two young boys Anton and John Schuessler?"

"Yes, sir."

"As I understand it, your boys also were going to a show last Sunday?"

"Yes."

"They did go to a show?"

"Yes."

"You gave them permission to go to a show?"

"I didn't know they were going downtown," Mr. Schuessler's voice was very quiet, almost defensive.

"They did go to a show?"

"Yes."

"Did John...by the way, what grade was he in school, the oldest boy?"

"Same as the Peterson's. Eighth Grade."

"Did your boy, at any time, ever tell you of any trouble, difficulty with a boy, or with boys, or a man or men or group, clique, or gang, teen-age group, ever tried to be nasty…threaten to hurt them or do anything as dastardly as this, did they ever report anything like that to you or to your wife that you know of…" He caught himself as he began to ramble. "You know, that is so important."

"To be honest, no." Mr. Schuessler seemed surprised at the question.

"They never did?"

"No. My boys have never been downtown without their parents. Never. This was the first time."

"Sir?" McCarron didn't understand Mr. Schuessler's response.

"My boys never left the house without their parents. Never. This was the first time. They were good boys…they were good," he said and began to cry.

McCarron cut it short.

"And you don't know why anyone would want to hurt them?" He asked one more time.

"NO!" Mr. Schuessler said loudly. It was obvious to everyone in the room that he was getting upset.

"I'm sorry." McCarron realized he had asked one question too many.

"You saw the bodies of your sons downstairs, and identified them?"

"Yes." Mr. Schuessler slumped in his chair.

"You have identified the bodies as those of your sons, Anton and John?"

"Yes." Bringing his hands to his face, Mr. Schuessler's anguished cries filled the room. "They were my life," he said. "My whole life."

The Deputy Coroner approached the court reporter. Rather than addressing the Coroner directly, he quietly directed his official statement to her.

"Let the record show that the corpus delicti has been duly established in the cases of Anton and John Schuessler."

McCarron nodded his approval of the Deputy's tact under the circumstances and then turned toward Mr. Schuessler.

"You are excused. We won't bother you any more. You can

go, and thank you very much." Addressing his Deputy, McCarron quietly added, "Will you help this man back?"

Coroner McCarron addressed the courtroom. "Mr. Victor Livingston?" He looked around the room, hoping the next witness would approach the bench.

"Is Mr. Victor Livingston present?" he repeated. No one moved.

"Any of the Forest Rangers here yet?" McCarron asked angrily. He turned to his Chief Deputy. "Do you know why none of the Forest Rangers are here?"

"No. They were notified," Glos was quick to respond. McCarron was clearly getting angry. He looked at Glos, then at his deputies on either side of the bench and expected an answer from someone.

"Do you know about this?" His question was directed to no one in particular.

"Is Chief Conway or any of his men from the Forest Preserve present?"

McCarron rose from his chair and faced the courtroom. He looked up at the clock, picked up the sheaf of papers he had been looking at during the inquest proceedings, then raised them over his head and threw them back down onto the bench.

"It is now 10:35 a.m., and this inquest was scheduled to be conducted at 10:00 a.m. This incident happened in the forest preserves. The forest preserve officials should be here, and should be very much interested in this case, as this comes under their jurisdiction.

"The fathers of these families, as crushed as they are, can be here. The Forest Preserve Department is involved in such a dastardly crime, and they are not here? I don't like that. That's no good. That is simply no good.

"And Victor Livingston is the most important person, in regard to seeing the boys, and he is not here. The Forest Rangers are not here. WHY?"

As he shouted, McCarron's face turned red, and he glared at every person in uniform as if they all bore some responsibility for the Forest Rangers' absence.

"I just want to state it is a very sad state of affairs when our agencies of government are not here, and these families who have this cross to carry are here. And these others don't think enough of this tragedy, a dastardly crime of this type, they don't think enough of it to be here. I DON'T LIKE IT. I don't think the people of Cook County like it either. The Sheriff's men are present, and the Chicago Police Department. Dr. Jerry J. Kearns, our pathologist and our toxicologist…."

McCarron could barely control himself. His rage apparent, none of his deputies said anything. What could they say?

One of the reporters from the City News Bureau abruptly stood up and interrupted the Coroner. "Coroner, you know about this man Dillon?" the reporter asked. It was bold move, but the reporter's aggressiveness had managed to refocus McCarron. Finally, he moved on.

"Dillon, yes—I didn't get to him yet. I will, though." The Coroner added a few more negative remarks about the absence of the Forest Rangers and then said, "We have here a Mr. Dillon I am told. If he will come up here."

"What is your name, please?" McCarron began his examination.

Dillon described his occupation as a maintenance man at the Monte Cristo Lanes, and went on to tell the Coroner and the jury about how Mr. Peterson had come to the bowling alley on Monday asking if anyone had seen the boys. He testified about the age groups of the kids at the alley, how on occasion a juvenile officer would show up to check on the pinsetters working there.

He told of his recollection of the boys' visit to the bowling alley on Sunday afternoon about 3:00 p.m. He couldn't recollect much of the visit, except that he was pretty sure it was Robert Peterson, who had asked about getting an alley to bowl.

McCarron asked Dillon a few questions about gangs hanging out at the Monte Cristo, whether Dillon had ever overheard conversations concerning gangs beating up other youngsters. Dillon responded that he never heard any of that kind of talk and this seemed to satisfy the Coroner, who excused the witness after a few more perfunctory questions.

McCarron then asked if anyone knew whether Victor Livingston had arrived. When he received no response, he continued the inquest by directing Assistant Chief Deputy Coroner Harry Glos to call Ernest Niewiadomski.

"Ernest Niewiadomski," Glos called out to the crowded courtroom.

The young man stood up from the second row of benches and slowly walked to the witness box.

"Step up here, son. Just raise your right hand and be sworn."

Ernest held up his right hand. Nervously, he scanned the courtroom and the sea of faces looking at him. He looked back at the Coroner and recited the oath, then took his seat in the witness box.

"What is your name, sir?" McCarron asked.

"Ernest Niewiadomski," he responded.

"And your address?"

"5730 North Major."

"Your age?"

"Seventeen."

"Your occupation?" Ernest looked puzzled.

"Do you work, son? Or do you go to school?" McCarron asked.

"Oh! Yes, sir. I'm a student at Gordon Technical High School."

"Live with your parents?"

"Yes, sir."

"All right, that is fine. Tell the jury and tell me just what you know about this incident."

Ernest told the Coroner and the jury about meeting the boys on Sunday evening at about 7:15 p.m., that he was a neighbor of the Schuessler brothers, and that the boys had told him they had been to a movie, "The African Lion" at a downtown theater. He told the Coroner and the jury that the boys left the bowling alley at about 7:30 or 7:45 p.m.

Ernest was asked whether he had seen anyone else talk to the boys. He responded that he hadn't seen anyone else speak with the boys while they were at the bowling alley. He didn't know of anyone who had bothered the boys that night or even since he had come to know the Schuesslers. After convincing McCarron that he knew of no gangs or others who might want to hurt the Peterson boy or the

Schuessler brothers, McCarron leaned back in his chair and asked if the jurors had any questions for the witness.

The procedures of a coroner's inquest differed from those in a criminal or civil matter. Members of the jury had the opportunity to ask a witness questions they might have concerning their testimony or any other evidence presented during the inquest. The questions were sometimes motivated by curiosity about irrelevant issues. On occasion, a juror might ask about some fact or testimony, which might have been overlooked by the coroner or the witness. But for the most part, jurors were silent.

This jury had no questions for Ernest Niewiadomski.

"All right, son, you are excused," Coroner McCarron said.

"I am going to continue this case now, and I am going to subpoena the Chief of the Forest Rangers. He should be more vitally interested and should be in here. Anyway, the law enforcement officers in that territory where this incident happened and who were the persons that originally took hold of this investigation didn't think enough of it to be here. And we are going to issue a subpoena for Chief Conway and his investigating officer. As far as the Prosecutor's Office is concerned, there is nothing more I can do with that.

"I am going to set a date, and a short one at that."

The reporters wrote down every word. It made great copy. Photographs were also taken of McCarron as he continued his tirade.

"I am going to continue this until October 24, 1955, and I am going to issue a subpoena for Captain Conway right now, as well as his investigating officer. What reason Captain Conway has for not being here, I don't know. But we will find out. Captain Corcoran is here, and I know you people are working around the clock. And I know other agencies are cooperating and are working around the clock. And maybe there is information at this time which you are working on that you probably don't want to divulge at this particular time, since those responsible may even be in this room."

The coroner's last comment brought an immediate response from the newspaper and radio reporters who stopped writing. He was beginning to repeat himself, but the mention that there might be someone in the courtroom who was involved in the murders brought the reporters' pens to a halt.

Corcoran thought that McCarron's last words were a little melodramatic. But he had to admit that he had investigated cases where the perpetrators were either on the scene, milling about in a crowd of on-lookers, or had returned to the scene of the crime to get some kind of satisfaction from their acts. It was possible.

Still, he thought McCarron shouldn't have mentioned that possibility. The public was in enough of a panic without the Coroner suggesting that the perpetrators could be sitting in the courtroom.

McCarron concluded the inquest by asking Captain Corcoran about progress on the case. Satisfied with the responses, he addressed the fathers.

"Mr. Peterson and Mr. Schuessler, there is nothing further we can do this morning, not much further we can go. I want to say that you not only have our sympathy, but that you have the interest of everybody in the city, the county, the state, and in the nation in relation to this case."

Mr. Peterson nodded then rose to his feet.

"May I say something?"

McCarron was somewhat taken aback by this.

"Yes, go ahead," he said.

"Mr. Schuessler claims his boys ate macaroni Sunday night, but what has macaroni got to do with this?"

"Son, we are trying to find out. I would rather not answer that right now. We have a pathologist and a toxicologist working on this matter. The toxicologist and the pathologists are doctors who are able to make chemical analysis and tests as to foods and the like found in bodies. We are trying to find out if these boys had anything to eat between six and eight in the evening on Sunday, October 16. We have reasons for asking that. I cannot go too far into it. If you and Mr. Schuessler will step into my office after the hearing is dismissed, I will go over it with you."

Mr. Peterson seemed satisfied with the Coroner's response and sat down.

"We will continue this on Monday, October 24, 1955 and a subpoena will be issued for Chief Conway." He turned to his Chief

Deputy. "You will see that it is served, sir." Glos nodded and made an entry in his notes, then summoned one of the other deputies and gave him the paper on which he had written the Coroner's instructions.

"We will stand adjourned until then, gentlemen." With that, McCarron slammed his gavel down one final time and quickly rose from his chair. He walked toward a side door of the courtroom and into his chambers. The crowd in the room rose and began to talk to one another in loud voices, which filled the courtroom. People began to move slowly toward the double doors of the courtroom and out into the hallway. The deputies struggled to control the large group trying to all leave at once.

The Chief Deputy Coroner and one of the other deputies approached Mr. Peterson and Mr. Schuessler and accompanied the fathers into the Coroner's chambers.

11:15 a.m.
Gale Street Station

I picked my way through a growing pile of small notes, memos, and messages on the desk, looking for something that needed immediate attention. The scraps of paper and telephone messages began to look alike—a name scribbled at the top, sometimes illegible; phone number and short message: "Janet Edmonds....RO3-7813.... heard boys talking in the alley behind her home late Sunday night.... Richard Melville....SP4-5362...thinks he saw two boys hitchhiking on Northwest Highway Sunday night…"

I was on the phone with what seemed to be one of the more interesting tipsters, but I could tell as soon as the conversation began that this was one tip that was going nowhere.

"Yes, ma'am…you were right to call us. At this point, everything is important. No, we don't have to come out and talk with you at this time, but we'll get back to you if we need more information."

Out of the corner of my eye, I could see Frank place a mark in the upper right hand corner of each phone message after he called back. Murphy told us to keep all the messages, note the date and time we responded, who we spoke to on the call, and then keep every phone message for filing according to dates, names, and times.

I made my final notes on the call, thanked the woman and hung up. I placed the note in the "to-be-filed" box at the edge of my desk and turned to Frank.

"What do you say we hit the Farnsworth School before lunch? Murphy wants us to talk to the principal today. If we don't leave now, we won't have time later this afternoon. I still have a lot of calls to make, and we have to go to the Peterson boy's wake."

"Sounds good to me. Let me make one more call, and I'll meet you at the car." Frank continued to scribble a few notes in red pen on one of the phone messages.

"I'll tell Murphy we're going out to the school for a couple of hours, and we'll be back. See you outside." I put my gray overcoat on and made my way out to the parking bay.

As I walked to the squad car, I went over my mental notes. It had been less than 48 hours since Frank and I made our first visit to the school and a lot had changed since then.

Murphy briefed us this morning on how the investigation was going to proceed with the boys' school, their teachers, and fellow students. Juvenile officers under the direction of Lt. Michael Delaney were going to be in charge of questioning the pupils in the upper grades. The officers were going to make an effort to pinpoint any information the children might have concerning the Schuessler brothers and Robert Peterson and what their activities might have been on the day the boys disappeared.

Captain Corcoran and Lt. Delaney had agreed that counselors at the school would do all preliminary questioning of the children. Counselors were assigned to each classroom, and interviews by the juvenile officers would be held during the evening in the school gymnasium. Every student would be interviewed along with his or her parents. Corcoran and Delaney decided that the most efficient way to interview the 175 students was to see them at the school at pre-arranged dates and times. This was more efficient than having teams of detectives visit each home, and the school setting was probably more reassuring for them.

My thoughts were interrupted when Frank opened the door. The engine already running, I gripped the steering wheel with both hands, shifted into first gear and drove the squad car out of the lot.

"Got anything new from those calls, Frank?" I inquired.

"Nothing. The people who think they saw the boys Sunday night couldn't positively identify them. They described boys who were either older than the Peterson and Schuessler kids, or else weren't close on describing the clothing the boys were wearing that night. I got notes on everything, though. Never know what'll happen."

I nodded and kept driving. It was a short trip to the Farnsworth School, and after a few minutes, we pulled up to the main entrance. Frank looked out the passenger window and saw several women and children standing outside the doors of the school. He also noticed that there were a few small groups of students talking to each other in the schoolyard. Some were laughing and playing tag while they waited for friends to join them on the short walk home for lunch. Others were standing quietly alone against the fence surrounding the playground, waiting for their parents to pick them up.

Since the news broke that the boys had been found murdered, the entire neighborhood was in a state of shock. Some of the women in the area had formed a group to keep an eye on the children in the neighborhood. Parents had become alarmed at the thought that three boys who went to school with their own children had suddenly disappeared and been murdered.

Mothers accompanied their children to and from school, not only in the morning and afternoon but also at lunchtime when the children who lived a few blocks from the school would go home and then return after lunch.

These women were gathered at the school to accompany their children and their neighbors' children when we arrived. They stood quietly, waiting patiently for all of the children. Several of them looked in our direction as we got out and walked to the front steps of the school. Before we could reach the entrance, two of the women stopped us.

"Are you gentlemen detectives?" one of them asked.

"Yes, ma'am." I showed the woman my badge and I.D. and introduced Frank and myself.

"I'm Mrs. Bernice Knoll. My family lives just down the street from the Schuessler family. My kids knew them and Robert Peterson." A few more students began coming out of the school. They stopped and looked at us, probably realizing who we were and why we were at the school. Mrs. Knoll looked in their direction and then turned back and resumed her conversation.

"If I could pick boys to be my own, I'd take Robert and the Schuessler brothers. They were never sassy or smart. They were wonderful boys." Her voice trailed off as she spoke and soon she began to cry.

One of the other women put her hand on Mrs. Knoll's shoulder, and then began to speak to Frank.

"You don't know who killed the boys. It could be anyone. I have three boys at home, and I'm watching every move they make. They don't go out of the house now without someone keeping an eye on them. I've put an extra lock on the doors. Even on the windows. And it's not just me. Everyone in this neighborhood is just terrified. We don't know what to do."

The mothers all nodded in agreement. We could see the looks of concern on their faces, how tightly some of them held the hands of their children after they greeted them and brought them to their side.

"My boys are not to go near the woods, they're not to take rides, and no hitchhiking," the woman continued.

Another woman spoke up. "My son Jim was very close to the Schuessler brothers. It was a miracle that he wasn't with them on Sunday. He would have gone with the boys downtown, but my husband and I decided to take our family for a drive instead."

Many of the children knew the boys, and they began to tell us about John and Anton Schuessler and Robert Peterson. A small girl about 10 years of age worked her way around the women who were speaking to us. She said her name was Ellen and that she knew Robert Peterson.

"Bobby was a nice boy. He wasn't a sissy or a bully. He was a lot of fun," she said.

An older boy standing next to her said he had known Robert since they were both in kindergarten, and that he had known John

Schuessler from the time John moved to the neighborhood.

"They were real nice guys. I'm really gonna miss them," he said. He looked down at the ground for a moment, then moved back from the small group and walked toward the playground. He walked quickly in the direction of a woman who was calling out to him, and joined her and two small children whom she held close to her as they walked away.

We heard how well liked the boys were and how frightened the parents had become. One woman, Mrs. E. J. Padal, lived a few doors away from the Schuessler boys. Her son was a close friend of the boys, and they had all been active in the Boy Scouts, had interests in building model airplanes, and were well-behaved.

"My son, Richard, was asked to go with them-all three of them-on their trip to the Loop movie on Sunday. But I wasn't feeling well, and I wouldn't let him go to the show. My husband and I decided a change in scenery might help me feel better, so we drove to Wisconsin. Richard went with us, and I remember him crying at first because he wanted to go to the movies so badly instead of going to Wisconsin with us."

I took out my notepad and wrote down the woman's name and that of her son. I made a note about the fact that this boy had planned to go downtown with the boys, then put the notepad back into my jacket pocket.

More children began to exit the doors of the school, either to meet their parents or walk in large groups toward their homes. The diversion gave us an opportunity to leave the group and meet with the principal. We thanked the women and children for their help and told them to call the 33rd District if they had any information they believed would help in the investigation.

We walked up the wide concrete steps and into the school. Working around the growing crowd of students who were headed out the front doors, we continued down the hallway in the direction of the principal's office.

Mr. Thornton was standing just outside his office, directing the heavy traffic of children as they left their classrooms and joined the moving crowd of students making their way down the wide hallway toward the front doors of the school.

"Good afternoon, detectives," Mr. Thornton said sadly. He opened the door to his office and motioned us in. "It'll be a little quieter in here."

Frank and I entered the office and sat in the two well-worn wooden chairs in front of his desk. Mr. Thornton closed the door and came around the side of his desk, picking up the phone before he sat down.

"Marge, will you ask Mrs. Schwachten to come to my office, please?"

He sat behind a large, gray metal desk similar to ours at the station, except Mr. Thornton's was much neater.

"Thank you for stopping by again, detectives. Sergeant Murphy called earlier today and told me that you would be making another visit. You know, this is just a tragedy. Every one of the children in this school knew those boys. We're all just crushed by this. And their poor families, my God." Like everyone else, he worked hard to fight back tears as he spoke.

"Mr. Thornton, Detective Czech and I appreciate how much help you and the teachers have been. The students have also been very helpful. We had a chance to talk to some of them and their mothers just now. We know the whole neighborhood is just sickened by this. They're also very scared. That's why Captain Corcoran and Lt. Delaney thought it would be a good idea to interview the children here at school, with their parents' permission first, of course. The Captain asked us to tell you we really appreciate the arrangements you've made with the Board of Education to conduct the interviews here."

"Yes, Detective, don't mention it. Anything we can do to help. But I need to let you know that we've had some problems with the news people here. I thought that the best thing for the students would be to continue with school. The Board agreed with me. That's why we didn't cancel classes.

"The school psychologists also agreed that continuing with classes was best for the children. But these reporters keep asking questions."

"What kind of questions?" Frank asked.

"Well, why isn't there some memorial service or something. Why do the students have to come to school…isn't it upsetting for them. I told the reporters that they should stay off the premises; the children are disturbed enough as it is."

"You mean these people—the reporters-they're going into the classrooms?" I was almost shouting. I couldn't believe it.

"Well, they've been hanging around the school, trying to talk to the children here…" Mr. Thornton did not have a chance to finish the sentence.

"Mr. Thornton, if you have any problems with reporters or anyone else trying to get into the school or classrooms to get stories from these children, we'll definitely lock them up for trespassing on city property. Don't wait for anything—we'll send a squad here at once. You tell them that, and if they have a problem with it tell them to call me or Detective Czech."

The principal thanked us for our support and assured us that if he had any problems he would call the District immediately.

There was a gentle knock on the door. Mrs. Schwachten timidly opened the door and entered the office.

"Yes, please come in. Thank you for coming. I think you met the detectives here when they came to the school on Monday." We stood and greeted her. She was visibly upset.

I asked how her students and her fellow teachers were doing, if she had learned anything from the students that might be important concerning the boys' activities last weekend. She responded that everyone was very upset after hearing the news. The horror of it began to sink today, she said. The teachers and school counselors were helping the students as best they could. She said that some of her students were very distraught, particularly those who were very close to the boys. And she was somewhat puzzled by a few of the children who did not seem very upset at all.

"Maybe it's so unbelievable that they haven't realized their friends are gone," she said, almost apologizing for them.

"That could be, Mrs. Schwachten," I said. It wasn't unusual even for adults to have difficulty comprehending and accepting the murder of innocent children. "Most of the people in the neighborhood can still hardly believe what happened."

I told Mrs. Schwachten that detectives and juvenile officers would interview every teacher and pupil. Should she or any of the children in her class recall anything about the boys' whereabouts last weekend, or if they know of anyone who saw them, they should let the officers know." Mrs. Schwachten and Mr. Thornton said they would not hesitate to do so.

I looked at my watch and realized that the school visit had taken much longer than anticipated. It was almost 12:25 p.m. and we had a lot to do before returning to the station. After thanking the principal and Mrs. Schwachten, we said we would return in a few days.

The school was nearly empty now and we walked down the quiet hallway, past the metal lockers on either side and out the double doors of the building.

1:15 p.m.

Frank called in our location. We got out of the car and walked towards a small store at the corner of Giddings and Milwaukee Avenue.

Sgt. Murphy assigned Frank and me to follow up on two calls received from local businessmen on Milwaukee Avenue. One operated a hobby shop. We interviewed Joseph Stranton, an employee who said he had worked the previous Sunday afternoon from 11:00 a.m. to 6:00 p.m. I showed him pictures of the three boys and Stranton identified them as the boys that came into the store.

"These were the boys. They looked around. It was somewhere around 4:30 p.m. on Sunday that they were in here."

I looked around the hobby shop. It would be a place three young boys would find fascinating—model trains, airplane kits, paints, sports equipment. Things they have or that they would be interested in.

We thanked Stranton, walked out of the store and a few doors north to a linoleum and tile store. The manager, Stanley Manski, spoke with us. He said that somewhere around 5:30 p.m. last Sunday afternoon, three boys entered his store and were looking at linoleum.

"They were looking for a birthday gift for their mother," he said.

Manski identified the Schuessler boys from the set of pictures.

"Those seem to be two of the boys," he said. We asked a few more questions about what the boys were wearing, if Manski noticed anyone with the boys when they were in his store, and whether it was dark out and what the weather was like at the time the boys were at his store.

Frank thanked Mr. Manski for his time and asked that he call the 33rd District if he remembered anything else.

As we walked away from the store and headed back to the car, we passed a neighborhood bar, Henri's Lounge. I stopped briefly, looked through the window and then looked back up the street toward the linoleum store.

"What's up, Jim?" Frank asked.

"What do you think of that guy Manski at the linoleum store?"

"The times don't match. He said the boys were in his store at 5:30 p.m. on Sunday. There's no way they could have left home at 3:00 p.m., gone downtown to the movie, and got back here by 5:30 p.m. The other guy at the hobby shop says the boys were in his place at 4:30 p.m. Same thing. No way."

"I'm with you on that one. I made a mental note to check on the date of Mrs. Schuessler's birthday. Can you figure that? Linoleum for a birthday present? I think the guy's just trying to get his name in the paper. He could have seen the kids' pictures in the newspaper yesterday or this morning."

I started toward the car, but Frank stopped.

"What's wrong?" I asked.

"Nothing, except my stomach is getting kind of small. How about we get a bite to eat before we go back to the District?"

"Good idea. I could use something myself. Where to?"

"How about Pete's?"

I had to think about that for a second. Pete's Hamburger and Chili was one of the many "ptomaine palaces" on Milwaukee Avenue. It was a small diner with about eight or nine counter stools and no booths. You had to have a good stomach to go there. Even before you walked in the place you could smell onions cooking on the grill. After you had eaten, the onions stayed with you and your clothes for at least three hours. The lingering odor was a dead give-away that you had been to Pete's.

2:45 p.m.

I turned off Milwaukee Avenue and drove ten feet down Gale Street before coming to a quick stop. Illinois Bell Telephone trucks, state trooper cars, Illinois government vehicles, news reporters and their sound trucks blocked the street in front of the station. Telephone work crews were setting up temporary phone booths outside the station and along the outside wall of the District. I carefully wove around the traffic and made a slow turn into the parking bay area.

"How was Pete's?" asked the desk sergeant as Frank and I walked by.

"We're still breathin' aren't we?" I shot back, noticing the Captain's door was closed. Probably meeting with the state people, I thought to myself. I also saw that the assembly hall was filled with city maintenance men. They were busy hanging bulletin boards on the walls. About fifteen new standing ashtrays were also placed around the room.

Telephone crews were hanging wires all over the place as they installed extra phones in the assembly room and in each office. Frank and I continued down the short hallway to Sergeant Murphy's office.

Murphy was placing bulletins on the new board hanging behind his desk.

"What's going on, Sarge?" Frank asked. He walked over and stood next to Murphy and began looking at the sheets as they were placed on the board. Some contained the description of the clothing the Schuessler brothers and Robert Peterson had worn on the night they were last seen. Others had lists of two-man teams of detectives and the search areas in Jefferson Park assigned to them to make door-to-door investigations.

"Well, the boards are for assignments and phone tips of people who call in—what time the calls came in and the action taken."

I was impressed to see that the most recent notes about phone tips Frank and I had completed that morning had already been written up and posted. Apparently, the "to-be-filed" box was being processed quite quickly.

"What's up in Corcoran's office?" I asked.

"I guess Governor Stratton called and ordered the state police to join in the investigation. The Superintendent of the state police, Phil Brown, and Ed Stanwyck of the criminal division will be working with us. They're both in the office with Corcoran. So are Sheriff Lohman and Chief Conway from the Forest Preserve Rangers. O'Malley's in there, too."

John O'Malley was the chief of detectives and coordinated the work of all of the detectives assigned to the case. These included detectives sent by other Districts and those working downtown at Police headquarters.

Murphy went on to say that the 33rd District would have two new people working in the unit. One would answer telephone calls on the hotline that was being set up by the phone company. The other would be filing reports for the day. Briefings would be held the following day in the morning with all the detectives in the unit. The clerical officers would put together any important findings for the day from officers and detectives. These summaries would be discussed at the morning briefings.

We informed Murphy of our visit to the Farnsworth School and discussions with Principal Thornton, the children and their mothers. Frank and I reviewed the remaining bulletins and summaries on Murphy's desk before returning to our office.

5:30 p.m.

We spent the rest of the afternoon writing reports. The summaries of interviews at Farnsworth School, with the manager of the hobby shop, and with the owner of the linoleum and tile shop were all completed and turned in to the file clerks.

Space was at a premium and detectives assigned to the case from other police districts had taken over every available desk. Juvenile officers and detectives had also started rounding up members of neighborhood juvenile gangs for interrogation. I still didn't think much of the theory that teenage gangs had murdered the boys. The gangs in the neighborhood could be violent, but there hadn't been any teenage, gang-related deaths in this District: beatings, a rumble now and then, but no murders. Not in Jefferson Park.

"Guys…we're going to need your desks." Murphy stood in our doorway and out of the path of patrol officers and detectives as they passed behind him in the crowded hallway, pushing young men and teenage boys into the other office for interrogation.

"I want you and Frank to get over to the Peterson boy's wake. How are you doing on your reports?"

"We've given our reports to the clerks, Sarge, but the calls keep coming in. Frank and I are doing what we can to follow up on them, but for every one that we answer and check out, we get four more." I pointed at the pile of messages.

"Do the best that you can. Right now, get over to the wake. I'll make sure nobody messes up your desks while you're out." He stopped speaking as a juvenile officer approached him.

"Sarge, can I use this office to talk to these mopes I got here?" the officer asked Murphy. He pointed down the hallway at two teenage boys dressed in worn jeans and black leather jackets. One of the boys was casually leaning against the wall, joking to his friend and smiling. His friend was combing his hair with a long, plastic comb as he looked at his reflection in the glass door of the other office.

"Yeah, you can use this one. Frank and Jim are on their way out for a while. Just be sure you don't mess up the office while you question those knuckleheads." Murphy made sure the two boys heard the sarcasm in his voice as he spoke in their direction. He seemed satisfied that he had gotten their attention, and now they were suddenly looking very worried about what kind of "questioning" they were going to receive.

We grabbed our coats from behind the open door and walked out towards the parking bay. As we passed the boys, one of them called out after us.

"Excuse me, sir," he said with more than a little feigned politeness. "Are we going to be alone with Officer Dooley when he questions us? Can't I call my dad first?" His polite tone was replaced by apprehension.

I turned and said, "Don't worry, kid. Officer Dooley won't bite. Just tell him what you know. He's real patient. Isn't that right, Dooley?" I didn't wait for an answer and kept walking. That kid was probably going to have to change his pants in a few minutes.

Frank was able to drive the squad car out of the parking bay and down a side street avoiding the congestion in front of the station. The wake was being held at the Drake Funeral Home on Western Avenue about twenty minutes drive from Gale Street. We sat quietly while a few bursts of static came over the police radio, followed by the voice of the dispatcher sending patrol cars to different locations within the district. One call was for a burglary in progress not far from our location on Western Avenue. Before Frank could reach for the radio, another patrol car responded telling the dispatcher he was one block away and would respond immediately.

"It's going to be pretty rough at this wake, Frank." I looked at the apartment buildings lining the street as we drove east on Foster Avenue.

"Yeah, I know."

Frank had worked a lot of homicide cases. Dealing with grieving families—distraught wives and children who at first could not believe the horrible news brought to them—was part of the job. Often the ones who brought bad news, detectives need to hold back emotions when communicating that a relative or friend has been killed. We must gauge the reactions of those interviewed and speak so that information can be obtained about the deceased: who disliked him or her; what their habits were; who their acquaintances were.

But this investigation was much different. The entire city was horrified. The boys could be anybody's sons. Innocent children on their way home from a movie on a Sunday afternoon, when out of nowhere someone grabs and kills them.

The reason we were sent to wakes and funerals on high profile murder cases was to mingle with the crowd of relatives and friends to keep our eyes and ears open and notice if there was someone present who didn't seem to belong there.

Like pyromaniacs, who return to the scene of a fire they had set to admire their work or to add to the thrill of their crime, criminals sometimes also return to the scene, or even to church services or memorial services to see the reactions of relatives and friends. People can be so damned crazy.

As we came to the corner of Foster and Western Avenues, Frank noticed the traffic beginning to slow down and back up.

"We better park wherever we find a spot. Looks like it's pretty crowded up there." I pointed in the direction of the funeral home. Lines had formed and stretched around the corner. Uniformed officers assigned from the Summerdale District were directing the heavy flow of cars to any open parking spaces on the street, even in "No Parking" zones.

Frank waved at one of the traffic officers. The officer noted our license plate and directed us to a parking spot next to a gas station. We got out and thanked the officer.

"We're from the 33rd District," I said as we showed the officer our badges. "How's it going out here?"

"It's better out here than it is in there, I'll tell you that." The officer pointed to the front entrance of the funeral home. Two uniformed officers stood at the doors. On the sidewalk, dozens of reporters and news crews stopped people on their way into the chapel to ask questions, taking pictures of the crowd.

We walked over to the doors of the chapel and greeted the two officers.

"What's it look like inside?" I asked one of them.

"You don't want to know," came the response. The officer shook his head.

The chapel was so crowded that the door could not be completely opened without coming into contact with someone in the vestibule. Frank and I politely pushed our way through the crowd and slowly arrived at the chapel at the end of a crowded hall.

At the front of the chapel, ten young honor guards of Boy Scout Troop 962 stood along the casket, five on each side. Mr. and Mrs. Peterson sat on a gray couch, facing Robert's body. Mrs. Peterson shielded her eyes with her hands. Mr. Peterson got up at once when he saw us.

We offered our condolences, but there were no words to express how we felt. We told Mr. Peterson that everything humanly possible to solve this crime was being done. That the men in the District, as well as other Districts, were working around the clock, every day, to catch the people responsible for the murder of their son and the Schuessler brothers. That at that moment, there were more than 400 men scouring neighborhoods, knocking on every door, searching roofs and basements, checking on every clue.

"That's our job, Mr. Peterson. We're going to do everything we can to catch whoever did this to your boy and the Schuessler brothers." I couldn't think of anything else to say. The sight of the Petersons, their family and friends, all grieving for this young boy who everyone loved was overwhelming.

"What really hurts is when I see those kids Bobby played baseball with," Mr. Peterson said. He fought back tears, as he looked at two boys wearing Cubs jackets approach the coffin accompanied by their parents.

We stood silently with Mr. Peterson as one by one mourners stepped past the Boy Scout Honor Guard, paid their last respects to Bobby Peterson then quietly offered their condolences to the Petersons. Many of the children, who I believe were Bobby's classmates, cried as they filed past the coffin, which was surrounded by flowers and wreaths from family, neighbors, and friends.

Frank and I moved a few steps from the front of the chapel to remain out of the way of mourners and to give the Petersons room to receive the many people seeking to comfort and console them.

We stood next to Rev. William F. Eifrig, the pastor of the Jefferson Park Lutheran Church on Northwest Highway, who introduced himself and began to talk about Bobby Peterson.

"Robert was just confirmed last spring at our Church. He loved all kinds of sports, and played baseball in the pony league at Norwood Park. If I counted the number of children who have been here tonight, it would probably be in the hundreds. Most of them were classmates of Roberts at Farnsworth School." Rev. Eifrig was visibly moved as he went on to talk about Robert's love of sports, how friendly he was and how all the children liked him.

Rev. Eifrig also introduced us to three Catholic priests from St. Tarcissus Church, where the Schuessler boys attended mass on Sundays and where their funeral mass was to be held this Saturday.

I recognized one of the priests, the Rev. Edward Kush. I attended mass on Sundays at St. Tarcissus, often either before or after working one of the weekend shifts. The pastor recognized me and mentioned a telegram the Archbishop of Chicago, Francis Cardinal Stritch, had sent to the parents of the boys. In expressing his deep grief and sorrow over the death of the boys, Cardinal Stritch said, "I beg almighty God and pray that out of this tragedy will come a better public consensus for the protection of our youth."

We mingled with the hundreds of people crowded into the funeral home. Captain Corcoran, Lt. Patrick Deeley, and Sheriff Lohman came to pay their respects. They, too, were immediately overwhelmed by the sight of the crowd of people outside the funeral home. It continued to circle the block for several hours.

Also present was Mrs. Schwachten; Mrs. Bernice Jonas, Anton's 6th grade teacher; and other teachers from the Farnsworth School. Principal Thornton was also there.

As 9:00 p.m. approached, the line of mourners continued to enter the chapel and the director of the funeral home announced that visitation would be extended until 10:00 p.m. to accommodate the many people still waiting to come into the chapel.

Frank and I scanned the crowd, looking for people who might not be mourners but curious members of the public or possibly someone who might have personal knowledge of the disappearance of the boys. If we spotted someone who was alone or seemed suspicious, we would carefully walk through the chapel and ease close to that person to overhear what they might be saying to someone else. We might even strike up a conversation to determine who they were, if they were family or neighbors. That evening, we saw no one who aroused our suspicions.

People began to leave as the hour of 10 p.m. approached. The funeral director spoke quietly to small groups of people, telling them that visitation was over and asking them to leave so that the family could spend a few moments alone in the chapel before it closed.

Frank and I positioned ourselves at the back of the chapel, looking carefully at each visitor as they left. We waited until the Peterson family left, then asked the funeral director if he minded if the two uniformed officers remained outside in a marked squad car, just in case they might be needed for any reason. The director thanked us for being there during the evening and said, yes, that would be helpful.

The Commander of the Foster Avenue Station had assigned the two uniformed officers at the front door. They told us that their Commander had assigned them to the funeral home from 10:00 p.m. through the next morning when other officers from their District would relieve them.

We walked back to our car and drove to the station to complete our reports.

"Long day, huh?" Frank said as he drove west on Foster Avenue. The traffic was light, and he drove the speed limit. He knew I was exhausted and needed time to decompress after the events of the last few hours.

I nodded and stared out the window. I gazed blankly at the rows of apartment houses, single-family homes, and small businesses lining the streets. We didn't turn on the police radio. Nothing we needed to hear, anyway.

How do the people in those homes feel right now, I thought to myself. Everyone in the city knows about the murders, the manhunt, and the search for the killer or killers. Were they thinking about how safe their neighborhood was? Were they wondering how long it would be before the killer or killers would be found? Could they feel safe at all?

I was wondering the same things as those people in their homes. Only I, along with the other police officers and detectives of the Chicago Police Department, was one of those who had to find the people responsible for the murders. No solid breaks in this case yet, mountains of paperwork, thousands of interviews to be made. Then I remembered Mr. Peterson's words: "They'll be caught no matter what." Sadly, I wasn't as certain as he was and that worried me.

Thursday
October 20, 1955
7:30 a.m.

I arrived at the Gale Street Station and met with a group of detectives assigned to the case from other Districts. They were all seasoned detectives, on the job for years and had investigated hundreds of murder cases, but you could tell by their conversations and demeanors that this particular case was getting to them. It was more personal than other cases. They all had families. Some of them had sons who were the same ages as the boys. The conversation was mixed with shock at the brutality of the crime, frustration at not having found any physical evidence near the bodies or any of the clothing worn on the night they disappeared. And there were still very few leads to work on.

Interrupting the discussions, Sgt. Murphy indicated the day's briefing was set to start in the assembly room. Captain Corcoran greeted us as we sat on the metal chairs and benches set up to accommodate the additional detectives and uniformed officers. Corcoran stood at the podium and waited until we were seated before beginning.

"Good morning, men. I'm going over some of the reports and passing them on to the other units who may be assigned to the investigations conducted yesterday. Things look a little better today." This bit of positive news got our attention and Corcoran continued the briefing. "This morning I learned that Captain John Olson of the State's Attorneys Police detached several teams of men to this unit. That's gonna be a little more manpower we could use. Also, I received reports from Captain Dan Conway of the Forest Preserve Rangers."

At the mention of Captain Conway, Frank leaned over and whispered, "I'll bet he got reports from Conway after he didn't show up yesterday. From what Koeppe told me about the inquest, Coroner McCarron's gonna have the Sheriff bring Conway to the next one in handcuffs," I smiled and waved away the small cloud of smoke from Frank's cigar that was moving in my direction.

The Captain continued addressing the men.

"Sheriff Lohman has given me his reports of the results of the search of Robinson's Woods, which has been going on for two days now. He's taken personal charge of the inch-by-inch search of the four square mile wooded area, using police, Army Reserve units, and citizen volunteers. They've turned up several possible clues which were turned over to us and which have been sent to the crime lab. As of now, none of them have been linked immediately to the crime.

"The first clues are fragments of charred blue jeans scattered around an old fire, possibly by campers but we just don't know. They found the fragments about 300 yards from the ditch where the bodies were found. As you know from the descriptions provided to you, the boys all wore blue jeans when they disappeared on Sunday.

"The second thing they found was a grease-stained tablecloth, like one you would use at your home. It was about four- or five-foot square. That was also located in the vicinity of the ditch. The cloth itself looked as if someone had wiped his hands on it.

"If you remember, the grease spots are considered significant because the heels and elbows of the boys had stains and grease marks on them. The cloth is also being examined at the crime lab. Sheriff Lohman has also offered a $2,500 reward for clues leading to the capture of the killer or killers of the three boys. This is a personal offer that the Sheriff said he would pay out of his own pocket."

A voice behind us muttered, "Big fuckin' deal. Must be an election year." No one laughed.

"Next, there was a young man who appeared at the search scene. He talked to Captain Conway, and he reported seeing two cars parked in the parking lot Tuesday morning, facing south. The cars were parked in a secluded area where the bodies were found. This man is identified as E.J. Malone, of 9916 Irving Park Road. That's in Schiller Park.

"As you know, we still theorize that the killer or killers dumped the bodies in the ditch Tuesday morning. That's according to the Coroner's Office. That's approximately the same time Mr. Malone reported he saw those two cars. The witness says the cars were a light green Ford convertible and a cream color sedan, probably a Chevy. Those of you from the 33rd District know that two cars were reported stolen before the boys disappeared Sunday night. Those of you who do not have this information, I'll repeat it now. One was a 1955 green Ford station wagon, reported stolen October 8 bearing the Illinois license number 11-87663; the other one was a 1948 black Chevrolet, bearing Illinois license number 17-03205, stolen October 11.

"Captain Conway and Sheriff Lohman had their men search the

surrounding areas where Mr. Malone saw these two cars, but they were unable to find any traces of tire marks. We will assign someone to talk to Malone and bring him in for questioning.

"Also, we have other clues from detectives' reports documenting the interviews of various people who have volunteered information about this case. One is a rubber mat found at Montrose and Cumberland, about a mile and a half from where the bodies were discovered. The mat is about 30 by 18 inches and was found in a garbage dump. It bore waffle-like markings, similar to those found on the back of Anton Schuessler. The mat was brought into the station and turned over to the crime lab.

"Finally, we received a letter at Headquarters postmarked 11:00 p.m. Tuesday, October 18. I first want to state that I think we're going to be getting all of the fruitcakes and wackos coming out of the woodwork on this one. These people want a little recognition and their names in the papers, so they're calling up with all kinds of information. But we're going to have to evaluate it and decide on every piece of information we receive in order to determine if it's valid. The letter contained only newspaper headlines telling of the slaying of the boys and a slip of paper bearing an Illinois license plate number. We're going to trace the whereabouts of the number, and if it's a legitimate number we'll question the person it's registered to.

"Remember, men, we're going to start getting a lot of strange calls and letters, but every lead will have to be investigated. This ends the briefing for today. Finish the investigations you're working on and then report to your unit supervisors."

The sound of dozens of chairs scraping the floor rose up as we filed out of the assembly room to return to offices or head back out to the streets to pursue investigations.

Sgt. Murphy assigned Detectives Duffy and Kakowinski, along with Frank and me to handle the investigation of Mr. Malone, who reported seeing two cars in the forest preserve parking lot. Murphy also briefed us on a report that had come in concerning a Harold Blumfield. The report indicated he picked up three boys hitchhiking Sunday night, October 16. Murphy instructed us to follow up on this lead as well.

After getting assignments, most of the detectives went to their desks to retrieve whatever notes and files they needed and headed to their squad cars. Frank and I stayed at our desks, completing reports and returning phone calls.

I heard Sgt. Murphy's voice from down the hall.

"Jim, can I see you for a minute. I need to talk to you." The tone of Murphy's voice made me uneasy. Placing the finished report into the to-be-filed bin, I walked into the hallway and toward Murphy's office. As I entered, Murphy was standing next to the door. He closed it and motioned for me to take a seat in one of the two chairs facing the desk.

"What's up, Sarge?" What the hell's coming off, I wondered.

Murphy came from around the desk and sat in the worn leather chair next to me. He casually picked up the nearest file, and without looking at anything in particular, thumbed through the papers loosely thrown into it. It was a distraction, a nervous bit Sarge went through just before he dished out bad news.

"Jim, I was wondering if you would volunteer doing some undercover work on this thing. Interested?"

It didn't take long for me to say yes.

"Sure, Sarge. What is it?"

"Well, you remember the guy who works as a caretaker and lives on the premises at the Monte Cristo Bowling Alley? His name's Dillon, right?"

"Yeah. He's the same guy who identified the pictures of the boys. Why?"

"The Captain's thinking the same thing you are. We need to get another look at this guy. From what the Captain and Koeppe told me about the inquest, Dillon left right after his testimony. The Coroner wanted to ask him some other questions, but the guy was gone. Could be he didn't realize they wanted to ask him other questions."

"You think the Coroner's going to call him again on Monday?" I asked.

"I doubt it. But that's where you come in."

"Me? What's up?"

"Jim, we need somebody on the inside. I want you to volunteer to go undercover at the bowling alley. There's a job advertised there for a pinsetting job.

"You've gotta be kidding, Sarge." The sergeant continued looking down at the file in his hand, still flipping through the pages. It allowed him to avoid eye contact with me.

"No, I'm not kidding. Somebody's got to get inside and keep an eye on this Dillon character. The jury's still out on him. I've received several reports that he's got strange interests, if you follow me. Put that together with him living at the bowling alley, the kids go in there, then they're found dead. Calls for a little follow-up, wouldn't you say? Of course, he's not going to admit anything. That's why we need somebody in there, close-up."

I got the drift of 'I want you to volunteer.' Like being in the marines, I thought.

"How much do they pay, Sarge?"

"I think it's about thirteen cents a line for letting the pins fly by you." Murphy was really buried in the folder now—pages began flying out, dropping to the floor, and the sergeant bent down to pick them up.

"What? I never did this before in my life, Sarge."

Murphy sat up in his chair again, shoved the loose papers back into the file and then sat the file on the top of his desk. Now he looked directly at me. The worst part was over, anyway.

"You'll learn. That is, if they give you the job," he smiled. I didn't smile back. "Why don't you try to get over there sometime today?"

"Hey, wait a minute! What do you mean if they hire me? Who said I would even take this goddam job for thirteen cents an hour? Am I insured for dental care if one of those pins whacks me in the face and knocks my teeth out? I'm not going around the rest of my life eating banana pudding." I took a deep breath then asked, "Who's going to know about this?"

Murphy became more animated. He could tell he'd gotten his undercover man, even if I had to be persuaded to volunteer.

"Well, I discussed it with Captain Corcoran and he discussed it with Lt. Deeley. They okayed it. I know about it, and I'll tell your partner, Frank, about it. Those will be the only ones who know about it. Don't worry Jim, it's only for a few days."

So it was already a done deal before Murphy talked to me. That's the way it worked. The top guys make the decision and to be polite they ask if it's okay. What are you going say? Anyway, it was good to know that Corcoran and Deeley had enough confidence to pick me from all of the other detectives assigned to the unit.

Murphy continued to brief me on the other reasons we needed undercover work at the bowling alley. There had been information that homosexuals were hanging around there, as well as rougher teenage gang members. This was consistent with two of the main theories about possible perpetrators of the crimes. It had to be checked out.

"According to Dillon and the owner, Mr. Davis, it's like heaven over there. Nothing bad ever happens, no problems, blah, blah, blah. We're just going to try to get as much information as we can from the pinsetters there. Keep an eye on Dillon and the gangs that hang out there. Keep your ears open, that's all."

I nodded, then added "Yeah, and I better keep my eyes open, too. Those bowlers make bets on how bad they can hurt the pinsetters. They throw real cannonballs down the alleys."

"Jim, it shouldn't take you too long to see what's really going on down there. Let Frank know what you're doing each day and let me know, and we'll try and coordinate your day and times."

"Sarge, don't worry about it. Whatever time I put in, I put in. Everybody's working double shifts and days off on this case. Besides, thirteen cents an hour is too good to pass up." That got a laugh from Murphy.

9:30 a.m.

"I guess you heard what Murphy wants me to do." Frank was driving as we pulled away from the station parking lot.

"Yeah. I hear you're going to be making some extra cash. Isn't that under the minimum wage or something?"

I looked straight ahead, thinking about how to pull this off. The bowling alley was pretty close to the District. Some off-duty police officers occasionally went there for a couple of drinks and to bowl after work. There was a chance of being seen by officers who knew me.

"You know, Frank, maybe you should drive me home, and I'll change into some old clothes. I can't go apply for a pinsetter's job looking like this. Then we can go to the Monte Cristo. If I get the job, I'll tell them I'll be back later. I'll have to check with Murphy about whatever shift they want me to work, maybe give them some bullshit to see if I can fit it around our shift. Then we can go over to the Peterson boy's funeral."

Frank nodded. "Yeah. I'll have to check with Murphy. Maybe he wants me to handle that Malone interview. I think Duffy's going to question that guy Blumfield. From what I heard this morning while you were talking with Murphy, Koeppe and Schulze are hitting the bowling alleys."

I turned quickly, looked over at Frank and said, "Shit, I hope those guys don't come over to where I'm at. We better get together tomorrow morning either before or after the briefing and get things straightened out. I don't want anybody coming over to the bowling alley while I'm there."

Frank nodded in agreement.

"Drive me over to the house," I said. "I'll change real fast."

Frank sped off heading to my house. It wasn't far from the station and was in a quiet, neat residential neighborhood. After pulling up to the curb, Frank pulled out a fresh El Producto from his inside coat pocket. He unwrapped the stiff cellophane wrapper, licked the tapered end and rolled down the driver's side window. He lit the cigar and took a few puffs, turning his head to blow the smoke out the window.

I hurried into the house and grabbed worn clothes that would be right for the job interview. My interview clothes consisted of a well-worn pair of pants with frayed cuffs, an old brown sweater, used to do work around the house, an old pair of shoes, with holes in both soles and cracks in the dull leather around the edges. Ready to get the job, I walked out the side door and up to the squad car.

"Jim, you look like a bum." Frank stared as I got into the car. "I don't want you sitting next to me. People will think that I'm driving around with some wino. Why don't you get in the back? At least they'll think I pinched some bum off the street." Frank started to laugh.

"Take it easy. You think I want anybody I know to see me like this? Just drive over to the Monte Cristo. I don't want to be late for my job interview." We looked at each other and laughed.

Frank dropped me off about a block west of the bowling alley. I walked the short distance to the front entrance, noticed the sign saying "PINSETTER WANTED," and walked in.

There were very few people in the alley at this time of the morning. Who would be in this place this early in the day, I thought to myself. Looking around the dimly lit room I noticed two or three bowlers, older men who were bowling a few lanes by themselves.

I approached the counter where a man stood next to a rack of bowling shoes. The man gazed out into the room, looking at the men who were bowling on the alley just in front of him. He pulled out a pair of bowling shoes from the rack, turned them over, looked at the worn soles then placed them back on the rack. The shoes were rentals, black and red in color with dirty gray laces. Large numbers were stitched on the back of each shoe indicating the size, just above the heels.

"I saw the sign on the door downstairs," I said to the man. "You still need a pinsetter?" The man found a space on the rack next to him and carefully placed the worn pair of size 13 shoes on the lower shelf. He continued to pull out shoes from the rack, never looking up at me.

"Yeah. Ever set pins before?"

"No, I haven't. But I'm willing to try." I tried to sound anxious to get the job, but not too anxious.

"When do you want to start?" Finally, he turned and glanced at me. Just as quickly, he turned back to the rack of shoes, pulling out another pair and inspecting them.

Jeez, I thought. This guy'll hire anybody. "I can start right away."

The man pulled some papers from under the counter and shoved them in my direction. "You're hired," he said, as he pointed to a ballpoint pen on the counter. "You start tonight."

I began to fill in the information. Where the form asked for my name, I wrote "Jim Goggin:" the name of a boyhood friend. As I completed the information, I asked about training on how to set pins.

"The other guys will show you what to do. You start at 6:00 p.m. tonight. That's when our men's league starts."

I hesitated for a moment, then asked, "How much do I get paid?"

"You get fourteen cents a line."

"That's it!" I tried to sound surprised. Actually, I was. It was one cent more than Murphy told me it would be.

"No, we pay seventy cents an hour besides that."

A bonanza, I thought. "I'll take it."

The man grabbed the application and looked at it quickly. He threw it into a cardboard box at the end of the counter.

"Okay, Goggin, make sure you're here at 6 p.m. tonight."

"You want me to take the sign off the door?"

"No, just leave it there. Never know."

That didn't sit too well with me. Never know what? Never know when a pinsetter will get knocked in the head and keel over dead? Or maybe the guy finally got a look at the way I was dressed and figured that they would need another pinsetter by the end of the night.

I walked cautiously down the steep flight of stairs and the short distance to where Frank was waiting in the car. The engine was still running.

Frank leaned over and opened the passenger's door. "I knew it wouldn't take you long to get that job. That's what happens when you dress for success, right Jim?"

"Just get me back home so I can get out of these clothes before we go back to the District."

10:50 a.m.

"Can you believe it, Murphy? They hired me!" I was now dressed in a work suit.

"That's great, Jim. They should only know what kind of experienced pinsetter you are. I'll let the Captain and Lt. Deeley know about this. When do you start?"

"Tonight, at 6:00 p.m. This guy was so anxious to hire me I thought he was going to throw a rope around me and have me start right then. By the way, I saw a guy walking back and forth down the side lane against the wall of the bowling alley. Looked like that guy Dillon. I looked at him, he looked at me and he didn't say anything. I don't think he's suspicious. Not yet, anyway."

Murphy reached for the phone on his desk and had the dispatcher notify Duffy and Schulze that they should call him as soon as possible. Then he turned to Frank and me, as we sat waiting for the call to end.

"I'm gonna send either Duffy or Schulze over to pick up Dillon and bring him back here. So keep in touch with me, Jim. I don't want you to accidentally stop in here while they're talking to him. If you can, call me before you come in. Otherwise, you'd better just stay away from the station. We'll pick him up today within the next hour or two and be finished with him sometime this afternoon."

"Sarge, that'll be fine. Frank and I will be at the Peterson funeral most of the afternoon. We'll be leaving right after lunch, then we'll get back to you later."

1:30 p.m.
Jefferson Park Lutheran Church

The Jefferson Park Lutheran Church was a small neighborhood church located on a quiet, tree-lined side street with well cared for homes and neat lawns. Gold and rust-colored leaves had fallen onto the lawns and side streets, shaken from the trees by the gentle, autumn breeze. A bright, October sun filtered through the remaining leaves as we drove down one of the side streets near the church.

As we neared the church, we saw what we had anticipated. Several squad cars were blocking the streets near the church, uniformed officers were attempting to control the heavy traffic, and a large crowd had gathered in front of the church doors. Reporters were taking pictures of the crowd, the traffic, and everything they thought might be of interest to readers of the late edition papers.

The officers handling traffic directed Frank and me to a 'No Parking' zone. Every possible parking spot was taken. As we walked toward the church, Frank walked over to several reporters taking pictures of those gathered on the front steps of the church.

"Don't you guys ever let up? Give 'em a break." By now, most of the reporters assigned to the case recognized Frank and knew enough not to say anything. They backed off a bit, but still had their cameras ready in case the opportunity for a good picture presented itself.

The mourners filed into the small church and the 350 seats were quickly filled. Those who could not find seats inside the church stood on the front steps while two ushers kept the doors open so that those outside could hear the service.

The children's choir began the service with "Jesus Savior, Pilot Me," and their voices could be heard on the sidewalk. Mr. Peterson later told me that this particular hymn had been Robert's favorite.

At the far end of the church, Rev. Eifrig began the service. The parents and family of Robert sat in the first several rows of the church, and soft muffled sobs could be heard throughout the small congregation gathered to pay their last respects.

Rev. Eifrig looked down from the pulpit at the gray casket covered by hundreds of beautiful flowers.

"Last Palm Sunday, Robert was confirmed in this church," Rev. Eifrig began. He spoke of Robert's devotion and strong affiliation with the Jefferson Park Church. "He was a wonderful boy," the Rev. Eifrig said. "He attended church regularly and never had a bad mark over his head."

"Our Savior meant it when He said on the cross, 'Father, forgive them for they know not what they do.'" The pastor reminded the Petersons that their son was taken from them by the evil that exists in men's hearts.

"When our emotions are aroused, our cry for justice should be mixed with righteousness and mellowed with mercy."

The sermon was brief, but so moving that it appeared that every person in the church was crying by the time Rev. Eifrig quietly finished and moved toward the casket. Honor guards from Boy Scout Troop 962, Robert's troop, moved toward the casket and slowly lifted it from the catafalque.

They walked slowly down the aisle of the church, past the family members, neighbors, and members of the congregation who had known Robert as a lively, loving boy. Now he was gone.

The Boy Scout Honor Guard walked down the steps of the church and across the sidewalk to the hearse waiting at the curb. Those gathered outside the church were hushed, even the traffic seemed to have stopped. All that was heard was the soft rustle of leaves.

The Honor Guard lifted the casket and carefully placed it into the hearse. Then the boys slowly stepped back from the large, black car and stood in a straight line along the curb. Raising their right hands in unison, they saluted their fellow scout.

Two squad cars, their lights flashing, led the hearse and the long line of cars behind it through the streets of the neighborhood where Bobby Peterson had lived. The funeral procession wound its way along the city streets, slowed down as it passed in front of the Peterson home on Farragut, then made its way east to Rosehill Cemetery.

In the quiet of the cemetery, Rev. Eifrig read the last words of the somber ceremony at the gravesite to the 100 mourners gathered to say their final farewell. Mr. and Mrs. Peterson had decided not to have their other children attend either the wake or funeral of their son, fearing it would be disturbing to them at their young ages.

At the end of the service, both parents walked to the casket, bowed their heads and sobbed, "Goodbye, Bobby. We love you always." Both of Robert's grandmothers were with the parents, holding them and trying their best to console them.

The friends and family of the Petersons walked quietly away from gravesite, heading to their cars. Some of them paused and looked at the Petersons, probably wondering how these parents could bear the tragic loss of their child.

Frank and I got into our squad car and drove slowly past old headstones and monuments, past old elm trees lining the winding, single lane road through the grounds of the cemetery and past the black iron gates. We drove in complete silence as we traveled west toward Gale Street.

Frank stopped the squad car at the edge of the parking bay

behind the station and I got out and went to my car parked next to the back stairs of the building and got in. As I drove home to change into my work clothes, I thought about the events of the afternoon.

Before leaving home, I called Murphy and told him about the funeral services and that I was about to leave for the Monte Cristo. Murphy said that he, Captain Corcoran, and Duffy were interviewing Dillon.

"He's not going to be back at the alley, Jim, because when we get finished with him here we're going to take him downtown for a lie detector test. So don't worry about seeing him tonight."

"That's good to know, Murph. I'm supposed to be at the Monte Cristo about fifteen minutes early tonight. That's about how much training I'm going to get. If anything happens while I'm there tonight, I'll give either you or Frank a call and keep in touch. If you don't hear from me tonight, I'll see you at the briefing tomorrow morning. Wish me luck, Sarge. I'm gonna need it with all them fuckin' pins flying around. And thanks for recommending me for this job."

"Don't mention it, Jim," Murphy said with a laugh.

5:45 p.m.
Monte Cristo Bowling Alley

I climbed up the narrow, steep flight of stairs at the Monte Cristo. Two men were coming down in my direction, both of whom were carrying well-worn, leather bowling bags and holding onto the wooden banister barely attached to the wall of the stairwell.

To let them pass, I turned sideways. There was barely room for two people to pass, and if either one was carrying a ball, one of the two had to put his back to the wall.

I wondered when the last time the place had been inspected by the Fire Department. If a fire started, nobody would make it out of there.

As I entered the lobby of the bowling alley, league play was just about the start. Making my way to the counter, I saw that there was a different person behind the counter than the man who had hired me earlier that afternoon. I introduced myself and said that I was told to be at work fifteen minutes early. I also told him I had never set pins before.

"Don't worry, we'll train ya." The new counter man barely looked up as he made change for the two young men standing next to me.

"You're gonna train me fifteen minutes before the leagues start?"

"Don't worry about it," he said gruffly. "I'll get Gordon. He's been around long enough to show you what to do." The man finished making change for the young men, picked up a microphone then flipped a switch below the counter.

"GORDON TO THE FRONT DESK," he barked. His voice echoed through the bowling alley and boomed over the noise of the balls rumbling down the alleys and wooden pins clacking sharply against each other.

Moments later, a man approached the front counter. He appeared to be about 30 years old, wearing a Hawaiian shirt, baggy green pants, and black and white "P.F. Flyer" gym shoes that seemed to be as old as he was.

"Gordon, this is Jim. Take him in the back and show him what to do."

I followed Gordon to the rear of the bowling lanes where the pins were racked by hand. We entered a long, narrow room extending across the bowling lanes. There were sheets of canvas behind each bay, stretched between two alleys. There was a small area above the back of the canvas sheet allowing the setters to sit down, but it was obvious there would be little time to do that.

As I looked down the narrow room, I could see the setters pick up pins from behind the canvas backstop, slip them into the rack and set the rack down on the alley. Then they scooted over to the alley next to them and did the same thing.

The noise was deafening. It looked like mass confusion, with a pin popping up over the canvas and the setter chasing after it. Racks were going up and down, and bowling balls were thundering down the alleys.

I raised my voice to be heard above the noise.

"Hey, Gordon. Is Dillon here tonight?"

"No. Dillon's not going to be here tonight. The guy at the counter is Ed Davis. He's the manager here. Don't pay any attention to him.

He's a lot of bullshit." He pointed to two alleys that were dark, with no bowlers using them. "You think you can handle one and two?"

"Are you out of your fuckin' mind? Handle TWO? This is my first night. I don't know what to do." I was now shouting as the noise of pins hitting the alley and canvas backstops started to increase.

"The only thing you do is sit in the middle here, where the canvas crosses both alleys. Rack the pins like this, push the button, hold the rope then pull it and the rack back up." He demonstrated the whole procedure as he talked. It seemed simple enough.

"You have to remember that when one person shoots on one alley, you go over to the other alley and set those pins. You're jumping over the rim here like a horse. When you're sitting up there, just make sure that when the pins come flying, you don't get hit with one." He pointed in the direction of one of the far lanes, and I saw a couple of pins flip up over the canvas. The setter at that alley made a quick jerk to his left and the pin went flying past him. The guy reminded me of a good fighter instinctively ducking away from a left hook.

That's some training, I thought. "Don't get hit with a pin."

Gordon continued his training session.

"A lot of guys really get hurt. You know, broken arms and legs. Especially broken legs and knees when they're going across alleys." He pointed down the alleys in the direction of the bowlers.

"You look through here, over the pins and over the rack. You can see the alleys down there. Make sure they don't double bowl on your alley, 'cause if they do, that means you'd be working the alley when pins are supposed to be put in. That's no good. That's when you can get hurt. Some of those assholes do it on purpose. I think they make bets to see if they can nail a setter."

That thought had already crossed my mind. I looked around the narrow room.

"What if you have to use the washroom real bad, something comes up and you gotta go?" I always thought of the basics. Like when you were on stakeout, sitting in your squad car all night. That was one of the first things you had to plan for—where to take a piss.

"Well, there's three things you can do. See that exit sign back there? Well, you can go out the door and take a leak off the fire escape. Or there's a can right next to you. Or there's a small little bathroom right at the other end by that exit. So you have three spots to go to. But since you don't have much experience yet, you better take a leak in the can. You might get some complaints if the bowlers have to wait for their pins to get set."

So that was the training, I said to myself. You put the pins here, pull this, push that, piss in the can. Oh, and don't get hit by the pins. Great, I'm gonna get killed tonight.

It wasn't hard to figure out why the bowling alley couldn't keep pinsetters for very long. The setters I saw working the lanes all looked like degenerates, bums just off the street with greasy pants and shirts, matted hair, and two days of stubble on their faces. I detected a familiar odor beginning to enter my nostrils. Like old piss in a filthy alley.

According to Gordon, these guys showed up every night. They got enough money for a few pints of whiskey and maybe a cot at some flophouse. But somehow they moved fast enough to rack up the pins. That's all that seemed to matter to the owners.

Gordon said he was going to work lanes three, four, five, and six. That meant he was probably the most intelligent guy back there and fast enough to earn more than double what the other pinsetters could make. He told me he would work close by to help out at first.

Suddenly, a bell sounded. It sounded like a school bell at the change of classes and rang loud enough to be heard over the noise of pins hitting the lanes and canvass backstops. It signaled the start of league bowling. Seconds later, scores of pins were being knocked down, the rolling thunder of bowling balls being fired down twelve lanes filled the small back room and the five pinsetters began darting back and forth between lanes. Racks began to rise and fall, and a half-dozen pins filled up behind the backstops and into upper portions of the back room.

I started to fill the first rack when I heard the pins in the second alley explode. After racking one lane, I jumped to the second lane and completed the same task. That's the way it went through the first game. One by one, the noise level fell as the last bowlers finished their tenth frames.

Gordon helped at first, but then after a few close calls and some fast thinking, I got the hang of it. Gordon walked over to the two lanes that I had been working, sat on the chair above the "trenches" and took a break. He looked down at me as I filled the rack on the first lane.

"So, what do you think? Not so bad, right?"

"Not when you get the hang of it. I don't think I'm ready to handle four lanes yet."

"Don't worry." Gordon got up from his chair and looked down the narrow space toward the end of the pinsetters room. Two pinsetters had gone out onto the balcony overlooking the small parking spaces behind the building. One was walking quickly toward the washroom.

"I have to check on the guys. You know, this is what Dillon usually does. He checks up on these guys to make sure they don't sneak a few nips out on the balcony or in the washroom. If they finish a pint, by the end of the night they won't be able to see any of the pins. How are you doing?"

I reached down to the small of my back and bent forward a bit. Then I straightened up and stretched my arms out in front of me, twisting my upper body from left to right to loosen a few tense muscles.

"I'm a little sore, but not from any of the pins hitting me. Bending down, picking up the pins, putting the racks down, picking them up, pulling the rope. I guess I'm a little out of shape."

"Well," Gordon said, "it's not really a bad job. You pick up some good money if you get experienced. Looks like you're handling it pretty good."

We talked a bit more about the leagues, what nights were busiest, who to watch out for. In another minute, the next game had begun, and we were at it again.

A couple of bowlers on my lanes yelled out a few curse words, and Gordon yelled back at them before I could react.

"Hey, take it easy. We got a new guy back here. Anyway, it's your fault we had to get a replacement. Take it easy or we'll close down the alley and you can set the pins yourself." Gordon looked over at me and smiled.

"Don't worry. That's just bullshit. We don't know what happened to Ralph, the guy you replaced. Those guys just need to know we don't take any more shit than we have to back here."

After the second game, I had to take a bathroom break. I made my way around the chairs and broken pins on the upper level of the back room and walked toward the washroom. Gordon was already there, keeping an eye on the rest of his "crew." I noticed a few empty half-pint bottles of liquor scattered near the door to the balcony and inside the washroom. Once inside the small restroom, I held my breath so I wouldn't be overwhelmed by the stench.

12:00 a.m.

I'd been on this new job for over six hours now, and the league bowlers had finished for the night. The action slowed down enough for Gordon and me to make some small talk again.

"Well, I guess you're doin' okay, Jim. Didn't get hit yet, right?"

"No, and I don't intend to, either."

Gordon laughed then asked if I was interested in staying on and doing some open bowling pinsetting. He explained that open bowling was after the leagues had finished playing. There were usually a lot of people waiting to bowl, since this place only had twelve lanes. I thought of the Peterson and Schuessler boys and how they probably had to wait for a lane to open up last Sunday night. I wanted to double-check my understanding of how this worked at the Monte Cristo.

"You mean these leagues play every night?" I knew what leagues were about, but needed to act as though this was all new.

"No, not every night. Usually before 6:00 p.m. and after midnight, there's open bowling. Also, there aren't any leagues playing here on Sunday. First come, first serve. You put your name on a list and you sit or stand around and wait for them to call your name. Like tonight, we'll have open bowling until two or three o'clock in the morning. Want to stick around and pick up some extra cash tonight? I'll talk to Davis if you want."

"No, that's all right. I think I'm done for tonight. Besides, it looks like you got a couple of new guys here. They probably could use the money. How do you get paid around here, anyway?"

"Just go up to the front and ask Davis. They'll have an envelope and have your money for your lines in there. At the end of the week they pay you for your hours separately. That's how it works around here."

I thanked Gordon for his help getting started and walked out of the pinsetters room and toward the front desk. Davis was busy assigning people on the waiting list to the alleys as they became available. He saw me coming and pointed to the small group of people waiting for lanes. I nodded then took a seat on one of the benches where the bowlers were changing into their bowling shoes.

I looked around at the people beginning open bowling and noticed there was a diverse mix of individuals waiting to get assigned to a lane. There were a lot of teenagers, which I thought a little unusual. The kids were mainly 15 or 16 years old. It was after midnight on a Thursday night, and I wondered what these kids were doing out so late. I made a mental note to discuss this with Murphy and talk to the juvenile officers working under Lt. Delaney.

From what I recalled of his conversation with Koeppe about Dillon's testimony at the inquest, this didn't look right. Dillon testified that there had been no incidents at the bowling alley involving teenagers or maybe one time last year involving some 18 year olds.

If that's what he testified to, he's full of bullshit. I was looking at three or four older kids standing right in front of me. They looked like they could tear up the place with no problem. I wondered whether the bowling alley had people around to act as security to be sure things didn't get out of hand, but didn't see anyone who could handle a bad situation with so many people in here.

The adults that I observed looked a little strange, too.

After noticing that most of the people waiting for open lanes had been assigned, I walked up to Davis and struck up a conversation with him. We figured out how many lines I had handled and Davis worked out I was due $3.60. He asked me to sign a small envelope, gave me the $3.60 and kept the envelope. Then he told me about the hour rates at the end of the week.

"There are a lot of kids up here for this time of the night, aren't there?" I tried not to sound to curious and attempted to say it in an off-handed way. "Don't they have school tomorrow?"

"It's none of my business," Davis responded. "My business is to control the alleys here and see that we don't have any problems collecting the money. You shouldn't worry about that either. If they're not your kids, don't worry about 'em."

I took the $3.60 and walked over to the bar area. I wanted to see if any juveniles were in there drinking. There were a few older people sitting around, some of the league bowlers were having a few more beers before heading home, but no teenagers. I walked back to the front counter and told Davis I might be a little late tomorrow night.

"I thought you were supposed to start at 6:00 p.m." Davis' voice was harsh.

"I can't make it at 6:00 p.m. I had some other things planned before I took the job."

"What time are you gonna get here, then?"

"I don't know. Maybe sometime after 9:00 p.m." I had to figure out my schedule at the District, clear any changes with Murphy, and there was the Schuessler wake to go to.

"Nine o'clock! What the hell's the matter with you guys? You get a job, and you come in when you feel like it? Tomorrow is Friday night and that's our big night. Fridays, Saturdays and Sundays. Are you gonna come in the rest of the week?" Davis sounded agitated. His eyebrows narrowed and his voice was loud enough for the bowlers standing across from us to turn their heads in our direction.

"Yeah, I'll be here the rest of the week. It just so happens that I might be a little late tomorrow."

Davis lowered his voice when he noticed that some of the bowlers could hear the conversation. "All right then, get here as fast as you can."

I walked to the stairs leading to the front entrance. I thought I was in pretty good shape, but my knees and lower back ached as I negotiated the steep flight of stairs.

Setting pins made me notice muscles I didn't know I had.

Friday
October 21, 1955
7:35 a.m.

Detectives started gathering in the assembly room nearly a half-hour before the scheduled 8:00 a.m. briefing by Captain Corcoran. Some shared information about their investigations the day before. Others were trying to confirm rumors they had heard from their informants on the streets. They traded information, a few contacts, and we were all becoming anxious as the investigation became larger in scope, but returned little in the form of solid clues and evidence about the murder of the boys.

Men worked around the clock, on their days off and put in as much of their own time on this case as they could. No one complained about the work, just about the frustration brought on by the lack of progress.

I passed through the assembly room and reported to Sgt. Murphy's office. The sergeant was handing out summaries of the most promising leads and the results of the most recent investigations by the various detectives in the unit. When he saw me in the doorway of his office, he asked me to come in and told the other officers and detectives to go on down to the assembly room and wait for the Captain's briefing. He closed the door and sat down behind his desk.

"So, how do you feel?" Murphy was placing the remaining summaries in a large brown legal file. He looked up and scrutinized me, looking for any dents and bruises.

"I feel great, Sarge. I had a shower and a couple hours sleep in a clean bed. That's more than I can say for my new fellow employees." I sat down in one of the two chairs in front of Murphy's desk.

"Get anything we can use?"

"The place has some strange people hanging around. Before I forget, I think the juvenile officers should start bringing some of those young kids in. They're at the bowling alley after midnight on a Thursday night. Where the hell are their parents?

"Anyway, I kept a low profile since I just started work there. This guy, Gordon, who showed me the ropes on the pinsetting job seems to be okay. The manager over there, Davis, he really doesn't seem to give a shit about what goes on there. All he cares about is getting paid. And those pinsetters, Jesus, no wonder they never take the sign down. They're all a bunch of bums. You should see the toilet back there. It's so bad that even those guys don't use it. They go out on the fire escape to take a piss."

I went on to tell Murphy about the way you have to sign up during open bowling times, the number of leagues using the alleys. All of that seemed to fit with what witnesses had said about how the boys had to wait for a lane to open up.

"What about this guy Dillon. What did you get from him?"

Murphy explained how he, Corcoran, and Duffy questioned Dillon for about four hours. The allegations concerning his sexual orientation and other information investigators had pieced together, Dillon corroborated himself. He denied taking any kids into his apartment, and also denied trying to pick up kids for sex acts. He was also asked if he tried to pick up any of the pinsetters for the same reason.

Murphy suggested that I look around the bowling alley and ask some of the pinsetters about their manager. If I had to, maybe I could try and get invited into Dillon's apartment and see what it looks like.

"Anything you want me to zero in on, Sarge?"

"No, just find out what kind of groups hang out there. Maybe some of these pinsetters are picking up kids. Oh, by the way, we did send Dillon downtown for a polygraph. He passed. You know the guy who gave the test—he's one of the best. As it stands now, this guy's eliminated as a suspect."

"Maybe he passed the lie box, Sarge, but in my opinion the jury's still out on that guy. If he didn't do something with the Peterson and Schuessler boys, he still might have his own little playground someplace. He should be back there tonight. I'll see what I can come up with as soon as Frank and I get back from the Schuessler wake. I told that guy Davis, the manager, I'd be late. He got hot about it, but I don't give a shit. Me and this guy Gordon are the only two setters he's got who don't fall down those fuckin' stairs at the end of the night."

We looked at the Monte Cristo as a promising source of information. If nothing else, we could file away the information gathered and keep tabs on the place in the future.

"By the way, Sarge, you were wrong about the pay. It's more than thirteen cents an hour."

"Oh yeah? How much are you making?"

"I made $3.60 last night. Plus a few more bucks at the end of the week."

Murphy laughed. "Don't forget to declare that on your income tax."

8:00 a.m.

Captain Corcoran called the briefing to order as the minute hand hit the hour. His voice was as pleasant as he could make it. Along with the other officers, detectives, and supervisors assigned to the case, the Captain had been working long hours. He had been keeping city officials briefed on all matters involving the investigation. Police Commissioner O'Connor was keeping the Mayor informed. But as the case continued to gain notoriety around the nation and the world, the Department began to feel the pressure from the public and city, county, and state officials to find the killer or killers. Soon.

"Good morning, men. First of all, the Commissioner and the Mayor want to commend you for all your hard work on this case. The Mayor has asked all citizens who live near bowling alleys on the northwest side, especially where the boys were last seen, to make a thorough search of their garages, empty lots, and alleys for any evidence like the clothing the boys wore on the night they disappeared. The newspapers have placed the description of the clothing in many of their editions and will continue to do so. The public has been informed that if they aren't sure of the clothing they are to call the hotline phone number.

"Mayor Richard J. Daley has announced that approval has been given by the City Council for a $10,000 reward for the capture of the killer or killers of the boys. County Board President Dan Ryan has offered a similar amount from the Board's contingency fund. Sheriff Lohman has personally offered $2,500; the Maryann Baking Company has offered a $1,000 reward and so has the Food Market

News office. A woman from Georgia has even offered a $1,000 reward.

"The Commissioner has appealed to the public to call us about anything they think might be related to this case. I know you men will have to answer and follow up on each of these calls, and they're in the thousands by now. But I can't emphasize it enough. Just one of those calls might provide a clue to these slayings.

"William L. McFetridge, the President of Local 1 here in Chicago of the Flat Janitors Union, has asked more than 1600 janitors on the northwest side to search basements and elsewhere for any clues or objects that might be related to this crime. He's asked his men to look for clothing or any items in garbage cans and trash piles that might help the Department locate the murder scene.

"The theory that the boys may have been victims of teenage gangs is being thoroughly investigated. So far, the teams of detectives that have been assigned to check out several schools in the area have found no evidence of gangs that might be involved in these murders.

"Lt. Delaney and his unit have begun a check of teenagers with juvenile records in the neighborhood where the victims lived. His men will also be rounding up every teenage sex offender who frequents the Milwaukee Avenue/Lawrence Avenue area. Every one of these individuals will be questioned thoroughly.

"We also received a call from Captain Conway who informed us his men are re-checking reports of teenage parties where trouble occurred through the year. He's going to pick up every person who has been arrested in connection with these activities.

"I had a briefing yesterday with Lt. Stanwyck, the Chief Investigator of the Illinois State Police. He informed me that his office is in possession of a brown suit coat found by two Schiller Park police officers near where the bodies were discovered. It's being inventoried and will be sent down to the crime lab.

"Also yesterday afternoon, I spoke with Captain Norman Hawthorne of the Sheriff's Office on Milwaukee Avenue. He informed me he was sending two deputies out to interview a patient who voluntarily committed himself to the Elgin State Hospital on Tuesday, the day the bodies were found. We have come to learn that this individual formerly worked at one of the stables about a half-mile from where the bodies were found. He also had once been a pinsetter at one of the bowling alleys in the Lawrence and Milwaukee area."

That got my attention. I looked over at Sgt. Murphy, who also happened to be looking at me. We nodded to each other then turned back to listen to the Captain as he continued his briefing.

"As of today, we received reports from the crime lab stating that they have been unable to find any link between the evidence that has been sent to them and the slayings. The evidence is being studied daily and results are being sent out on a regular basis from the crime lab to all units.

"Three suspects were brought in last night and were questioned by us during the night, but they have been released upon determination that they had no connections with the murders.

"The consensus of all the detectives working on this case, and their supervisors, is that we need to focus our attention on the clues we have at the present time: the location of the bodies, the clothing the boys were wearing at the time they were last seen; and the time they were reported to have last been seen.

"You men on the street, those of you going door-to-door, and every uniformed officer need to get us the answers to two questions as soon as possible: Did anyone see Robert, John, and Anton alive after 8:55 p.m. Sunday night, and second, we need to find the owners of the two vehicles that the witness, Mr. Malone, said he saw in the forest preserve parking lot on Tuesday.

"You detectives who are assigned with Lt. Michael Shannon of the stolen auto division, be sure you go through every car registered with the description given to you in the summary reports Sgt. Murphy handed out this morning.

"Those of you making a house-to-house search, pay special attention to the garages. Lt. Shannon has informed me that he and the men in his unit are going to widen their search for these two cars over the entire City of Chicago. He'll also be contacting the Sheriff and State Police as their search expands to the whole county.

"I received a report from Sheriff Lohman informing me that there will be thirty-seven new deputies assigned to this particular phase of the search. I also received a report from Dr. Kearns at the Coroner's Office. Those imprinted marks that we've been discussing—the waffle-like imprints and marks across Anton Schuessler's chest —indicate that his body had been pressed against a rubber mat, possibly in the killer's car. Dr. Kearns' office views this as a possibly significant clue. So be on the lookout.

"Finally, we have a lot of interviewing to do with all of the telephone calls we've received. We have one woman, Mrs. Margaret Crimmans, who stated that she saw three boys enter a car Sunday night. We have a Mrs. Eloise Alsterlund who stated she saw a Pontiac sedan about 8:30 a.m. on the morning in Robinson's Woods where the boys' bodies were found. They're going to be interviewed today.

"That's all we have for you now. You have your assignments, so join your units and bring back some good information. Good luck."

10:00 a.m.

Frank and I were given our assignments for the day by Murphy. We were to interview Elmer Malone about the two cars he claims he saw in Robinson's Woods. Sgt. Murphy called Mr. Malone and asked him to stop by the District to be interviewed.

Detective Bill Duffy would assist in interviewing Harold Blumfield, who claimed he picked up three boys hitchhiking at Montrose and Kimball Avenues near the Drake Bowling Alley. Then Frank and I were to follow up with Mrs. Crimmins and Mrs. Alsterlund, who called in to report that they might have witnessed something related to the slayings.

Frank and I completed reports, returned phone calls and tried to transfer the pile of messages from the tops of our desks to the to-be-filed box as quickly as possible.

Shortly after 10:15 a.m., one of the uniformed officers stuck his head into our office.

"There's a guy here to see either Jim or Frank. Says he was told by Murphy to stop by the District."

"Thanks, Bill." I put the last of several phone messages into the wire bin for the filing clerks to collect.

"Frank, that's probably Malone. Do you want to sit in on the questioning?" Frank nodded his head and finished the conversation he was having on the phone, then pushed himself away from his desk and joined me on my way to the front desk. The desk sergeant pointed to a man in his early fifties standing at the desk, trying to keep out of the way of the officers and detectives who were now running out of office space and trying to work wherever they could find room.

"Mr. Malone, my name is Detective Jack. This is my partner, Detective Czech. We're working on the Peterson-Schuessler case. As you can see, it's kind of crowded in here. If you don't mind, maybe we could talk right here rather than go into our office. That's even more crowded."

Mr. Malone said that would be fine. He was a little nervous, since this was the first time he'd been in a police station or involved in anything like this.

He went on to say that he lived in Schiller Park and worked at a heating supply firm, the Bell and Gossett Company in Morton Grove, Illinois, as an engineer on the night shift.

"I finished my shift at 7 a.m. in the morning on Tuesday. I drive home west on Lawrence Avenue every day, and that's what I did on Tuesday. I was passing the driveway of Robinson's Woods and noticed two old cars parked very close to each other in the woods there. They were about twenty-five feet from the entrance and facing south on the west side of the driveway. They were parked along side each other over the curb and on the grass."

The location Malone described was about fifty feet south and across the driveway from where the bodies were found. He went on to say that the cars looked like they were about eight or nine years old and were in pretty bad shape. He described the first car as a green convertible with a black cloth top; the second was a cream colored sedan, also in very bad condition.

"I wondered to myself why cars were parked there so early in the morning. I pass that spot every day on my way home from work, and I never saw anything like that before. That's why I remembered it." He said he could identify the cars again if he saw them.

I interrupted him and asked if he had seen any persons in the vicinity.

"I was driving by, you know when you drive by something and notice it. I didn't see anybody standing outside the cars or anybody walking across the road or anything. I just continued on home. Like I say, I didn't pay too much attention to it until I found out later that this was where the bodies were found. It was just unusual for me to see two cars parked there at that time of the morning, that's all."

Frank and I thanked Mr. Malone for his assistance and asked him to call us if he could remember anything more about that particular morning and the cars he observed.

Later in the day, Bill Duffy asked both Frank and me to join him in the Captain's office to interview Harold Blumfield, age 20, who had called and reported that he had picked up three boys hitchhiking on Sunday evening in the vicinity of Montrose and Kimball Avenues. This intersection was within two blocks of both the Monte Cristo bowling alley and the Drake Bowl, where other witnesses said they had seen the boys on Sunday.

Blumfield identified the Peterson boy from the photo published by the newspapers and shown on television. He called the police to report that he had picked the boys up at Montrose and Kimball and then dropped them off at Kenneth and Montrose Avenues at about 8:25 p.m. He told the detectives that Robert Peterson sat in the front seat and the other two boys sat in the back seat of his car. He didn't get a good look at the two boys in the back seat.

"I didn't think about it until I read about the boys in the newspapers," he said.

"Was there any reason why the boys wanted to get out at Kenneth Avenue?" Frank asked. Frank and I were familiar with the area and knew that there were no shops or businesses at that intersection. There was a viaduct and some industrial buildings. Why would the boys have gotten out at that location when they had just gotten a ride?

"I don't know why they got out. I just let them off."

"But you're sure you saw the Peterson boy?" I showed him pictures of the boys again.

"Yes, I'm sure. That's him. But like I said, I didn't get a good look at the two boys in the back seat. It was raining and dark that night, and I really didn't pay that much attention."

"What did you do when you dropped the boys off?" Frank asked.

"I drove over to a friend's house and then stayed there for a little while and went back home."

Frank pressed on with questions about the identity of the friend, where he lived. As the young man responded, we assessed his answers, his tone of voice. We asked and re-asked questions about what kind of car he drove, where he picked up the boys, what he could tell us about what they were wearing, what they talked about.

We came to the conclusion that the young man was being truthful. The information he gave concerning the boys was consistent with other witnesses. And the way he answered questions led us to the conclusion that he was not being evasive or seeking publicity.

"Is this all you can tell us about what you saw and did on Sunday night?"

"Yes. I told you everything I know."

We thanked the young man for his cooperation and asked him to call if he remembered anything else.

We sat in the Captain's office for a few minutes and talked about what, if anything, was learned from Blumfield's statements. Duffy wrote a few notes in his notebook. I took out my notebook that contained a timetable indicating where the boys were seen on Sunday. I made several new entries, with the information obtained from Blumfield. I had a few ideas but wanted to know what Duffy and Frank thought.

"The time checks out with the statements of the other witnesses. The boys were in the area at about that time. The kid sounds convincing. He didn't back down or change his identification of the Peterson boy. And if he was looking for publicity or trying to bullshit us, he could just as well identify the Schuessler brothers. But he didn't. What do you guys think?"

Duffy looked up from his own notes.

"There's nothing at Kenneth and Montrose. You guys know where that is. The boys made a visit to both the Monte Cristo and the Drake bowling alleys already, and they walked west to Kimball

Avenue where Bloomfield picked them up, and he dropped them off several blocks west on Kenneth Avenue."

It didn't make sense. At least not now, but that's how most investigations go. If you do the work, get all the pieces you can find, sometimes they fall together and make up a bigger piece—or even the whole picture. You have to keep every bit of information, make decisions about them then make decisions about them again after you have more information.

The last stop on our follow-up assignment today was in Des Plaines, a suburb just northwest of the city, to speak with Mrs. E. Alsterlund. She gave a statement about her observation at about 8:30 a.m. on Tuesday, October 18 in Robinson's Woods parking lot. She stated that she saw an old Pontiac sedan, either black or blue, parked about fifty feet south of the entrance to the parking lot off Lawrence Avenue. She recalled that the car had a damaged rear fender. She couldn't recall anything else, except that she remembered seeing the car because she thought it was odd that a car would be in the parking lot that early in the morning.

Like Mr. Malone, she recalled seeing the car after reading newspaper accounts about the murders and the location of the bodies.

Frank and I thanked her, gave her the number to the District and asked her to call should she remember anything else about the car or anything she saw Tuesday morning at Robinson's Woods.

On the way back to the station, we discussed our notes and assignments for the day. We discussed the information obtained from the interviews and how it fit in to the investigation so far.

Frank made a sharp turn south at River Road and headed toward Lawrence Avenue. He turned the volume on the police radio down then looked over at me.

"Jim, the interesting thing about this last lady is that she saw some old, beat up car in the parking lot at about the same time Malone says he did. Nothing's been in the papers or on the radio about this yet. Two independent witnesses say they saw something. I think that's important."

"Are we headed to Robinson's Woods?" I asked.

Frank nodded. "I just want to drive by. The place is probably still cordoned off and the Sheriff and Forest Rangers are still there. We don't need to stop, but I just want to see what you can see from Lawrence Avenue as you drive by. Like what those two witnesses said."

The squad car made a left onto Lawrence Avenue, headed east and crossed over the Des Plaines River Bridge. He slowed down as we passed the entrance to the forest preserve lot. It was closed to the public, with two Forest Rangers at the main entrance securing the driveway.

Driving by, it was possible to see into the parking lot from Lawrence Avenue for at least 200 feet. The two witnesses could very well have seen one or two cars in the parking lot. Frank picked up speed and continued toward the District.

We were less than a mile from the station when the dispatcher notified us to proceed to North Sheffield Avenue. One of the detectives manning the phones at the district had just received a call from a woman reporting that her son and a friend had been picked up at a bowling alley on Monday night. The boys were safe, but after reading about what had happened to the Peterson and Schuessler boys, they had told their mothers about the incident.

Frank and I arrived at the address given to us by the dispatcher. A woman answered the door and after introducing ourselves, she invited us into her home where another woman was sitting in the living room, obviously distraught.

Their sons had gone bowling at the Lakeview Bowling Alley, not far from their homes. The mothers had decided to call the police after their sons told them what had occurred there. They contacted the police while their sons were at school, so that they could speak with the detectives first and keep the incident from becoming public for the protection of their sons.

According to the women, the boys got into a conversation with a man at the bowling alley, and the boys went for a ride with him. He took the boys to the lakefront at Belmont Avenue where he took off his shirt and had the boys whip him with his belt.

Frank and I looked at each other, took out our notebooks and began writing down a brief summary of the statements. As one of the mothers continued, the other woman excused herself and went into another room. I thought she was probably uncomfortable about the entire incident and found it too difficult to continue.

The other woman went on to tell us that her understanding, from hearing the account from her son and his friend, was that after whipping the man a few times, they all got back into the man's car. Then he drove them to an alley in the rear of the 3200 block of North Halsted Avenue, and they repeated the same act.

Frank and I thanked the woman and asked her to thank her friend. We told her that the juvenile officers at their District would be informed and those officers would contact both parents and the boys, probably that evening. We reassured the woman that she and her friend had done the right thing in contacting the police. The investigation conducted by the juvenile officers and other detectives would be as discreet as possible in order to protect the boys' identities and their families from publicity.

After returning to the car, I got in and started shaking my head.

"What's the matter?" Frank asked.

"Can you believe the number of crazy fuckin' people out there? They're comin' out from under all sorts of rocks. I never heard such weirdo shit in my life. And that's just what WE'VE been hearing. Just think about all the weirdos the rest of the guys in the unit are finding out about."

8:10 p.m.

The day continued with more leads followed up, calls made, and reports completed. Our last official assignment of the day was the wake for the Schuessler boys at the Koop Funeral Home.

As with the wake of Bobby the night before, traffic officers from the District directed hundreds of cars. They were double and triple parked for blocks and every side street seemed to have its own traffic jam.

Frank located a spot next to a fire hydrant about two blocks from the funeral home and parked the car. Walking down the darkened side street, we merged with small groups of people who were also on their way to the wake.

Uniformed officers were stationed for blocks around Koop Funeral Home. They were at every parking lot and side street. Their numbers increased the closer we got to the funeral. The sidewalk outside the entrance was packed with reporters and onlookers, and a line formed at the front doors and stretched nearly a full block down Milwaukee Avenue.

Frank and I said 'hello' to the uniformed officers at the door and walked past the dark bronze doors of the mortuary. Hundreds of mourners were jammed into its rooms, which could comfortably accommodate only half the number of people inside.

Edging past the men, women, and children packed into the main reception area and hallway, we made our way to the front of the main chapel.

There we saw two beautiful twin white and gold caskets, one containing the body of John and the other of his brother Anton. The brothers were attired in identical brown suits, and each had a bible resting under his hands.

Once again, the Honor Guard from Boy Scout Troop 962 stood beside the coffins. Frank and I said a prayer at the front of the chapel.

Across from the coffins sat the Schuessler family. Mrs. Schuessler sat next to her husband. It was apparent she was still in a state of shock. She murmured softly to herself, over and over, but I could not understand what she was saying. As we moved closer to the family, the words Mrs. Schuessler repeated became clear.

"I want my boys…I want my boys," she said softly. Her husband stroked her hair and held her hand.

As Frank and I respectfully made the parents aware we were there, they attempted to stand but couldn't. Mrs. Schuessler's face was covered with tears, her eyes dark with sadness and grief. This time, she recognized us and extended her hand to greet us. She was so weak, spent from the shock of the sudden loss of her two sons.

"Thank you for coming, officers," she said. Her voice was a whisper. She met our eyes, and tears began to stream down her face. We stood silently.

Mr. Schuessler put his left arm around his wife's shoulders, looked at us and said, "Please find them…please…"

"We will," I replied.

Slowly stepping away from the Schuesslers, neighbors, family, and friends took our place, filing one-by-one past the coffins and extending their condolences to the parents. Frank and I walked to the back of the chapel and observed the mourners in the room. Once again, we made sure to note those who looked as if they did not belong.

We spoke with the funeral director, Mr. Koop, on the way out of the chapel. I had met Koop on prior occasions, either at his funeral home or at inquests, which Koop attended in his capacity as a funeral director. Mr. Koop said he'd been counting the number of people who had come in so far that evening and estimated that nearly 5000 people had viewed the bodies. He went on to say that there would be a high mass held for the two brothers tomorrow at St. Tarcissus Catholic Church. He also wanted us to know that he appreciated the 33rd District's help in directing traffic and providing security.

"Thanks, Mr. Koop. You be sure to let Captain Corcoran know if you need anything. Tomorrow's going to be pretty tough, and the Captain's made arrangements for special traffic control from the church to the cemetery. Frank and I will be attending the funeral, so if there's anything you need let us know."

Frank and I left the funeral home and tried to move through the crowd still gathered on the sidewalk and now spilling onto the street. Traffic was at a standstill.

"Frank, I can't believe these people," I said, "What's there to see out here? Why don't they just go home? And these reporters. Every time they see somebody, they gotta snap their picture. I'd like to snap the noses off some of their faces."

"Take it easy, Jim. You're starting to sound like me."

9:05 p.m.

I thought about my next shift as Frank drove back to the station. Tonight, I would probably meet Dillon. There was something about him that I didn't like. Maybe it was personal. Maybe it wasn't.

When the squad car pulled into the parking bay I got out, went to my car, grabbed the bag containing my "work clothes" and took the back steps into the station.

Every room was occupied with detectives interrogating suspects. I stood in the doorway of Sgt. Murphy's office, but saw that he was busy going over reports and preparing a summary of results. The summary had to be ready for tomorrow's briefing so I thought it best to just let Murphy know I was checking in and going back out to my undercover assignment.

"Hey, Sarge," I yelled over the sounds of clacking typewriters, phone conversations, and uniformed officers getting ready for the next shift. "I'm going back to work." I reached into the bag containing my old clothes, pulled out the torn sweater and showed it to Murphy.

Murphy briefly looked up, smiled, and gave me a "thumbs up" sign with his right hand. Just as quickly, he returned his attention to the paperwork and reports on his desk.

I ducked into the small washroom at the end of the hallway and changed. I didn't change clothes in the officer's locker room, since no one was supposed to know about the undercover assignment. After changing clothes, I made a dash for the door to the parking area.

9:25 p.m.

I could hear the sounds of the bowling pins crashing and the muted rumble of bowling balls as they thudded on the lanes of the second floor of the building. I grabbed the wooden banister on the wall of the staircase and pulled myself up the steep flight of stairs. A few people were leaving, and I had to turn my back to the wall so they could get by.

Smoke filled the darkened room, and scores of people were standing behind those bowlers already hurling their balls down the alley. Most of them were either watching their friends bowl, drinking bottles of beer, or simply chain-smoking unfiltered cigarettes.

I walked up to the counter and saw that the man standing behind it was Dillon. A group of men stood between us, wearing bright yellow bowling shirts with "Richie's Auto Shop" embroidered in thick black lettering on the backs.

"If you guys wouldn't fire those balls down the alleys so damned hard, we wouldn't have to fix the racks every night." Dillon pointed past them to another league just in front of the counter where a bowler had just fired a 16-pound ball down the alley so hard that two pins flew into the alley next to it. A pinsetter ran up the alley and retrieved the pins. He ran to the far wall then along the side and back into the room behind the alleys.

I waved my arm at Dillon to get his attention. "I'm supposed to work tonight." He probably couldn't hear my voice over the noise in the room.

Dillon peered over the group of men, saw me waving then shouted something. He pointed at the end of the counter and motioned for me to stand there. He finished talking to the group of men, who were moving toward their assigned alley, and walked to the end of the counter where I was standing.

"Oh, you're the guy that was coming in late," Dillon said. He looked at my clothing then stared at my face.

"Do I know you? Didn't you work here before?"

I shook my head. "No, I just started last night."

"Oh, okay I'll call Gordon. You know him? He'll give you some lanes to handle tonight. You gotta start right away." He walked back behind the counter, picked up the microphone lying next to the cash register and put it directly on his mouth. He bent down, hit a switch behind the counter then yelled into the microphone.

"GORDON, UP FRONT!"

Gordon came out from the room behind the alleys and met me at the counter. We walked back to the room behind the lanes. After asking whether I remembered how to set the pins or had any questions, he walked to the far end of the room and stood near the open door leading to the fire escape. He kept a watchful eye on the pinsetters occasionally yelling at one of them to fill the racks faster.

I spent the next three hours dodging pins, filling the racks on my assigned lanes, and trying to keep up with the leagues bowling my alleys. Shortly after midnight, the league play ended, and the slower pace gave me time to go back out front to speak with Dillon.

"Listen, I'm not going to set pins during open bowling tonight,"

I told him.

"What?" Dillon threw a pair of rental shoes on the counter. He took a crumpled dollar bill from a young man, hit the "No Sale" key of the cash register and gave the man his change.

"What do you mean you're not going to do open bowling? You didn't come in here until almost 9:30 p.m." Dillon was visibly upset and his face began to redden.

"Look, I just worked two lanes for three hours straight. You've got two other guys sitting back there doing nothin'. They want to work for a few hours, and it's crowded back there. So Gordon told me to tell you he doesn't need me for the rest of the night."

"Fine. I'll get your envelope when I got time. Come back in twenty minutes or so." Dillon seemed to calm down after he heard it was Gordon who told me to knock off for the night.

I decided to walk over to the bar and wait. I could use the chance to strike up a conversation with some of the regulars and see what they knew about who hung out here.

The men I spoke with at the bar were mostly league bowlers having a few beers before going home. They were mostly guys from the neighborhood, or friends of people who had a business in the area and sponsored a bowling team. None of the small talk gave me any new information.

A half an hour later, Gordon stopped by the bar to have a beer and took a seat on one of the barstools next to me. He talked about how hard it was to find reliable people to work the alleys and tried to find out a little about who I was and why I was working here.

I answered without trying to sound too evasive. If my story didn't sound convincing, most of the guys who worked here had something to hide. Maybe a problem with booze or betting the horses had left them broke. Maybe they just got out of the joint and needed a few bucks to live on. It wouldn't be the first time Gordon had heard a bullshit story.

"I had a couple of bad breaks a while back. I just need some extra money. You know, pay off some bills and stuff." I took out a dollar and laid it on the counter then asked the bartender for two beers.

"Yeah, I know how that goes," Gordon said. He grabbed the dollar bill I had just put on the bar and put it front of me. Then he called out to the bartender. "Tony, these two are on me."

"Thanks, Gordon." I looked around the bar.

"Gets a little slower after the leagues leave. Lot more kids in here late at night." I was just making comments, not being pushy or wanting to sound too inquisitive.

The bartender put two bottles of beer in front us.

Gordon agreed that some of the young kids still in the place should probably be at home.

"The owners don't give a shit," Gordon said. "Just as long as they don't cause any trouble."

"I heard that those three kids who were killed were in here last Sunday night." I took a sip of beer then turned on my barstool and looked in the direction of the teenagers who were bowling with friends, or who were standing and watching the bowlers. I was careful not to look at Gordon when mentioning the boys, hoping not to sound too curious.

"Yeah. Dillon seen them," Gordon said. "That's all he talks about. His name got mentioned in the newspapers and now he thinks he's important. Big deal."

"Did he talk to the kids when they were in here?" I kept looking in the direction of the bowling lanes.

"I don't know," Gordon answered defensively.

I decided not push it at this point and arouse suspicion. I really did need the job, but not for the money.

We talked a little more about what were the busiest times of the week at the bowling alley; how I should be sure to check the envelope with my pay to be certain I got what I earned. Gordon suggested I might want to come in late tomorrow afternoon. Saturdays were pretty good days to work at the alley.

It was almost 1:00 in the morning, and I was tired. After thanking Gordon for the beer, I went home. In less than seven hours, I had to be back at the District, and after working almost sixteen hours straight, I needed as much sleep as possible.

Saturday
October 22, 1955
7:50 a.m.

I knocked on the door, waited for a second, and then opened it just enough to see if anyone was in the office. Murphy was at his desk, the phone receiver tucked between his chin and his right shoulder as he read a list of names from an open file he held in his hand. He looked up from the file when he heard the knock on his door and waved for me to come in. He gave a few more instructions to the person on the other end of the line.

"Yeah, I want all those names checked with the Bureau of Identification…I know it's a lot…yeah, we're real busy here too. Who isn't? Put those names ahead of everything else you've got. If someone beefs about it, have 'em call the Commissioner." He hung up and threw the file onto his desk.

"So how'd it go last night?" Sgt. Murphy asked.

"Not bad, Sarge. Not too much information yet, other than what I already told you yesterday. That guy Dillon's an asshole, real arrogant. I guess he thinks he's important now he got his name in the paper and testified at the inquest the other day."

I told Murphy of my observations at the bowling alley, the large number of teenagers there until the early hours of the morning.

"They looked like they could be in gangs. Frank and I interviewed some of the neighbors the other day, and they said that kids are always hanging around outside the place. I don't know how much of that is true. We might want to check with the juvenile division about any complaints. Maybe we could do that after I've been there for a few more nights. I don't want to spook the owners if the detectives from Juvenile Division go in there and make a few checks for any underage drinking and stuff."

Suddenly there was a sharp knock at the door. We turned to watch it open. Frank poked his head around the opened door.

"Come on in, Frank," Murphy said. "Have a seat. Jim and I were just talking about his new job."

Frank sat down next to me and stared at my mouth.

"Well, you still have a few teeth left. I guess you're fitting right in with that bunch at the Monte Cristo." Frank smiled and then turned to Murphy. "Did he tell you he got a raise, Sarge? What is it, Jim, about fourteen cents an hour?"

"Yeah, fourteen cents. That'll buy a dozen of those cigars you chew on all day." It was my turn to smile, now. Then I brought Frank up to speed on what I told Murphy and what I observed at the bowling alley.

"I'll handle it, Jim. Don't worry about it. Just keep a low profile when you're in the place. We already questioned Dillon and put him on the lie box. He's clean, at least as it concerns the three boys. In the meantime, keep an eye on him and see what you can dig up. I know you guys have been putting in a lot of hours, and I want you and Frank to go to the Schuessler boys' funeral this morning. You won't get to be at the Captain's briefing. Let me give you a rundown on what's been going on."

The Captain was initiating a new mass search today, this time covering the area from Foster Avenue on the south to Howard Street on the north, and from Cicero Avenue on the east to Canfield Avenue on the west. This search was to include teams of investigators going door-to-door to each residence and business in the area. Each team would include one uniformed officer and one detective. The presence of a uniformed officer would get people's attention and immediately convey both police identity and authority.

The team would ask each property owner for permission to search the premises. If permission were not granted, they would note the name and address of the individual. Then they would notify the District and get a search warrant issued if they had to.

The search was to focus primarily on efforts to recover physical evidence. Any clothing that was found resembling the clothes worn by the boys when they were last seen would be recovered and sent to the crime lab. We were also instructed to be on the lookout for any automobiles matching the description given by witnesses concerning vehicles seen in the Robinson's Woods parking lot on the morning the bodies were discovered.

Murphy wrapped up the briefing. "You can read the briefing

summary when you get a chance. Meanwhile, I want you guys to work on your reports from yesterday then go to the funeral. After that, come back to the District and report in to me. We've got a lot of work to catch up on."

9:30 a.m.

St. Tarcissus Roman Catholic Church was located two miles from the 33rd District, directly north up Milwaukee Avenue and one block into a residential area. Anticipating the congested traffic and crowds which would surround the church, we took side streets and parked a few blocks from the church.

Walking west on one of the quiet side streets, hundreds of people ahead of us spilled onto the sidewalks and lawns of neighboring homes. The traffic detail was doing its best, but the combination of normal Saturday morning traffic and the huge crowd of mourners and onlookers made it difficult to reach the steps of the church.

Frank and I made our way through the crowd of people in front of the church and past the group of uniformed officers who controlled the entrance. As soon as the doors closed behind us, we were stunned by the number of people who already filled the church. I saw familiar faces among the more than 1500 mourners sitting in every pew and standing in the aisles. Many of these people had also attended Bobby's wake and funeral.

Classmates and teachers of the Schuessler brothers were present, as was Mr. Thornton. Neighbors of the Schuesslers were there, along with their children who had known the boys from the time John and Anton had moved to their home on Mango Avenue.

Also in attendance were representatives from city government and the Police Department. Captain Corcoran was standing in the back of the church, occasionally speaking with other detectives and police officers who were present and providing security inside the church.

Frank and I went back outside and saw that the crowd had grown even larger. Just as we were about to re-enter the church, the crowd suddenly grew quiet. All heads turned toward a line of cars that had turned from Milwaukee Avenue onto Ardmore Avenue. Two

Chicago Police Department squad cars, their mars lights flashing, were the first of a long line of cars stretching down Milwaukee Avenue. Behind them were two black and gray hearses from the Koop Funeral Home.

Three flower cars from the funeral home filled with hundreds of roses and lilies followed behind the hearses. Then a black Cadillac with Mr. and Mrs. Schuessler and the immediate family inside, followed by more than one hundred other vehicles in the longest funeral procession I had ever seen.

The Cadillac stopped just in front of the steps of the church. The driver got out and slowly opened the back passenger door. Mr. and Mrs. Schuessler got out, helped along by Mrs. Schuessler's mother and brother-in-law. As she took a step toward the church, she collapsed on the sidewalk. The crowd gasped, then fell silent again. No one said a word as her husband and mother helped her to her feet.

They waited as one group of eight Boy Scout Honor Guards took John's casket from the first hearse. Then another group of eight Honor Guards took Anton's casket from the second hearse. They walked carefully and slowly up the steps and into the church, past the uniformed officers, and up the main aisle to the front pews. Mr. and Mrs. Schuessler followed behind, overcome with grief, barely able to walk. They slowly sat down in the front pew of the church, next to the two white and gold caskets that held the remains of their sons.

The Reverend Raymond Carey said the high solemn mass, assisted by Rev. Theodore Stone and Rev. Thomas Seity. Nine of John and Anton's closest friends served as altar boys.

Father Carey did not refer to the murder of Bobby Peterson, John Schuessler, and Anton Schuessler. He spoke of the love the boys had for their family and their friends, and how everyone who knew them loved them.

"John and Anton share God, not for life, but forever," he said.

The service ended and the nine altar boys led the procession down the main aisle of the church. The sixteen Honor Guards of Boy Scout Troop 962 immediately followed them carrying the gold and white caskets. Tears streamed down the faces of every boy as they struggled to walk straight, heads held high, carrying the heavy caskets of their friends down the aisle and through the doors of the church.

The crowd outside parted to make room for the procession as it left the church and walked slowly down the steps. The first group of Honor Guards carefully placed John's casket into one hearse, then waited until the other Honor Guard placed Anton's casket into the second hearse.

The boys lined up along the curb next to the hearses and stood at attention, while the Schuessler family entered the black limousine. After a few minutes, the two squad cars at the front of the procession of vehicles turned on their lights, and the cars filled with mourners pulled out slowly onto Milwaukee Avenue for the journey to St. Joseph's Cemetery in the suburb of River Grove.

The service at the gravesite was brief as Fr. Carey led the family and friends in prayers for the souls of John and Anton. After the final words of the last prayer were said, the only sound was the gentle rustling of the last golden leaves of autumn. Then the grief stricken parents began to sob and Mrs. Schuessler reached out with her right hand to touch the caskets of her sons.

"Goodbye Johnny, Goodbye Tony," she cried softly.

1:45 p.m.

When Frank and I returned to the District we reported to Murphy, and he asked us about the funeral services for the brothers.

"Don't ask, Sarge," I responded. "It was one of the worst experiences we've ever had. I don't think we want to talk about it."

Murphy looked at us and understood from the expressions on our faces that he shouldn't pursue it any further. He knew we had seen the worst of what people are capable of doing to each other. Murders, beatings, victims of rape and unspeakable acts of violence and cruelty were things we had to deal with every day. He also knew what Frank and I had seen since beginning the investigation of this case was unlike anything ever seen before.

"I understand," he said. "The best thing for us to do now is get down to business and keep working. There are two calls that came in that I want you to check out. We got reports on some clothing that was found that may be connected to the boys. Detective Robert Lane is already at the scene, and the Captain is going out there himself. I want you guys to help Lane and check out the clothing. The call came in from a reporter from the Chicago American. Said he found one leg of a boy's blue jeans and some navy socks in a vacant lot at 4700 N. Milwaukee. Right where the boys were last seen on Sunday night.

"Captain Norman Hawthorn and two of his deputies from the Sheriff's Department are here to talk to us about what they found. His men found some blue jeans, a black rubber car mat, and a man's blood-stained handkerchief that were found along the side of Montrose Avenue, three blocks east of River Road. That's a half-mile south and a mile east of Robinson's Woods. Captain Hawthorn is getting those items inventoried right now, and we're sending them down to the crime lab to see if the blood on the handkerchief is human blood.

"The other call is from a guy at the May's Funeral Home. He says he found a pair of jeans and a wallet in the alley behind the premises there. Frank, you stay with Lane and the Captain at the vacant lot. Jim, after you check that out, meet up with Bill Duffy at the funeral home and see what he's got over there. Then get back here and fill me in. Captain Hawthorn's down the hall. Let's talk to him before you go."

The rubber floor mat would be examined to see if it could have left markings consistent with those found on one of the bodies.

"Excuse me, Sarge, but Jim and I have to get over to that vacant lot on Milwaukee Avenue. We don't want Captain Corcoran to get there before we do." Frank didn't want to interrupt the meeting, but he knew that Murphy wouldn't want their Captain to start looking for them.

"Right. You guys get out of here. We're just going to compare notes on what our unit has found so far with what the Sheriff's Department has found."

After we left, Sgt. Murphy continued to talk with the Sheriff's Deputies about the progress of the investigation and what the Sheriff's Department was working on. The Sheriff's Department would take over the investigations of bowling alleys being conducted throughout the city and surrounding suburbs. They could easily cover all areas of the county without any problems of jurisdiction, including the nearby suburbs.

Bowling alleys, restaurants, and movie theaters were the initial focus of the investigation, and in the last few days the Chicago Police Department's manpower had been stretched to its limits. Uniformed officers and detectives from the Department were limited in their jurisdiction outside the city limits, so assignments were given to other departments and law enforcement agencies to maximize the efficient use of available officers assigned to the investigation.

3:45 p.m.

The Gale Street station continued to be surrounded by reporters, neighbors and people who traveled from different parts of the city to visit the building that continued to be front-page news in every daily paper.

When reporters left the station, those in the crowd asked about the newest developments. Now the press was experiencing what they had been doing to detectives assigned to the case. They were followed by curiosity-seekers who almost demanded that the reporters let them in on any breaking news.

"Buy a copy of the paper," some reporters began to say.

Our squad car slipped unnoticed into a parking space as on-lookers ran to the front of the station. Spotting two photographers and a reporter leaving the building, they surged towards the front steps. The journalists elbowed their way through the crowd to get to their cars.

Frank had the slightest of smiles on his face as we left our squad and dashed up the back steps, taking advantage of the commotion at the front of the building.

"I'm glad those news guys get to see how it feels to be surrounded by a pack of dogs, picking at you, grabbing your coat to slow you down so they can ask you all sorts of shit that's none of their business."

We reported to Murphy after arriving at the station. I knocked sharply on his door, turned the doorknob and walked in. Taking our usual seats, we waited as he finished a phone conversation.

"Two of my guys just came in, Chief." Murphy said as he put his right hand over the mouthpiece of the phone. He looked at us and held up his index finger, signaling he would be off the phone in a few seconds.

"Yeah…uh huh…I'll put together a summary of the results we've got so far."

Murphy rolled his eyes and held the phone out so Frank and I could hear the tinny sound of a thin voice coming out of the phone. The Chief kept talking while Murphy occasionally interjected a few grunts and "uh-huhs" into the phone, just to be sure the boss didn't think he was talking to himself.

Finally, the conversation was over. Murphy hung up and sat back in his chair.

"So, what's the latest?"

"Frank and I met Detective Lane at the vacant lot. The reporter from the Chicago American met us there too. Captain Corcoran and Duffy came by just after we got there. You know, Sarge, that vacant lot is right across the street from the Jefferson Park Recreation Center and just down the block from Henri's Lounge. Right where the bus driver said he dropped the boys off on Sunday night."

Murphy got up and walked to one of the new filing cabinets placed in his office just a few days before. Every drawer was filled with files, briefing summaries, telephone reports, and copies of the results of hundreds of interviews and witness statements detectives had compiled during the last six days. He pulled open one of the drawers, grabbed a thick file then turned around and looked at us.

"I remember. You guys also said that after you interviewed the owners of the Jefferson Park Recreation Center, you thought the boys never made it there. Nobody I.D.'d their photographs." He flipped through the first few pages in the file and pulled out a thin yellow sheet of onionskin paper. He walked over to us, reading the sheet of paper. I could tell it was one of my reports from the heading and the initials scribbled in red ink in the upper right hand corner.

"That's right, Murph. So what we found at the vacant lot might be pretty important. We showed the Captain the leg of the jeans and the navy socks. All three pieces of clothing had grease smudges on them. We figured that was significant since the boys had grease on the soles of their feet. One of the socks had rust colored stains on it. Looked like it could be blood. Captain Corcoran said we should bag the items and send them to the lab. We came back here and Frank did the paperwork and reports and sent the clothing to the crime lab.

"Then Duffy and I went over to May's Funeral Home to talk to the handyman." I paused for a second as Murphy shoved the yellow sheet back into the file and walked back to the filing cabinets.

"Did he tell you anything?" Murphy asked over his shoulder. He pulled out the drawer marked "JJ/FC REPORTS-PSS" and put the file back.

"The guy's name is Henry Fiedler," I continued. "He said he's been the handyman around the mortuary for several years. While he was walking around the building cleaning up he found a wallet outside. It didn't have any identification inside, but it did have some pictures of teenage boys and family pictures. He didn't think much about it until a little later when he was across the street burning trash he'd picked up. Some woman passed by and pointed to the blue jeans. He picked them up then suddenly thought about the stories in the papers about the boys. That's when he called the District."

"Did you get a look at the stuff?"

"We did, Sarge. Duffy and I bagged it up after we took a look at the pictures. We were careful not to touch anything. The pictures weren't of the Peterson or Schuessler boys, but Duffy and I decided to be sure so we stopped off at the boys' homes and had the family take a look at what we had. They couldn't identify any of the articles. We brought them back, checked them in, and they're going to the lab today. Frank and I went out again to check on some phone tips, but they were nothing. We just got back and wanted to check in with you before we got to our reports."

"Good job," Murphy said. "Let me know what the lab says about those items as soon as you hear anything. One more thing before I forget to tell you, Jim. I talked to the Sheriff's guys today. They've been assigned to check bowling alleys here in the city and in the suburbs. So you don't have to worry about one of our guys recognizing you at the Monte Cristo. I didn't tell them we had you inside the place, so you're still covered."

"Thanks, Murph."

"You guys better get to those reports. You heard the Chief. Jeez, he must think I just got out of the academy the way he kept going on and on."

"Sarge," Frank said. "The guy's probably got the Commissioner and the rest of the brass downtown breathin' down his neck. Not to mention City Hall."

"You don't have to tell me, I know. We're all under a lot of pressure. Anyway, you guys need to do your paperwork and Jim needs to get to his other job on time so he doesn't get fired. Right?"

"Yeah, right. Listen, Murph, I was thinking about going in there a little early tonight. There are a few things I want to check out. You know, look around a little bit."

I was hinting that I might be crossing a line or two. If any police procedures or state laws were violated, I was on my own. But I wanted to let Murphy know what I was planning to do, and more importantly, that backup might be needed if things got out of hand.

"I hear ya," Murphy answered. "Just be careful. Looks like I'll be here until ten or eleven o'clock tonight."

4:30 p.m.

I changed clothes, putting on the same ones worn the night before. I hung my suit and put it on a metal hook on the wall behind the door of our office. I put on my overcoat then walked quickly down the hall and out the station to my car.

It was Saturday afternoon and traffic was heavy on Milwaukee Avenue. I parked my car on one of the side streets and walked a short distance to the bowling alley. Before reaching the building, I turned off the sidewalk and into the alley, not stopping or looking to see if I was being watched. Walking at a deliberate pace down the alley, I casually looked up at the back of the buildings.

Soon I recognized the two fire escapes located at the rear of the Monte Cristo. They ran from the second floor down to the first floor and against the back of the building. At the base of the rusted steel stairs was a short flight of cement steps that led to the basement. From where I stood, I could see the basement door with its peeling gray paint.

I looked up at the fire escapes as I walked toward them. No one was standing outside where the pinsetters usually take a break or a piss. Still too light outside, I thought. They're like cockroaches; they don't like light.

Cautiously, I walked down the cement steps and stood facing the door. Taking a deep breath, I turned the doorknob.

The door swung open. I quickly backed away from the doorway and stood next to the wall. My detective's instincts suddenly kicked in at full tilt. You never just walk into a place like this, or stand in front of a door unless you damned well knew who is behind it. You knock then stand next to the door along the wall. This way, if the person on the other side starts firing, you don't catch a bullet in your gut like some mope.

I swore at myself. Damn, that was stupid. I was thinking like a pinsetter and not like a detective.

Slowly I entered the room. My eyes focused on the blackness inside until they adjusted to the dark. Soon forms and shapes became visible: an old furnace, some heating equipment and a lot of discarded junk. Boxes, pipes, and stacks of old newspapers littered the floor.

The room wasn't that large, maybe 12- by 15-feet. Only a sliver of light shone through a small window. Without creating a sound, I closed the door behind me. I knew Dillon lived on the floor above, and if I made a noise, the shit would hit the fan.

My eyes adjusted more. That's when I noticed something familiar in the corner of the basement. Next to the furnace lay a set of rubber car mats. It was difficult to see, but the patterns looked similar to the markings on one of the bodies. They looked like the waffle iron patterns described by Dr. Kearns. I continued to scan the room. Just a few feet away, I saw a wide wooden board about six feet long by two feet wide. The board had dark stains on it.

Suddenly, a cold chill went down my back, and a flood of information came rushing into my head: mats, patterns, clothing, stained socks, and jeans. My mind began to race.

Then just as suddenly, I remembered where I was. Nothing could be taken at that moment. If anyone caught me or saw me, things could get ugly and even dangerous. I couldn't even touch the stuff.

Walking quietly past the scattered piles of newspapers and heating equipment strewn on the floor, I carefully opened the door. I listened for sounds coming from the alley or the fire escapes. Nothing.

I closed the basement door softly then cautiously took a few steps up the flight of stairs. I looked around, down the alley, and up again at the fire escapes. Good, no one. I walked swiftly up the steps, into the alley and back to my car.

I drove down the block to a side street then turned onto Montrose Avenue. Turning west, I found a public telephone just a few blocks away at a Sinclair gas station. I pulled in, got out of my car and called Murphy's direct line.

"Murphy, I think we've got something here." I looked around to be sure no one was standing nearby. The attendant was the only person inside the station and had run outside to pump gas for a customer.

Hurriedly, I told Murphy what I'd seen in the basement. "I've got to get back so I can start work. I don't want to be late again."

Murphy said he would send the Sheriff's deputies right over. He was pretty sure they wouldn't need a warrant if they just showed up and asked for permission to search the place. He was going to instruct the deputies to station one of their men at the rear of the building while the others go up to the bowling lanes, just in case someone tried to remove the items. "Sounds good, Murph. I'm gonna grab a quick bite to eat then get to the bowling alley."

6:15 p.m.

"You gotta wait like everybody else," the man behind the counter yelled out. The clatter of bowling pins exploded against each other and the occasional shouts from the league players made it difficult for the man's voice to be heard. Four men in blue bowling shirts and black trousers were standing impatiently in front of the counter. I could tell by the voice that Dillon was there and, from the sound of it, was having a bad night already.

Before I could maneuver around the group of men standing between us, I heard the voice again. This time it was louder.

"Hey you! Goggin! Are you ready to work?" Dillon screamed.

I almost forgot that my new name was "Goggin." Working my way around the league players, I stood in front of Dillon.

"Yeah." I didn't like being talked to like some kind of bum off the street. But if I dove over the counter and kicked the shit out of this guy, there went the whole operation.

"Well? Get the hell back there where you belong and start working." Dillon turned his attention to the large sheets of lined paper spread out on the counter in front of him. They contained the alley assignments and had lane numbers listed across the top and the names of the bowlers or leagues written along the left margin. Dillon circled one of the names along the left side of the sheet with a red pen. He picked up the microphone next to him and flipped a switch.

"SAM'S AUTO REPAIR ON LANE SIX," he shouted. His voice boomed and echoed above the noise. The group of men in front of me moved away from the counter and headed toward lane six. Saturday night was the busiest night at the Monte Cristo, and the place was jammed with open bowlers, teenagers hanging out, and people who weren't interested in bowling at all but came there to drink at the bar.

Gordon was already in the back room behind the bowling lanes making sure no one was pissing off the balcony, at least not this early in the evening. This was the busiest time on the busiest night of the week and pins were already flying over the canvas barriers. I noticed that the pinsetter, handling lanes six and seven, had what looked like a fresh bruise along the right side of his face. He held a wet towel against his cheek with his left hand and was doing his best to grab and set the pins with his right.

"Hey Jim," Gordon shouted. "Take over six and seven from Lenny. He caught a 7-10 split in his face a minute ago, and he can't keep up. Dillon's pissed off already, and the play is starting to slow down."

I nodded and walked to the chair between lanes six and seven and took off my coat. The injured pinsetter continued filling the rack as I leaned down to help.

"Thanks, pal," Lenny said. He looked relieved and grateful that he could leave without getting injured again. If play slowed down too much because a pinsetter wasn't working fast enough, some league players tossed the ball down the lane to make things worse.

"Forget it," I responded. Picking up the remaining pins scattered behind lane seven, I quickly put them in the rack then punched the button.

For the next four hours, I dodged pins flipping over the barriers and balls zooming down the lanes. More than once, I fell behind in setting the pins, and the guys bowling for "Sam's Auto Repair" fired two 16-pound balls down the lane, just missing my leg.

"Assholes!" I didn't care at this point about getting fired. That would be fine. Then I could knock the living shit out of those guys with one of these pins and not give a shit what happened.

I had just set three racks of pins when I heard a commotion from the front. The voices were louder than the usual grumbling and shouts of the bowlers. It sounded like a fight had broken out.

Along with the other pinsetters, I bent over, peered from underneath the rack, and looked down the alley. You couldn't see much. But the bowlers using lane seven had stopped bowling and were looking towards the front door. Most of the other people were looking in that direction, too. Then Dillon's voice came booming over the loudspeaker.

"ATTENTION, EVERYBODY. EVERYTHING'S UNDER CONTROL...GET BACK TO YOUR LANES OR YOU'LL LOSE THEM."

The entire bowling alley was suddenly quiet. The only sound was a bowling ball rumbling down lane one. Two pins fell, then silence.

All at once, as if the volume on a jukebox had been turned up, the sounds of men's loud voices filled the room and bowling balls hit the alleys with loud thumps as play began again.

I looked up and saw Gordon walking past.

"What's goin' on?" I asked.

"Ya got me. I'll be right back." Gordon opened the side door and slammed it shut behind him.

A few minutes later, Gordon came back and said there had been some kind of argument between two customers out front. "Some guy was talking to a couple of kids and another guy came over to him and some kind of argument started. Somebody said one of the two guys was the father of one of the boys that were killed."

"No shit?" I didn't have to try to sound surprised. I was stunned. If it were true that either Mr. Schuessler or Mr. Peterson had been there, what were they doing? And what was that stuff about some guy talking to two kids?

"Listen, Gordon. You mind if I take my break now? It's after ten o'clock, and I haven't had time to take a leak."

"Sure. I'll watch your lanes. Just don't take too long."

I walked toward the side door leading to the main room of the bowling alley.

"Hey, where're you goin'?" Gordon called out before I could reach the door.

"I gotta get something to drink. Just a Coke or something."

"Well, okay. But don't let Dillon see you hanging around out there. Just get what you've gotta get and come back in here. Take your break out on the fire escape. If Dillon asks you anything, tell him you're getting something for me."

"Thanks, Gordon."

10:20 p.m.

I walked quickly down the narrow strip of linoleum leading from the side door and along the base of the wall parallel to lane one. Dillon had his back to the counter exchanging bowling shoes for customers.

Walking quickly through the crowd, I kept my eyes on Dillion. His vision was blocked, and he couldn't see me standing behind a group of people lined up to return their rental shoes and pay for their lanes. When he turned his back to place some rental shoes on the shelf, I walked past the customers and into the bar area.

Just then three uniformed officers came up the steep flight

of stairs and were headed to the desk. Right behind them was Mr. Peterson.

I quickened my pace and walked in front of another group of men headed to the bar, lessening the chances of being seen by the officers who responded to the call and by Mr. Peterson. The Monte Cristo was in the Albany Park Police District, so the officers probably wouldn't recognize me.

Reaching the pay phone in the corner of the bar, I called Murphy.

"Murphy," the voice said.

"Yeah, this is Jim. Listen, could you tell Frank I'm over here at the Monte Cristo? I can hardly hear you, but just tell him I'll be here until midnight."

"Jim, is everything okay?"

"Yeah. I'll meet him at the front desk in twenty minutes."

Murphy understood that I wasn't in any immediate trouble or the words "thirty-three" or "Nick's Place" would have used during the conversation. I was telling him to call Frank and also letting him know that something was up at the Monte Cristo.

"I'll let Frank know."

"Thanks."

Murphy immediately called Frank at home and told him to meet me in twenty minutes.

I walked away from the telephone and took a seat at the end of the bar. After a few minutes, I finally got the bartender's attention and ordered a Coke. When the bartender returned with my drink, the two men next to me stopped talking, looked at me then at the Coke.

"I heard that stuff will kill you if you drink enough of it." The man pointed to the Coke then looked at his friend as both men laughed.

"Let me buy you one, pal," the friend said.

"No thanks, I've had my limit. You guys bowl tonight?" I asked casually. Now I really had to be careful. These two might be the jerks that tried to break my legs earlier in the evening. It wouldn't be good if they found out I had been the pinsetter on their lane.

"Yeah. We beat the pants off those guys from 'Sam's Auto Repair.' I don't think they'll even show up next week, they got beat so bad."

"What happened earlier? I didn't get to see what was going on. Somebody took a punch or something?" I took a sip of Coke and sat it back on the bar.

"Naw, just some guys got into a shouting match about something. One of the guys ran out and the other guy chased him down the stairs. Then somebody called the cops."

The bartender came to our end of the bar and began wiping it off. He asked the men if they needed another round then looked at me. He leaned across the bar and talked directly to the men, lowering his voice a little.

"One of the guys was the father of one of the boys found dead last week. You know, the kids they found in the forest preserve," he said. He continued to wipe the bar, looked at me and raised his eyebrows then nodded in the direction of the front counter where Dillon was working.

I knew what that meant. The bartender recognized me as one of the pinsetters and was letting me know Dillon wouldn't be pleased.

"You mean those three boys who lived around here?" said one man. "Man, that's terrible. I've been reading about it all week in the papers. No wonder the cops got here so quick."

I leaned to my right to look around the people seated at the front of the bar and in the direction of the counter. The three uniformed officers were still there questioning Dillon.

I sat for a few minutes listening to the men talk about the radio, television, and newspaper coverage of the killings. Reporters have been keeping the public informed about the investigation. From what I was hearing from these men, they knew the cops had conducted a huge manhunt but had yet to come up with any suspects.

"Yeah," one of the men said. "Our tax dollars at work. You'd think they could have caught the killers by now. I heard they picked up every pervert in the city, asked them a lot of questions and then let them all go."

"Is that why you could make it here tonight? They let you go, too?" his friend asked and laughed.

"Hey, go to hell, asshole." Then he laughed along with his friend. "Where the hell's that bartender? And where are you goin'? You gotta buy us the next round." He looked at me, as I pushed my stool away from the bar and stood up.

"I've been here too long guys. Gotta go." I thanked them for the Coke and walked out of the bar area and towards the front of the bowling alley. As I reached the counter, the bartender was talking to Dillon. Both of them just happened to turn and see me walking toward them.

"Hey you! Goggin! Come over here." Dillon's face was flushed and from the sound of his voice I could tell he wasn't happy. I made my way through the crowd and got to the desk just in time to pass the bartender.

Fuckin' snitch, I thought as I walked by.

"Listen, buddy. You get paid to work around here. What are you doin' askin' a lot of questions? You a reporter or something? Get back behind those alleys."

"Gordon said it was okay if I took my break." I didn't say anything else. This guy was really starting to get to me. I made my way back to the room behind the alleys and saw that Gordon was still working my lanes.

"Where you been?" Gordon asked.

"Sorry, Gordon. Thanks for covering for me. I had a Coke at the bar, and Dillon got all pissed off at me. I told him you said it was okay." I had to be careful not to put Gordon in the hot seat, and I wanted him to know what had happened in case there was a problem.

"I told you he would. Don't worry about it. If he gives me any shit, all I have to do is threaten to quit. You think he'd last more than a minute back here?"

Both Gordon and I laughed at the idea.

11:10 p.m.

"What are you lookin' for, Jim?" Gordon asked. He had been standing at the far end of the room and walked over to where I was working my two lanes. Gordon noticed that I had been bending over under the rack and looking down the alley. I would set a few racks, then bend over and look down the alley again.

"Oh, nothing. Just seeing how many guys are down there. Looks like it's thinning out a little bit." I was lying. Frank hadn't arrived yet, and I was keeping an eye out. Every so often, I would peek between the racks and pins to see if he had shown up.

An hour had gone by and the uniformed police officers were still standing near the counter. I looked down the lane again. Finally, another person joined them. It was Frank.

"Still some cops out there," I said to Gordon, who was now standing behind me.

"Yeah, that's what I heard. Tony told me they've been here for a while. Some guy tried to pick up a couple of boys here, and I guess the father of one of those murdered kids tried to talk to the guy. I guess he's conducting his own investigation or something."

"Guess so." I stood up, filled the rack over lane six then pushed the button.

I decided not to look down the lanes while Gordon was watching. Tomorrow Frank would fill me in on what happened.

All I really wanted to do was go home and go to bed. My back was creaking and every muscle in my body was sore. Although no flying pins had hit me, I was beat. And there was one more hour to go before calling it a night.

Sunday
October 23, 1955
8:00 a.m.

"How's it goin', Jim?" Frank greeted me as I walked into Murphy's office. "You look like shit. Except your clothes. Those look a lot better than what you were wearing last night."

"Where did you see me last night?" I asked. I couldn't recall leaving the back room of the bowling alley while Frank was there.

"Oh for Christ sake, Jim. I was looking down the alleys for those sharp pants and shoes you have on when you work there. Every so often I'd see you dance around behind lanes six and seven. You move pretty fast."

"Yeah, and I guess I'm working too hard to figure out the obvious. What did you find out last night about Mr. Peterson? What the hell was he doing there?"

Frank told me that he got Murphy's call as soon as he walked into his house last night.

"Murphy told me to get over to the Monte Cristo and meet you at the counter. I figured something was up since you wouldn't blow your cover by meeting me right in the middle of the place. By the time I got there, the Albany Park District guys were already asking your buddy Dillon about what happened. He didn't know anything, of course, except that there was some shouting and two or three guys started to chase another guy down the front stairs and out of the bowling alley.

"After I talked to a few people, including Mr. Peterson and his friends, I got the whole story. Seems Mr. Peterson and two of his friends are doing their own work on this case and not keeping us informed. They've been visiting different places, trying to find out who might have seen the boys last week. Bowling alleys, restaurants, and movie theaters. Guess they've been as busy as we have.

"Anyway, Peterson sees some guy about 5 feet 11 inches, stocky, about 45 or 50 years old, with real bushy hair talking to two young kids. He watches this for a while, wonders what this guy wants from the kids then goes over himself to investigate.

"The guy with the bushy hair gets nervous and runs out, and Peterson and his pals chase after him. He makes it to the corner and disappears. Then Peterson calls the Albany Park Station and reports it. They sent a couple of squad cars over, checked out the place and drove around the neighborhood with Peterson, but they didn't find the guy.

"I asked around when I got to the Monte Cristo and found out that this bushy haired guy is well-known around there. He hangs out at some of the bowling alleys and places along Montrose Avenue. We're looking for the two boys who were talking to him. We got a good idea of who the guy is and where he lives."

"That fuckin' guy Dillon..." I pounded my hand on the desk

then began pacing around the office. "Koeppe told me that when Dillon gave his testimony, the guy says 'Oh, there's been no trouble in the bowling alley.' What bullshit. The last few nights I've been there, there's been an awful lot going on. And from what I've heard just from asking around, that place has a reputation for being full of all kinds of weirdos and teenagers who I'm sure are in gangs and just hang out there looking for trouble. If that guy Dillon gives me any more shit, I swear I'll kick his ass."

I stopped for a moment as Murphy entered the office.

"Take it easy, Jim," Murphy said. He closed the door and walked over to me. "I could hear you all the way down the hall. Guess you had a rough night, huh? Frank filled me in before you got here." Murphy sat down behind his desk and looked at the reports other detectives had just completed.

"Let me fill you guys in on what's been going on here. About what you were just saying, Jim, the Commissioner called Captain Corcoran last night. The Commissioner wants us to extend the citywide roundup: members of teenage gangs and social clubs, anybody with a history of sex crimes, any suspects we have on other open cases. We're supposed to bring them all in for questioning.

"I talked to Captain Hawthorn of the Sheriff's Department about what you saw in the basement yesterday. He told me they got the rubber mats and the large board with the stains on it. They were both sent to the lab.

"We're also looking for the two boys that talked to that bushy-haired guy. Detectives from our unit are looking for the guy right now. We got two other calls we checked on last night. One was on a shell-shocked veteran we picked up after we got an anonymous tip that he might know something. We put him on the lie box and he passed. How the hell they could give a guy that's shell-shocked a polygraph and say he passed, I'll never know. Anyway, the other call was from the Provost Marshall at the Air Force Reserve Unit at the airport. One of his airmen reported that he saw a car parked in Robinson's Woods at 7:25 a.m. on Tuesday morning. Says it was a '40 or '41 dark blue sedan. We got somebody following up on that, too.

Murphy stopped his briefing and picked up the phone. He dialed the front desk and spoke quickly into the phone.

"Bob, this is Murphy. See if you can get Koeppe and Duffy in my office as soon as possible. Ask Lt. Delaney to come in here when he gets a chance." Murphy hung up and then continued.

He went on to explain that Coroner McCarron had deputized Capt. Corcoran, Lt. Deeley, Lt. McMahon, and Chief of Detectives John O'Malley the day before, so that they could operate throughout the county without jurisdictional problems. The rest of the men in our unit, including detectives Czech, Koeppe, Duffy and myself were to be sworn in by special deputies the following day. Murphy told Frank and me to go to the morgue to be sworn in.

I was given the assignment to visit every movie theater in the downtown area after leaving the inquest. Every manager, usher, and anyone else who may have seen the boys was to be interviewed.

The door to Murphy's office swung open suddenly, and detectives Koeppe and Duffy walked in followed by Lt. Delaney. He was in charge of the juvenile officers and knew every gang in the District, their members, where they hung out, and what each member's rap sheet contained.

"Morning, Murph," Duffy said as he closed the door behind them. He nodded to Frank and me and then sat down. Koeppe sat next to him, while Lt. Delaney stood off to one side of the room.

"I'm glad you guys could make it," Murphy said. "You all know Lt. Delaney, here. He's going to give us a rundown on what his unit's been doing on this case."

We knew Delaney but hadn't worked with him too often since he handled juvenile cases. Juvenile homicides had been rare occurrences in the 33rd District—until this case.

Delaney summarized his work with the gangs in the area. He said he found that gang violence had increased in the last sixteen months and that most of this violence was motivated by revenge. It included the burning of garages and acts of vandalism to other private property as well as gang fights at local dances.

Three gangs were named as having a history of violence: the Naturals, the Kav Knights, and the Marquees. Several of their members had been arrested during the weeks prior to the murders.

"They're a tough bunch of little sons of bitches," Delaney said. "Don't turn your backs on them. They hate police officers, and they'll give you a hard time. That's why Murphy and I decided that when you pick them up, we want you to go out two at a time. If you need help, I've detailed one of my men on each shift to help out."

We agreed that since we weren't that familiar with juvenile gang members, having Delaney's men would be helpful. The detectives working juvenile knew how to handle those kids.

"Lt. Delaney, a few of us were talking about the motive on the crimes. There doesn't appear to have been any clear motive behind those killings." Duffy was referring to the ongoing discussion among the detectives that the boys weren't involved with a gang and all three were unknown to authorities.

"I know what you mean, Bill," Lt. Delaney responded. "When you think about it, what's the motive behind what kids do in gangs? Some of these gangs will jump out from nowhere and assault people for no apparent reason. That's one of the things we believe supports our theory that this crime could have been their handiwork. Those boys could have run across some gang who initially intended just to rough them up. Things could have gotten out of hand, and they were killed.

"There hasn't been any evidence about the boys' having been sexually molested. The fact that the boys were slapped around and beaten in the face seems hard to figure out in the absence of any physical evidence of molestation. And the removal of their clothing, the binding and gagging...all that is still a mystery."

The three gangs that Delaney mentioned had been arrested as suspects in the one or two rare cases where some young kid had been killed. But every detective working homicide agreed that although it was possible that the murders could have been the result of an assault by gangs that went wrong, it was very unlikely.

If teenagers had been involved in something so brutal, word would leak out. In our experience, teenagers tended to brag about their "exploits." Someone would have talked by now, especially since it was almost certain that we were looking for more than one person.

Also, the boys didn't have any record of involvement with gangs. Gangs had been known to retaliate against other gangs, and sometimes that resulted in the death of a rival gang member—but not three innocent kids.

Lt. Delaney was one of the higher echelon detectives in the Department and very few police officers had more experience with gangs than he did. We couldn't completely discount the gang theory, just as we couldn't be 100 percent sure of anything at this point. Still, I wasn't putting any money on the theory that teenagers killed the boys.

"Thanks for your time, Lt. Delaney," said Murphy. "I'm sure all the detectives working this case will be happy to call and ask for your advice."

Murphy came around his desk and shook hands with Delaney, thanking him again for his time as the two walked to the door of his office. The sergeant held the door open and the lieutenant walked into the hallway and toward the front of the station.

"Okay, men. You heard him," Murphy said as he closed the door behind him and walked back to his desk. "I don't care if you guys give much weight to his theory, we're bringing in every mope in every gang we know of. They'll be interrogated in detail, and if you have to, hold them for further investigation."

Before sitting down, he stopped momentarily and reached behind his chair to the bulletin board on the wall behind it. He picked off one of the thin, yellow sheets of paper tacked to the board.

"Now, what we have up for today is quite a lot. First, I want Jack, Czech, Duffy and Kakowinski to look at a new case we have from a guy who says he was a victim of a teenage sex gang. Carpenter should like this one, so we need to pick the guy up and question him as soon as possible. You guys decide when you want to bring him in.

"Next, O'Neal and I and are going over to Henri's Lounge on Milwaukee Avenue. We've heard it's a bar for homosexuals. We'll be picking up the owner, Larry Smith, sometime later this afternoon.

"Like I said earlier, and just so you don't forget, all of you have to be down at the morgue tomorrow morning to be sworn in as special Cook County Deputies.

"Jim, you're going to spend the rest of the day at the movies downtown." The detectives looked at me and started to laugh.

"Hey Sarge," Koeppe shouted. "You're giving Jim all the easy jobs. He gets to watch movies and eat popcorn all day. I think he needs a date. How about, it?" Another round of laughter rose up in the room.

I didn't wait for Murphy to respond. "Okay, Fred. Tell you what. You take my job at the theaters, and I'll take your job sitting around at the inquest."

"Okay, guys, listen up. Jim, you won't have time to eat any popcorn. I want you to interview every person who works there. We have to know if any of them saw the Peterson and Schuessler boys last Sunday. Get a schedule of the times the movies were shown, especially at the Loop Theater where the boys were supposed to have seen that movie. What was it?"

"The African Lion," I said.

"Yeah, that one. Make sure you talk to everybody. If they're off from work, go to their homes."

"Got it, Sarge."

"Finally, we got a call from Capt. McCann from the Sheriff's Department. This one looks to be pretty hot. The phone tip was anonymous but said we should be picking up some guy named Dahlquist. The guy lives about five blocks away from the Schuessler home, and he was supposed to have molested some young boy a few months ago. This one's a priority. McCann said he's a little short on personnel today, and I told him we'd handle it. I want Jack, Duffy, and O'Neal to go over to this guy's house right after we're finished here. Bring him in and question him about whether he knew the boys, what he knows, and what his background is. That's it, men. Check in with me later this afternoon and have your initial reports done by 5:00 p.m."

9:20 a.m.
Peterson Avenue

Our unmarked police car pulled slowly to the curb in front of 5915 Peterson Avenue. Duffy carefully brought the car to within inches of the vehicle in front of us, then stopped and cut the engine. It was Sunday morning, and most people were still in their homes, enjoying a late breakfast or reading the Sunday paper.

On the drive, we talked about the progress of the investigation. We were all in agreement that things weren't going as well as we'd hoped. One lead after another had led to a dead end. The crime lab was still examining the articles of clothing found the day before. Suspects had been questioned and released when no hard evidence could incriminate them as being involved in the murders.

Newspapers, radio, and television reports continued their coverage of the story. They kept the public as informed as the Police Department and other authorities conducting the investigation would allow. But now they were starting to become impatient. Along with the citizens of the city, county, state, and the rest of the country, the reporters wanted someone to be identified as the killer, and soon.

We talked about how you could read between the lines in some of the more recent stories: "Manhunt continues...killers elude dragnet despite the work of hundreds of police investigating the crime... Parents want those responsible brought to justice..."

"We've got suspects," I said. "What about Dillon? I can't put my finger on it, but believe me, he's hiding something."

"Every mope we've brought in is hiding something, Jim," O'Neal said. "We've uncovered more weirdo shit on this case than I've seen in years. They're coming out of the woodwork, for God's sake. Stuff I've never heard of before."

"You got that right, Al." I said.

"Well, guys, what do you want to do?" Duffy interrupted. "Stay here and gab or get out and bring in the guy who lives here? If we don't get a move on, he'll spot us just by looking out his window. Then we got a rabbit to look for."

All at once, the conversation stopped as Duffy opened the driver's side door and got out. O'Neal got out of the passenger's side door, and I exited the back seat. We slowly walked up the narrow walk to the front steps of the house. Reaching the front door, O'Neal pushed on the white plastic doorbell next to it.

The muffled sound of door chimes could be heard through the

heavy wooden door, followed by the faint thumps of heavy footsteps coming closer to the front of the house. The door opened a few inches, and a man's voice asked, "Yes, who is it?"

"Mr. Dahlquist? I'm Detective O'Neal, Chicago Police Department. This is Detective Jack and Detective Duffy." Our identification and police shields were held out so they could be seen. "We'd like to ask you some questions down at the station about what you may know about the Peterson and Schuessler boys."

The man opened the door a few more inches. He was wearing a T-shirt and pajama bottoms and was barefoot.

"I don't know anything about them," he quivered.

"It'll only take a few minutes, Mr. Dahlquist," O'Neal said.

"Can't I just go down there this afternoon? I'm not even dressed."

O'Neal began to inch toward the door and got ready to push it open if he felt the man was going to slam it shut. Dahlquist's eyes darted back and forth. He could sense we weren't taking no for an answer.

He opened the door to let us inside. As soon as we entered the small foyer, Duffy and I grabbed his wrists as O'Neal searched him, patting him down to check to see if he had any weapons.

"Hey, what are you doin'?" the man cried.

"Take it easy pal," O'Neal said." Now why don't you go along with Detective Duffy there and get your coat."

"But I'm not dressed. And I told you I don't know anything about what happened to those boys. I live in the neighborhood, that's all…. I don't even know if I saw them before this thing happened…."

I interrupted him. "Hold your thoughts there, Mr. Dahlquist. We'll straighten this out down at the station. Now why don't you and I go and get some clothes for you, if that'll make you feel better." O'Neal and Duffy waited in the living room, casually looking at the furnishings in the room and the pictures hanging on the wall.

Dahlquist led me through the living room and into a small bedroom just off the hallway leading to the kitchen. I watched as he took a pair of brown slacks off a chair in the corner of the room, put them on over his pajama bottoms, and then put on a tan colored woolen sweater. He and I walked out into the living room, and he reached into a closet next to the front door. He took out a black trench coat and a pair of worn, scuffed shoes and finished dressing. We led him out of his house and walked him to the squad car at the curb.

I got into the back seat with Mr. Dahlquist, while O'Neal joined Duffy in front. Duffy started the engine and pulled away, heading back to the District.

10:10 a.m.

Dahlquist sat next to my desk in the detectives' room. He looked around the office. Although the phones on other desks were ringing, no one was answering them. I was busy looking over the phone messages that had been put on my desk, and Murphy had just walked in the room. Murphy closed the door behind him and took a seat at Frank's desk. He introduced himself then began the interrogation.

"Do you know why you're here?" Murphy began.

"Yeah, they told me you wanted to talk to me about the boys that were killed last week."

"What's your full name?"

"Charles L. Dahlquist."

"How old are you?"

"I'm 31."

"Do you work?"

"No, I'm unemployed."

Murphy paused for a moment.

"I see," Murphy said. "Do you know where you were on October 16 and through the evening of Sunday through Monday?"

"Yeah."

"Well, where were you?"

"I was home alone. I was watching TV that night. I could tell you what programs I was watching, too. In detail." His voice carried a tone of defiance, as if he was more prepared for these questions than we thought he would be.

"Good for you," Murphy said. "Ever been arrested before?"

The man hesitated just long enough for us to guess what was coming.

"Yeah."

"Okay, now why don't you tell us what you've been arrested for,"

Murphy said with as much sarcasm as he could.

"Well, some minor sex charge. Exposing myself."

"How nice," Murphy smiled. "Anything else?"

"No, not that I can remember."

I suddenly stood up and leaned down so that my face came within inches of Dahlquist's face. "What do mean you can't remember?" I shouted. "Maybe we can help you out. Sarge, I think he needs some time to remember." I picked up the phone and called the front desk.

"Yeah, Roy, this is Jim. Get a patrolman into my office. We got a guy in here who needs some time to remember. He's going in the holding cell for a while. Then he's going downtown."

3:30 p.m.

"Get that Dahlquist guy out of the lock-up, Mike. Bring him into the office here. Frank and I want to go over a few things with him again."

I stood in the doorway of our office and looked down the narrow hallway at the uniformed officer standing just in front of the barred door of the lock-up. Officer Mike Reardon nodded and pulled out one of the large metal keys from the ring hanging from his thick black leather belt. Officer Reardon inserted the key into the door's worn metal lock and swung the heavy barred door open.

"Let's go, Dahlquist," Reardon shouted into the dimly lit cell. After a few moments, the prisoner walked out of the doorway of the lock-up and both he and the officer walked to where my partner and I were standing.

"Thanks, Mike," I said. "You better stick around. If this guy doesn't start remembering things, you'll have to take him down to Cook County Jail tonight."

The prisoner sat down on one of the gray metal chairs and looked nervously around the room. When he saw Frank's glare, his eyes quickly looked away and down at the floor.

I walked slowly around the man and took a seat behind the desk. After pulling out a pad of paper and a pen, I looked at Dahlquist.

"Okay, now let's start all over again. You know why you're here?"

"Not really. I don't know anything."

"Not anything about WHAT?" I shot back.

"I guess you think I know something about those three kids who got killed last week." His voice was lower now and his eyes remained focused on the floor.

"Well, what about it? Do you?" My voice rose in volume. I didn't wait for an answer. "You ever been arrested? And don't give us any bullshit."

"Ah...well, yeah."

"What for? We'll get your sheet anyway, so just tell us now."

"Some small sex offenses, that's all."

"Small sex offenses?" I didn't try to hide any of the sarcasm in my voice. What the hell kind of a person was this. Does he think there's a sex offense that isn't serious?

"Where do you work?"

"I don't have a job," Dahlquist said quietly. He looked up at me then shifted his eyes back to the floor.

"Listen, asshole, we want to hear where you were every minute from when you got up Sunday morning on the sixteenth of this month all the way to last Tuesday night, the eighteenth. Where you went, what you ate, who you saw, where you work. Everything. Now let's have it."

Dahlquist sat up in his chair, suddenly realizing he was a suspect in a triple homicide. His face tensed and his eyebrows narrowed, almost as if he were about to start crying. He looked straight ahead and past Frank and me as we waited for an answer, not wanting to make eye contact with either of us.

"I don't remember. . . Tuesday? You want to know about where I was Tuesday?"

Frank got up from behind his desk and slowly walked toward Dahlquist, then stopped and stood right behind his chair.

"No, not Tuesday. Start with Sunday, the sixteenth. Where were you Sunday morning?"

Dahlquist said he left home Sunday morning and went to Tam O'Shanter Country Club in Niles, just northwest of the city limits. He said he stayed there until 4:00 p.m. When he returned to his home, he ate supper with his parents. He said he spent the rest of the evening with them, watching television and went to bed at 11:30 p.m.

On Monday, the seventeenth of October, he said he ate breakfast and then went back to Tam O'Shanter again.

"Are you a member there?" I asked.

"No." He went on to say that on Monday he played a round of golf, then went home Monday afternoon. After reading the newspaper, he ate supper, cut the lawn, worked on his golf clubs, and watched television again until 10:30 p.m., then went to bed. He emphasized that his parents knew that he was home the entire time on Sunday and Monday evening.

"Who did you play golf with?" Frank asked.

"Just some of the guys there...I'm a caddy."

"You said you didn't have a job. Are you tellin' us you have a job? At the country club?"

"I'm a caddy at Tam."

Frank walked back to the chair behind his desk and sat down. He looked at me, made a few notes on the pad in front of him and leaned back in his chair. Both Frank and I glared at Dahlquist, who was now shifting uneasily and nervously scratching the thumb of his right hand across his pant leg.

Frank tapped the pen against the top of the desk, getting impatient with Dahlquist's answers.

"What about Tuesday, the eighteenth? What did you do all day?" I asked.

"I got up about 9:00 a.m., had breakfast and went to Bob-O-Link Country Club...up in Highland Park. I waited around to caddy a foursome and finally got out at about 11:00 a.m. I got through about 4:00 p.m. and got home at about 4:30 p.m. I gave my mother the $10 I made from caddying. Then my parents and I had dinner at about 6:00 p.m. I read the paper then watched television."

"Did you go out at all on Tuesday night?"

"No. My parents were with me the whole time."

"When did you first hear about the Peterson and Schuessler boys?" I asked"

"I think it was Tuesday night. My mother came home from shopping and had brought the newspaper."

Frank looked at me then quickly said "You just said you were with your parents all night Tuesday. Now you got your mother out shopping that night? Which is it?"

"That's what happened. She went to the store behind our house...across the alley...after we ate dinner."

"Frank, let me talk to you a minute." I stood up and flipped over the pad of paper. I walked to the door and waited for Frank, and then we stepped out into the hallway as I kept my eyes on Dahlquist.

The loud voices of detectives and officers working in the assembly area filled the hallway, along with the clacking of typewriters and conversations from other offices.

I raised my voice just enough so that my partner could hear me.

"What do you think, Frank?"

"That guy's story has more holes in it than Swiss cheese. First, he doesn't have a job. Then, he works as a caddy. He says he went from Highland Park to Chicago in thirty minutes. That's bullshit, unless he took a plane. Then he says he read the paper after dinner but his mother doesn't bring it home until after she goes shopping that night."

I nodded in agreement. The guy was hiding something, but just what we couldn't be sure of.

Let's get him to run over the details again. It looks like we'll have to send him to Griffin for a polygraph, but let's see if we can pin him down on whatever it is he doesn't want to tell us."

Monday
October 24, 1955
9:15 a.m.

I turned up the volume on the police radio while driving the squad car down State Street. My first stop was the Roosevelt Theater. It was one of a half-dozen movie theaters in the north end of Chicago's downtown district, known as the "Loop." Located just south of the intersection at Randolph and State Streets, it was directly across the street from Marshall Field's Department store. Although the early morning traffic was heavy, few cars parked in front of the businesses and theaters on what was then known as "The World's Busiest Street." The officers in the Traffic Division were given strict instructions to enforce the parking ordinances so that traffic on State Street flowed easily and it didn't become a parking lot.

I pulled into a parking space in front of the theater and got out of the car. Just then a uniformed patrol officer walked over hurriedly and pointed at the car.

"Hey, pal, move that out of there, or I'll have to write you up," the officer said.

I turned and smiled. It was Joseph Walsh. Walsh and his partner, William Lyman handled the traffic on Randolph and State Streets. They weren't there when I went through the intersection, but that wasn't unusual.

To keep the flow of traffic going on State Street, they occasionally walked the street and wrote parking tickets or told motorists to move on.

Joe recognized me immediately. "What's up, Jim? Going to the early show?"

"How you doing, Joe?" I said. "Where's your partner?"

"He's down the block. You know how it goes down here. My Sergeant drives up and down the street every chance he gets to make sure nobody parks in front of the businesses. The merchants want it clear, they talk to the alderman, he talks to the District Commander who tells my supervisor, and so I got a dozen people looking over my shoulder and counting how many violations I write up every day."

We laughed at the way things worked in the Department, something that every cop understood. Before we had a chance to continue the conversation, a young woman entered the ticket booth at the theater. She looked at us then pointed to the sign hanging in the booth showing the starting times of the movie.

"We're not open yet," she said through the metal screen in the center of the window.

I held up my police badge up for the woman to see. "I'm Detective James Jack, Chicago Police Department. I'd appreciate it if you would get the theater manager."

The woman stared blankly for a moment then nodded her head and opened the narrow door that allowed her to exit the booth. I could see her through the glass doors of the theater, as she walked quickly across the lobby.

"Peterson-Schuessler case?" Walsh asked.

"Yeah." My answer was short, but polite. I didn't say anything else, and we stood silently for a few seconds. Soon Joe looked past me as a driver began to park his car in front of mine. He reached into his back pocket, pulled out his ticket book then stopped and looked at me.

"Jim, I hope you get the guys who did it," he said. "I can't even think about what those parents are going through. Good luck."

"Thanks," I said as Walsh left to deal with the driver. I turned back toward the doors of the theater just as the young woman returned. She opened one of the double doors and asked me to come into the lobby.

"The manager's not here yet, but maybe his assistant can help you. Her office is the first door on the right, just at the end of the counter."

I thanked her and walked into the small lobby of the theater. A few employees were vacuuming the carpet, and a young man behind the candy counter was cleaning the popcorn machine. As I reached the counter, a woman in her mid-forties stood in the doorway of the manager's office. She introduced herself as the assistant manager and asked how she could be of assistance. After identifying myself and explaining the purpose of the visit, I asked her whether she and the employees present had worked on Sunday, October 16.

"I did and so did Susan, the young lady who works the ticket booth. The ushers and counter people may not have worked on the sixteenth, though. I can check the work schedule and tell you who did work on that particular Sunday."

I thanked her and told her I would interview the employees present while she checked the list of employees. I interviewed the young man at the counter, the young woman in the ticket booth, and the employees vacuuming the carpet. They were shown the pictures of the boys, but none could identify them as being in the Roosevelt Theater the week before.

The assistant manager came out with the list of employees, indicating the ones who would have worked on the sixteenth. Some of the people on the list were not scheduled to be in today. I wrote down their names and addresses. Then I showed the woman the pictures of the boys and asked if she recalled seeing them in the theater last Sunday.

"No, I don't remember them. We get a lot of people in here, even on a Sunday night. But everyone who works here knows what happened from the newspapers. I'm sure someone would have said something to the manager or to me if they remembered anything. But I'll be sure to let the manager know you were here."

I thanked her, gave her a card, and asked her to call the direct number in case any of the employees recalled seeing the boys. I jotted down the manager's name and phone number in my notebook. I decided to call him personally after getting back to the station.

Leaving Roosevelt Theater, I walked to the corner and crossed Randolph Street to the Oriental Theater where I went through the same process of showing pictures of the boys and asking if anyone had seen them Sunday night. I did the same thing at the United Artists Theater, just across the street, with similar results.

I walked back to State Street and a half-block north to the Loop Theater, the destination of Bobby Peterson, and Anton and John Schuessler. The Loop was a small movie theater, just across the alley from the much larger and older Chicago Theater. If it weren't for the narrow black and white marquee over the sidewalk, it could easily be mistaken for just another small business.

No one was in the ticket booth when I got there, a small sign in the window indicated the first showing was just before noon. The theater was closed, and no one responded when I knocked on the doors.

I stood under the narrow marquee for a moment and thought of the boys and that they probably had been standing in that same location just one week ago.

Did they really come down here? What would they have done if they had arrived and the movie had already started? Had they somehow spent or lost the money they had and couldn't get in?

I looked around at the marquees of the other theaters then took out my notebook. The starting times at the theaters already visited were marked as well as the names of the movies shown last Sunday. No, I thought, those boys came down to see the movie. And Ernest Niewiadomski told us the boys had seen the movie at the Loop.

I looked at the huge marquee of the Chicago Theater. The movie being shown that week was "My Sister Eileen," starring Janet Leigh and Jack Lemmon. The smaller billboards in front of the entrance advertised a stage show later in the week, starring Liberace. The famous entertainer was going to be in town to promote the opening of his new movie, "Sincerely Yours."

Large movie theaters, especially the ones downtown, still had live entertainment between movie showings. It was a holdover from Vaudeville as well as an effort by the larger theaters to draw people away from their television sets and into the movie theaters.

In the late '40s, I worked as an usher at the Chicago Theater. It was an ornate movie palace that showcased some of the biggest names in show business. I saw the best of the big bands there: Tommy and Jimmy Dorsey, Benny Goodman, and Glenn Miller. But it had been a while since I'd been in there.

I didn't think that the boys would have been interested in seeing a picture like the one playing at the Chicago Theater, but every downtown theater had to be checked.

I walked up to the ticket booth at the Chicago Theater, showed my identification and said I wanted to see the manager. The attendant in the booth directed me into the lobby and showed me the location of the manager's office, just beyond the front doors of the theater.

When I walked into the lobby, I immediately remembered those days as an usher. Nothing seemed to have changed. The tall marble pillars, replicas of Old World furniture and tapestries along the walls on either side of the theater, and a grand staircase leading up to the balcony all looked as they did years before.

The door to the theater manager's office was open, and I knocked as it swung open. I identified myself again and stated the purpose of the visit. The manager looked at the photos and said that some of the employees who had worked on October 16 were either at the theater already or would arrive shortly. I got the manager's permission to interview the ushers and other employees who were present but asked if I could wait until all of the employees reported to work.

"Sure, Detective. Take any seat in the house. You have about 1480 seats to choose from this morning. We really don't get busy until early afternoon. I'll double check the work schedule and get you the names and addresses of our people who worked last Sunday but won't be here today."

I thanked the man and walked to the doors leading to the theater seating area. The movie had already begun and the soft light from the screen allowed me to look over the rows and rows of empty seats to determine just how many people went to a movie on Monday morning. I counted about two-dozen people spread out amongst the empty rows.

The voices of the actors sounded like echoes in a canyon. Because of the small number of people in the theater, the acoustics were noticeably different from what I was used to. I walked down the aisle of the main floor to a row in the middle of the theater, went several seats down into the row and took a seat.

Although I looked at the screen, my mind continued to work over the facts of the case. I added and subtracted the minutes it would take to travel by bus downtown, to walk from one theater to another, to get back to the northwest side, to go from the Drake Bowl to the Monte Cristo to the intersection of Lawrence and Milwaukee. I thought of the different permutations and combinations of each trip, and how it would fit the time frame already established of where and when the boys were seen by reliable witnesses.

Suddenly, my thoughts were interrupted by the movement of someone walking slowly down the row of seats. I turned my head slightly to the left and noticed a man in his late-twenties. When he got to the seat next to me, he pushed the seat cushion away from the back of the chair and sat down.

I can't fuckin' believe this, I thought. Fifteen hundred empty goddamn seats and this son of a bitch sits right next to me.

I calmed down and paid attention to the movie. I wasn't going to be sitting there that much longer anyway, so why get bent out of shape over somebody sitting in the next seat.

The theater had become quiet during a lull in the dialogue between the actors. Janet Leigh and Jack Lemmon were looking longingly at each other, when I heard a strange sound. It sounded like a cricket in one of the cushioned seats, a muffled clicking noise. Then I glanced to my left. The man had unzipped his pants and exposed himself. A few seconds later, I felt a hand on my knee.

My first impulse was to smash the guy's face in. Instead I sat motionlessly as his hand began to move up my leg.

I couldn't believe this. Just one week ago three boys had attended a movie right next door at the Loop Theater and had later been found dead. The story had been front-page news for nearly a week, everybody in the city was looking for some crazed degenerate, and this son of a bitch is sitting in a downtown theater grabbing his thing and playing with my leg.

I turned to him and quietly whispered, "Why don't you and me go to the back of the theater?"

The man looked at me and took his hand off my leg.

"Okay," he said. He put himself back into his pants and zipped up. Then he got up from his seat and, with me following closely behind, walked up the aisle of the theater toward the lobby.

Just before we reached the door, I announced that I was a police officer and that he was under arrest.

Suddenly, the man threw himself at the heavy double doors with his right shoulder causing them to fly open. I ran after him as he dashed down the corridor, past the candy counter and towards the front doors of the theater.

I tackled him about twenty feet away from the entrance. My right arm, placed across his neck, held him to the floor as he kicked and struggled trying to get free.

"Get off of me you asshole! Help! He's choking me!" the man yelled.

Two ushers standing in the lobby rushed over and tried to pull me off. I kept my right hand on the man's neck, pushing his face into the bright red carpet while elbowing the ushers to keep them from interfering with the arrest.

"I'm a police officer, and this man's under arrest! Get the hell out of the way!" I shouted. "Go get the police officer outside. He's right on the corner at Randolph. Tell him an officer needs assistance."

The man continued to kick and scream, saying that he hadn't done anything and that this was a false arrest. By now I had my knee in his lower back as well as my hand on the back of his neck. I used my other hand to grab his left arm, pinning it behind his back.

Minutes later, Officers Lyman and Walsh burst through the front doors and into the lobby. They rushed over and grabbed the man, lifting him off the floor and patting him down for weapons.

"Joe, I want this guy locked up. Take him down to 11th and State, and I'll get a wagon from my District to pick him up so we can interrogate him."

After the officers completed their search for weapons, I pulled out my handcuffs and asked the man for some identification.

"Show me something…who are you?" I pulled the man's hands behind his back and clicked the cuffs around his wrists.

"None of your fuckin' business," the man shouted.

"None of my fuckin' business? You just made an unwanted pass on a police officer in the theater. If that isn't my business then I'm Mickey Mouse, you slime ball."

"I don't give a shit who you are, asshole: a cop or Mickey Mouse."

"Listen, scumbag. You've got some kind of problem. But when I get finished with you, this is going to be one of your worst nightmares. You'll wish you never came in here."

Soon the movie patrons began to gather in the lobby, talking to one another in increasingly louder voices. Several had heard the Peterson-Schuessler murders mentioned. I heard the word "suspect" jump out from some of the conversations, and I also noticed angry looks among the crowd.

"Joe, we better get this guy out of here. These people are starting to get upset. I don't want them to lynch the guy right here in the theater."

Walsh agreed, and we led the man out the front doors.

Meanwhile Lyman asked the manager if he could use the phone to call the First District.

In those days, black police vans, known as "paddy wagons," were used to transport prisoners to and from district stations or to Cook County Jail. While Walsh and I stood waiting for the wagon, we were able to get the prisoner's name. It was Robert O'Connor. He was 31 years of age and lived at 4334 N. Wilson Avenue.

"What do you guys want from me? I was minding my own business, watching the movie," the man said to Walsh. He nodded at me. "Then Tarzan over here tackles me and starts beating me up for no reason. What's he doing going to the movies when he's on duty, anyway?"

"Listen, asshole, I'm here investigating a triple homicide. Did you hear about it? Three kids who were right in that theater over there." I pointed at the Loop Theater. "And from what you did just a while ago, I think you're a good candidate for a long interrogation about what you might know about that."

The smug look on O'Connor's face suddenly changed to shock, then anger.

"Hey, wait a minute. That's bullshit and you know it! You can't scare me with that shit."

I turned to Walsh and calmly said, "Joe, this guy's a suspect in a triple homicide, and he wants you to know he's not scared."

Walsh looked at O'Connor, then at me. I smiled sheepishly, "He might change his mind when he gets to the lock-up. We still have guys we picked up over the weekend who haven't made their bond. They get pretty bored sitting in the holding cell after forty-eight hours with nothing to do."

"Yeah, well maybe you cops should keep 'em company."

The sound of a police siren echoed in the distance. Coming up State Street, a flashing red light weaved back and forth among the hoods of cars until the black van pulled up in front of the theater.

I told the two policemen in the cab about the arrest, while Walsh took O'Connor to the rear of the wagon and opened the doors. He waited until I joined them, then we stepped up into the back of the wagon with O'Connor.

11:10 a.m.
Police Headquarters
11ᵗʰ & State

The paddy wagon entered the alley behind Police Headquarters and backed into one of the loading bays on the ground floor of the building. After feeling the rear bumper of the wagon tap the loading bay, Officer Walsh stood up inside and pushed open the back doors. I stood up and led O'Connor by the arm out of the doors and up to one of the rear elevators of the building.

These elevators were used to bring prisoners directly to the lock-up area or to one of several courtrooms, known as branch courts, located on different floors of Police Headquarters. As the elevator doors opened, Walsh, O'Connor, and I entered and stood against the back wall. The first thing I noticed was the smell, as if twenty people who hadn't taken a shower in a week had just gotten off at one of the other floors.

The elevator stopped at the eleventh floor, the doors slowly crept open, and the cab of the elevator bobbed twice until it came level with the floor. Two sergeants working behind the counter at one end of the room greeted Walsh.

"What've you got there, Joe? Did the guy park in front of a fire hydrant or something?" The two officers smiled at each other as one of them came around the end of the counter. He came up behind the prisoner and took hold of the man's arms, raising them a bit in order to unlock the handcuffs around his wrists.

"You better wait until you get him into the cell before you take the cuffs off," I told the sergeant. "I'm Detective James Jack from the 33ʳᵈ District, and this guy's going to be interrogated about the Peterson-Schuessler murders."

Both sergeants stopped smiling. The one taking custody of O'Connor let the prisoner's arms drop back down behind him then quickly took him around the counter and led him to a holding cell.

I waited until the sergeant came back from the detention area and returned with my handcuffs. I also wanted to be sure the two sergeants and other officers in the room heard what I said next.

Remembering my days on traffic detail, I knew how much a pat on the back from a fellow officer was appreciated, especially in front of peers.

"Thanks for your help on this, Officer Walsh. And let your partner know I appreciate what you guys did," I said. "I'll be in Lt. Deeley's office upstairs. Let me know when the wagon from the 33rd District gets here to pick that guy up."

"Don't mention it, Detective," Walsh said. He looked at the two sergeants standing behind the counter and smiled.

I opened the door leading from the lock-up to the main corridor of the eleventh floor and walked to the stairway at the far end. After walking up two flights of stairs, I reached a large, wooden door with a sheet of paper taped to it with the letters "S.I.U." written by hand. Inside, I saw scores of detectives seated behind gray-metal desks. Some were talking to uniformed officers, while others were conducting interviews at their desks with civilians. Several men were shouting over the ringing of telephones, trying to make themselves heard over dozens of conversations going on in the room.

The Special Investigations Unit located at Police Headquarters was under the command of Lt. Pat Deeley. The detectives and officers working out of 11th and State were coordinating their investigations with the investigators at our District. Because of the 33rd District's location, detectives and officers assigned to the SIU focused their investigations on neighborhoods near the crime scene and the surrounding areas within that vicinty. The Loop movie theaters were located in the First District, so Lt. Deeley needed to be aware of the arrest and interogation, which would occur at our station.

The unit downtown was given the task of coordinating the efforts of city, county, state, and federal investigative agencies working on the case. As with any investigation that involved several governmental agencies, there was some duplication of effort and, on occasion, even confusion as to what each agency was doing.

"Hold it. Let's see some identification." A uniformed officer stood in front of me as I entered the room.

I showed my police badge and asked to see Lt. Deeley, explaining that I was a detective from the 33rd District. The police officer pointed to an office at the back of the room. "He's back there. Hang on a second, Detective." The officer walked to the desk closest to him and got the attention of one of the detectives.

The man looked up as the officer pointed in my direction and spoke a few words that I could barely hear. The detective got up from his desk and walked over to where I was standing.

"I'm Detective Larson," the man said as he extended his hand.

I shook Larson's hand and told him I was doing a follow-up investigation of movie theaters in the Loop. Detective Larson was informed of the man Walsh, Lyman and I arrested in the Chicago Theater and that I wanted to check in with Lt. Deeley and write up a report before taking O'Connor back to the 33rd District.

"I'm sure the Lieutenant will be glad to hear that. Come on, I'll show you back there."

As we walked around the desks and dodged tangles of telephone wires on the floor, Larson explained that their unit had run out of room days ago. New officers were being assigned to the investigation nearly every day. And the unit had received more than 2000 telephone calls from the public concerning tips or other information about the case.

"Same with us," I said. "Let me guess what your boss told you: 'Every fuckin' one of 'em has got to be checked out.'"

Larson laughed and nodded as we reached the back of the office where Lt. Deeley was speaking with three detectives.

"Hey, Jim! Come on in. We were just going over Dr. Kerns' pathology report," Deeley said. Lt. Deeley introduced me to the other detectives. "What brings you down here?"

I told Lt. Deeley about the arrest.

"It's great to hear that Captain Corcoran has got you guys out there hitting the streets like that. This mope might not know anything, but at least we're out there putting the heat on. Somebody's got to know something about those boys and where they were Sunday night.

"Jim, I know your District's been getting the same information we have down here. We were going over Dr. Kerns' report just now and all indications are that those boys weren't sexually molested. That's critical as to where this investigation is going to go. I know Captain Corcoran has given the men in your unit specific assignments: house-to-house canvassing of your area, follow-up investigations like the one you're on today, and checking out the files of known sex offenders.

"But it's starting to look like McCarron might have a point. He thinks these murders could have been the work of a teenage gang. Something went wrong; they panicked and killed the boys. We just don't have any physical evidence to support a sex crime here. Kearns' report was specific. The boys were not sexually molested. And we've got to use whatever manpower we have in the best way we can."

I didn't say anything for a moment and thought about what Deeley was saying. We were looking for killers, not people with different sex drives. But those categories weren't necessarily exclusive, either, I thought to myself.

"Lieutenant, I guess I have to go along with the evidence we have at this point and give less weight to the theory that these murders were sex crimes. I still have a gut feeling about this thing. Like everybody in charge of these investigations has been saying, I don't think we can eliminate any angles. We've got to keep an open mind and look for the most unexpected things, not close any avenues on this investigation."

"I hear what you're saying, Jim." Deeley said. "At this point, we can't be sure of anything. We get something unexpected every day, I guess. Like your arrest this morning. Unbelievable. Let me know what you get from that guy, okay?"

Just then another detective stepped into the small office. He looked around the room and asked, "Who's Jim?"

"That's me," I said.

"The sergeant in the lock-up told me to tell you the squadrol from the 33rd District is waiting for you downstairs."

"Thanks, Officer. Tell the sergeant I'll be right down to pick up the prisoner." I stood up and shook hands with Lt. Deeley first, then the other detectives in the office.

"Good job, Jim. Keep the pressure on. Like I said, eventually we're going to find somebody that knows something about what happened to those boys. I'll probably be seeing you at one of the briefings up at Gale Street."

"Right, Lieutenant." I stood up, turned, and moved toward the exit. Nodding in the direction of the other detectives as I left, "Good to meet you guys," I said.

I took the elevator down to the first floor of Police Headquarters, then turned right and headed toward the front desk. I reached for my police shield and flashed it at the desk sergeant as I walked quickly down the narrow hallway.

The squadrol from Gale Street was in one of the parking bays, motor running and with the driver's door open. A uniformed officer stuck his head out the driver's side window and turned to look in my direction.

"Come up front, Jim. Billy O'Rourke's in the back with your guy," the officer called out.

"Be right there," I answered. I knocked sharply on the double doors. Seconds later, the right door opened and officer O'Rourke peered out the door, stooping down to avoid bumping his head on the low ceiling of the squadrol.

"How's it goin' Jim?"

"Fine, Billy. Is that knucklehead giving you any problems? He's got a smart mouth. The guys upstairs fill you in on this mope?"

"Yeah, but he hasn't said much since my partner and I got here."

I stuck my head into the squadrol to look at the prisoner. The only light inside came from a dim yellow overhead lamp encased in thick wire mesh.

I made sure the officers had taken custody of the right suspect and checked to see that he was securely handcuffed.

Satisfied, I closed the back door and walked to the passenger side of the cab. "I'm not going back to the station with you guys," I said to the driver who had already put the vehicle in gear. "Drop me off at State and Randolph. I left my squad car there. I didn't think I would be arresting any weirdos when I started out this morning. I'll meet up with you back at the station. And thanks for the lift."

After a few minutes, the squadrol came to a stop on State Street. I got out and walked a short distance to where I had parked the car earlier today in a "No Parking" zone.

October 24, 1955
2:25 p.m.
Gale Street Station

"Listen, shithead, you weren't arrested up for jaywalking this morning. Now tell us what you were doing at the Chicago Theater. And don't tell us you went to see Liberace."

Murphy was standing directly in front of O'Connor who was seated in a steel chair next to my desk. Handcuffs were securely snapped over both wrists, and he held his hands between his knees.

"Murph, this guy's been a wiseass all morning. He's been giving me bullshit since I tackled him in the lobby. Why don't we just send him down to 26ᵗʰ and California so he can play with his buddies?" I got up from behind the desk and walked to one of the filing cabinets at the far end of the office. I turned and gave a mean look to the suspect then opened a cabinet drawer.

At the mention of Cook County Jail, the suspect's right leg began to move nervously back and forth. He looked up at Murphy, then back at me.

"I told you. I went to see a movie. I didn't do anything."

I slammed the cabinet drawer shut and the sudden noise caused O'Connor to jump from his seat.

"You didn't. What the fuck were you doing putting your hand on my knee, then moving it up and down! You're lucky you still have your teeth. Now cut the bullshit. You know why you're here. Don't you know that three boys were killed last week? They went to a movie not fifty yards from where you were sitting this morning."

"I don't know anything about that. I just heard about it."

"Heard about it? How?"

"From the newspapers and the radio where I work."

"Where do you work?"

"Club Laura."

"Where's that?"

"Foster and Broadway. Customers talk about it every night. Some of the bartenders talk about it too. You know…it's a big story."

I walked over and stood next to Murphy. We both stared down

at O'Connor. His leg began to tremble.

"Do you know of anyone who would have killed the boys? Or any reason why they were killed?"

"No. Not at all."

"Have you ever been in Robinson's Woods?"

"No. I haven't."

I walked past Murphy and sat down behind the desk. He picked up a brown file folder and opened it. On one side was copies of the arrest reports filled out earlier that morning. On the other side was the man's driver's license and other identification taken from his wallet.

"Well, you must be some kind of saint, then. Never did anything to get yourself pinched?"

"No, I haven't."

I closed the folder, slid it to the right side of the desk then slammed my open palm down on the desktop.

"No, no, no. You sound like a broken record. Let me ask you something you DO know about, then. While you were in the theater, did you know that exposing yourself and touching somebody is a lewd act?"

"Yeah, I guess I did. I'm old enough to know better, I guess."

"You guess? What would make you do something like that?"

The man looked down at his hands.

"I really can't answer that," he said then looked down at the floor.

I got up slowly and walked to the front of the desk again. I stared scornfully at this guy, O'Connor.

"I can answer it. You're a sick fucking person. I think you're an exhibitionist. You like to play with your joint in public places and hope you're gonna get lucky. But this time you struck out. I'm gonna lock you up for indecent exposure, assaulting a peace officer, resisting arrest, and disorderly conduct. When you go to court you can tell your story to the judge. If you can't think of an answer when HE asks you the same question, you can use my answer. You're a sick fucking asshole."

The man just sat there. His leg stopped trembling and a small

,pool of water began to creep around his shoes.

"We're gonna lock you up. We're gonna fingerprint you and send you down to the Sex Bureau and have sex sheets made out on you. Then you're gonna go down to the polygraph lab, and you're gonna go on the box and be asked questions about the murders."

"Wait a minute," the man cried. His eyes were filled with tears, and he held up his wrists and wiped his eyes with the back of his right hand. "I didn't do it…. I don't know anything about that."

"You've been bullshitting us here all day. Soon as the guys at the polygraph lab have a chance to take you—maybe tonight, maybe tomorrow morning—we'll see if you pass. It's as simple as that."

I turned and walked out the door. Halfway down the hallway, I found a patrolman to take O'Connor to the lock-up. I also told the officer to get the custodian to mop up the water next to my desk.

5:00 p.m.

"Murph, Frank and I got the report back from Griffin this morning. He put Dahlquist on the lie box three times, and the results weren't conclusive. But, he saw something that backs up our opinion that the guy's not tellin' us the whole story."

Murphy looked up from the file folder in his hands. He leaned back in his chair and scratched his neck.

"Yeah, I know. I just read it." Murphy brought the file folder up close to his face and squinted his eyes as he read from one of the pages. "'There was a slight emotional disturbance indicative of deception in the subject's polygraph, but not of sufficient magnitude or consistency to enable the examiner to state the subject was involved in this particular murder.'"

Frank smiled. "So basically Griffin agrees with Jim and me that the guy's full of shit. We just can't put our finger on just what he's lying about."

Murphy put the folder back down on his desk. "Took the words right out of my mouth, Frank. Listen, we had to let the guy go. I read your report and from what you tell me, there's no question the guy's hiding something. I let Lt. Deeley know about it this morning, and we sent a team of detectives over to Dahlquist's house today.

They got the family's permission to search the place and didn't find anything that would tie him in with the murders. But what we didn't find was more interesting. According to your report, Dahlquist says he was home 'working on his golf clubs' Monday. He didn't have any golf clubs at his house, in his garage, or anyplace else. I ran this by Spiotto, and he agreed that we have to keep an eye on this guy. You guys know that Mike's got a good nose."

All three of us laughed.

Detective Sgt. Mike Spiotto was one of the sharpest detectives in the Police Department. He had been with the department since the early '40s and one of the first cases he solved as a patrolman was the apprehension of an arsonist at the scene of a large warehouse fire. While helping with crowd control, Spiotto found himself standing next to one of the many on-lookers watching as firemen attempted to control the blaze.

He noticed a distinctive odor coming from the man standing near him and determined that what he smelled was gasoline. After engaging the man with small talk about what a large fire this was, and knowing that many "firebugs" like to observe the results of their work, Spiotto eventually got the man to unwittingly admit that, yes, he did in fact set the fire. The man was arrested and convicted for arson.

"What about the Coroner's Inquest this morning, Murph?" I asked. "Anything new come out?"

"No, not much. The State's Attorneys Office made sure they sent somebody over there. So did the Forest Rangers. Koeppe can fill you in on what happened. What we have to talk about now is where we're going on this investigation."

"Frank and I are going to follow up on O'Connor this week. He gave me a lot of smart talk yesterday, but it seems like he's taking things more seriously now."

"That's good," Murphy said. "Let me know what you guys come up with." Murphy reached for the telephone.

As he lifted the receiver, he looked at his wristwatch then back up in my direction. "Shouldn't you be leaving for work about now?"

For a moment, I didn't understand what Murphy was talking about.

"What? Oh, yeah! Gotta be behind the pins by 6:00 p.m. or that son of a bitch boss of mine will fire my ass."

8:45 p.m.

The sound of the muted thunder of bowling balls began to fade as I hurried to fill the pin rack at the end of lane six. The entire room suddenly became quiet as balls stopped rolling down bowling alley.

Gordon yelled out from the end of the narrow room.

"Hey Jim, hold up a minute. Dillon wants to see everybody out at the front desk for a minute."

"What's going on?" I pulled the pin rack's frayed rope and brought it to rest just above the end of the alley.

Gordon lowered his voice, almost to a whisper, so that he wouldn't be heard by the other pinsetters. He didn't want them to bolt out onto the fire escape and run out the rear of the building.

"Couple of detectives are out there. They're questioning everybody about those kids who were killed. Guess they want to know if anybody saw them here. Just get out there before Dillon gets pissed. I told the cops I'd make sure nobody working back here left without talking to them first."

For a split second, I thought about bending down to see if I recognized the detectives. Then I realized it would only arouse Gordon's suspicion.

I started to get angry. "Dammit," I thought. Everybody was starting to step all over everyone else's investigation. Things like this happen when you have a high profile case. Somebody doesn't check with the local District's Commander before they go into a place in another District. Or maybe it was the guys from my own District station or the guys from downtown who decided to drop in on the Monte Cristo. At this point, it didn't matter. I was stuck. I couldn't beg off, or Dillon and whoever was out there would wonder why I wasn't out at the front desk with the rest of the pinsetters.

"Good," I said with a little too much false confidence. "I could use a break." I followed Gordon and the pinsetters toward the door.

As I walked behind the other pinsetters, I attempted to see the detectives who were talking to Dillon and a few of the other employees gathered near the front door.

One of the plainclothes detectives looked familiar, but I wasn't sure I had seen him before. None of them were from the 33rd District, but I had just been downtown that morning and walked through the offices. There was a good chance somebody might either say something to me that would give me away, or that some look of recognition on their faces would tip off Dillon or Gordon that something was up.

"Is that it?" one of the detectives called out to Gordon as we reached the door.

"Yeah. These are all the pinsetters we've got working tonight. They're all here."

One of the detectives showed us his badge and identified himself as Detective Kenneth Lewis. He told us he and his fellow officers wanted to ask all the employees whether they had ever seen the Peterson or Schuessler boys.

It was useless to try to hide behind the other pinsetters. I would only draw attention to myself and one of the detectives would make a beeline straight for me. Instead, I tried to act like the other pinsetters, bored and a little pissed off that we were losing money standing here waiting to be interviewed.

Detective Lewis looked over to where we were all standing, and for a brief second his eyes stopped and looked straight at me.

Oh, shit, I thought. Here we go.

Immediately, I made eye contact with Lewis and purposely shifted his glance toward the front doors of the bowling alley, hoping he would get the message that this grubby pinsetter wanted to talk to him, but not in front of his fellow employees.

Lewis kept staring, at first wondering what this shifty-eyed bum was looking at. Then he suddenly barked out, "You three guys come outside with me." Then he turned to the detective standing to his left. "Dave, you and Phil take statements from the rest of these people. I'll question these guys outside where I can hear myself think."

I felt my entire body relax. My fellow officer got the message and was doing what I had done a hundred times before when I had a feeling that someone wanted to talk to me alone, but not let anyone else know about it.

We followed Lewis toward the front door of the bowling alley. "You two stay here," he said pointing to me and one of the other pinsetters. He opened the door and led the third man out to the top landing of the stairs.

After a few minutes, Detective Lewis opened the door and said, "Okay, next." The man Lewis had questioned walked back into the bowling alley, and I stepped out onto the landing and let the door close behind us.

"What's your story, pal? What do you know?" Lewis asked impatiently, his eyebrows narrowing into a suspicious frown.

I looked over the detective's shoulder and down the steep flight of stairs to be sure no one was coming up.

"I'm a detective working undercover for the 33rd District trying to find out the same thing you guys are." I noticed a sudden change of expression on Lewis's face as I gave him information about what I'd seen since I started working there. "I can't believe you guys are over here. Why didn't you check with Sgt. Murphy at the 33rd District?"

"For Christ sake," Lewis muttered, barely able to control his frustration. "We got sent out here from downtown. We're checking out bowling alleys in the city. The Sheriff's Office is checking them out in the suburbs. Guess a few wires got crossed. I had a hunch this was probably the first place you guys would check out. But hell, we just follow orders. You know how that goes."

"Yeah, well you better tell your 'bull dick' to give Sgt. Murphy a call. Nobody except him Lt. Deeley, Capt. Corcoran, and my partner know about me being here."

"Listen, you better go back in there. I'll ask your buddy inside to come out here and answer a few questions so you can stay covered. My guys and I will stick around for a little while so nobody suspects anything, then we'll get out of here. By the way, good luck."

I nodded, turned and opened the door to the bowling alley. I walked in and joined the rest of the pinsetters standing next to Gordon and Dillon at the front desk. After a few minutes, Lewis and the last pinsetter he interviewed on the landing came in and walked up to the employees standing with the two other detectives.

"These guys can go back to work," Lewis told Dillon as he pointed to me and the other pinsetters. "We still want to talk to a few people before we go, but let 'em start bowling again."

The other pinsetters and I hurried down to the far lane and walked quickly along the narrow catwalk between the last alley and the wall of the large, smoke-filled room.

In a few minutes the room began to fill with a familiar noise: muted thuds and soft rumblings of bowling balls combined with the sound of wooden pins clacking against each other.

Tuesday
October 25, 1955

The day started too early. After finishing my shift at the Monte Cristo the night before, I went home and had a bite to eat. I fell asleep right after watching the late news on television.

For the past seven days, the lead story of every news program was about the progress of the investigation of the Peterson-Schuessler murders. Once or twice, I had even seen myself for a few seconds in short film segments the television stations used to supplement the most current news items about the case. Some of the film clips showed the front entrance of the 33rd District. Others showed frames of home movies of one of the boys taken a few months before his death.

It seemed as if everyone had a theory about who had perpetrated the crime. All that was lacking was any physical evidence pointing to specific individuals. That certainly didn't stop people from voicing their opinions.

Coroner McCarron was sticking to his theory about the possibility that teen gangs committed the murders. One of the psychologists from the Circuit Court of Cook County Psychiatric Institute reiterated his belief that a sexual deviant had committed the crimes. It seemed that every politician also wanted to put his two cents, and his face, in every available television camera or newspaper photo while he editorialized on the outrage everyone felt about the crime.

Although very few people said it for the record, there was

a growing sense of frustration with local, state, and federal law enforcement agencies and our failure to apprehend the killer or killers.

The families of the slain boys had been cooperative and patient throughout the ordeal. But Anton Schuessler, Sr. came right out and said it.

"This isn't the first time this happened," Mr. Schuessler told the press. "What about the other boys they found dead? What is it going to take to get these criminals locked up?"

Schuessler was referring to the murder of Peter Certik, a 14-year old boy who resided in suburban Bannockburn. His body was found on September 12 near Libertyville, Illinois, north of Chicago. An autopsy determined that he had been strangled, just like the Peterson and Schuessler boys.

On August 14, the body of an Evanston boy, Peter Gorham, age 12, was found near Muskegon, Michigan. The boy disappeared on July 5, 1955 from a Boy Scout camp near Muskegon, and the local coroner reported that the cause of death was a gunshot wound.

I knew about those cases. I'd read the reports of the meetings with the police investigators who came down from Michigan after the bodies of the Peterson and Schuessler boys were found. Detectives investigating the murders had also been in contact with local law enforcement agencies and investigators concerning the case in Bannockburn. Those two cases had provided little more physical evidence than the present investigation. There was no basis to believe those murders were related to the murders of the boys.

But I didn't need to read between the lines of newspaper stories to know about the growing fear and frustration of the public. I heard it in the sound of the voices of my neighbors, from friends who weren't police officers, and from my own family.

"How's the investigation going? Do you have any suspects?" they would ask. They were starting to sound like the reporters Frank and I had to deal with every time we came out of the station.

7: 45 a.m.
Gale Street Station

Frank was already at his desk when I walked into our office. Even at this hour of the morning, a cloud of cigar smoke hung in the room. An El Producto cigar was in the ashtray next to Frank's Underwood typewriter, and a thin veil of smoke danced across the keys as he punched out the first of his daily reports.

"Mornin', Jim. How was work last night?"

I took off my overcoat and hung it on the wooden coat rack behind the door. I grabbed a small pile of phone messages from the top of my desk and began flipping through them.

"Some guys from downtown stopped by. Almost ruined the whole thing. I've got to let Murphy know as soon as he gets in," I continued to read the scribbles on the thin slips of paper.

"He's already in," Frank said as he grabbed the cigar from the ashtray and jabbed it into the right side of his mouth. "He just went in to see the Captain to get him up to speed on what's been going on. By the way, we got the polygraph results back on your buddy from the Chicago Theater. The guy came up clean on the homicide, but not a hundred percent on other stuff they asked him. Who knows what he does when he's not tryin' to pick up cops. Duffy and me also checked out the bar where the guy works. Same thing...guy's a little strange. But plenty of people know where he was last week, and it wasn't at Robinson's Woods."

10:35 a.m.

"Jim, Sgt. Murphy wants to see you in his office right away," said the uniformed officer who stood in the doorway while I was on the phone. The officer waited for some indication that he had been heard. I looked up and nodded while I spoke quickly into the phone and jotted down a few numbers in my notebook. The officer nodded back then disappeared into the narrow corridor.

After putting my small notebook into the inside pocket of my suit coat, I got up from the desk and headed toward Murphy's office. As it had been for the past week, the hallway leading to the reception area was crowded with detectives and uniformed officers, clerks, and other personnel. I walked past two clerks waiting outside Murphy's office, their arms loaded with files: the most recent reports from downtown and the daily reports generated at the District.

"What's up, Murph?" I said, walking into the sergeant's office.

"Take a seat, Jim. I'm going over a report here I just got from Spiotto and the unit downtown." Murphy didn't look up, but instead kept his eyes on the folder in front of him. He flipped back and forth through the pages then bent the upper right hand corner of one and finally looked up.

"Looks like we got something here," he said.

Spiotto's unit at headquarters received a call from a Mr. and Mrs. Frank Kruell. They saw Dahlquist's picture in the evening newspaper after he left the 33rd District station. Mrs. Kruell told Spiotto that she and her husband had seen him with one of the Schuessler brothers in July of this year.

"Lt. Deeley is picking them up and taking them downtown. They live nearby, and Spiotto said they sounded very certain about what they told him. I'm on my way downtown to meet them and I'll let you know what happened when we're done."

"Right, Sarge."

2:25 p.m.
Police Headquaters

Lt. Deeley interviewed Mr. and Mrs. Kruell along with Sgt. Murphy. The Kruells were an older couple, in their mid-fifties. They had one daughter who was married, and lived by themselves in a home on the west side of the city, just across the southern boundary of the area covered by the 33rd Police District.

Mrs. Kruell told the detectives that on July 23, 1955 at about 1:00 p.m., she and her husband were out for a walk on Irving Park Road and the Des Plaines River, not far from Robinson's Woods parking lot. They were about one hundred yards away from a bridge, which crossed the Des Plaines River in the forest preserve, when they noticed a brand new bicycle parked in the middle of it.

As they crossed the bridge, she recalled that her husband remarked to her that it was very odd for a new bicycle to be left unattended. Mrs. Kruell stated that she remembered telling her husband that perhaps the bicycle belonged to someone who was fishing in the river. She told the detectives that once she and her husband had reached the bicycle, she leaned over the railing of the bridge and looked down at the riverbank.

She said she stared right into the face of a man and a boy, and was so frightened at seeing someone so unexpectedly that she screamed. What she said she saw just before she screamed also frightened her.

The detectives noticed that Mrs. Kruell's face became noticeably flushed and red at this point. She turned to her husband, and Mr. Kruell patted her arm and reassured her that she must tell everything that she had seen.

Mrs. Kruell averted her eyes as she began to speak again with an embarrassed look on her face. Speaking very slowly and purposefully, she told the detectives that she had seen a boy and a man engaging in a sexual act. When she screamed the man ran away into the woods while the boy remained standing on the riverbank.

After telling her husband what she had seen, he told her that they should leave the forest preserve immediately. They both walked to a tavern at River and Irving Park Roads, just beyond the limits of the forest preserve, where they had a glass of beer and tried to calm themselves. They left the tavern and were waiting for a bus just down the street. The couple waited nearly an hour for the bus. Within this period of time, they saw the same man walking with the boy who had the bicycle. The boy walked the bicycle right past them and cut across the street.

Feeling uneasy, Mrs. Kruell told her husband that she didn't want to wait any longer, and they walked east on Irving Park and took the bus at a stop well into the city limits.

Lt. Deeley then showed Mrs. Kruell photographs of the boys and asked if she had seen any of them. She pointed to the picture of Anton and said he was the young boy she had seen under the bridge that day in July.

"Lieutenant, can I speak with you for a minute?" Murphy asked. He got up from his chair and both he and Lt. Deeley walked into the hallway.

"I know this lady saw something from the way she talks about it, blushing and everything. I doubt she's making it up," Murphy told

Lt. Deeley. "But the fact that she saw pictures of Dahlquist and the Schuessler boy in the paper could be a problem."

Deeley nodded his head in agreement. "You're right, Murph. She could have seen something in the forest preserve, then she sees pictures in the paper, sees that the bodies were found close to where she saw the man and the boy, and puts it all together into a story she believes really happened. See if we got anything on either Mrs. Kruell or her husband. From what I've seen, they look like pretty upstanding citizens. But let's cover all the bases. Ask them if they can stick around for a while."

During the first seven days of the investigation, teams of detectives and uniformed officers continuously generated reports and canvassed the neighborhoods on the city's north side. Reports were filed each day at police headquarters and at the 33rd District. The paperwork was reviewed and select items were cross-referenced and categorized.

The names and current addresses or locations of individuals with prior histories of sex offenses were one major category. In addition, reports of unsolved cases of assault, battery, and sex crimes were also indexed and categorized by date, location, district, as were the names of any suspects questioned concerning those crimes.

There was also a category for the hundreds of anonymous tips called into both units and nearly every police district in the city. Each tip was documented by date, time received, general subject, and assigned to a team of investigators for follow-up. Although there were hundreds of anonymous phone calls, every one was investigated. More often than not, they proved to be unfounded.

After we completed our initial interrogation, Dahlquist had been allowed to go home. But the investigating team at the 33rd District ran a background check on him. Detectives also reviewed the hundreds of reports completed, filed, and categorized by other investigators. They scanned names, dates, locations of arrest, and criminal charges in an attempt to determine if Dahlquist's name, physical description, or address had come up in the cross-referenced reports.

Detectives were also assigned to question residents living in the area where Dahlquist lived. They asked the neighbors specific questions about him: Did they know him or ever hear anything about him?

The exhaustive search paid off.

During the second day of house-to-house questioning, detectives located a young boy, Billy Dayton, who admitted that he had known Dahlquist for almost two years. The boy was initially reluctant to speak, since his parents had no idea that he had been acquainted with the much older man. But they sensed that the boy knew a lot more than he was willing to tell them in front of his parents. They asked Mr. and Mrs. Dayton if they could take Billy to the 33rd District for further interviewing.

Dayton was interviewed at the station. Present were two juvenile officers, along with Mr. and Mrs. Dayton who consented to their son being interviewed and giving a statement about Dahlquist.

Billy told the juvenile officers that he first met Dahlquist two years earlier. He had been walking down the sidewalk in his neighborhood with one of his friends when a man in a 1953 Hudson pulled over to the curb. His friend knew the man and said that the man lived in the neighborhood. They got into Dahlquist's car and "just drove around."

The boy recounted how he and the friend had taken rides with Dahlquist in his car several times. Dahlquist would buy beer for the underage boys, and on one occasion they drove out to Fox Lake in the far northwest suburbs to go ice fishing.

After several hours of questioning, Billy became less anxious about being asked specific questions concerning his relationship with Dahlquist. In order to minimize the parents' reaction to explicit questions concerning any sexual contact between Billy and Dahlquist, I was given the task of talking to the parents in private and preparing them for what the officers were almost certain they would hear from Billy.

He admitted to having engaged in sexual acts with Dahlquist. The last time was two months before, in July, on a bridge at the Edgebrook Golf Course.

Mr. and Mrs. Dayton signed a criminal complaint charging Dahlquist with violating Chapter 38, Paragraph 131 of the Illinois Criminal Code, known at the time as "Crime Against Nature (Sodomy)."

6:25 p.m.
Police Headquarters

"Why are you guys bugging me? I already told you, I don't know anything about those three kids that were killed. I was home all night. Ask my mother."

Dahlquist was sitting in a worn gray metal chair next to a desk in the detectives' office. He had been picked up at his home and brought downtown.

Several detectives gathered and stared at Dahlquist, his left hand securely cuffed to a thick steel ring. Detective Larson was seated at his desk punching the keys on his typewriter finishing a report.

"For Christ sake, shut up. I'm working here," Larson shouted at the man seated a few feet from him. The detectives gathered around began to laugh at Larson's outburst then suddenly grew quiet and backed away as Spiotto made his way through the group.

"Okay, guys, I'm sure you're as busy as I am, so what do you say you finish those reports I'm supposed to read," Spiotto said with a smile.

"Mr. Dahlquist, I would like you to come with me."

At the mention of his name, Dahlquist sat up straight in his chair and pulled at the handcuff holding his left hand. Spiotto conferred privately with Larson. The detective stood up, pulled out a key then reached over and unlocked one link of the cuffs. He clicked the open cuff over the man's other wrist and pulled him carefully to his feet.

"Won't hurt a bit, I promise," Larson said with a smile. Spiotto led Dahlquist past the police officers and clerks, out the doors then down a hallway. The men walked silently to a separate area of the building to a small, sparsely furnished room.

"What's going on?" Dahlquist asked. "What are we doing here?"

Spiotto turned to Dahlquist and unlocked the handcuffs. "You're not going anywhere yet. Just stand up straight and wait here." Soon several other men joined Dahlquist. They were told to stand along the wall and face the mirror.

7:05 p.m.

"You want to tell us everything, Mr. Dahlquist?"

Larson tapped his pen on a pad of paper and looked at him, seated in a chair. The man was rubbing his left wrist with his right hand and appeared not to have heard the question. Standing across from Dahlquist were Spiotto and Murphy.

"Before you do," he continued, "we have to tell you that you were positively identified as the man who had sexual relations with a young boy in the forest preserve out by Irving Park Road and the Des Plaines River last July. Oh, and we have another complaint against you. You know Billy Dayton, don't you?"

The mention of Billy Dayton's name got Dahlquist's full attention. He stopped rubbing his wrist then looked up at the detectives looking back at him.

"Wait...wait. Okay. Yeah, I know Billy. But I don't know anything about those boys. Billy lives in the neighborhood. We goofed around a few times in my car."

"Goofed around?" Larson shouted at him. "Listen, you better tell us everything you did with Billy Dayton and anybody else. You're 31 years old and you're "goofing around" with minors? You're being charged with a felony, Dahlquist, Crime Against Nature. Get it? And we think that's not the only thing you've done. So you better lay it all out for us right now!"

Dahlquist began to talk. He admitted having sex with Billy Dayton on the bridge in the Edgebrook Golf Course. He also admitted that he had known Billy for approximately two years and had engaged in sexual relations with other boys for several years. He was adamant; however, in his denial that he ever knew any of the Peterson or Schuessler boys.

He went on to tell the detectives that he owned a Buick automobile, not a Hudson as Billy Dayton had described. Yes, he had purchased beer on several occasions for young boys and had taken them up to Fox Lake and other places.

The interrogation of Dahlquist went on for several hours. Dahlquist's arrest record and the reports, which had been completed after he was brought in for questioning, were reviewed.

By the time Murphy returned to the District, my partner and I were nearing the end of our shift.

"We put that guy on the lie box last week, remember Murph?" I said. "We got no positive response when the examiner asked him about the Peterson or Schuessler boys, but the examiner did say Dahlquist wasn't 100 percent honest. Maybe what he's telling us now is what he was hiding from us."

Murphy agreed. "That's what I think, too, Jim. We're seeing this an awful lot in this investigation. When we put these suspects on the box, we get mixed results. The examiner knows the guy's not honest, but we can't put a finger on it. It's like they're hiding all this weirdo shit they're doing, then we wonder if they're hiding something about the Peterson-Schuessler case"

"Yeah, but this guy Dahlquist's got to be looked at real close. He lives in the same neighborhood as the boys, "goofs around" with minors, has prior sex offense charges, and hangs out in the forest preserve. Let's check his house again, talk with his parents and people he works with. He's not going anywhere now, at least until he gets to court tomorrow. Even then, he shouldn't be let out on bond."

"I hope not," Murphy said. "But you never know."

Wednesday
October 26, 1955
12:17 p.m.

"So what happened?" Frank asked. He looked up from the files scattered on the desk in front of him and in the direction of the open door of the detectives' office. He noticed that I had already taken off my overcoat but still had my hat on. My charcoal gray Borsalino fedora was spotted with small dots of water where the rain hit it as I raced into the station house. I carefully took off my hat and let it drop on one of the hooks of the coat rack.

"The judge let Dahlquist out on a $10,000 bond. Murphy's pissed off, Spiotto's pissed off, and I'm not too happy about it either." I walked to my desk and sat down hard on the chair.

"Who was the judge?

"Judge Emitt Morrissey. Dahlquist's parents were there, and they were cryin'…his lawyer made a big deal out of the fact that we didn't have anything solid on him for the Peterson-Schuessler kids, and that the charges were only about the one kid."

"Only? What the hell's that all about? This guy admitted he's a child molester. Now he gets to hang out in the forest preserves again?" Frank stubbed out his cigar in the ashtray already overflowing with remains of a half-dozen other cigar butts.

"The guy's parents put up their house as security. I guess the judge doesn't think Dahlquist is going to skip town and leave his parents out in the street." I reached across my desk and picked up the Dahlquist file, flipped it open and reviewed the notes and reports I, and the other detectives, had made during questioning of the suspect.

"Listen, Frank, all we can do is keep looking at this guy." My eyes darted across the pages of the reports and back up at Frank. "Lots of people must have known Dahlquist from the golf courses he worked at. Let's check them out before he goes back to court. He's got a continuance 'til November 23. If we work on it, maybe we can come up with something so the judge can change his mind about letting the guy out on bond.

"How about getting out there right now?" Frank didn't wait for an answer but instead stood up and headed toward the office door. "I've been doing these reports since I got here this morning. Besides, it's raining out, and I don't think there'll be too many duffers out on the links today. Where do you want to start?" Frank already had his coat on and began to walk down the narrow hallway to the back entrance of the station.

I was caught short by his rush to leave the office and quickly scooped up a small pile of phone messages and a manila folder containing the notes from the Dahlquist interrogation. I grabbed my hat and coat and raced to catch up with him.

"Jesus, Frank, wait a minute. I think we should start at Tam O'Shanter Country Club out in Niles," I said as we walked down the short flight of steps to the parking lot.

Frank nodded and kept moving toward the unmarked squad car.

"Dahlquist said that he was working there as a caddy. I don't think he'll be there today. The guy's probably still shook up from being in court this morning."

We got in the squad car and sped off, heading north on

Milwaukee Avenue toward the edge of the city limits and the suburb of Niles.

Tam O'Shanter Country Club was located about a mile past the northern edge of the city. Its members included doctors, lawyers, as well as individuals considered to be in the top management of organized crime in Chicago. Over the years, the club had been the site of numerous national golf tournaments, especially the Western Open.

Most of the caddies at the club were older high school and college students who liked golf and were interested in making some money during the summer months. Another attraction was that the club allowed the caddies to play a free round of 18-holes on Mondays when the course was closed.

Frank turned into the entrance of the club and stopped at the small, wooden guardhouse halfway up the driveway. It had just started to rain again as we looked out at the parking lot. There were very few cars.

He rolled down his window and showed his badge to the man standing inside the small guardhouse. The man looked down for a second at the badge, then back up and leaned down to peer into the squad car.

"He's with me," Frank said as he pointed at me. The guard nodded and waved the car through.

"Where do they get those guys?" Frank laughed as he moved the car into one of the scores of empty parking spaces and turned off the ignition.

"Don't laugh, Frank. I think he used to be with the Department. And we might be looking at his job if we don't come up with something pretty soon on this case."

We got out of the car and walked to a white frame building not much larger than a two-car garage located at the far end of the parking lot. A freshly painted sign identified it as the "Caddy Shack."

Two teenage boys were sitting at a picnic bench under a large green awning extending from the flat roof of the building. The screen door of the shack was held open by a set of golf clubs and Frank and I could hear the sound of a radio coming from inside.

Just as we reached the open door, a tall, thin man wearing a well-worn cap with the words "Tam O'Shanter" stitched across the front came and stopped abruptly.

My partner and I showed the man our badges and identified ourselves. "We're looking for the golf pro here. Know where he is?" Frank asked.

"That's me," the man said. "My name is Fred Seibel. Can I help you?"

The two boys turned around and were now listening intently. I looked over at them, and then asked Seibel if we could speak privately with him for a few minutes.

"Sure, come on in. Little slow today 'cause of the rain." He led us into the caddy shack, picked up the golf bag holding the screen door open, and let it shut. He put the bag down in a corner of the small room then walked over to where a radio sat on a narrow counter littered with Coke cans and paper bags. He turned the radio off and brushed the soda cans and paper bags from the counter into a large wastebasket just below it.

"Mr. Seibel, do you have a caddy working here named Charles Dahlquist?" I asked.

The man responded that, yes, Dahlquist worked as a caddy at the club, but no one had seen him since last week. He went on to say, that he had heard some of the caddies talk about seeing Dahlquist's picture in the newspaper the week before and that he himself had read about Dahlquist's arrest.

"The club members really got crazy over that whole thing," Seibel said. "My boss told me not to let Dahlquist come back. Like I said, nobody's seen him since last week. So I don't know what else I can tell you."

Frank and I asked about how long Dahlquist had worked at the club and were told that he had worked there as a caddy for about four years, on and off. I asked if there was a list of caddies who had worked at the club during the past season.

"Sure. Just a minute." Seibel disappeared into another small room just behind the counter and rummaged through a desk at the far end of the room. He came back with a typewritten list and handed it to me.

"That's a list of every caddy who worked here this year. Most of them quit right after Labor Day to go back to school."

I looked at the list of thirty names. Before each name was a series of numbers, then the name of the caddy, and his address and telephone number. "What's the number just in front of these names?"

"That's the point system. Each caddy gets points every time they go out on the course. They get more points if they caddy a foursome alone. The guys with the most points get to work as caddies for the big tournaments like the Western Open. You know, for the golfers on the tour who don't have their own caddies."

I nodded as if I was well aware of how this all worked, but I had never played a round of golf in my life. Growing up in the Garfield Park area, the only guys with clubs were loan sharks looking for gamblers behind on their weekly payments.

"How about Dahlquist? Did he ever caddy one of the tournaments?"

"Sure. He was always in the top ten, but that's probably 'cause he was a lot older than most of the caddies. They'd start the season late because they're still in school."

I asked if we could take the list and make a copy. "I'll see that you get it back tomorrow. In the meantime, if you remember anything else about Mr. Dahlquist, we'd appreciate hearing from you."

Seibel responded that he would be happy to help the detectives any way that he could.

We made a copy of the list of caddies. Most of them attended local high schools and colleges in the Chicago area on the north side of the city or in the northern suburbs.

For the next several days, teams of detectives interviewed each young man on the list. Most of them recalled either knowing or caddying with Dahlquist. What the detectives learned from their interviews with the caddies, as well as the meticulous records kept by the caddy master at the country club, was that Dahlquist's account of how he spent the days of October 16–17 appeared to be accurate. His statement that he was caddying at Bob 'O Link Country Club in Highland Park, Illinois until 4 p.m. on the eighteeth of October was also verified.

But the only people who could corroborate Dahlquist's statement of where he spent the evening of October 17 were his parents. We considered what had been learned about Dahlquist: his admissions about contacts with young boys; that he lived not far from the Peterson and Schuessler boys; the discrepancies in his answers to our questions during interrogation of him; and his identification by Mrs. Kruell as the man she saw with the boy just months before the murders. All this was balanced against what Mr. and Mrs. Dahlquist had told detectives about being with their son.

The unit continued to regard him as one of the prime suspects.

During the course of the interrogation of the caddies at the country club, detectives found a young man who could not recall ever seeing Dahlquist. But he did reveal something investigators believed deserved attention.

William Melford had just started his sophomore year at a local college. He was an above-average student, commuted to school from his home, and worked part-time two evenings each week in the school library. When Detectives Edward Nucio and Jeffrey Wolfe interviewed him on October 26, 1955, they sensed something about the way Melford answered their questions. He wasn't evasive nor did he appear to be less than honest with the detectives. But there was an underlying uneasiness in his demeanor and facial expressions, which both detectives noticed.

Convinced that Melford was telling the truth about not ever having met Dahlquist, Detective Nucio began asking more general questions in an effort to determine what made the detectives believe he was hiding something.

They talked about his new course in school, how much money he had earned that summer from caddying, and how he liked his new part-time job. The subject then turned to his supervisor at the library. He got along with him fine, the young man said.

Nucio noticed small beads of perspiration appear on the young man's upper lip, then across his forehead. He saw the man shift nervously in his seat then begin to tremble. Finally his face tensed up, and he began to cry.

Melford told the detectives about his supervisor. How he had lured Melford to his apartment downtown on the pretext of wanting to show the young man some rare manuscripts he had collected while studying in Europe. When Melford met with his supervisor at his apartment, he told the detectives he was coerced into posing for nude pictures. He wasn't the only one who had done this. His supervisor had shown him dozens of similar pictures of other young men and boys.

Nucio and Wolfe asked Melford for the name of his supervisor, but he was reluctant to tell them.

"I can't do that. I don't want to get thrown out of school. He's the chief librarian, and I'm just a student. Can't you just forget about what I said? He didn't hurt me or anything," Melford said. He was starting to tremble again and the fear in his voice was something both detectives had heard before from victims of sex crimes. The victims were often afraid. They were embarrassed. They were both relieved and sorry that they had ever told anyone about what had happened to them.

Detective Wolfe leaned toward the young man and spoke softly, but in a firm tone of voice.

"Listen, William, we didn't come here to hurt or embarrass you. We're here investigating the murders of three young boys. I don't know if your supervisor knows anything about it, but that's not for you to decide. You're not going to be punished for anything."

Melford straightened up in his chair and wiped away the tears in his eyes.

"His name's Detmer. Richard Detmer," the young man said quietly.

4 p.m.
Park Ridge, IL

In the days immediately following the discovery of the bodies of the boys, Captain Corcoran had instructed several teams of detectives to conduct an intensive search of a two square mile area next to Robinson's Woods. The area consisted of a farm, several riding stables, and a few residential homes at the edge of the forest preserve.

Among those individuals interviewed were two people who had called the 33rd Police District and reported that they had heard screams coming from the area of the forest preserves on the night of October 16. Murphy assigned Frank and me to interview two residents of suburban Park Ridge who claimed to have heard these screams.

The Salerno's lived in a tri-level home with an open breezeway connected to the house. Directly west of the Salerno home, two doors away, lived Mr. Stanley Panek. Both Mr. Salerno and Mr. Panek called the District after the bodies of the boys had been found and reported that they had each heard screams coming from the forest preserve on Sunday night.

I interviewed Mr. and Mrs. Salerno, who recounted that Mr. Salerno had been talking to a neighbor when they heard the first scream. Then, they heard another scream. Both recalled that they thought it might have been an animal or possibly some teenagers who were known to hang out in the forest preserves at night.

But a few days later Mr. Salerno ran into Mr. Panek, who also heard the screams. They both decided to report this to the 33rd District.

Mrs. Salerno told me she had heard two screams, the first one loud and piercing. It sounded like a frightened scream, and she had gone into the house. Then she told us about the second scream she heard, after she had been convinced by her husband to come back outside. Both voices sounded to her like a younger voice.

"From what direction do you think the screams came?" I asked her.

"Definitely from the fields south of our house and a little to the west. Somewhere around the stables," she said.

"What stables?" I asked.

"The Idle Hour Stables, at Cumberland and Higgins Road."

Two other individuals who resided east and south of the Salerno home also reported hearing screams on the night of October 16. Although they could not be sure from which direction they heard the screams, they believed that the sounds came from just west of their homes. Their statements concerning the approximate times that they heard these sounds corresponded with the information received from the Salerno's and Mr. Panek.

After reporting the results to Captain Corcoran, he instructed us to join several other teams of detectives who were conducting interviews of persons who owned and worked at the various horse stables along Cumberland Avenue.

Frank, Officer Alice McCarthy, and I visited the Idle Hour Stable at 8600 Higgins Road. We interviewed John Lyda, who told us he worked as a night watchman at the stables and also resided on the premises. He said the stable closed on Sundays at 6:00 p.m. and that on the night of October 16, he did not hear anything unusual. We asked if we could inspect the premises, and Lyda responded that certainly we could.

We toured the property, including the stables and the office area. We looked carefully for any indications of the presence of oily stains or heavy machinery around the area, consistent with the smudge marks left on the soles of the boys' feet. While we toured the premises, we asked Lyda about the nature of the Idle Hour's business.

This was one of several riding stables located along a stretch of Cumberland Avenue. The stables boarded private horses, made horses available to the public for rides through the forest preserve, and provided riding lessons.

In addition, he said there were five other employees who also lived on the premises. I asked him to give us the names of those employees. As he was writing the names down in his small spiral notebook, two men approached.

One had thick, white hair and a rugged face; the other was a taller, younger man.

"This is the owner, Mr. Jayne," Lyda said. This is Detective Jack, Detective Czech, and Officer McCarthy. They're investigating the killings of the three boys that were found in the woods."

My partner and I looked at the two men. The younger man looked like a bouncer. He was well built, handsome and had a smirk on his face. Jayne didn't say anything at first then turned and introduced the man he was with.

"This is one of my hired hands, Ken. Is John helping you out?" Jayne asked.

"Yeah," I answered. "We want to talk with everybody who works here."

Neither man answered. Jayne nodded his head, and he and Ken walked back across the small parking lot.

I continued the interview with Lyda and completed taking the names of the other employees Lyda said lived on the premises. I asked Lyda if we could obtain the names and addresses of the private owners of the horses who were boarded at the stables.

"I'll have to ask Mr. Jayne about that," he said. He looked past us, across the parking lot, where Jayne and the man were standing. He waved his arm. When he finally got their attention, the two men walked back over.

"Mr. Jayne," I said, "We would like a list of the private horse owners and anyone else who may have been out riding on Sunday, October 16."

Jayne's face narrowed into a deep scowl, and he turned to the man standing next to him.

"Oh, listen to this. Now we have to stop everything we're doing here and do their job for them," he said with a gruff voice. The man standing next to Jayne smiled at the sarcasm in his boss's voice.

"Hey, I don't know where all that stuff is. You'll have to call me. That's going to take a lot of time to put down on paper." Jayne shrugged his shoulders as if to say the request would be unreasonable then turned and smiled again at the employee standing next to him.

"Mr. Jayne, we're investigating a triple homicide, and the bodies were found not far from here. We'd appreciate your cooperation on this," I said. tryimg to hide my annoyance at his response.

"Like I said, give me a call, and when I got time, I'll get somebody to get that stuff together. I got to get back to work. I'm not on the city payroll."

Before I could say another word, Frank reached for my notebook and looked at it then said, "We got what we need for now, Jim. Let's get going. I'm sure Mr. Jayne will have what we need when we come back."

Jayne and his hired hand had already turned away and were walking toward the barns.

We thanked Lyda for his help and left to continue our

investigation of the other horse stables in the area. For the next several days, we interviewed the owners and employees of the Rainbow Ranch on East River Road; Maple Tree Stables; Tally-Ho Stables; and Rancho Russell Stables.

During our visit to the Happy Day Stables at 4400 N. Cumberland Avenue, we learned the owner was George Jayne, brother of Silas Jayne who owned the Idle Hour Stables that we had visited a few days earlier.

George Jayne invited us to examine any part of the premises we wished and accompanied us as we looked around the property. He told us there were about 116 horses on the premises, eighty-one of which were privately owned, ten of which were his and the rest were owned by the lessee of the property, William Kaczmarek.

The Happy Day Stables, like most of the stables we visited in the area, consisted of three barns; two corncribs; a huge hay barn; an indoor riding area, and a clubroom that was rented out for dances and parties. The public could also rent hayrides through the forest preserve.

We interviewed the employees of the stables and asked George Jayne to provide us with a list of horse owners and people who may have been on the premises or rented horses on Sunday, October 16.

George Jayne, like his brother, balked at this request. He was unwilling to volunteer this information.

Not wanting to antagonize Mr. Jayne, who had been more accommodating than his brother, Frank and I decided the records of private horse owners could be obtained either through subpoena or in a more indirect fashion.

The last stable visited during our initial investigation was the Mello-Rust Farm. It was owned by Don Gudeman, who along with one of his employees, Gene Price, and Ranger Byrne, had gone back to Robinson's Woods with Victor Livingston on the afternoon Livingston found the bodies of the boys.

At first Gudeman and Price were not cooperative when we visited them. Gudeman told us that after he and Gene Price had given their statements to other investigators both men were "roughed-up" by Sheriff's Deputies.

The ranger who came out and found the three bodies went back to call his supervisor. He left Gudeman, Livingston, and Gene Price at the scene. They got out of the car to see what was there and Gene started taking movies of the bodies. He was still taking movies when the other Rangers arrived at the scene and told him to stop.

"The Sheriff came by here a little later and wanted to know where the film was. They were like the Gestapo. They roughed us up and took the film, then they took Gene into custody and gave him the "third degree" about what he knew. They even gave him a lie detector test, but when they were satisfied he really didn't know anything other than what he already told them, they let him go.

"Both Gene and I looked at the pictures the police photographer took of the bodies, and we told the Sheriff and the Chicago Police Department guys that nobody touched the bodies before the cops came—we didn't touch anything. The pictures you guys took show exactly how we found the bodies."

"Where's the film?" I asked.

"Hell, I don't know. Last I saw it was when the Sheriff's Office took it. Gene told me that the film probably wouldn't turn out anyway. Red Heuer said the film in the camera was for indoor movies."

"What kind of asshole would take movies, for Christ sake?" I asked, shaking my head in disgust.

"Shit, I don't know. It was just that Livingston said he saw a body, and I knew Red had a movie camera. I didn't know it would be three kids out there."

November 1, 1955
4:10 p.m.

Detectives Nucio and Wolfe had obtained a search warrant for the residence of Richard Detmer, located on the north side of the city. They were parked in an unmarked squad car just south of Belmont Avenue and Lake Shore Drive and kept their attention focused on the apartment building on the southwest corner of the intersection.

They had visited the college library earlier that afternoon, and observed Detmer as he sat at a large desk behind the main counter on the first floor of the library. They watched him from their seats in the general reading room for nearly forty-five minutes as he instructed several students and library employees concerning new acquisitions for the library's history section.

The two men had been sitting in the squad car for nearly an hour, waiting for Detmer to arrive at his apartment. Suddenly, Detective Nucio poked Wolfe in the ribs.

"There he is," Nucio said.

Detective Wolfe sat up and looked straight ahead through the windshield. Detmer had just come around the corner and was headed directly toward them.

"Let's give him five minutes, then we'll go up and see what he's got in the apartment," Wolfe said. He watched as Detmer entered the front door of the apartment building.

A few minutes later, both men got out of the squad car, went to door and entered the building. The building's doorman met them at a second set of double doors. Detective Nucio showed the man his badge, asked him what apartment Richard Detmer lived in, and asked the man to go with them into the elevator and up to the 10th floor. After getting the doorman's name, Wolfe asked if there was only one entrance to Detmer's apartment and was told every apartment had only one way in and out.

When they reached apartment 1016, Wolfe told the doorman to wait by the elevator until he was told to go back downstairs. Nucio stood with his back to the wall right next to the door and reached his arm across and knocked on the door, announcing his name and office and that they had a warrant to search the premises.

Wolfe and Nucio heard the muffled sound of a door slam shut from inside the apartment and stared angrily back at the doorman ten steps behind him, holding the elevator door open.

"There better not be another way out of there," Nucio shouted in the direction of the elevator. The doorman shook his head, then ducked into the elevator and peered around the open door. "Wait down in the lobby and send that elevator back up here," Nucio ordered.

A few seconds later, the door to the apartment opened slightly and Detectives Wolfe and Nucio burst inside, knocking Richard Detmer to the floor.

"We've got a warrant to search the premises. Stay on the floor and don't move," Nucio shouted, as he stood over the man and gave him a menacing look.

Detective Wolfe began searching the living room first then went into the bedroom. He emerged a few minutes later with several photo albums and dozens of pictures, all of young, naked boys.

"You are under arrest for production, distribution and possession of pornographic material," Wolfe said. Detmer remained on the floor of his apartment. "Get up and put your hands behind your back."

Wolfe and Nucio handcuffed him and led him to the elevator.

On the ride down, the man asked Nucio where the detectives were taking him and how long he would be there. Nucio told Detmer that they would be taking him downtown for interrogation, and then he would be placed in the lock-up and charged. Whether he would be able to post bail and in what amount would be up to the judge. If he posted a bond, he might be out in twenty-four hours. If not, he should expect to be held in Cook County Jail for a while.

"Listen, you've got to let me call my parents. They're expecting me to call them this afternoon. They'll get worried if I don't. And I don't want them to know anything about this."

"No phone calls," Nucio said. "Call them when you get out."

Detmer pleaded with the detectives. His parents would be frantic if they didn't hear from him for days while he was in the County Jail.

Wolfe asked Detmer where his parents lived, and when the man explained that they lived only a mile south of his apartment Wolfe considered giving the man a break. He looked at Nucio who was holding the man's cuffed wrists. Nucio shrugged his shoulders.

"It's on the way," he said. "As long as he doesn't give us any trouble." Wolfe nodded. The elevator door opened and the three men walked briskly through the lobby of the apartment house and out the front doors of the building. The detectives rushed down the sidewalk, practically carrying Detmer along with them to their squad car.

5:10 p.m.

Wolfe drove the unmarked car into a parking space a block away from Detmer's parents' modest bungalow located at 1237 W.

Wabansia. He kept the motor running and turned to talk with Nucio who was in the back seat with Detmer.

"So how are we going to do this, Eddy? He's not going in there by himself."

Nucio stared back at Wolfe for a few seconds.

"Listen, Jeff, this was your idea. I don't care one way or the other. You bring him up to the house." Then he turned to Richard Detmer. "You got any ideas about how you're going to explain Detective Wolfe to your parents?"

Detmer had been craning his neck and looking out the windows to see if any of his parents' neighbors could see him in the unmarked vehicle. At the sound of Nucio's question, he quickly turned his head back to face the detective sitting to his left.

"I'll just tell them you're a friend of mine from the college…that I'm going up to Wisconsin for the weekend and that you're going to give me a ride to the train station…and I stopped by to pick up some stuff I need." Detmer looked first at Wolfe, then at Nucio to see if his suggestion made sense to them.

"If you think they'll go for that. What do you think, Eddy?"

"I think we better do something or the neighbors here are going to call the local police station about three guys hanging out in a car."

"Okay, I'll take him up there," Wolfe said. "Take the cuffs off him." He turned forward in the front seat, then looked up into the rear view mirror of the car and caught Detmer's attention. "But if you make like a rabbit, we'll make sure you won't be going to Wisconsin for a long time."

"I won't," he said honestly.

Nucio reached over and undid the handcuffs while Wolfe got out of the car and came to the right rear door of the vehicle. He opened the door, Detmer slid out and both men walked slowly down the darkened sidewalk toward Detmer's parents' house.

When Wolfe and Detmer reached the front door, Nucio reached up to the overhead light and flipped the switch so the inside of the car would remain dark. He waited quietly and kept his eyes on his partner and Detmer as they waited on the front porch of the home.

After he was sure he would not be seen, he got out of the car and walked down a narrow walkway between two homes just down the block from the Detmer house. He quickly walked past a rear garage and into the alley. He counted the number of houses between where he stood and the Detmer house, then proceeded down the alley until he arrived at the small backyard.

He silently opened the back gate and walked to the rear of the house, noting that there were no other entrances to the home except the door on the back porch. He stood quietly at the edge of a short flight of stairs leading to the rear porch. He could hear the faint sounds of conversations coming from the front of the house where Wolfe and Detmer were talking with another person.

"Mom, I hope I'm not disturbing you and Dad, but I'm going up to Wisconsin this weekend and need to get a few things. This is Jeff. He works with me, and he's giving me a ride to the train."

The woman smiled and nodded at Detective Wolfe and asked him to come in.

Wolfe entered the small foyer of the home and saw that an elderly man was sitting in the living room watching television. The detective smiled at the man then turned to Detmer who was standing next to him.

"Better get what you need. Don't want to be late," he said.

Detmer said he would be down in a minute and rushed up into the darkness of a flight of stairs just to the right of the foyer.

"So you work with Richard at the college?" Mrs. Detmer asked as the two of them stood waiting in the foyer.

Wolfe had been looking up the flight of stairs then turned his head in her direction.

"Uh huh," Wolfe responded. He looked back up the flight of stairs and noticed that they remained dark, and there was no sign of light on the second floor. He heard footsteps and a door being opened at the top of the stairs.

Seconds later, a loud noise rang out, startling both Detective Wolfe and Mrs. Detmer. She went swiftly to the bottom of the stairs and shouted: "Richard! What was that noise?"

"Richard?!"

November 2, 1955
9:17 a.m.
Police Headquarters

"Jesus Christ, Eddy. What the hell happened?" Lt. Deeley paced nervously back and forth then suddenly stopped. He peered through the windows of his office and looked down at the "El" tracks running next to Police Headquarters. Detectives Nucio and Wolfe sat quietly in front of Deeley's desk, neither one wanting to be the first to speak.

"Lieutenant, we were just trying to give the guy a break," Nucio said. He hesitated a moment and looked at his partner.

"We get to the guy's apartment and find hundreds of these nude pictures," Wolfe said as he rose to his feet. He held the albums of black and white photos he and his partner had taken from Detmer's apartment, now wrapped in a clear plastic evidence bag, and placed them on Deeley's desk. "He didn't resist arrest, he was polite and quiet. He didn't want his parents to worry, so we figure, no problem. How the hell were we supposed to know he'd go up to his room and blow his brains out?"

Deeley turned away from the windows and looked at the photo albums on his desk.

"You guys go over these pictures with the unit up at Gale Street? Did they find any pictures of the Peterson or Schuessler kids in there?"

"No, Lieutenant, they didn't. Two of the guys from the 33rd District came down here last night, and we went through all of the pictures," Wolfe said.

"Did you find anything else at the Detmer house after this happened?"

"No, nothing. We searched the guy's bedroom after the technicians were done. Then we went through the whole house, the basement, the garage, everything. He kept all of this stuff in his apartment. The parents' house was clean."

Deeley sat down at his desk. He rubbed his eyes and leaned back in his chair. He stared at the two men seated across from him then leaned forward and put his hands firmly on the top of his desk.

"I read your reports. Are you sure neither one of you mentioned the Peterson-Schuessler case when you had him in custody?"

Both men shook their heads.

"Not a word, Lieutenant," Wolfe said. "We figured that would be the first thing you'd ask him when we got him back here for interrogation, and we didn't want to spook him. Then the guy shoots himself. Looks like he might be the one we've been looking for, and he took the short way out."

"Maybe," Deeley said. "Or it could be he's not who we're looking for. We have to check him out like anybody else, find out where he was the night before the boys' bodies were found or if he knew them.

"Anyway, you two know what happens now. You finish your reports; I'll review them. Then Internal Affairs has to look into what happened. I'll back you up as much as I can. Detmer's connection to the school makes this a pretty hot situation, and a lot of the details aren't going to come out. So just follow procedures and refer all inquiries you get from the press to the Department's public relations office. Got it?"

Nucio and Wolfe nodded their heads.

"Fine. We're going to interview all the people that Detmer worked with, where he spent his off hours, and look at anything else that might get us some information. I've assigned Thomasen and Gornick to do the legwork. You two guys are still assigned here, but you're off the street until this whole situation gets straightened out. Handle the phones and do whatever follow-up you can from your desks. That's it for now."

Further investigation in Detmer's background revealed a sad history of child pornography. His parents were aware of these activities, and he had been referred for counseling. A psychiatrist who had moved to Florida conducted the sessions. Through interviews with Detmer's father, it was learned that he had been treated for only two months. The psychiatrist said he was "cured" and no further intervention or observation was needed.

November 5, 1955
8:37 a.m.

"Glad you stopped by, Jim. I've got something a little sensitive that needs to be handled, and Captain Corcoran said you would be the guy to help us with it." I took my hat off and walked into Murphy's office. Instead of taking a seat, I leaned against the wall.

Murphy said there had been speculation by the media and some local residents about the parents of the boys. Every suspect in the case had been sent down for polygraph examinations after being thoroughly interrogated. Gossip and innuendo concerning why the parents had not been required to take polygraph examinations had come to the attention of Lt. Deeley, Captain Corcoran, and Cook County State's Attorney Gutknecht.

"They want the parents to go on the box?" I asked. The frown on my face only emphasized the incredulity in my voice. "That's nuts. Haven't they seen those people? Their lives are destroyed. Mr. Schuessler can barely put two words together. Frank and I have talked to the parents from the time those kids disappeared. Now we're going to treat them like suspects?"

"Jim, it doesn't matter what we think. You know how the system works. Somebody's brother or son gets picked up as a suspect then they're cleared. The relatives get pissed off, start asking 'what about the parents of the boys?' They start rumors, and it gets out of hand."

"So now what? We politely ask them 'Oh, and by the way, did you kill your sons?' Jesus, Murph." I shook my head in disbelief.

"I know, I know. But if they don't go through the routine like everybody else, it'll just get worse. Up to now, nothing's been said about it in the press. The Captain agrees with the State's Attorney that we should have them do it and end the rumors."

"And I'm the guy that has to ask them?"

"No, you don't ask them. The State's Attorney is the one who's going to ask them. You're the guy who has to set up the meeting. You're not even going to be there. Just ask the parents if they would agree to meet with the State's Attorney. He'll take it from there."

"Do I get to tell them to bring their attorneys, too? What the hell is this?"

"Take a few steps back, Jim. Everybody's a suspect in this case. Nobody gets a free pass. And it's the best thing for everyone involved here. Think about it. The only people who haven't been given polygraphs are the parents, and so far we haven't got any evidence or solid suspects. If you're a hot shot reporter on a slow day, does that sound interesting to you?"

November 8, 1955

After meeting with State's Attorney Gutknecht and agreeing to undergo a polygraph examination, Mr. and Mrs. Anton Schuessler were brought to an office at 33 N. LaSalle Street in Chicago's Loop by Lt. Walter Fleming of the Sheriff's Department. They were given separate polygraph examinations and were asked questions about the disappearance and murder of their sons and Robert Peterson.

Mr. and Mrs. Schuessler were each given two tests. It was the opinion and conclusion of the examiner that the parents neither had anything to do with the murders nor did they have any knowledge as to who might have committed the crimes.

Mr. Schuessler had agreed to take the polygraph test on the condition that it would not be made public. Sheriff Lohman gave Mr. Schuessler his word that it would remain a secret from the press, and he swore all those who had knowledge of the test to secrecy.

The parents of Robert Peterson also met with State's Attorney Gutknecht and agreed to take a polygraph exam. Mr. Peterson was anxious to be cleared and believed that it would clear up any doubt in anyone's mind that the parents had knowledge about who had committed the crimes. They, too, passed the examinations.

December 1955

Each time the investigation identified an individual who appeared to be a promising suspect the same procedure was used. Background checks were run; extensive interviews were conducted of family members, friends, acquaintances, neighbors and employers. Each interview covered the same ground: where was the suspect during the time the boys were first reported missing; where were they during the following forty-eight hours.

Then each suspect was interrogated again. Finally, every individual that detectives suspected of having any knowledge of the crime or who could reasonably be deemed a suspect was questioned at length through use of several polygraph examinations.

A posthumous investigation of Richard Detmer determined that there was ample proof of his whereabouts for the entire weekend preceding the murders as well as during the critical hours before the boys' death and the discovery of their bodies.

During this time, the media slowly began giving their front-page coverage to other news stories of the day. National and international events pushed the coverage of the Peterson-Schuessler case farther back into the pages of their local papers.

But on December 3, 1955 that changed. Another story brought the case back to center stage.

By the end of November 1955, Mr. Schuessler had become more despondent about the loss of his two sons. His physical condition deteriorated to the point where he was exhausted. From the time his sons went missing to when their bodies were found, he became increasingly withdrawn and depressed.

At times, he would vent his anger at his wife, then at his friends and family who had tried to console and support him. He would express his opinion about the inability of investigators to discover those responsible for the death of his sons in ways that surprised his friends and neighbors.

At first he had tried to continue working, hoping this would help him manage his sorrow and grief. But this, too, seemed hopeless.

Finally, he was admitted to a private psychiatric hospital not far from his home. Physicians diagnosed him as suffering from severe clinical depression.

One of the methods of treating severe cases of depression in 1955 was electroshock therapy, and Mr. Schuessler was given an initial series of treatments. While undergoing treatment, he had a heart attack. He died six weeks after the bodies of his sons were found in Robinson's Woods.

News of Mr. Schuessler's death was not unexpected by those who knew him. The news stories after his death included quotes from friends and relatives who said that "another victim has been claimed by those responsible for the deaths of Robert Peterson and Anton and John Schuessler."

A fund, established by one of the city's newspapers to help the families of the boys, received additional donations at the news of Mr. Schuessler's death. The Schuessler family fund had now increased in value to nearly $60,000.

With the death of Mr. Schuessler, Lt. Deeley and Sgt. Mulvey disclosed the information about the boys' parents taking the polygraph tests. It was wisely decided there could be benefit in letting the public know that the parents had taken the examinations and cleared of any suspicion. This ended the speculation and rumors that the parents had knowledge of who was responsible for the killings.

The news of Mr. Schuessler's death deeply affected the men in our unit. Many had young children close in age to the Peterson and Schuessler boys. We had offered our sympathy to the families at the wakes and funerals, and now we would see the Schuessler family again: still offering sympathies, but feeling discomfort and embarrassment that we could offer little else. The killer or killers were still at large.

January 16, 1956
2:47 p.m.

"What? When was he supposed to be there? Dammit!" Murphy slammed the receiver down and shot up from his chair. "Czech! Jack! Get in here!" He shouted in the direction of the open door of his office. His voice echoed for an instant through the small corridor.

Murphy's yelling had alerted us to the fact that something was wrong. We were already out of our chairs and in the corridor by the time he shouted out our names.

"What is it, Murph?" I reached the Sergeant's office before Frank, who was right behind me.

"That son of a bitch Dahlquist, he never showed up in court. Lt. Morris had Grogan and Maher, two of his guys from downtown, detailed to watch the guy all day. They kept up with him all the way down to 26th and California, followed him up to Morrissey's courtroom where he meets his lawyer in the hallway, and they leave. The asshole just walked away and disappeared. He must have spotted Grogan and Maher trailing him then made like a rabbit after they left the courtroom. Morrissey ordered his bond forfeited. His parents put up their house as bond, and now the State's Attorney wants it.

"I want you guys to get over to his house right now! They've already issued a warrant for his arrest for jumping bond and a stop order was issued for him at the Bureau of Investigations. Get his parents to give you the names of every person the son of a bitch knows."

Murphy's face was red and streaks of sweat ran down in front of his ears. He began to stomp down the hall in the direction of the Captain's office but stopped and looked back at us.

"And don't leave Dahlquist's house until Grogan and Maher get there. If it's the last thing I do on this case, those two knuckleheads are going to live in their car outside that asshole's house until we find him."

January 24, 1956
8:33 p.m.

"What do you think, Murph? The kid was held prisoner for five hours, she was abused, and whoever it was took her to a forest preserve. Thank God the only difference from the Peterson-Schuessler case is that she's still alive."

I looked up from the notes made a few hours earlier after getting off the phone with a detective from one of the western suburbs. An eight year-old girl had been abducted and molested. Our unit was alerted of the crime by the Elmwood Park Police Department, and I was reporting what little information had been received to Murphy.

"Yeah, I know. It all sounds very similar to our case. But the obvious difference is we have three boys that were abducted and killed. From what the experts downtown have been telling us, we're looking for people who are attracted to boys, not girls."

I knew all about the "experts," the psychiatrists, who had expounded on their theories of the possible motivations the killer or killers may have had.

"Sarge, don't forget we haven't got any evidence the boys were molested or sexually assaulted. From what I was told this afternoon by the Elmwood Park Police, the little girl was sexually assaulted."

"We've got three of our guys looking into this, plus a half-dozen sheriff's deputies are already on their way to Park Ridge to interview the little girl. Lt. Morris called me a little while ago and told me that headquarters is checking it out like everything else. They'll keep us informed."

"How's Joe like his new job?" I asked. Lt. Joseph Morris had replaced Lt. Deeley as head of our unit. Deeley was now Chief of Detectives.

"Joe has his hands full on this case. The Mayor, the Commissioner, the press...everybody wants it solved like yesterday. It's a good thing he was assigned to it from the beginning. He knows it hasn't been easy for any of us. We're lucky he's the boss."

February 7, 1956

The holidays had come and gone for the citizens of Chicago, and the cold, gray days of February were passing slowly. The Peterson and Schuessler families had suffered their first Christmas without their sons; the coverage of the investigation of the triple slaying continued to be pushed from the headlines by other stories; and the trail of the killer or killers became as cold as a Chicago winter.

But the detectives on the case refused to give up. Hundreds of people were interviewed, mountains of reports were generated and collated, and the monotony of combing through thousands of police files and arrest records continued.

On February 7, 1956, my partner Frank and I, accompanied by police officers Alice McCarthy and Toni Quinn, drove to the home of Mr. and Mrs. John C. Holtz, the grandparents of the Schuessler brothers. Frank and I had met Mr. and Mrs. Holtz on numerous occassions. We had also spoken with the couple several times by phone over the past few months to keep them informed about the progress of the investigation.

Mrs. Holtz told us that John and Anton would often visit them, accompanied by Mr. and Mrs. Schuessler. On occasion, the boys would go to a movie theater across the street from the Holtz home on Southport Avenue in Chicago, or visit their cousins who lived nearby on Damen Avenue. She reported that nothing unusual had ever happened during the visits the boys had with either their grandparents or their cousins.

"They didn't play with any of the children in this neighborhood.

I don't think they really knew any of them. You know, they were very well behaved and just stayed together when they visited with us here."

Mrs. Holtz told the detectives that she was especially close to Anton. "He always bragged to me that he wanted to be a priest," she said. He would often tell her about things he and his older brother did, things he was reluctant to tell his parents.

She recalled Anton telling her that he and his brother had once thrown rocks at "some bums" who lived in boxcars at the Forest Glen Station of the Milwaukee Railroad. She said Anton told her that the bums would then chase the boys along the railroad tracks and into the nearby forest preserve.

"He said one of their friends was with them. A boy named Robin." She had scolded Anton about that behavior but hadn't told the boys' parents about it.

During another visit, Anton told her the boys would often go into the forest preserves located at Milwaukee and Devon Avenue, considerably farther from their homes. She also remembered that on October 15, the day before the boys disappeared, the brothers had gone to the Natoma Bowling Alley in Niles, Illinois.

Mrs. Holtz said that despite these "childish pranks," she considered her grandsons to be fine young boys, who really never caused their parents any trouble. Although they attended a public school, they attended classes for religious instruction every Wednesday at their parish, St. Tarcissus.

Mrs. Holtz thought very highly of her son-in-law and said that Mr. Schuessler was very involved with his sons' educational and recreational activities. In fact, she said, Mr. Schuessler had just spent $1,600 to have the basement remodeled into a playroom for the boys.

On the night the boys disappeared, Mrs. Holtz said her daughter called to tell her how worried she was about the boys. Mrs. Holtz went to their home the next morning, and the first thing her daughter thought of was to visit the Natoma Bowling Alley in Niles to see if the boys had gone there.

After talking with people at the bowling alley, the two women continued to look for the boys at the many small stores located in the area. All of them were closed, Mrs. Holtz recalled. They even went through the forest preserves late that night, calling out the boys' names but to no avail.

"This has just destroyed us all," she said as her eyes began to swell with tears. "First the boys, then their father. Poor Anton, he was such a wonderful man. I went to visit Eleanor last week, around the end of February. That was so terrible. She was looking at some clothing of the boys and her husband, you know, sorting them. She picked them up and held the clothes to her chest and broke down crying. It just ripped my heart out to see her that way."

We thanked Mrs. Holtz and reminded her that if she were to remember anything else about the boys' activities, or anything else she believed might help them in the investigation, she should not hesitate to call.

It was starting to snow as the four of us left the Holtz residence and got into the parked squad car. I got behind the wheel, with Frank in the front seat and the two officers in the back seat. As the car moved slowly through the slush and ice that had piled up from an earlier snowstorm, I asked what my colleagues thought about what Mrs. Holtz had told them.

"Throwing rocks at bums?" Frank said as he cracked the passenger's side window open. "Sounds like the boys were a little more adventurous than we thought."

"They were just kids, Frank. Didn't you ever do stuff like that when you were that age? Oh, I forgot. You were born old."

"Yeah, I guess so." Frank reached into the inside pocket of his suit coat for one of his cigars. "I forgot I was talking to the youngest lightweight boxing champ of the Garfield Park area." He peeled the cellophane from a new cigar and pushed the crumpled wrapper into the ashtray in front of him.

"Come on, Frank, don't light that thing. We've got to breathe back here. Can't you wait until we get back to the station?" The firm, loud female voice from the back seat caused Frank to turn and look at the officers behind him.

"Good idea, Alice," I said glancing in the rear view mirror. "Frank,

I only beat the crap out of the punks who were picking on my friends, the Wolfson brothers. Otherwise, I was pure as the driven snow."

"I just meant to say that maybe the boys got into something that got out of control the night they disappeared. Everybody we've talked to says they were good kids. But something went wrong that night. Maybe they aggravated the wrong person. Let's go back over those interviews with the kids at the school. Maybe interview that boy Robin."

Frank put the cigar back in his pocket and rolled up the window.

March 20, 1956
8:10 a.m.

"Lt. Morris called me at home this morning," Murphy said. He looked at the faces of the group of detectives standing in the reception area. The room was crowded, as usual, and some of the men were already sipping on their second cup of coffee. Murphy got right to the point.

"Downtown got a Teletype last night about our latest missing person, Mr. Dahlquist. Seems like he's been a real traveler since he jumped bond in January. Lt. Morris said the Arizona State Police reported they found our boy's Buick in Ashford, Arizona. The car was found abandoned there about four days ago. When they ran the plates, the name "Dahlquist" came up with a Chicago address. Then the Arizona highway patrol called the Dahlquist home, and when the mother was told about the car, she asked where her son was. They got his first name, ran it, and the warrant popped up. That's when they called downtown."

One of the detectives looked up from his cup of coffee. Like the rest of us, he was bleary-eyed from too much work and not enough sleep. This latest bit of information didn't cause him to perk up. We had gotten our hopes up of finding a suspect too many times in the past few months, only to be let down when they were cleared of any link to the murders. But the detective asked the question anyway.

"Any chance they have any good leads on where Dahlquist is?"

Murphy looked back at the man. He was getting just as tired giving out the same answer.

"No, not yet. But you know what we have to do next. I'm assigning one team of detectives to visit Mr. and Mrs. Dahlquist and get their side of the conversation they had with the Arizona highway patrol. They're going to ask the parents if they have any relatives out West, if their son knows anybody out there, and the names of every one of his friends. Then the same team is going to watch their house and jot down the license plate of every car that pulls up to the house and visits them. Bill Duffy and Jim Fitzgerald get to do that."

There was no response from either of the two detectives who had just been detailed to the Dahlquist house. In a way, the assignment wasn't so bad. It kept them in one place for a few days. Watching the Dahlquist house would be boring, but at least they wouldn't have to be driving around the entire city pursuing leads. Not for a while, anyway.

The results of the interview Duffy and Fitzgerald had with the Dahlquists later that afternoon indicated that the parents didn't know where their son was. They insisted their son had not spoken with them for over two months.

"The guy lived with them, for God's sake," Duffy said to Fitzgerald as they sat watching the Dahlquist house from their unmarked car. "They posted their house for that knucklehead's bond. And we're supposed to believe that they just "wondered" what happened when he jumps bond? They never got a call from him?"

Fitzgerald took a slow sip from a thermos of coffee that had now become lukewarm during the six hours of their stakeout.

"Yeah, I know. And the car they found is registered to the father. He's still making the monthly payments on it for his son. If it were my kid who jumped bond and they were going to take my house, he'd wish the cops found him before I did."

April 21, 1956
8:04 a.m.

The meeting in Murphy's office had just begun. I was there along with Frank and Duffy. We all had our overcoats and hats on because we knew this wasn't going to last long. Two representatives of the Park Ridge Police Department were also in the meeting.

"Chief Jones of Park Ridge is in charge of the investigation. We've been assigned to assist because of the similarities of this little girl's case with the Peterson-Schuessler murders," Murphy began.

"You guys know Sgt. Schuenemann's cousin here at the District. The family's got a long history with the Department, and they go way back in police work, so we'll get along well with the Park Ridge Police on this."

On April 20 at around 3 p.m., a six-year-old girl was enticed into a car and raped. She was in fair condition at the local hospital and could not be questioned. From what the Park Ridge police were able to determine from questioning the parents, the girl said the man took her to a location where there was "lots of water and trees." The first thing we thought about was Robinson's Woods Forest Preserve. In this newest case, however, the assailant dropped the girl off a few blocks from her home after he raped her.

"Sarge, I can't understand how this little girl could have been allowed to walk home alone. It's not far from where we found the boys' bodies," I said, shaking my head in disbelief.

"I know what you mean. People in this neighborhood haven't unlocked their windows since October. They won't even let their kids go to the park alone," Murphy said. He stood up from his desk, took a few steps toward the coat rack and reached out to grab his overcoat.

"I'm going out to Park Ridge with you guys," he said as he shoved his right arm into the sleeve of his dark blue overcoat. "We can interview the girl's parents again, but the doctors said the kid's in no condition to talk to us until Monday."

We walked down the narrow corridor leading to the back exit of the station, not saying a word to each other but thinking about the most recent victim of yet another unknown assailant.

May 2, 1956
8:17 a.m.

I was just about to leave my office and follow-up on several new leads concerning the location of Dahlquist.

Just before reaching the back door, I heard someone shout my name.

One of the clerks was standing at the other end of the corridor, waving a telephone message note.

"Jim, it's from Lt. Morris. I thought you left already. He wants you downtown right now. Says it's urgent."

I walked quickly toward the officer and took the message. Jeez, I thought. Good thing I know his direct line. I couldn't read this thing for the life of me.

"Jim, glad we got ahold of you this morning." Lt. Morris was seated at his desk and looked up only briefly. He motioned for me to sit down and then stood and walked to one of the filing cabinets along the wall. He reached for several files resting on the top of one of the cabinets, opened one of them and pulled out a sheet of lined paper with scores of names on it. He handed the sheet to me.

"It's a sign-in sheet from the Garland Building on Wabash Avenue. One of the guys in the unit down here found it last night. For the last several months, we've been going over the reports of our guys taken from people all over downtown: every office building, business, department store, and small business in the Loop. Mike Flannery found this in a file on the Garland Building at 111 N. Wabash."

I looked down at the lined sheet. At the top was the date "October 16, 1955" and under it were scores of names. In columns next to the names were sign-in times from 6:00 a.m. to midnight. Next to that was a column indicating the times at which visitors had signed out.

I scanned the names until my eyes suddenly stopped, three-quarters down from the top of the page.

'9- / Robert Peterson   /6:00 /6:15'

It was a child's signature, clearly legible and having the steady hand of someone who was not in a hurry to sign his name to the lined sheet of paper.

"Do you think it could be his?" Morris asked, looking over my shoulder. "I called you because I want you to show it to Mr. and Mrs. Peterson and verify that the signature is Bobby's."

"Lieutenant, I can tell you right now that it's probably his signature. Mr. Peterson told me that his daughter's eye doctor was in the Garland Building. He said Bobby took her downtown to her appointments. It fits with what we know about him going downtown before the boys went to the Loop Theater that Sunday."

"I think so, too. But we've got to be sure it's his. Ask the parents if they have any of the boy's homework papers. Maybe check with the school and his teachers, too. It's the only thing we've got on these boys since they left home to go downtown that day." Morris walked back to his desk and sat down.

"But why would they go into the Garland Building?" I asked. "Did you talk with the doorman or whoever was on duty that afternoon?"

"Not yet. We just got his name. Flannery is out looking for the guy right now. We'll bring him in and show him the pictures, ask him if he remembers the boys. Maybe it was just Bobby Peterson who went there. At this point, we don't know. You've got to put this ahead of anything else you're doing right now, Jim so get to it. I've got a meeting with the Commissioner and the Mayor this afternoon. The way this investigation's been going, I've got to let them know about this. It's our biggest break so far. Try and get to the parents right away. Once this gets out, the papers and reporters will be all over them again."

May 5, 1956
State's Attorneys Office
26th Street & California Avenue

"It's something that's got to be done. I don't care how we do it. If the parents don't cooperate with us, we'll get a judge to order that it be done."

Cook County State's Attorney John Gutknecht paced in front of his desk. He didn't bother to look at the two men seated on the leather couch at the far end of his office. Instead, he continued to walk back and forth, emphasizing his frustration by pounding the fist of one hand into the palm of the other.

He stopped suddenly and looked out of the windows of his office for several seconds. Gutkneckt stared at the skyline of the city, barely visible through the mist of early morning.

"Six months…and what have we got? I'm telling you, we better clear up all this confusion and argument. The people of this city won't put up with it. It's bad enough we haven't found the killers. Now with all this about the autopsies, we look like the 'Keystone Kops.'" He wheeled around and looked at the men sitting on the couch.

"I'm sorry, let me be specific. You're the ones who look bad, not me. I'm just waiting for you to bring me somebody to prosecute and the evidence that will put them in the electric chair."

Gutkneckt was speaking with the authority of a man who knew how things worked, both legally and politically. Before being elected as State's Attorney, he had been in private practice for many years as a skilled and influential attorney. Among his clients had been some of the most influential and powerful people in the city. He knew how to get things done.

But this was a case unlike any he had ever had. Finding those responsible for the triple homicide had turned the city upside down. Every law enforcement agency on every level of government had expended thousands and thousands of man-hours and resources in an attempt to solve the crime. Yet not one suspect had been charged.

This latest problem just fueled his anger and frustration.

"What the hell's going on at the Coroner's Office? Who's responsible for this dissention over there? Now I read in the papers there's a 'disagreement as to the accuracy of the autopsies.' Where's that coming from?"

The two men shifted nervously on the couch.

"John, wait a minute. We made inquiries at the Coroner's Office to find out if this came from somebody who is employed there. One of our investigators works with them every day, and he knows everything that goes on over there. He doesn't think it came from anybody over there." The man looked at his colleague sitting next to him.

"Everybody's frustrated," he continued. "Some of the guys in the Sheriff's Department blame the police department for not sharing information, and vice versa. You talk to some of the detectives on the street, and they say 'the Coroner didn't give us enough.'"

"Dr. Kearns made the initial autopsies," the second man on the couch added. "Coroner McCarron agreed with the results. You know how it is, John. Everybody's an expert now that we don't have any indictments. The newspaper reporters want a target, they want to cause a stir and sell more papers. They find some wacko unemployed doctor who probably had his license pulled, and they get another theory about what the pathologists should have found. Talk is cheap."

"Maybe talk is cheap, but it does a lot of expensive damage," Gutknecht snapped back. "I've talked it over with the Coroner and the Mayor, and they told me to tell you what's been decided. What's going to happen is that the bodies of those three boys will be exhumed. In order to keep everybody happy and so as not to throw stones at any one individual or agency, it's been decided that we're going to have several people involved.

"Dr. Edwin Hirsch from St. Luke's Hospital and Dr. Alvin Bates, the Coroner's acting pathologist, will be doing the new examination. We're also going to have Dr. Kearns included on this, too. He's taken a lot of unfair criticism on this whole autopsy "controversy." Everybody agreed it's the right thing to do."

Gutkneckt walked past the two men he had been speaking to and placed his hand on the doorknob of the solid oak door to his office, his way of telling them that the meeting was over.

"When all that talk about the parents of the boys not taking a polygraph test started circulating, we dealt with it head on," Gutkneckt said. "We asked them if they would submit to a test and that ended all the talk about the parents. We're going to do the same thing with this issue about the autopsies. I'm going to call the boys' parents myself, and I'm sure that they'll cooperate with us just as they have all along."

May 22, 1956
Park Ridge, Illinois

In conjunction with Sgt. Schuenemann and Detective Christensen of the Park Ridge Police Department, Frank and I continued to search for the assailant who abducted and sexually assaulted the young girl one month earlier. Through interviews with her and two other young girls, whom the assailant tried to abduct before her, we were able to piece together what happened.

The first girl he approached was about ten years old and waiting for traffic to clear before crossing the street.

"Excuse me," the man called out. He was approximately fifty years old, with long strands of gray and black hair covering his ears. He wore farmers' overalls and a blue shirt. She could also see that the man was wearing a small hat, which didn't seem to fit.

What the little girl noticed most of all, however, was his long sharp nose. It reminded her of a comedian her father liked to watch on television, Bob Hope.

"Could you tell me where Higgins Road is?" the man asked.

"It's that way," she said, and pointed to her right. "I think it's about five more blocks."

At first she thought the man hadn't heard what she said. He didn't move but instead kept staring at her.

"Do you need a ride home?" he asked.

The girl turned away and looked at the passing traffic in front of her.

"I could give you a ride," the man said, a little more forcefully this time, but still in a friendly tone of voice.

The girl heard him, but did not look back in his direction. Instead, she quickly walked into the street after the last of a line of cars had passed and then quickly ran the rest of the way across the busy street.

As she glanced over her right shoulder, she saw him make a quick right turn and disappear in the direction of Higgins Road.

Just ten minutes later, Melody Rice had left school an hour early than usual. The children in her class were dismissed at 2:00 p.m. so that they could prepare for their confirmation the following Sunday. Melody had stayed up late the previous night preparing her dress and shoes so that everything would be ready for the services. Not needing to prepare her clothes, she decided to sell her Girl Scout cookies instead.

Melody was standing at an intersection two blocks away from her home when she noticed an old, dark car come to a stop a few feet away from her. She heard a voice call to her from inside the car.

"How much are the cookies?"

Melody turned and looked behind her. A hand grasping a dollar bill stuck out of the passenger's window. She reached into a shopping bag resting on the sidewalk next to her and pulled out three boxes of cookies, one of each kind. Boxes in hand, she ran up to the open window.

"Forty cents," she said.

"Here, give me a box. The mint ones." The man said as he stretched out his hand.

Melody took the dollar, gave the man the box of cookies, and was about to ask him to wait until she could go back to the shopping bag for his change.

"Don't worry, keep the change," the man said. "I know where you can sell a lot of those cookies. Let me drop you off at Canfield and Higgins. There are lots of stores there and more people than at this corner here."

"No thanks," the girl said. "I'm not supposed to go that far without my parents with me." She turned and walked quickly to the corner to retrieve her shopping bag then started to walk in the direction of her home.

She heard the gears of the car engage and the sound of the motor fade away behind her as it pulled toward the intersection and turned the corner.

But as she approached her house, out of the corner of her eye, she saw the car again. It slowed down for a moment, then sped up as she raced up the sidewalk. The car turned quickly around the corner and disappeared.

Instead of running up the front steps of her house, Melody cut across the lawn of her neighbor's house, ran along the side of their garage then into her own backyard. She ran up the back steps and pounded on the back door until it opened, and she heard her mother's startled voice.

"What's the matter, honey?

Linda Madison was on her way home from school. She had left with three of her friends. The four young children lived a few blocks away from each other. They said goodbye to one another as they reached their homes. Each child had hurried inside so as not to miss a popular television program, which began each weekday at 3:30 in the afternoon.

Linda lived the furtherest and was walking the short distance to her home alone. Only blocks from reaching home, a dark car pulled up to the curb next to her.

"Excuse me, I'm looking for Glen Lake Avenue. Do you know where that is?"

Linda walked slowly toward the car. She could see an older man wearing overalls and a blue shirt sitting behind the wheel.

The man shifted into park and moved across the front seat toward the open window. He reached up to the dashboard and grabbed a box of Girl Scout cookies. He opened the box, removed a cookie, and began eating it. Then he held the box out through the open window of the car. "Here, take one for yourself."

Linda reached up but couldn't get her hand into the box of cookies, they were just beyond her reach. He drew the box back through the window and opened the passenger door with his other hand.

"Here you go, now you can reach." He drew the box towards himself, and Linda had to take a small step into the front of the car.

Fortunately, Linda lived to tell us this story and based on her information we were searching for dark colored Plymouth automobiles and their owners were being identified and interrogated.

Linda was only six years old. But she was able to draw sketches of the location where she had been assaulted. She drew a picture of a bridge with three arches over the water and a road with a gate at the end of it. On one occasion, a detective escorted the girl and her parents as they toured various forest preserves and lakes in the vicinity of her home.

After the girl's sketches were circulated among the detectives at the unit, the Sheriff's Office and the Forest Preserve Rangers, one of the detectives believed that he could identify the location the girl had drawn in her sketches.

Accompanied by her parents, the girl was taken by Frank, Schuenemann and me to a location on the banks of the Des Plaines River near the location of a campsite used by the Girl Scouts in the summer.

"This is the place," Linda said. She pointed to the trees along the river and three arches of a bridge that spanned the river a short distance from where she stood in the parking lot. The scene was almost exactly like the one she had sketched for detectives during her interview.

1:27 p.m.
Park Ridge Police Station

"Jim, there's a call for you." The police officer standing at the front desk called out to me in the reception area. We had just dropped off the Madisons and their daughter, Linda, at home, and Sergeant Schuenemann and I were discussing the importance of the girl's identification of the location where the offender had taken her.

"Sergeant, is it all right if I take the call in your office?" I asked.

"Sure, Jim. Come on, it's right down the hall."

The suburban police station was in better shape than the 33rd District. Park Ridge didn't have one-tenth the caseload our District had to deal with. I noticed the newer furniture, the well-polished floors. It was a lot quieter, too.

"This is Detective Jack." I looked out of the large window in Schuenemann's office. I could see trees and grass, and a cool breeze came through one of the windows that was opened just enough to keep the room smelling fresh. The lack of the distinctive odor of my partner's El Producto cigars was what I noticed most of all.

"How's it going out there, Jim?" Murphy asked.

"Murph, the girl identified the location where she was molested. It's near Euclid Road."

"That's great, Jim," Murphy answered. "You better sit down for this, though. We just got two big breaks." Murphy responded.

He told me that a man named Walter Mertees called the 33rd District with startling information concerning Dahlquist. Mertees, a golf-pro at a local country club, had gone to California to play golf during the winter. While at the Brentwood Country Club in Los Angeles, he ran into a person who he recognized. His caddy that day was Charles Dahlquist.

Mertees was unaware that the Chicago Police Department had been searching for Dahlquist since Mertees left for California the previous fall. When he returned to Chicago, he heard from several of his caddies about the search. Mertees then contacted the 33rd

District.

Murphy notified Lt. Morris and Lt. Deeley, who immediately contacted J.C. Bowers, Chief of Detectives of the Los Angeles County Sheriff's Department, and requested assistance.

The LA Sheriff acted immediately. Bowers' dispatched several detectives to local golf courses and country clubs, including the Bel-Aire Country Club and the Riviera Country Club. They interviewed caddies and golf pros at the clubs to determine if they knew of anyone fitting Dahlquist's description.

Lt. Deeley also contacted the Chief of the California Bureau of Identification in Sacramento, asking him to issue an all points bulletin. Acting on information received from police headquarters, Deeley also sent a letter to Francis J. Ahern, the Chief of Police of San Francisco, asking if his department could investigate the possibility of Dahlquist's sailing on merchant ships to the Far East.

Two shipping companies, Compangie D'Etransport & Ocianiques and The French Line, were contacted as well as the U.S. Coast Guard and the Merchant Marine Exchange.

Confident that virtually every California law enforcement agency had been notified of the warrant, if Dahlquist was in California, the odds were very good that he would eventually be apprehended.

"Now get ready for more good news, Jim," Murphy continued. "We received a report from the Melrose Park Police. They were notified by the police in Indiana of a suspect in a child kidnapping case that occurred on May 11, 1956 in Warren, Indiana. It fits the M.O. of the Park Ridge case and the one in January in Elmwood Park. Except this time, we got the license plate number. The guy they're looking for lives in River Grove. His name is Morris Downs."

May 28, 1956

Morris Downs had a history. His arrest record went back more than twenty years which included state and federal arrests and convictions for auto theft, burglary, rape, and two escapes from prison. Now an all points bulletin was issued for his arrest in connection with the rape and kidnapping of an eight year-old girl in Indiana.

After receiving the suspect's name, identification, and last known address, Lt. Morris from the Chicago Police Department and Lt. Stanwyck from the Illinois State Police decided to handle this investigation themselves. They went first to Park Ridge to interview the girls who had been accosted by the man in the dark Plymouth.

Pictures of Downs were obtained from federal and state prison authorities and Morris and Stanwyck showed them to the three girls who had been accosted by a man fitting Downs' description. They positively identified him. So did the young girl who had been abducted in January 1956 in Elmwood Park, Illinois. Downs was now being sought in connection with all of these crimes.

A team of detectives from our unit was assigned to search for the 1947 dark colored Plymouth the young girls said the man drove. Over the next several days, they located a number of vehicles matching the description, but each owner was thoroughly investigated as to their whereabouts on the dates of the incidents, and none matched the description of the suspect.

Upon further investigation, detectives discovered that Downs had recently married, and that only three months after the marriage, his wife had filed for divorce. It was also learned that Downs was employed by Dernhoff Florists on Cumberland Avenue, near his home. When a deputy from the Sheriff's Office attempted to serve him with the divorce papers at his place of employment, Downs ran out the rear door of the greenhouse and raced away in his sedan.

The deputy who attempted to serve the summons wrote down the license plate number. After the plate number was entered in the warrant system, investigators were able to put the pieces of information together. It's possible Downs believed the Sheriff's deputy came to arrest him for child molestation, rather than merely serve him with divorce papers. So really, we simply got lucky.

Downs' wife and friends were interviewed, as were two men who had escaped from prison with him several years earlier. None of them was able to tell investigators of his current whereabouts.

"Last time I heard from him was about a week ago," his wife told Detectives Morris and Stanwyck. "I got a package in the mail with a note and his wristwatch in it." She seemed unfazed by the fact that she was married to a man police sought in connection with three child abductions. "I'll bet that's the only thing I get out of the divorce." She showed the detectives the note and the package, and it was later determined that the return address on the package was an empty lot on the south side of Chicago.

"Let us know if he contacts you or if you hear of anyone else who's heard from him," Lt. Morris told the woman.

"Does this mean I can't get divorced until you find him?"

Lt. Morris didn't answer.

June 5, 1956
Cook County Coroner's Office

The bodies of John Schuessler, his brother Anton and Robert Peterson were exhumed on June 1, 1956. As predicted by State's Attorney Gutkneckt, the families cooperated with authorities seeking to dispel any rumors that the initial autopsies had been incomplete.

On May 28, 1956, the parents of Robert Peterson, along with Mrs. Schuessler, attended a meeting at the Office of the State's Attorney. During the meeting, which was also attended by representatives of several law enforcement agencies, the need for verification of the findings of the original autopsies was discussed.

More importantly, the discussion dealt with the hope that additional information might be obtained from a re-examination of the bodies that might assist in the investigation.

The families agreed to the exhumation of the bodies with the stipulation that it proceed without publicity.

Several days later, Drs. Edwin Hirsch, Alvin Bates, and Jerry Kearns conducted examinations of the tissue samples taken from the bodies. One of the samples had been taken from the head wounds found on Robert Peterson. After careful testing and examination, particles taken from the wounds were determined to be finely divided soil, known as diatomaceous soil, with microscopic pieces of bone meal.

From the distinctive patterns of the wounds on Bobby's scalp, the examiners believed that a small, three-pronged gardening rake might have caused them.

Investigators initially believed that the black smudges found on the boys' feet and elbows could have come from a machine shop. Over 2000 such shops, factories and manufacturing facilities had been contacted and searched with no positive results.

Diatomaceous soil, like the particles of bone meal, which were also found in the Peterson boy's scalp wound, was not typically used by home gardeners. It was a very fine-grained soil used by groundskeepers on golf courses, cemeteries, and in greenhouses.

The results of the second autopsies brought a dramatic re-evaluation of the entire investigation. The presence of bone meal and diatomaceous earth in a patterned scalp wound caused by a rake turned the investigation away from machine shops to golf courses, cemeteries, florists, and greenhouses.

June 7, 1956
9:23 a.m.

Lt. Morris received a Teletype message. Lt. Frank Earl of the Hollywood Division of the Los Angeles Police Department described an arrest: Dahlquist had been apprehended. The previous evening, LAPD Officers Henley and Young pursued him after he made a sudden u-turn on Sunset Boulevard.

After being apprehended and fingerprinted, the LA Police became aware of Dahlquist's outstanding warrant in Chicago. Further investigation revealed that he was driving a stolen vehicle, which he admitted he had stolen a month earlier.

Dahlquist would also be questioned in connection with the murder of a Los Angeles woman. He would not be extradited to Chicago until that investigation was complete.

June 8, 1956
7:23 p.m.
Police Headquarters

"And you're giving me this information only now? Where's it been? I had to hear about it from a press conference? For God's sake, what the hell do you think we've been doing for the last eight months?" Lt. Morris threw the nine-page report down on the desk.

He was more than upset. He was furious.

Coroner Walter McCarron had announced the results of the autopsy and tissue examination conducted by the new team of pathologists at a press conference at St. Luke's Hospital earlier that afternoon. Now McCarron was in Lt. Morris' office with a copy of the autopsy and tissue examination report.

McCarron called Lt. Morris after the press conference and told him he would bring a copy of the Coroner's Report down to Lt. Morris' office later that evening. It hadn't taken Morris long to read the report. He had already heard of its contents from people who had attended the press conference and called him seeking his reaction.

It wasn't the first time Joe Morris had been placed in an embarrassing position by a subordinate or, even more complicated, one of his superiors. But that was why the Commissioner had appointed him as head of the investigation, replacing Lt. Deeley who now was Chief of Detectives.

Morris was a good cop, with a good reputation. His superiors and those under his command respected him and knew that he had come up the hard way: no political sponsors, no political debts.

He knew when he was selected to head the investigation that it wasn't going to be easy. By January of 1956, we had a lot of leads and only a handful of real suspects. Still, Morris believed that with the continued dedication and hard work of the men in the unit, plus a few breaks, the Peterson-Schuessler case could be solved.

The lieutenant stood up from his chair and flipped to the last page of the report.

"I really like this last sentence, Coroner McCarron: 'The results of these investigations have been discussed and reported to the Coroner of Cook County.' Can you tell me who discussed the results with Lt. Stanwyck?

"And just what does Stanwyck think he's doing? I hear he's been putting golf course groundskeepers on the lie box for the last few days. Hiding in some room at the Evanston police station without telling anybody what he's been up to. Conducting his own investigation, for Christ sake. If the public finds out about it before those who are responsible for the investigation get informed, who knows what the hell Stanwyck's been doing or how he's screwed things up!"

McCarron remained seated in one of the two leather chairs facing Lt. Morris' desk. He looked down at the linoleum tile floor in Morris' office and struggled to find a response.

"Coroner McCarron?"

The sharpness in Morris' voice momentarily startled him.

"Listen, Lieutenant. I don't know how this information got to Stanwyck. I don't have to tell you how things have been between the Police Department and the State Police during this investigation. Everybody knows that all of the law enforcement agencies involved haven't been as cooperative with each other as they should be. I'll try to find out how he got the information."

"Thanks just the same, Coroner," Morris said. His anger had subsided a bit, but he was still agitated about the entire situation. "But I've got a pretty good idea how this report got out before you brought it to me tonight." Morris wondered if the sarcasm of his last remark would register on McCarron. He sat down again in the swivel chair behind his desk and re-read sections of the report he had underlined.

"If it's all right with you, Coroner McCarron, I want to take this opportunity to discuss this report with you in detail. It's obviously going to affect how we proceed in this investigation from now on. I just hope this situation with Stanwyck's secret investigation doesn't foul things up."

The two men then discussed the significance of the newest findings, particularly concerning the possible sources of manufacture and use of diatomaceous soil.

McCarron pointed out that although the deaths of each of the boys was by strangulation, the Peterson boy had been hit on the left side of the head behind the hair line by some sort of object. He agreed with Drs. Kearns and Hirsch that although the lacerations were deep, they were not the cause of death since there was no fracture or penetrating injury to the bones of the cranium. These findings had been consistent with the first autopsy.

Photographs of the head wound on the scalp showed a group of three lacerations in the left occipital region. These lacerations were arranged in the form of a triangle, suggesting that an object with at least three claw-like prongs had been used as the weapon.

During the second autopsy, the distance between the three wounds was measured and the dimensions corresponded to those of a commonly used hand garden tool. The characteristics of the wounds also indicated a downward drag of the striking object and that the object had been held in the right hand of the assailant.

Materials that had been dragged deeply into the wounds by the striking object were analyzed and found to contain diatomaceous earth mixed with small pieces of old bone.

The initial autopsies also revealed that the killer or killers used tape to cover the nose and mouths of the boys.

During this latest examination, solubility tests of the tape residue suggested that it was not surgical tape, as some investigators had originally suspected.

Morris questioned Coroner McCarron about certain technical procedures used during the second autopsies and exactly how the particles of diatomaceous soil had been identified.

"We had a clue about the make-up of the smudge marks on the boys' feet back in November of last year. We had samples analyzed by Standard Oil's research department in Whiting, Indiana. They had help from the Armour Institute. Then another independent analysis was done at the Henry Baird Favill Laboratory at St. Luke's Hospital. They both found that the smudge marks were not grease."

"I remember. When the bodies were found, at first we thought that the smudge marks were grease or oil," Morris interrupted McCarron.

"That's right. They guessed the particles were some sort of soil or combination of dirt and some kind of chemical like protein or glue.

"So what did we find out this time?" Lt. Morris asked.

"The marks were left by some sort of rake or tool, like a garden tool. We suspected some kind of pronged tool. One of the newspapers ran a picture of something like it last year. This time we measured the marks, and they correspond to something with three prongs.

"The most important thing we found was the diatomaceous soil and bone meal fragments inside the head wound. The particles were probably on the rake used as a weapon. As the rake, or whatever it was, came into contact with the boy's scalp, it embedded these particles of soil and bone meal into the wounds."

"What about the insecticide?" Lt. Morris asked.

"Insecticide?"

"Yes, insecticide. The people I talked to who were at your press conference today said Kearns and Hirsch found insecticide in the scalp wounds."

"They didn't find any insecticides in the wounds. Does it say that in the report?"

McCarron stood up and moved to the front of Lt. Morris' desk. He leaned toward Lt. Morris and twisted his head in order to read from the front page of the report Morris held in his hands.

June 9, 1956
7:50 a.m.

"Men, I want to thank you all for getting down here this morning," Corcoran began. The assembly area of the 33rd District was packed with detectives and uniformed officers, reminding me of the very first of many meetings that were held in this room since October.

A lot of things have changed, I thought. Of the hundreds of detectives and uniformed officers originally assigned to the case, only twenty-seven remained.

Lt. Deeley had become Chief of Detectives replaced by Lt. Morris. Mrs. Schuessler had just remarried over the weekend and appeared to be trying to start a new life.

One thing hadn't changed. The investigation was now into its eighth month, and no one had been arrested and charged with the murders. While there had been a few strong suspects, all but two had been tentatively cleared of any involvement. Dahlquist was going to be extradited from California and would be questioned extensively, but Downs was still a fugitive.

"I know some of you in this room have been working for the past sixteen hours, so I'll be brief. We just received the preliminary results from the second autopsy, and it will be changing the course of our investigation. Lt. Morris is here to fill you in on the details, and it goes without saying that although the general public has been given some of this information, they haven't been given all of the results. So it's for your ears only."

Corcoran stepped aside from the podium and Lt. Morris addressed the group. He told us of the results of the lab tests on the particles found in the scalp wound and how the investigation would now change in direction. Lt. Morris also told us about the patterned head wounds, and that the theory the wounds were caused by a garden rake or similar tool seemed to have been substantiated by the second autopsies.

"We're going to be taking a closer look at golf courses, greenhouses, farms, florists, and cemeteries. These particles found by the Coroner's Office are not the kinds of things found around your house. We're looking for substances the Coroner's Office has described as bone meal and diatomaceous soil. These are things that are used by very few people. Taken together, these ingredients and the unique scalp wound should lead us to the location where the boys were murdered and to those responsible.

"I know that we already have a few places and people in mind. But we're going to be as thorough and systematic as we were when we started this investigation almost eight months ago. That means a lot of double shifts, a lot of legwork. But these latest results have given us hope that we'll be able to find those responsible for the murders.

"Each of you will check with your team unit supervisors this morning about your new assignments. I know I speak for the Commissioner, the Mayor, and all of the citizens of Chicago in thanking you for all of your fine work in this case. Good luck."

8:17 a.m.

Murphy didn't wait for the assembly room to clear before meeting with the detectives under his command. He called out to Frank, Duffy, Koeppe, Schulze and me right after Lt. Morris left the podium and motioned for us to gather along one wall of the assembly room.

"Before any of you guys say anything, let me get a word in edgewise," Murphy said. He raised his voice so he would be heard over the sound of detectives and uniformed officers on their way out of the station.

"First, I can read your minds: golf courses and greenhouses; Dahlquist and Downs. Those were the first things Captain Corcoran, Lt. Morris and I put together this morning before the meeting. Dahlquist worked at Tam O'Shanter Country Club and confessed to committing sex crimes at Edgebrook Golf Course. Downs worked in a greenhouse. Dahlquist is in the Los Angeles County Jail, and the LA cops have already questioned him. Once the extradition process is complete, we'll be able to do our own interrogation. Downs is another matter. All we have to do is find him."

Murphy read us correctly. We didn't say anything, so he took the opportunity to continue.

"While we're looking for Downs and waiting for Dahlquist to be sent back here, we're also going to go back to the golf courses and the greenhouses and find out if they use any of that stuff. Jim, Frank… you're going to do the follow-up on Downs, Tam O'Shanter, and the Billy Caldwell and Edgebrook public golf courses. You've been there before, and they're close to the boys' homes.

"Duffy and Koeppe, you'll be investigating the florists and greenhouses around Robinson's Woods. Schulze, you're with me. We're going to look at the golf courses and country clubs in the same area as Duffy and Koeppe. We're having a meeting in my office this afternoon about how we're going to coordinate each team's investigation.

"Oh, and by the way, don't forget to keep up on the other assignments. I need your reports on those, too."

The Coroner's report concerning the results of the second autopsies shifted the direction of the investigation substantially. Since the end of October, theories about who the killer or killers might have been and where the murders occurred were formulated, investigated, and then changed.

A great deal of time and effort had gone into checking out Coroner McCarron's theory about the possible involvement of teenage gangs committing the crimes. Scores of known gang members had been interrogated, but eventually, this theory was discarded.

Similarly, hundreds of man-hours had been spent investigating machine shops or other locations that used heavy machinery and steel, based on the findings of minute particles of stainless steel in the smudges on the heels and elbows of the boys. The theory that the boys had been killed in a garage, machine shop, or other location where steel was used or manufactured had led nowhere.

The trail had gone cold.

Homicide detectives know that with the passing of time, the chances of finding a killer diminish significantly. Eight months had passed, and now we had new evidence that pointed in an entirely different direction. A lot could happen to evidence in eight months, and who could be certain that this newly discovered information was correct.

"Starter sheets." I looked over at Frank who was busy typing up the latest reports he had promised to give to Murphy. Frank continued to punch the keys on his typewriter and chew on the last bit of an unlit El Producto cigar. Satisfied with his progress, he stopped and turned to look at me.

"What?" The cigar wedged in his mouth muffled the word.

"Starter sheets. The sheets you sign at a golf course that tell you when you get to tee off."

"I don't play golf," Frank said. He turned his attention back to the typewriter.

I was reviewing notes and reports from interviews with the Peterson and Schuessler families. I recalled asking Bobby's parents what kinds of sports activities he liked. Mr. and Mrs. Peterson told me that he enjoyed baseball and bowling.

Since the beginning of the investigation, Mr. Peterson had been following the progress and activities of the unit by visiting the station several times each week. The Peterson home was barely six blocks away, and Mr. Peterson would often drop in and talk to detectives about new leads in the investigation. On one of these occasions, I remember Mr. Peterson said that Bobby played golf at two public golf courses near his home. One course, Edgebrook Golf Course, was just two miles from their house.

Putting down the files, I picked up the Coroner's report from the second autopsies. My eyes scanned the paragraphs until I found the sentence I was looking for.

"Top dressing with black soil enriched with fertilizers and insecticide spraying is a usual practice in the care of golf courses."

"The kid played golf, Frank. We need to find out when he played and who he played with. We'll have to talk to the parents again to see if they can tell us. But if he played at those courses, his name and whoever he was with might be on the starter sheets"

Lt. Morris, Captain Corcoran and Murphy had met earlier to plan this new avenue of investigation. A form was developed for us to complete as information was obtained from various sources. The form was similar to that used at the initial stage of the investigation in October, when we had to inspect machine shops and locations that manufactured or processed steel products.

Murphy assigned one team of detectives to start the new investigation with a visit to the General Headquarters of the Cook County Forest Preserve District at 536 North Harlem Avenue in River Forest, Illinois. Detectives met with the Deputy Comptroller and asked him if he had starter sheets for the year 1955. They were told the Forest Preserve District had discontinued keeping the sheets. They did have sheets for the summer of 1954 for Billy Caldwell Golf Course, a 9-hole course about two miles from the homes of the Schuessler and Peterson boys.

Over the next several days, nearly one hundred starter sheets were reviewed and checked to determine whether the names of Robert Peterson, Anton or John Schuessler were among the thousands listed.

We discovered that an "R. Peterson" had signed in on June 21, 27, and 28, 1954. In addition, we saw the name "R. Peterson" on July 3, 5, 6, 8, 18, 23, and 24, 1954. Detectives copied all of the names listed on starter sheets for those dates and later showed the names to Mr. and Mrs. Peterson.

The Petersons were able to identify only one name on one starter sheet, "B. Peterson" who they thought could be Mr. Peterson's cousin, Bert Peterson. They said that he'd occasionally take Robert golfing and to baseball games. Bert Peterson was subsequently interviewed and said that he could not recall anything out of the ordinary that had occurred on those occasions when he and Robert played golf.

During the visit to the Peterson home, Mr. Peterson allowed us to look in Robert's golf bag where we found an undated scorecard from the Caldwell Golf Course. Mr. Peterson told us that Robert usually played golf with two friends from the neighborhood who were not the Schuessler brothers.

He also told detectives that perhaps the reason Robert's name wasn't found on starter sheets for the Edgebrook course was because sometimes the boys would sneak onto the course without paying.

While another team followed-up on the starter sheets provided by the Forest Preserve District, my partner and I were assigned to the Edgebrook and Billy Caldwell golf courses. The form sheets to be completed asked for information concerning the use of adhesive tape, buffing machines used in pro shops or in maintenance work, pronged instruments, different types of soils used on the grounds, lawn mowers and other tools used on the premises. The name of every individual employed at the golf course was recorded and later checked with the Bureau of Identification for any history of arrests.

Other teams assigned to Ridgemore Country Club, River Forest Country Club, and Big Oaks Golf Club conducted similar investigations.

Detectives visited the golf courses on more than one occasion, and by the end of June we had filled out scores of forms and generated more reports. More inspections of the premises were conducted, more people interviewed, more background checks completed. All with the same results: no positive leads or new information, which would lead to the location of the murders or to any new suspects.

June 14, 1956
10:45 a.m.
Police Headquarters

"I don't care what he said, or what his theory is. He was wrong to do what he did and he knows it. What the hell are the detectives in my unit expected to do in this situation? They get assigned to investigate golf courses and question employees. What do they get as an answer? I'll tell you what they get: 'We already talked to the State

Police. We were given lie detector tests. What more do you guys want from us?' I told McCarron this would happen."

Lt. Morris became aggravated all over again. He was in Capt. Deeley's office.

"Take it easy, Joe," Deeley said. "Remember, it wasn't that long ago that I was sitting in your desk. The lack of cooperation with the agencies working on this case has been going on from day one."

"Yeah, I know. But Stanwyck gets the Coroner's report before anybody else and decides to give polygraph tests to twenty groundskeepers without anybody knowing what he's doing. Okay, so let's say he's a genius. He's got it all figured out. But do we get reports on who was tested and what the results were? No, we don't. Come on, it's ridiculous. We look like idiots."

"Joe, we've got to work with these people." Deeley tried to remain calm and detached, but what he just said sounded strange even to him. He had been in the same situation himself plenty of times before. Only now, he was the one trying to smooth things over.

"And another thing," Lt. Morris continued. "I have to read about how the exhumation was his idea, that he was the one who pressed for a new examination. Does that mean he was the one who was criticizing Dr. Kearns' first autopsy? His theory is bullshit. I bet the guy didn't even read the Coroner's report. 'Insecticide found on body of victim,' and he's going along with that. That came from the newspapers. The Coroner didn't find any insecticide in the Peterson boy's head wound. Stanwyck's out there looking for bug spray, for Christ sake."

"Joe, I read the newspapers. I also saw the report. We don't know how the press managed to mangle it the way they did. It happens all the time, and you know that. Listen, we're going to have to deal with these differences of opinion somehow. Otherwise, we'll never solve this case."

July 6, 1956
6:10 p.m.
Police Headquarters

Sgt. John J. Hartigan, along with two detectives investigating the Peterson-Schuessler murders, walked the prisoner off American Airline Flight 44 on their arrival at Midway Airport. They left Los

Angeles Airport that day at 9:30 a.m., pacific time and the four men looked tired after the long flight from the West Coast. They were met at the gate by two other detectives who hurried them through the airport and into a waiting squadrol.

On July 5, Lt. Morris received a telegram from Los Angeles Chief of Police that Dahlquist had waived extradition to Illinois at a hearing earlier that day. Chief Parker reported that Dahlquist was not going to be charged as a murder suspect in the death of the young woman and, since he had waived extradition, would be placed in the custody of Detective Sgt. Hartigan and sent back to Chicago.

Upon arriving at 11th & State, Dahlquist underwent extensive interrogation by Sgt. Hartigan, Lt. Morris, and several other detectives.

Dahlquist told the detectives he jumped bond and failed to make his January 16 court date because he didn't want to embarrass his parents. He didn't seem to care that his parents had lost their home.

He said that after leaving Chicago he worked for six weeks in an iron ore factory in the Mesabi Range near Duluth, Minnesota. He left and intended to go to California, but ran out of gas in Holbrook, Arizona and abandoned his car because he had no money for gas and repairs. From there, he hitchhiked to Los Angeles, then to San Francisco for a few days. He returned to Los Angeles where he worked as a caddy at a country club until the time of his arrest.

He denied involvement in the murders and knowing anything other than what he had read in the newspapers. He reiterated what he had told detectives during his interrogation in October of last year.

Dahlquist was then given a series of polygraph examinations. The examiners believed that Dahlquist was truthful when he stated that he was neither involved in, nor knew anything about, the Peterson-Schuessler murders. Detectives checked out the statements of his activities and whereabouts on the days preceding the discovery of the bodies in detail and several independent witnesses corroborated those statements.

Investigators became convinced that, despite Dahlquist's decision to jump bond and flee to avoid prosecution, he was not the person who killed the Peterson and Schuessler boys.

However, it was the opinion of the administrators of the

polygraph tests that emotional disturbances "indicative of deception" concerning the July 1955 molestation of Billy Dayton were present.

Rather than face trial, Dahlquist pled guilty to the charge of Crimes Against Nature involving Billy Dayton, and Judge Crowley of the Criminal Court of Cook County sentenced Dahlquist to Illinois State Penitentiary for a period of one to five years.

July 22, 1956
2:00 p.m.
Norwood Park

Frank and I stood in the back of the Moe-Seaver Chapel of the Norwegian Lutheran Children's Home on North Canfield Avenue in the Norwood Park neighborhood on the city's far northwest side.

More than 300 people were in attendance for a memorial service for Robert Peterson. Reverend Eifrig, again, conducted the service.

The Norwood Park Kiwanis Club had sponsored Bobby's Little League team and collected funds for a memorial. A baseball backstop on the athletic field of the Norwegian Lutheran Children's Home was constructed with Bobby's name on it and would be dedicated to his memory at the conclusion of the services.

The girls' choir from the Home sang hymns, followed by prayers, an invocation, more religious songs, and finally a sermon by the Reverend Eifrig.

From the chapel, the crowd moved to the athletic field for the dedication ceremonies. As the American flag was raised, Boy Scouts from Bobby's troop sang the Star Spangled Banner and the crowd joined in.

Mr. and Mrs. Peterson were present. They acknowledged and thanked those in attendance. Then Mrs. Peterson unveiled the plaque dedicated to her son.

The family, neighbors, and friends of Bobby Peterson stood quietly for several minutes on the baseball field under a bright blue July sky. Some of them could almost see a young boy playing baseball, right there, on a Sunday afternoon.

For Frank and I, the memorial services bought back memories of another sad day in October 1955 when we attended the wakes and funerals. But in addition to paying our respects to the Peterson family at the dedication ceremony, we, and fellow detectives, were again present to find those responsible for the deaths.

We observed every one of the more than three hundred people in the crowd. Our observations began before the memorial service. Months earlier, a list of Norwood Park Little League team members had been obtained from Juvenile Officer Toni Quinn. Each team member was interviewed about their recollections: did Bobby know anyone in a gang, did they ever see him talking to a stranger?

As my partner and I attended the memorial services inside the chapel and on the field, other detectives were busy recording approximately 160 license plates of people attending the service and parked nearby. Each license plate was run for identification of the owners, and those names in turn were assessed by the Bureau of Identification for any history of arrests.

Time marched on. The number of detectives assigned to the investigation diminished, but those who remained were as thorough and determined as we were the day the boys went missing.

Office of the Police Commissioner
9:00 a.m.

"The Commissioner will see you now." The uniformed police sergeant seated at the desk in the reception area still had the receiver of the telephone wedged between his chin and shoulder. He looked across the large room at Capt. Deeley, seated in one of the half dozen chairs lined up against the far wall.

Deeley didn't get down to City Hall very often. In fact, he preferred to avoid the place. Too many politicians and "ward heelers"—political appointees who had a lot of side businesses going on.

"Thanks," he replied. He walked across the room as the sergeant got up from the desk. The officer rapped on the door, then slowly opened it and showed Capt. Deeley in.

"Good morning, Capt. Deeley. Come in and have a seat." Commissioner O'Connor rose from his chair behind a huge mahogany desk. On the wall behind the desk, scores of photos and awards were arranged in meticulous rows. There were pictures of the Commissioner with the Mayor, the Governor, former President Harry S. Truman, and one Republican: President Dwight D. Eisenhower. Capt. Deeley sat down in one of the chairs in front of O'Connor's desk.

"I'll get right to the point," the Commissioner said as he returned to his chair. "I received your report on the exhumation yesterday. Or should I say Sgt. Otto Kreuser's report, which you approved." O'Connor reached across the top of his desk and picked up the two-page, typewritten report. Capt. Deeley couldn't help noticing that the only other objects on the Commissioner's desk were a telephone and two framed pictures.

"Is Sgt. Kreuser going to law school?" O'Connor asked with a smile. He picked up the report and turned to the second page. "He certainly writes like a lawyer. 'In the light of the limitations established by the frequency of availability and the need for additional refinements, no immediate plan can be formulated to make an extensive search that would require the combined unified efforts of investigative authorities. The pathologist is continuing his search. It is recommended that each authority proceed individually as they may be influenced by interpretation.'"

Deeley shifted nervously in his chair. By the tone of O'Connor's voice he wasn't sure what the Commissioner thought of either Kreuser or his report.

"I guess that says it all," O'Connor said, without betraying any emotion. He looked squarely at Capt. Deeley and waited for him to say something.

"Commissioner, I had Kreuser draft the report to you. You're right. He's got a knack for these kinds of things. I would have been a lot more blunt about the entire situation, and that's why I had him write it. So I appreciative you inviting me here to talk about it."

Deeley told the Commissioner about the long history of tense relations among law enforcement agencies working on the case. He also told O'Connor he believed Lt. Morris was doing a fine job. Deeley mentioned the fact that Morris was still angry about the secretiveness with which Stanwyck had conducted his investigation before giving the 33rd District the Coroner's report.

"Commissioner, I'm sure you've heard what Lt. Morris thinks

about Stanwyck's theory, the insecticide issue, where we should be looking for evidence."

"Captain, I am very aware of all of that. From what I've been able to determine from reading the report, somebody misinterpreted what it said. I like how Kreuser says only 1 percent of that particular soil is used with insecticides. He gets the point across."

The Commissioner placed the report back on his desk, then crossed his arms and leaned back in his chair.

"Is that your recommendation, then? Let each investigating authority proceed according to how they interpret what we've got so far? In other words, since we can't work together on this, it's every agency for itself?"

Deeley hesitated for a moment then responded in a very confident voice.

"Commissioner, it wouldn't be the first time. You've tried, the Mayor's tried, just about everybody's tried to get all the investigative agencies to work together on this case. Maybe we were wrong. Maybe it would be better for each agency to proceed, within limits of course, to either prove their theory or fail. At this point, we've tried everything else."

Commissioner O'Connor slowly nodded his head, indicating he understood.

"I appreciate your candor, Capt. Deeley. I'll have to give the matter more thought."

August 25, 1956

The search for Downs intensified in the weeks after the Coroner released the results of the second autopsies. Warrants had been issued for his arrest in connection with the child molestation cases in Park Ridge and Elmwood Park. National bulletins had been issued to notify all law enforcement authorities that Downs was also being sought in connection with the Peterson-Schuessler murders.

Detectives interviewed his employer at length.

After identifying Downs from a photograph shown to him by detectives, the owner told detectives that Downs had worked for him from February of 1955 until May 1956 when he was fired. He had not used the name Morris Downs but was known to his co-workers as Murray Dorhn. A review of his employment records showed that Downs had been off work on October 16–17, 1955 but did work from 6:45 a.m. to 4:00 p.m. on Tuesday, the eighteenth of October.

The owners led detectives through a tour of the premises, including the greenhouses where two samples of fertilizers were obtained. One of the samples contained bone meal.

The investigators also took pictures of the various gardening tools used by workers in the greenhouses or offered for sale to gardeners in the retail store located on the grounds of the nursery.

Tips had been received that Downs at one time resided in a trailer park in Des Plaines, Illinois and a team of detectives was assigned to check the park and several others located nearby.

Another team of detectives was sent to the L. Fish Furniture Company located at Grand and Harlem Avenues after learning that Downs had recently purchased furniture there. They obtained the list of references Downs had given the store when he applied for credit then interviewed those individuals about their knowledge of Downs' whereabouts.

In July, the Secretary of State of Illinois was contacted to obtain the chain of titles of a 1947 Plymouth. In a very short time, we received information that the vehicle was registered to Murray Dorhn, the name under which Downs had worked while at the florists shop.

Mrs. Downs was interviewed again by Sgt. Mulvey to determine Downs' whereabouts during the period of October 16–18, 1955.

She said that on Sunday, October 16, 1955, she, Downs, and her mother had driven to Logan's Furniture Mart in the 4500 block of W. Madison St. in Chicago. There, they happened to meet a co-worker of Downs and spoke with him for a bit. Then they returned home at about 5:30 p.m. She and Downs stayed in his apartment adjoining the grounds of the nursery until 9:30 that night, then she went home.

During her questioning by detectives, Mrs. Downs told them she had received a collect long distance call from Downs at 12:30 a.m. on August 20. He refused to tell her where he was, but Mrs. Downs remembered that since it had been a collect call, the operator had told her it was from San Francisco, California.

Sgt. Mulvey immediately contacted Special Agent Elliot Anderson of the FBI's Chicago office and informed him of what he had learned from Mrs. Downs. He asked Agent Anderson if a record of the call could be located with the assistance of the phone company in both Illinois and California. Mulvey also contacted police in San Francisco to alert them to the fact that Downs might be in their city.

A few days later, Mulvey received a call from the FBI, informing him that the FBI's San Francisco office had traced the call made to Mrs. Downs to a pay phone in the parking lot of Chuck's Park and Save Supermarket at High and 14th Streets in San Leandro, California. Their agents canvassed the area with photos of Downs and learned that he was an employee of a nearby florist and nursery. He had been employed there since June and had resigned two months later on August 15.

Agents learned that he had returned only hours before to pick up his last paycheck. They also learned where he lived. On August 22, during their visit to the Washington Hotel in San Leandro, agents just missed him again shortly after he checked out. He had registered under the name of Charles Newman, an alias he had previously used in Chicago. From interviews with hotel employees and guests, the agents learned that he had purchased a 1941 blue Desoto on June 12, 1956 from Peterson Auto Parts in San Leandro.

An auto repairman told the two agents that Downs would be returning within the next several days to pick up his car, which had some work done on it.

On the morning of August 25, 1956, Downs was arrested as he got out of his blue Desoto.

August 26, 1956
Oakland, California

Lt. Morris, Assistant State's Attorney Robert Cooney, and Sgt. Andrew Young of the State's Attorneys Office took the earliest available flight to San Francisco and were met at the airport by Special Agent James R. Donleavy of the FBI's San Francisco office. The four men proceeded directly to the Alameda County Courthouse in Oakland, where Downs was being held on an unlawful flight warrant.

During the drive from San Francisco to Oakland, Agent Donleavy brought the Chicago group up to speed on what he and the Alameda Sheriff had obtained from their initial interrogation of Downs.

"He's been telling us his name's not Downs, it's Charles Newman," Agent Donleavy said. "Same name he used at the Washington Hotel, but the manager and everybody we showed the photos you sent us said it was Downs.

"The other thing is that he fits the I.D. of a guy the San Leandro police are looking for in connection with a sex assault on a young boy last week. And we also got a call from the Indiana State Police about a kidnapping and sex assault on a little girl down there. Of course, he's denied knowing anything about all this. Looks like you guys are going to have to get in line on this one."

Sheriff Pete Gleason, who arranged for Cooney and Morris to interview Downs, met them at the Alameda County Courthouse.

"I'm not Downs," the man told his interrogators. "I got hit on the head a while back, and the next thing I remember is that I'm working at this Twin Nursery place in San Leandro."

After confronting Downs with his prison photos and police mug shots, it did not take long to get him to admit to his real name. They began their interrogation of him by asking what he knew about the rape charges pending against him in Park Ridge and Elmwood Park. Then they asked him about the Peterson-Schuessler murders.

He denied any involvement in any of the crimes, but later admitted that he had fled Chicago because he feared he would have been interrogated about the murders of the boys because of his past record.

"Well that was pretty stupid of you, don't you think?" Morris asked the prisoner. "If you believed you were going to be questioned and then ran, what do you suppose we would think about that?"

Downs didn't answer.

"What about this boy in San Leandro?" Morris asked Downs. "He identified you as the one who molested him last week."

Early in the day, Downs had been held in the jail's "bull pen," a large cell holding twenty-five prisoners. The young boy had identified Downs as the man who assaulted him by picking him out of the group of prisoners. A few hours later, Downs was among five men who formed a line-up for the purpose of a second identification.

The boy had viewed Downs through a one-way glass mirror on both occasions and positively identified him as his assailant.

When Downs was confronted with this information, he became physically ill. At one point, Lt. Morris thought the suspect was going to throw up all over him.

After regaining control of himself, Downs volunteered to take a polygraph test concerning the Peterson-Schuessler murders. Arrangements were made with Lt. Everett King of the Alameda County Sheriff's Office to conduct the examination.

Later that evening, Lt. Morris learned that questions concerning the Park Ridge and Elmwood Park child molestation cases had been included in the polygraph examination. This was a cause for concern since Lt. Morris was aware that questions concerning one criminal case should not be included during the polygraph examination of a separate and distinct criminal case.

Since he was not in his own jurisdiction, Lt. Morris decided not to protest or complain about the test procedures. The Alameda Sheriff's Office had been very hospitable, and he decided to maintain the cooperative and cordial relationship between the two agencies.

He'd already had enough of inter-agency friction in Chicago and didn't want to make waves two thousand miles from home.

After being given four subsequent polygraph examinations by three different examiners, the unanimous consensus of the examiners was that Downs was truthful in his answers concerning the murders.

However, authorities in Illinois still had to wait in line for Morris Downs. He was first extradited to Indiana to face charges in the kidnapping and molestation of the young girl there.

Sgt. Mulvey and Lt. Stanwyck drove to the small Indiana town where Downs was being held to interview him. As a result of their extensive questioning of him and their earlier interviews with his wife and co-workers who had corroborated his statements, Sgt. Mulvey and Lt. Stanwyck agreed that Downs could no longer be considered a likely suspect in the murders.

After consulting with the local prosecutor and having a telephone conference with the Cook County State's Attorneys Office, Mulvey and Stanwyck were informed that the prosecution of Downs would proceed in Indiana on the charge of "stealing a child." Local prosecutors had made a deal with Downs that in return for his guilty plea to that lesser charge, he would be given a sentence of two to fourteen years. The basis for the plea bargain was that the young girl would be spared the ordeal of testifying at trial.

Before his Indiana trial, the two young girls from the suburbs of Chicago positively identified Downs through his photographs as the man who had abducted and molested them. A Cook County grand jury indicted Downs in connection with these cases.

1957

By the end of 1957, the detectives on the investigation become less confident that the perpetrators of the murders would be identified and apprehended. With the exclusion of Downs and Dahlquist, detectives had very few individuals to consider as possible suspects.

Many of the investigators assigned to the case were re-assigned. During the next several years, news items about the murders appeared less frequently and were replaced by coverage of more recent homicides that were just as horrific as those of the boys.

1961

In May 1961, Police Superintendent O.W. Wilson changed the assignment and command structure of detectives working in the Department. Detectives were to be assigned to one of the six Area Districts, rather than local police stations. Because of my seniority, I was given the opportunity to select the District I preferred. I chose Area Five Homicide, which was the station formerly known as Shakespeare Street. Sadly, Frank was no longer my partner. He retired in 1960 and died the next year.

The investigation unit responsible for apprehending the murderers of Bobby, John, and Tony continued its task, but by 1961, the crimes remained unsolved.

Nearly every year after the crime, newspapers would report the anniversary of the boys' deaths, along with the facts surrounding their disappearance and the discovery of their bodies. Occasionally, an individual who had been apprehended for child molestation would be identified in news stories as having been interrogated about the murders. But the story usually ended with a statement that investigators were still looking for the boys' killer or killers, and the suspect had been released pending further investigation.

Every investigator who worked the case continued to check on the progress of those who were still assigned to it. We followed the news reports and always kept each other informed of anything new.

On November 27, 1961, Coroner Andrew Toman held another inquest at the Cook County Morgue concerning the Peterson-Schuessler murders. The two previous hearings held on October 19, 1955 and October 24, 1955 had been continued "in order to allow law enforcement agencies an opportunity to complete their investigation."

Many of those who testified had done so at the previous hearings. Victor Livingston, the liquor salesman who found the bodies, was present. So was Forest Ranger Byrne, who followed Livingston and two others to the location of the bodies in Robinson's Woods. Also in attendance were Captain Corcoran, Sgt. Murphy, and Captain Deeley. Their testimony was brief, re-iterating for the most part prior testimony at the previous inquests.

After deliberating for a short time, the jury returned. Like the two juries before them, they found that the boys had been murdered by "a person or persons unknown and unidentified at this time...we deplore the situation which presents itself wherein we are forced to return a verdict without naming the responsible person or persons for said crime...and recommend that the police and other law enforcement agencies continue their search for said person or persons responsible for said act, and that when apprehended, -HE, SHE, or THEY be held to the Grand Jury of Cook County, Illinois on a charge of MURDER until released by due process of law."

The case remained open and listed among the many in the "Uncleared Homicide" files. Most of these individual case files were less than an inch thick. By the 1960s, the Peterson-Schuessler case filled three drawers of a gray metal file cabinet. As police districts were re-mapped and the Department restructured, the metal cabinet followed the respective detective unit responsible for the "open file."

The case would remain open for more than forty years.

The Trial

September 6, 1995

Judge Toomin asked the bailiff to seat the jurors who would hear the State's evidence against Kenneth Hansen for the murders of Robert Peterson, John Schuessler, and Anton Schuessler, Jr. on October 16, 1955. The State was represented by two veteran Assistant State's Attorneys: Patrick Quinn and Scott Cassidy. Two highly skilled and successful defense attorneys represented Hansen, Art O'Donnell and Jed Stone.

The judge looked in the direction of the two assistant state's attorneys seated at the prosecution's table. Just behind them were benches filled since early that morning with spectators eager to be present at the trial.

"Mr. Quinn, Mr. Cassidy, you may proceed," Judge Toomin said, his voice echoing in the large courtroom.

Patrick Quinn rose from his chair and walked to the jury box; seven men and five women were selected to serve as jurors. For a few moments, there was silence as the jurors looked at Quinn. He stopped a few feet from where they sat, looked at them for a moment and then began his opening statement.

"Defense counsel, Scott, ladies and gentleman of the jury, let me start by telling you what this case is about. This case is not about homosexuality. What this case is about is child molestation and murder."

Quinn told the jurors there is no statute of limitations for the crime of murder and murder cases never close until the case is solved.

And that was what the jurors would hear in this case. How through the efforts of several law enforcement agencies, a crime that had occurred forty years ago had been solved.

He described how the boys disappeared on the night of October 16, 1955 and that their nude, beaten, and strangled bodies were found two days later in a forest preserve and led to one of the most intensive criminal investigations ever conducted in the city's history.

"The details of the crime, ladies and gentleman, I tell you are horrific, and you cannot imagine how horrific they are," Quinn continued. "Let me tell you the reason you should convict Kenneth Hansen. It is not because the details are horrific. It is because it is his handiwork that you will see in this case. You should convict him because he did it, not for any other reason."

Quinn told the jurors that they would hear how Bobby Peterson signed a registry sheet at the Garland Building in Chicago at about 6:00 p.m. on the evening they were last seen. Earnest Niewiadomski would tell them that as a seventeen year old, he saw all three boys at the Monte Cristo Bowling Alley on West Montrose Avenue at about 7:30 p.m. that same night.

The jurors would also hear from Ralph Helm, who saw the three boys hitchhiking on Milwaukee Avenue, and from a witness who would testify that she heard a child screaming in an area near her home at about 9:30 p.m. that night. The jury would hear from the photographer who took photographs of the bodies shortly after they were found in the forest preserve. They would also see those photographs.

"You'll hear from Dr. Donoghue who will tell you, he reviewed the post-mortem examinations, or the autopsies of the boys, and he will tell you that from his review, Bobby Peterson was beaten with some kind of object on the head, he was strangled with some type of device, and he was killed in that manner.

"He will tell you that John Schuessler was beaten and that his throat was crushed. He will tell you that Tony Schuessler was manually strangled."

Quinn then began to tell the jurors about the other testimony they would hear. About how one week after the boys' bodies were found, Kenneth Hansen told one of his close friends that "he had killed those kids, the kids everybody is investigating."

The jury would also hear from another friend of the defendant, Quinn continued. This witness would also testify that Hansen admitted he had killed the three boys after he had picked them up hitchhiking and had taken them to the Idle Hour Stables, molested two of them, and then killed all three after they threatened to tell their parents and the authorities.

"You will hear from people who knew Ken Hansen at the Idle Hour Stables in the year 1955," Quinn said. "You will hear how two young ladies thought he was a very attractive fellow and being somewhat smitten they remembered him, and they will tell you why they remembered him. And they remember him being at the Idle Hour, specifically in 1955."

He told the jurors that they would hear from other witnesses about how Kenneth Hansen would pick up young hitchhikers and take them to the stables and have sex with them.

"And in his first interview with the Chicago Police Department, he admitted to being a homosexual all his life and his preference for sex was oral to be performed on males twelve to twenty-two years of age."

His voice remained calm as he neared the end of his opening statement, describing what several witnesses would tell them about how Hansen admitted to killing the boys.

"Ladies and gentleman," Quinn concluded, "you will find that justice delayed is not always justice denied. And you, ladies and gentleman, will play the most important part in this case, to do that all you have to do is watch and listen. Thank you."

Quinn returned to his seat at the prosecution table. Judge Toomin then looked in the direction of the two defense attorneys and nodded, indicating that they would be allowed to make their opening statement.

Art O'Donnell stood and walked calmly and deliberately to a spot in front of the jury. Like Quinn, he first addressed the judge, then his opponents, his co-council Jed Stone, and then turned to look at the jurors and began his statement.

"Mr. Quinn's opening statement to you started out by saying… telling you that this is not a case of homosexuality. I say this because it's fresh in your mind to review what you've just heard. And that if 95 percent of it didn't deal with the question of homosexuality and pedophilia, then I didn't hear the same thing you heard, and that is one of the real problems of this case."

O'Donnell told the jury that the evidence would show that Kenneth Hansen was born in 1932 and lived on the northwest side of the city, attended school there, and married his high school sweetheart.

Hansen worked for his father who had some horses that he used for pony rides at carnivals and church functions. He then went into the service and served in Korea. After being honorably discharged in January 1955, he worked for his father again. Later, he and his wife purchased a stable in June 1955 near Willow Springs, IL.

The time frame was important, O'Donnell stated, because at the time the murders were committed Hansen was not living or working in the community on the north side of the city. Hansen's wife would take the pony riders to different locations, and Hansen would stay home and handle the business there.

The attorney then turned to the night of October 16, 1955. He told the jurors about how the evidence would show that the three boys intended to go to the Loop Theater in Chicago and how the bodies were found two days later.

Then O'Donnell began to tell the jurors about "the one single hard piece of physical evidence in this case," which turned up twenty months after the murders. He told the jurors that Robert Peterson went to the Garland Building at approximately 6:00 p.m. on the night of October 16, 1955 and that the boy's signature was on the registry of the building.

"…I respectfully submit to you, ladies and gentlemen, that Robert Peterson went there to meet someone. He checked in at 6:00 p.m., and he immediately left the building at 6:05 p.m. He then went with these other two boys, the Schuesslers, who waited down on the sidewalk, didn't go upstairs with him, they didn't sign the registry, and they proceeded to go on the way back home, but not directly.

They went to a bowling alley, the Monte Cristo Bowl on Spaulding and Montrose.

"Now maybe they went there to bowl. They were seen there at about 7:30 p.m. by young Mr. Niewiadomski, and I think also by his sister. You'll hear evidence by the state's witness that they asked them, the boys, if they wanted to bowl. They said they didn't have any money. They said if you pay for it, we'll bowl. They spent all their money at the show.

"So what was their reason for going to the Monte Cristo at all if they didn't even have the money to go bowling? I respectfully submit they could have been looking for the same person that they were looking for on the ninth floor of the Garland Building."

O'Donnell's defense argument would be that Robert had met someone in the Garland Building and that someone was the murderer, not Kenneth Hansen.

His theory was based on the speculations of Detective John Sarnowski of the Chicago Police Department. Sarnowski and his partner had found the Peterson boy's signature in the register at the Garland Building during a follow-up investigation. All the tenants in the building had been interviewed, and one had told investigators that she recalled seeing a young teenager "with a head like a potato" hanging around the building.

Twenty-five years later Sarnowski would speculate that John Wayne Gacy was the "potato head" teenager, that Gacy frequented the Garland Building, and that he would be a likely suspect in the Peterson-Schuessler case. Because of pre-trial evidentiary motions, the jury would not hear the specifics of Sarnowski`s theory nor would they hear from Sarnowski, who was seriously ill at the time of the trial.

O'Donnell, undaunted by earlier rulings by Judge Toomin, continued to press his theory. "Sarnowski worked on it for five years, and Mr. Sarnowski, who is a witness, in this case, unfortunately is in Resurrection Hospital having two weeks ago suffered a relapse of lymphoma, lymphatic cancer, and we asked to continue the case…"

"Objection," Scott Cassidy interrupted.

"Objection sustained," Judge Toomin said.

"...But the court would not grant that," O'Donnell continued.

"Objection sustained," the judge said in a louder voice than before. "I'll strike that comment and instruct the jury to disregard it."

"The absence of the witness..." O'Donnell began to argue.

"I sustained the objection, Mr. O'Donnell. Continue your argument in a proper manner," Judge Toomin sternly instructed.

O'Donnell turned the subject of his opening statement to the witnesses the State would be presenting in their case.

"Sometime in about 1993 or so a very talented ingenious person saw an opportunity. His name is William Wemette, and you're going to meet him. Mr. Wemette has been a paid—I underline that—paid government witness in one form or another at different times or other since 1971."

O'Donnell went on to tell the jurors William "Red" Wemette had testified for the FBI and the IRS and that "98 percent of the interviews conducted in this case with respect to this murder were conducted by ATF agents. He told the jurors that the ATF "was probably the most discredited law enforcement agency on the face of the earth after the "Waco" disaster and Ruby Ridge. They desperately needed to rehabilitate their image before the public."

O'Donnell told the jurors that the present case grew out of the horse industry fraud investigations, the Brach case, where, like before, it remained unsolved. It was not solved, he said, because there was not sufficient evidence to charge anyone in the Brach murder.

Then the defense turned to the other witnesses the State would introduce in their case and O'Donnell questioned the quality of the evidence they would provide.

Finally, the defense stated that there was a total lack of evidence against Hansen, and in fact, the only hard evidence in the case strongly suggested that someone else had committed the crimes.

"If you listen carefully to the evidence, you will see that there is no physical evidence, no fingerprints, no eyewitnesses, nothing but a few isolated circumstances plus the testimony of these two principal paid witnesses and another pathetic character by the name of Hollatz. None of these people who heard about these horrible crimes ever told another single human being about it. And you have the right to ask yourself why, because ladies and gentlemen, that is the quality of the evidence that they have here…we ask that you listen carefully to the evidence and keep an open mind because that desire at the closing will be very important in light of the unfortunate circumstances and the lifestyle that was involved here. Thank you very much."

The first witness in the State's case was Beatrice Blane, Eleanor Schuessler's sister and the aunt of Anton and John Schuessler. Her testimony was brief, and chiefly served to introduce evidence that prior to October 16, 1955, the Schuessler boys had been alive.

She told the jury her sister, Eleanor Schuessler, was no longer living and that her brother-in-law, Anton Sr., died one month after his sons were murdered. In response to Scott Cassidy's request, she identified the photographs of her two nephews and testified that before October 16, 1955, they had been alive and in good health. She then stated that after the boys' bodies had been found she was at her sister's home constantly until the wake.

The next witness was Ernest Niewiadomski, who testified about meeting the Peterson and Schuessler boys at the Monte Cristo Bowling Lanes at 7:30 p.m. on the evening of their disappearance. He said the boys told him they had just gotten back from seeing "The African Lion" downtown, and they had stopped in the bowling alley on their way home. They stayed at the bowling alley for about twenty minutes and then left, he said.

Niewiadomski was shown pictures of the boys by Cassidy, and he identified each one and turned the photos toward the jury as he pointed at each picture.

"This is Tony Schuessler, Anton…this is his brother John…and this is Rob," he said.

"Bobby Peterson; is that right?" Cassidy asked him.

"Yes."

Niewiadomski testified that the boys had been wearing Cubs and Sox jackets. He said that the photos shown to him by Cassidy of examples of these jackets were similar to the ones he saw the boys wearing on October 16, 1955 at the Monte Cristo Bowling Alley.

On cross-examination, O'Donnell asked Niewiadomski if it was possible for another person to have been with the boys that night.

Niewiadomski responded that he didn't see anyone else with the boys and that the three boys "stuck together" and that he saw no one else with them.

Next to testify was Ralph Helm, now a fifty-five year old police officer. In 1955, he had seen the boys hitchhiking at the corner of Lawrence and Milwaukee Avenue while walking his girlfriend home from the movies.

Helm testified that between 8:30 and 9:00 p.m. on October 16, 1955, he and his girlfriend were walking on the sidewalk on the eastside of Milwaukee Avenue heading toward Lawrence Avenue. It was raining, and as Helm and his girlfriend were just south of Lawrence Avenue, he saw a young boy standing on the curb facing south with his right hand extended and his thumb out as if to be hitchhiking.

He estimated the boy was about eleven or twelve-years old and described him as wearing a waist length baseball type sports jacket. As he came within two feet, he noticed two other boys standing out of the rain in the doorway of a store. These two boys were approximately six feet north of where the young boy was standing at the curb.

He described these two boys as also wearing waist length sports jackets.

"I thought it was a dangerous situation," Helm testified.

"Why is that?" Cassidy asked.

"To have a young boy hitchhiking that late at night."

He told the jury that after he dropped his girlfriend at her home, he returned to the corner of Milwaukee Avenue and Lawrence Avenue to take a southbound Milwaukee Avenue bus home. It had taken him about fifteen minutes to drop off his girlfriend and return to the corner where he had seen the boys, but when he returned they were gone.

Helm said that after he heard about the three boys being found dead, he told his mother that he believed he had seen the boys on Milwaukee Avenue and then his mother notified the police. After being interviewed by three detectives, Helm said he went to the wake of the Schuessler boys to make a positive identification. There he identified Anton Schuessler.

During cross-examination, O'Donnell sought to show that Helm had not known the boys before seeing them hitchhiking. He also had the witness confirm that he had not seen them enter a car.

The State's next witness was Hetty Salerno, who told police investigators she heard screams coming from the direction of the Idle Hour Stables on a rainy evening forty years ago.

Mrs. Salerno told the jury she was born in Liverpool, England and had married her husband there and then moved to the United States. She described how the family had moved to Park Ridge, IL. In 1953, the area was nothing but fields, farms, and stables. The family lived in a tri-level home on Peterson Avenue, she said, with an open breezeway, which faced west and was attached to the garage.

"We were...my husband and I, were sitting in the breezeway talking to Mr. Panek who was standing across the street."

"Did anything unusual occur at that time?"

"Yes"

"Would you please describe to the jury what happened?"

"We heard...I heard two screams. The first scream was loud, piercing, it was a young voice and it was a frightened voice. It scared me. Then a little while later the next scream came lower than the first scream."

"Had you ever heard a scream like that prior to that night?"

"Never. And I haven't now, up until now, never."

"Could you tell whether it was a male or female voice?"

"It sounded like a boy's voice."

"An older or younger boy?"

"Younger."

She told Assistant State's Attorney Cassidy that after she heard the screams, she heard her neighbor, Mr.Panek, come across the street and talk to her husband. She was scared, she said, and went into the house.

Mrs. Salerno was shown an aerial view of the area as it appeared in 1955, at the time of the murders. She pointed to the area in which her house was located, and the location of the Idle Hour Stables. Mrs. Salerno placed an S over the location of the Salerno home, and also placed a P where the Panek home was located, across the street.

Finally she placed a B where the Idle Hour barn was located.

The photo was mounted on an easel for the jury to see it, but Mrs. Salerno had drawn the letters so that Judge Toomin was able to follow her identification. Now, she was asked to leave the witness stand, and after the enlarged photograph had been turned in the direction of the jury, she repeated her identification and pointed to the letters she had placed on the photo, showing the jury exactly where her home and the stables were located on the photograph.

"Is that the direction you heard the screams coming from?" Cassidy asked her.

"Absolutely, yes," Mrs. Salerno said.

On cross-examination, O'Donnell asked the witness if, when describing the screams on that night, Mrs. Salerno was suggesting that the screams she heard came from inside the barn as opposed to an open field.

"I'm saying that Mr. Panek, my husband and I heard it directly down Peterson, not from the side where the fields were," she said with confidence.

O'Donnell asked the witness if she could tell the jury how far the screams were from her house.

"About a block and a quarter from our house," she answered.

"The time that you heard the screams you told Mr. Cassidy that you thought it was between nine and ten o'clock at night."

"I know it was that time."

"How is it that you know it was between nine and ten o'clock at night?"

"We had at that time four small children. They went to bed at eight or nine o'clock every night, whether it was rain, hail, or snow, we'd go out on the breezeway, enjoy our coffee and just talk alone, put our jackets on if it was cold..."

Mrs. Salerno told O'Donnell that two days after she had heard the screams, she saw thirty police officers walking through the fields near her home.

"They were walking through the field presumably looking for evidence?"

"They were looking for something, yes."

"Did you ever think to say to them, no, gentlemen, don't be walking over here in the field, go further south towards the barn, did you say that to them?"

"No, because my husband handled it at that time, I didn't."

"Did you ever talk to the police forty years ago in October 1955 about what you had heard that evening?"

"Yes. Yes, the Chicago Police."

"And I know that you know that this is the Idle Hour Stable but you never told the police in 1955 that these screams came from the Idle Hour Stable?"

"My husband did."

"Okay. I'm asking if you ever directed the police who were searching in the field for evidence to the area of the stables? Is that a no?" O'Donnell said forcefully.

"That's a no, sir."

O'Donnell ended his cross-examination and returned to his chair at the defense table.

Cassidy slowly approached the witness, and paused briefly before beginning his redirect examination.

"Mrs. Salerno, your husband passed away several years ago isn't that correct?"

"Twenty-five years ago, sir."

"Counsel asked you to speak a little about how loud these screams were. When you were in London there were bombings then, weren't there?"

"I was an ambulance driver during the war, yes."

"Following the bombings in London you heard screams, did you not?"

"Yes, I had children…"

Before she could finish her answer O'Donnell's loud and insistent voice cut through the courtroom.

"Objection."

"Sustained," Judge Toomin ruled.

"Were these the loudest screams you ever heard before when you heard them on that night?" Cassidy asked again.

"Objection," O'Donnell said. "That's been asked and answered by her on direct and well beyond the scope of my cross."

"Sustained."

"No further questions, your Honor." Cassidy said. He had made his point.

Cassidy's fellow prosecutor, rose to his feet after the next witness to be called had taken her seat on the witness stand.

The next witness was Violet Sable, a neighbor of the Salerno family in 1955, who still resided in the same home on Peterson Avenue since 1953. She testified that she recalled that at the time, the area was still sparsely populated and consisted of open farm fields and the Idle Hour Stables.

She told of seeing police officers searching near her home, just as Mrs. Salerno had testified. Like the witness before her, Mrs. Sable walked to the aerial photograph placed on the easel next to the witness stand and pointed to the location of her home, marked it with the letters "Vi" and pointed to the area she saw the police walking in the fields and the location of the barn of the Idle Hour Stable.

Jed Stone briefly cross-examined the witness. In response to Stone's questions, she told the jury how she attended a barbecue at her next door neighbors home, Mr. Panek, and that she and her husband had returned to their home at about ten o'clock that night. She said that she hadn't heard any screams that night, but that it had been raining, and she had closed all the windows as it began to rain harder that evening.

Mrs. Sable was asked several questions about the location of her home and the four other homes that were located near hers in 1955, and was then excused.

Roger Hammill had just celebrated his eightieth birthday the week before and would be marking his fifty-fifth wedding anniversary in two months. His demeanor, however, was not that of a man well-past retirement. He spoke in a clear, firm voice and those in the courtroom could see a spry man who continued to live an active life.

He told the jury that he had been a photographer for more than forty years beginning in 1938 while working for a testing company. His wife had bought him a camera, and he eventually progressed from that small camera to the larger professional type that he used for years afterward.

By 1942, he had moved to Franklin Park and had begun to work part-time as a photographer. He began working for the fire department and police department, and then did work with the county and state police and most of the fire departments in the west suburban area where he lived.

In those days, he told the jury, the police would call him if they wanted him to take pictures of a crime scene. He also had direct communications with the fire and police departments in the area, known as "Car 99" on the police frequencies.

In October 1955 Hammill recalled, he received a call from the State Police Headquarters at Harlem and Irving Park Avenues directing him to the forest preserves at Lawrence Avenue and River Road.

"I believe I was at lunch and got the call, and I left immediately…"

"Would you please describe what you saw when you pulled into the forest preserve area," Cassidy asked the witness.

"Well, there wasn't too many people there when I got there because I was there real early, and they waved me in off Lawrence Avenue and then took me over to the area and, of course, I carried my cameras all ready to take pictures. I used a great big four by five speed graphic camera at the time, took four by five pictures and they directed me in there, and I started immediately to take pictures before anybody else got there or before anybody else started to move anything."

"And what did you begin to take pictures of, that is, what did you see?"

"Well, there were three young boys, and I would say they were ten, eleven and twelve or twelve and thirteen, something like that. It looked like they had just been dumped out, and they were badly bruised. I could see… I could show you my photographs that I took, and they're badly bruised, and then they just laid there and it was just a few people, and I took a photograph to show how they were laying and that showed the area where it was. And then later on, well, other people came, of course. Later on this deputy or assistant coroner,

Harry Glos came on the scene and then, well, he took over."

"Okay. Did you happen to take photographs of the boys as you saw them before they were moved?"

"Oh, yes. There wasn't that many people there so nobody touched them."

Hammill testified that he had an open and unobstructed view of the bodies that he described as "laying crisscross on top of one another."

He was shown People's Exhibit 22, a photograph showing the bodies and Harry Glos starting to examine the boys. "He touched them all and turned some of them over after that point," Hammill said.

The witness was shown several photographs that he identified as the ones he had taken at the scene, and with each photo he described as best he could the investigators who had begun to arrive at the scene.

"Was the crime scene protected in any way that day?" Cassidy asked.

"No, no. Nobody ever heard of yellow ribbon around anything. We didn't have anything in those days. You just...we hoped that the police would keep the people out of the way. But, no, as you can see we got a lot of people in here that have the right to be there."

After questioning Hammill about several other photographs and what they showed in the background, Cassidy addressed the issue of the defense's contention in its opening statement that there was no physical evidence to connect the defendant to the crimes.

"To the best of your knowledge did the police recover any physical evidence from that crime scene besides the boys' bodies?"

"Objection," Stone said.

"No, not to my knowledge," Hammill continued, answering the State's question.

"To his knowledge he may testify to," Judge Toomin said.

Cassidy restated his earlier question.

"I don't think there was any other evidence but the three bodies."

"Judge I move to strike the answer. Objection," Stone said.

"Overruled. The answer may stand."

The State then asked that the photographs taken by Hammill be admitted into evidence, and after no objection from the defense that reserved its right to subject the photographs and the witness testimony on cross-examination, the gruesome black and white photographs were admitted into evidence.

"In 1955 it wasn't unusual for police officers to move bodies, roll them over, reposition them, even before the coroners office got there, was it?" Stone asked.

"It was unusual. A good police officer wouldn't do that."

"Who was the first police officer on the scene in Robinson's Woods?"

"I would have to think that was Peters, Sergeant Peters from the State Police but I can't vouch for that for sure. He was there when I got there but I can't say who got there first."

"You say he was there when you got there and we know that Mr. Glos was there when you got there?" queried Stone.

"No, he wasn't. He came in later."

Hammill testified that he was unable to tell the order the photographs had been taken in. He also could not identify all of the persons in the photos.

The next witness, Patrick Mason, testified that he had grown up in Chicago and had frequented the Bro-Ken H Stable in 1956 with his sister and her friend. He would go to the stables every weekend, he said, and work around the stable feeding horses and taking riders out as a guide. Because he was only 11 years old, he would not get paid for his work but instead he would be allowed to ride for free at the end his day's work.

Scott Cassidy asked the witness if he recalled the last day he spent at the stable.

"That day my father gave me a ride from our house. I went into the smaller of the two barns to get a horse to take out a group of riders, and half way through the barn I looked to my left in an empty stall, I saw Mr. Hansen performing oral copulation on a boy."

"Objection," O'Donnell said from his seat at the defense table. "Move for mistrial, your Honor."

"Objection overruled," Judge Toomin said, his voice matter of fact and perfunctory. "The answer may stand."

Cassidy asked the witness to repeat his answer then asked if he knew the identity of the boy he saw in the stable with the defendant.

"Yes." He identified the young boy by name, and stated that the boy and Hansen were about five or six feet away from him.

Then Mason continued his testimony and told the jury that Hansen looked at him. The witness then said he turned around and left the barn and went into another barn to saddle up horses.

"I was in the process of saddling a horse when Mr. Hansen came up behind me, grabbed me by the crotch. I shoved him away with my elbow, he told me I had to go along with the program that he had going there or I would not be allowed to work there anymore."

"What happened next?"

"I told him I was not interested, just to get out of my way, I was leaving...He stuck his finger in my face and told me that if I told anybody about what I saw him doing I'd wind up in the woods like those other boys."

Cassidy then asked the witness if he saw Hansen in the courtroom. The witness pointed to the defendant.

"That's the man sitting in the middle there," he said pointing to the defense table where Hansen sat with his attorneys.

Cassidy then showed the witness a picture identified as People's Exhibit #29, and asked if he recognized who it was.

"Yes, sir... Kenny Hansen."

"Does that picture show how he looked in 1957?"

"Yes, just about. Possibly just a little bit older looking than this."

Cassidy thanked the witness and walked back to his seat next to fellow prosecutor Pat Quinn.

Now Stone approached the witness and asked about his background. He had been a Chicago Police Officer, he said, and after he retired he had moved out West.

Stone pointed out discrepancies in the dates and addresses the witness had given in his statements to Agent James J. Grady of the Bureau of Alcohol, Tobacco and Firearms concerning the witness' recollection of the events he had just testified to seeing.

"I told him 1957. I pointed that out to him that it was a mistake, the year that's put on that report," the witness told Stone.

Stone asked the witness if he could recall the names of any of the more popular horses that were boarded at the Bro-Ken-H Stables in 1957.

"Sarge, Hong Kong, Blackjack," Mason responded in a confident voice.

"Do you remember a horse named Spice?" Stone asked.

"No sir, But I remember a horse named Tom Collins who was owned by Mr. Hansen."

"And you say that you saw Mr. Hansen in the small stable with a young man?"

"Yes, sir."

"And following that Mr. Hansen said something about winding up in the woods like the other boys?"

"Yes, sir."

"To the best of your knowledge were those the very words that you remember?"

"Yes, sir."

Stone then referred back to the witness' statement to Agent Grady and the corrections the witness had made to his earlier statement, attempting to raise the inference that this witness' recollection and statements about what he had seen forty years ago were not infallible.

After a few more questions, Stone wound up his cross-examination.

"Do you remember telling Mr. Grady that on that same occasion in that same report, August 19, 1994, that Hansen never had approached him in a sexual manner, him meaning you?"

"That's right."

"…No further questions, sir."

Judge Toomin excused the witness, then asked to see both sets of attorneys for a side bar conference and asked that the jury return to the jury room for a brief recess.

"Call Roger Spry," Quinn said in a loud, firm voice.

Roger Lee Spry was 46 years old, he told the jury, and was born in Logan, West Virginia. His father had been a coal miner and when Spry was 10 years old, the mine his father worked in closed down. His father moved to Illinois to find work and the family, including

Roger Spry's seven younger brothers and sisters, followed six months later.

The family settled in Calumet City, Illinois, a southern suburb of Chicago. Elements of organized crime in Chicago had run the strip bars and illegal gambling in that suburb for years during the '50s and '60s, and "Cal City" was known as the Midwest's "Sin City."

Spry testified that his mother was a stripper and prostitute, and a few months after the family had moved to Calumet City, his mother left home taking Spry's two younger brothers with her. The remaining children were then split up among relatives.

Shortly after the family split, Spry worked at his uncle's gas station and while working there met a man who was in the horse business. Spry began to work for the man on weekends, taking ponies out to the suburbs and taking pictures of kids sitting on the ponies. For an eleven-year-old, making $25 each weekend was good money.

Spry testified that his employer would rent the ponies from Ken Hansen and pick up the ponies from the Bro-Ken H Stables.

Shortly after his mother left the family and about six months after meeting Hansen, Spry moved into the apartment Ken Hansen and his wife shared with their two children. Seven months later, the Hansen's and Spry moved to the second floor of a two-story building on the premises of the Bro-Ken H Stables at 82nd and Keane Avenues.

Then only a few days after moving to the property, Spry testified, Hansen attempted to molest him. When Spry wouldn't let him, he said, Hansen made him move into the dog kennels on the first floor of the building where Spry slept on an old bed.

Spry then testified that he lived with Hansen off and on for the next twenty years.

Quinn conducted his direct examination of the witness from where he stood at the far end of the jury box, about twenty feet from the witness and a few steps from the short divider that separated the jury from rest of the courtroom.

"Now during the twenty years that you lived with Ken Hansen off and on did he occasionally have sex with you?"

"Objection," Stone called out from the defense table.

"Overruled," Judge Toomin ruled.

"Yes," Spry answered.

"Judge," Stone said in a loud voice, "could we be heard?"

Stone and Quinn walked up to the bench where another side bar conference was held. The attorneys argued about what testimony could or could not be admitted. After a few minutes, the judge made his decision.

"The motion is denied," Judge Toomin said. "You may continue."

Spry went on to testify to his relationship with Ken Hansen and that Hansen had sex with him for the next seven years after the first time he had been molested when he was eleven or twelve years old.

He lived with the Hansen family again when they moved to the High Hopes Stable in the late '60s, and then again when they moved to the Sky High Stables in south suburban Tinley Park, Illinois in the early '70s. During this period of time, Spry said, he saw other young boys working at the stables. They would clean out the barns and clean the horses and lead the horses from the barns out to riders.

"Sir, did you see how many of these boys arrived at the stables?"

"Objection," O'Donnell said. He knew where Quinn was going during his direct examination.

"Overruled," Judge Toomin said.

"Yes"

"And how is that?"

"Pick them up hitchhiking."

"Were you on occasion with Ken Hansen when he picked up young boys hitchhiking?"

"Yes."

"What would he say to young male hitchhikers when he first picked them up?"

Stone then got up from his chair to record his objections to the testimony.

"Judge, objection. We're talking about events fifteen years after 1955."

"I understand," Judge Toomin responded in an even-tempered tone. "Objection overruled."

"Sir," Quinn continued," what would he say to the kids to get them to go with him?"

"Where ya going, you know, where ya going to? What are you doing? Do you like horses? Do you need a place to stay? If you come to the barn and help us with the horses, you know, we'll give you some food and give you a place to stay."

"And when you were with Ken Hansen did many young boys take him up on that?"

"Yes."

"Where would he take them when he took them up on that?"

"Take them back to the barn."

Spry testified that the boys he saw Hansen pick up were between eleven and sixteen years of age and that he would not pick up older boys. He said that on many occasions he would have conversations with Hansen in which Hansen told him he had sex with the boys he had picked up.

"Did Ken Hansen have a name for the young boys he took to the stables and that he had sex with?" Quinn asked.

"Yes."

"What was that?"

"Chicken."

Quinn paused for a moment, letting the last word drift and echo throughout the courtroom. He turned and took a few steps back from where he stood at the far end of the jury box, then stopped and slowly turned around to look at Spry. He paused again, then in a calm, matter of fact tone, continued his questioning.

"Sir, do you know a person by the name of Silas Jayne?"

"Yes, I do," Spry answered.

He went on to testify about how he first came to know Silas Jayne, meeting him when Spry was fifteen or sixteen years old at Jayne's farm in Elgin, Illinois. Over the objections of Stone as to the relevancy of testimony concerning events ten years after the murders of the boys, Spry was allowed to continue his testimony.

He recalled that he was with Ken Hansen when he first met Jayne at the farm in Elgin, and that he also recalled meeting him at the Idle Hour Stables. Spry testified that Hansen had described his relationship with Jayne as a "business, personal relationship."

Now Quinn moved from his position at the end of the jury box and took a few steps in the direction of the witness. It was a nonverbal cue that what would be coming next would be important testimony.

"Sir, directing your attention now to back when you were about fifteen years of age did you have occasion—were you at that time living at the Bro-Ken H still?"

"Yes."

"While you were there, did anything unusual happen to you in terms of a conversation with Ken Hansen?"

Spry told the jury that while he and Hansen were preparing saddles in the tack room at the Bro-Ken H, Hansen had told Spry to go upstairs and get his bottle of scotch, and when he returned the two of them continued to work on the saddles. Hansen had been drinking the scotch and talking with Spry when he brought up Silas Jayne.

"And Kenny goes you don't want to ride for that man, you don't want to have anything to do with him, he's crazy," Spry testified.

"I said, what do you mean 'he's crazy?' Kenny says…he was about half in the bag…he said he picked up these three kids, took them to this barn and he sent [Robert] off somewhere to do something, to brush horses or something, so he could have sex with the two younger boys."

Spry testified that Hansen told him that when the older boy returned, he had surprised Hansen while he was having sex with the younger boys. When one of the boys threatened to tell, Hansen said he grabbed the older boy by the throat with one arm, and he tried to keep the other two boys from getting away with his other arm.

He went on to describe how Hansen told him that one of the boys was screaming and that he accidentally choked the older boy to death.

"What did he tell you he did after he accidentally choked the older boy to death?"

"He said he had no other choice but to kill the other two kids, so he said he killed the other two kids."

The courtroom was silent as Spry's last words faded into smaller echoes in the huge, crowded room.

Quinn asked what Hansen said happened after he killed the remaining two boys. Spry said that Hansen told him that Silas Jayne showed up and was angry at what had happened.

"Si told him, he said 'why do you have to get into this stuff?' He said 'this could ruin me.'"

Continuing to describe what Hansen had told him, Spry said that Hansen told him that Hansen and Jayne placed the bodies in a car and dropped them in a forest preserve.

"The older boy, he said he accidentally strangled, did he tell you his last name?" Quinn asked.

"Peterson."

Quinn asked if Hansen had ever mentioned the boys again in any conversations he had with him after this.

Spry testified he had taken money from horse riders at the stable without documenting it on the sign-in sheet and put the money in his pocket. One time, after he had pocketed about $5.00, he said that Hansen discovered what he had done and confronted him.

"He said 'why didn't you sign the people up' and I said I forgot. And he said, 'Rog, you're going to keep it up, and you're going to end up just like that Peterson kid.'"

Spry testified that he first talked to authorities about the murders in July of 1994, and that as a result of cooperating with authorities, he and his girlfriend had to relocate and find new jobs. As a result of moving and being out of work, he said, the government had given him approximately $4,000 in rent payments and other stipends.

Quinn asked the witness, "I'd like you to look around the courtroom right now, and tell the ladies and gentlemen of the jury, do you see the person that you had these conversations with that molested you and that you lived with off and on for twenty years?"

Spry pointed to the man seated between his two attorneys at the defense table. "That's him right there."

"Your Honor," Quinn concluded, "I would ask that the record reflect an in-court identification of Ken Hansen."

O'Donnell stood to cross-examine the witness.

First O'Donnell asked Spry about the money he had taken from horse riders without logging it in, putting the money in his own pocket, and telling Hansen he had forgotten to log it in.

"And when Mr. Hansen confronted you, you told him the reason you didn't put people's names down on the registry was that you forgot?" O'Donnell asked Spry.

"Yes, sir."

"That wasn't true, was it, because you indicated to us you took the money because he hadn't been paying you anything, is that right?"

"Right."

"So, by your own admission then you are a thief; is that correct?"

"Objection," Cassidy said for the record.

"Overruled," Judge Toomin stated in a calm, firm voice.

"Is that right?"

"Yes."

"And you also, then, are a liar by your own admission because you told him you forgot to put the names down but you didn't forget. You did it deliberately; is that correct?"

"Yes, sir."

Then O'Donnell pressed on, believing that there was additional information the jury should hear about the State's witness.

"Have you ever stolen anything else from the stable?"

Judge Toomin overruled the State's objection to the question.

"No, sir."

"Do you recall a Palomino horse?" O'Donnell continued.

"Yes, sir."

"And did you take that horse from the stables and take it over to Michigan and sell it?"

"Yeah, because Kenny owed me money."

"Because he hadn't paid you money you felt he owed you, is that it?"

"Yes."

"So really, then, you stole the horse but it was really Kenny's fault?"

"He owed me money."

"Now have you ever stolen any saddles from the stable?"

"No, sir."

"Well, didn't you put a saddle on the Palomino."

"Yes. I did that."

"And you didn't bring it back from Michigan, did you?"

"No, sir."

"And that was part of what you got, the money from...the Michigan stables isn't that correct?"

"Yes, sir."

Next, O'Donnell focused his cross-examination of Spry on why he hadn't told anyone about his conversation with Hansen until one year before the trial.

"That was when the police came and wanted to talk to you; isn't that correct?"

"Yes, sir."

"And they were going to arrest you for a crime; is that correct?"

"Yes, sir. Yes, sir."

"As a matter of fact, Mr. Spry, you have a case pending in the Circuit Court of Cook County, don't you?"

"Yes, sir."

"And the charge is what?"

"Arson."

"Arson of what?"

"Burning a barn down."

"So, you are not only a thief and a liar and a horse thief you are now an arsonist; is that correct?"

"No, sir."

"Well are you denying that you burned the barn down?"

"No, sir."

O'Donnell went on to elicit Spry's testimony that he and his girlfriend had been relocated at government expense, and assisted in finding housing and employment. That he lived on and off with the Hansens for twenty years; and had known one of the prosecution witnesses in the late '60s but had not communicated with him since that time, learning only two days before the trial that this other witness would be testifying at Hansen's trial.

O'Donnell concluded his cross-examination by asking Spry about other specifics of his agreement with the government concerning his testimony.

"Didn't you agree with the government that your arson charge would be dismissed or it would be reduced or that you would get a sentence of probation, for criminal damage to property?"

"Six months later I knew, yeah."

"So you did get a commitment from the government your sentence would be reduced, right?"

"No. They just said since you were going to testify they would just reduce it."

"And that you probably wouldn't have to go to prison, you would get probation; is that correct?"

"Yeah. Eighteen months probation."

"You didn't want to go to prison, did you?"

"No. Who wants to go to prison?"

Satisfied that he had done his job, O'Donnell turned in the direction of Judge Toomin and said, "That's all."

September 1995

"Gentlemen, do you want to identify yourselves, please?" Judge Toomin looked at the four men standing before him then nodded in the direction of the court reporter sitting to his right.

"Jed Stone and Arthur O'Donnell on behalf of Mr. Kenneth Hansen, who is before the Court." Stone said as he turned slightly in the direction of the court reporter. The reporter began to tap the keys of her steno machine.

"Scott Cassidy and Pat Quinn, assistant state's attorneys," Cassidy said.

The attorneys discussed the issue of Dr. Edmund Donoghue's testimony, which the jury would hear in a few hours. As Chief Medical Examiner of Cook County, he directed the Office of the Medical Examiner that conducted, among other things, the autopsies and investigations surrounding violent or suspicious deaths that occurred in Cook County. After considerable discussion, a ruling was entered and the trial continued.

"Mr. Quinn," Judge Toomin said, "you may proceed."

Quinn called Judith Mae Anderson to the stand as the State's next witness.

Mrs. Anderson recalled how in the summer of 1955 she was a 17-year old girl who liked horseback riding. She told the jurors that in August 1955, she had just returned from a month's vacation in California with her parents. She and a friend had gone riding and rented horses from the Idle Hour Stables. As they were riding back to the stables, the saddle on her friend's horse came loose throwing her onto the bridle path next to the Des Plaines River.

After helping her friend up, they walked their horses back to the stable. When they arrived, Ms. Anderson testified, she recalled that she had forgotten to pay for their horse rentals and approached a young man she saw standing in the yard.

"I asked him, you know, would he take my money, I forgot to pay. He said 'Well, I can't take your money, only Mr. Jayne can take your money.'"

"What happened after he said that to you?" Quinn asked the witness.

"He said that Mr. Jayne would be back in a few minutes, you'd have to wait. He was waiting, too. So while we were waiting—I had seen him there before, very good looking man, and I asked him his name."

"And what name did he tell you?"

"He said Ken Hansen."

Ms. Anderson testified that she and Hansen continued to talk, that he told her about how he and Mr. Jayne 'go back a long way,' and how he did odd jobs around the stable and helped Mr. Jayne.

"He had showed my girlfriend and me some tricks with the neck rein when we were on the bridle path. We had a lot of conversation about this," she said.

Anderson told the jury about how she would ride at the stables every other weekend in the summer, and that she was interested in Hansen. At one point, she said, she told him that if he was interested in getting together, he could look her up in the phone book.

She also told the jurors about how she had spoken to the agents of the Bureau of Alcohol, Tobacco and Firearms in August 1994. She was an artist, she said, and she had attempted to sketch a drawing from memory of what she believed Ken Hansen looked like. Unable to do so, she picked up some clay and did a sculpture sketch of him from memory.

Quinn then showed her a photograph, which had been marked People's Exhibit Number 34 and asked her if she recognized anyone in the photograph.

"Yes, I recognize Ken Hansen."

"And this is what Ken Hansen looked like when you saw him in the summer of 1955?"

"Yes, yes."

Stone approached the witness for his cross-examination of her.

"Miss Anderson, if I understand you correctly, you read about this case in the newspaper?"

"Yes, the first time that I saw his name was in the newspaper."

"And then having seen it in the media you decided to call the ATF?"

"Yes, I think that would be correct."

Stone went on to ask the witness about her forty year old recollection of a fifteen minute conversation with the defendant, and read Agent Rotunno's report where Anderson was quoted as having said "she was at the stable (Idle Hour) two times in the summer at the end of her school term (high school) possibly in June or July 1955."

"Well, that's not correct," the witness said.

"That's not what you told Agent Rotunno?" Stone asked.

"No, no, no. I told him that I had been in California for the month of July and it was at the end of the summer of 1955 that I was at the Idle Hour Stable several times with Linda Hoffman."

"You were shown this report and you corrected it, didn't you?"

"I corrected almost half of it before I handed it back to Agent Rotunno and I said, 'you have misunderstood most of everything that I told you on the telephone."

"So Agent Rotunno took down information and got it wrong?"

"He just said 'I'll do the whole thing over again.'"

"And in any event, you told Agent Rotunno that you couldn't identify any of the photographs of the person that you were remembering as being Ken Hansen from forty years ago?"

"I looked at forty different photographs that day, and I couldn't identify Ken Hansen from any of the photographs. Whoever these other people were, I don't know. So, that's correct."

"Thanks," Stone said. He turned and walked away from the witness and took his seat.

The State's next witness was Linda Hoffman-Trivers, who was able to recall that she had gone riding with Judy Anderson one day in 1955. She testified that she had an accident and fell from her horse after the cinch came loose and the saddles slipped from the horse. She and her friend then walked back to the stables. Although she remembered that she and Judy Anderson took a bus to the end of the bus line to reach the stables, she was unable to recall the name of the riding stable or the specific address of the stable.

On his cross-examination of Trivers, Stone was brief but made his point.

"Miss Trivers, you were interviewed by the ATF, the Alcohol, Tobacco, and Firearms, people?"

"Correct"

"They found you and called you up and talked to you?"

"Correct."

"And you gave them the best information you could from a forty year-old memory?"

"Correct."

"And as you sit here now, you certainly want to tell the truth to the Court and the jury and do the best you can?"

"Indeed."

"But forty years is a long time?"

"Long time."

"So you've done the best you could with the forty year-old memory?"

"That's right."

"Thanks," Stone said.

"Thank you," Ms. Trivers said.

Quinn didn't wait for Stone to reach his chair before he took his turn at the witness.

"Are you still a friend of Judith Mae Anderson?" Quinn asked.

"I am."

Quinn paused, his timing deliberate and reasoned.

"How is her memory?" he asked.

"Phenomenal," Trivers answered.

"Objection." Stone snapped the word out but it was too late.

"Sustained," Judge Toomin said.

"Nothing further," Quinn said as he sat down. It was hard for him not to smile.

The State's next witness was Dr. Edmund Donoghue, the Medical Examiner of Cook County. The coroners who had conducted the original and subsequent autopsies of the bodies of the Peterson and Schuessler boys were no longer alive, nor were any of the investigators from the old Coroner's Office who had originally been assigned to the case. But because the case was an unsolved, "open" case, the current Medical Examiner was called to render his opinions as to the causes of death.

Dr. Donoghue had been with the Cook County Medical Examiner's Office since July 1, 1977 and was now the Chief Medical Examiner, responsible for the work of 114 employees.

Quinn asked Dr. Donoghue about his experience and background as a forensic pathologist. Dr. Donoghue told the jury that he was a graduate of the University of Notre Dame and Marquette University Medical School, and licensed to practice medicine in Illinois, Wisconsin, Michigan, and Minnesota. He served his medical internship at the Mayo Clinic, in Rochester, Minnesota. And then, took two years of specialized training in the field of anatomic pathology at the Mayo Clinic, one year of forensic pathology with the Medical Examiner of Wayne County, Michigan and then further training at the Armed Forces Institute of Pathology while serving in the United States Navy.

In addition to being the Medical Examiner of Cook County, Dr. Donoghue was also the Director of Residency Training in Forensic Pathology, a Clinical Associate Professor of Forensic Pathology at the University of Illinois College of Medicine, and Board Certified with the American Board of Pathology in both anatomic and forensic pathology.

Quinn asked Dr. Donoghue about his experience in cases where the cause of death was by strangulation or asphyxiation.

"Well, I've probably performed at least ninety examinations in strangulation deaths myself and had the opportunity to observe many others."

Quinn then asked Dr. Donoghue if he had reviewed the reports, charts, or records of patients prepared by colleagues and whether he had ever drawn any conclusions from these records within the bounds of reasonable medical certainty.

"Yes, I have," Dr. Donoghue responded.

"On approximately how many occasions?"

"Well, probably hundreds of occasions."

Dr. Donoghue stated that he had reviewed the reports of Dr. Kearns concerning the bodies of the Peterson and Schuessler boys. And that he relied on the report of the postmortem examination prepared by Dr. Kearns, the Coroner's verdict, photographs of the location where the bodies were found, and photographs taken during the course of the autopsies.

Quinn then directed his questioning to Dr. Donoghue's review of the postmortem examination of Anton Schuessler. Dr. Donoghue testified that Tony Schuessler was 11 years old, weighed 90 pounds, and his height was 5 feet 1 inch.

The witness addressed each point of evidence of injuries noted on the body, including the external and internal injuries noted during the initial autopsy, and spoke slowly as he carefully enunciated each word he read from the report. Included in the report was a description of residue of adhesive tape noted over the nose and mouth area.

After he had finished his recitation of the numerous injuries found on the body, Dr. Donoghue paused for a moment then looked up at Quinn.

"Doctor, do you have an opinion based upon a reasonable degree of medical certainty as to the cause of death of Tony Schuessler?" Quinn asked.

"Yes, I do."

"And what is your opinion?"

"It is my opinion that Tony Schuessler died of strangulation."

"And, doctor, would it be consistent with your opinion that Tony Schuessler died of manual strangulation?"

"Manual strangulation, that's correct. That would mean he was strangled by someone's hands."

Quinn then proceeded to ask the witness about Robert Peterson and the evidence of external and internal injuries the autopsy report showed.

"Robert Peterson lived at 5519 West Farragut in Chicago, he weighed 110 pounds, and he measured 5 feet 3 inches in length, and appeared at the stated age of 13 years." Included in Dr. Donoghue's testimony was the description of seven lacerations or tears of the scalp that were arranged in two rows. There were three lacerations in the upper row and four lacerations in the lower row, varying in size from one centimeter to four centimeters. Also among the evidence of injury were fragments of adhesive tape found on the mouth and nose area, and a constricting bruise with abrasion in the neck area measuring two centimeters wide and completely encircling the neck.

"Do you have an opinion, Dr. Donoghue, within a reasonable degree of medical certainty as to cause of death of Robert Peterson?"

"Yes, I do."

"And what is that opinion?"

"It's my opinion that Robert Peterson died of strangulation."

"Dr. Donoghue, is it consistent with your opinion that Robert Peterson died of ligature strangulation?"

"Yes, it is because of the two-centimeter wide band of abrasion and bruising that encircled the neck."

"And can you please explain what you mean by ligature strangulation?"

"Well, ligature strangulation would be when you would take some sort of ligature, like a belt or a rope, and place it around the neck and put pressure on the neck."

"We can move now, doctor, to John Schuessler," he said.

"John Schuessler lived at 5711 North Mango in Chicago, he weighed 100 pounds, he measured 5 feet 3 inches in length, and he appeared at the stated age of 13 years," Dr. Donoghue continued in a clear firm voice.

He explained the evidence of external and internal injuries, including evidence of an incised wound approximately 10 by 4 centimeters on the front of the left thigh, made by an instrument with a sharp edge. It appeared to be a postmortem wound, occurring after John Schuessler had died.

"Do you have an opinion within a reasonable degree of medical certainty as to the cause of death of John Schuessler?" Quinn asked.

"Yes, I do."

"And what's your opinion?"

"It is my opinion that John Schuessler died of strangulation."

"And in your opinion, doctor, would the cause of death of John Schuessler be consistent with someone having held him in a choke hold at the time of his death?"

"Yes, it would."

"In your opinion, doctor, would the cause of death of John Schuessler be consistent with someone having held John in a choke hold at the same time with his free hand striking him in the head?"

"That would be consistent," Dr. Donoghue answered.

Quinn then asked if Dr. Donoghue would point out the injuries he had just described by referring to the photographs he relied upon, and which had been marked earlier as exhibits and had been enlarged and placed on an easel in front of the jury.

Dr. Donoghue stepped off the witness stand and walked to where the photographs were placed, then took a pointer and began to point out to the jury the location of the abrasions on each body, which he had just described in his testimony.

After he had finished his testimony, Dr. Donoghue returned to the witness stand and awaited Stone's cross-examination.

"Good morning, doctor," Stone said. His voice was pleasant, but not ingratiating.

"Good afternoon, Mr. Stone, Dr. Donoghue corrected.

"You are right," Stone said with a wry smile. "Dr. Donoghue, you have told the jury that you examined certain photographs, and we've seen the photographs that you have examined."

"That's correct."

"Could you tell the ladies and gentlemen how you got those

photographs?"

"Those were brought to me by Mr. Cassidy, the state's attorney."

"The state's attorney hand-delivered the photographs to you?"

"Yes, he did."

"And there's nothing unusual about that?"

"No."

"I mean, that's customary?"

"Yes."

Stone continued to ask the witness how Dr. Donoghue came to obtain the photographs and reports inferring that perhaps this procedure was out of the ordinary but denying that was the intention of his questioning.

"Nothing unusual about somebody bringing you a report and asking you to look at it?" Stone continued.

"No."

"And those reports were brought to you by whom?"

"Well, by Mr. Cassidy, the state's attorney."

"And again, nothing unusual about that. I'm not suggesting nor should you that there is anything sinister about that, is there?"

"I didn't think there was anything sinister."

Stone pointed out that the witness never saw the bodies and relied upon the reports of others and upon photographs that were taken. He asked Dr. Donoghue if he had read any reports by Sgt. Murphy or Captain Corcoran. Dr. Donoghue replied that he hadn't.

Stone then referred to the reports that had been the subject of evidentiary rulings earlier in the day. These included the autopsy reports and re-autopsy reports, which were unsigned but had the names of Drs. Kearns and Hirsch at the bottom of the page.

"In that same report there's some comments about black stains on the boys' feet," Stone continued. "Are you familiar with the fact that the boys' feet had black stains on them?"

"Yes, I am."

Stone continued his questioning after Judge Toomin sustained objections as to the use of the document being presented to Dr. Donoghue.

Stone continued his cross-examination and focused on the report that showed diatomaceous earth had been found in the wound of one of the boys.

"Now, doctor, based upon your experience as a coroner...as a medical examiner...would this kind of information assist you in arriving at an opinion as to the cause of death of these children?"

"Well, no," Dr. Donoghue responded. "I had already arrived at an opinion without ever having seen this report. So, no, I don't think it adds anything."

"Did you find any evidence that any of these children's bodies bore any evidence of hay?"

"No. I didn't find any evidence of hay."

"Straw?"

"Straw? No."

"Manure, horse manure specifically?"

"No."

"Oats?"

"No oats."

"Barley?"

"No barley."

"Horse feed?"

"No horse feed."

Dr. Donoghue responded to Stone's additional questions about diatomaceous earth.

"I suspect that you're going to find that diatomaceous earth occurs in a lot of places. I don't think it's going to be too helpful."

"Are you aware that the Chief of Detectives reported that nothing was found in the rectums of these boys and that in his words there was no evidence of any sexual molestation?" Stone cited the paragraph of the March 4, 1958 report he had given to the witness earlier in his cross-examination.

"Well, that's what the Chief of Detectives said, yes." After additional questions about whether Dr. Donoghue had gotten all of the reports generated by detectives in the case, Stone asked his final question.

"Sir, do you have any evidence that you can give to this jury that these boys were killed in a stable?"

"No."

"Your witness."

Scott Cassidy rose slowly from his chair at the prosecutor table.

"Dr. Donoghue," Cassidy began. His voice was slow and deliberate.

"If the victim of a homicide had oral sex performed upon him would you find evidence of sexual molestation… are you likely to find evidence of sexual molestation?"

"No."

"Can you yourself draw any inference of sexual molestation in your opinion in this case?"

"Yes," the medical examiner responded.

"Objection," Stone shouted. The veteran defense attorney also knew what was coming.

Judge Toomin had anticipated the entire exchange before Cassidy even finished his initial question.

"What's the basis?" Judge Toomin asked.

"Well beyond the knowledge and scope of this juror," Stone said.

Cassidy looked up in the direction of Stone and looked quizzically at his opponent. Stone had mistakenly referred to the witness as "this juror." If he realized his mistake, it did not interrupt his fluid recitation of the basis of his objection.

"He's already told us he's not a criminalist, and we're not asking him an opinion to a reasonable degree of medical certainty. So because of the form of the question and because it's beyond the scope of his expertise, objection."

"Overruled. If he's able to answer it, he will tell us so."

Cassidy asked the court reporter to read back his last question to the witness.

The reporter picked up the loose roll of shorthand tape flowing out of the back of the stenographic machine. She flipped through it, expertly passing the thin, continuous tape between the thumb and index finger of her right hand. She stopped, then passed another few inches of the tape between her fingers until she found the question she had typed. "Can you yourself draw any inference of sexual molestation in your opinion in this case?" she said matter-of-factly.

She let the loop of paper fall back into the tray.

"Yes," the medical examiner said.

"And your opinion is what?"

"Well, it is my opinion that there's at least evidence that's suggestive of a sexual nature of this attack because the deceased were found without any clothing."

"I have no further question, your Honor."

Stone asked if he could begin his re-cross examination of the witness and walked to the far end of the jury box.

"Dr. Donoghue," Stone began, "clothing can be removed and destroyed because it contains evidence, yes?"

"Is that a question?"

Dr. Donoghue's response made him sound like a snobbish professor demeaning a student.

"Yes," Stone responded politely.

"Yes, it can."

"And, of course, that has nothing to do with sex?"

"If it's...well, it could. That might be the evidence you'd want to get rid of it."

"And it may not have anything to do with sex?" Stone re-iterated the question for effect.

"Well, it also might not."

"And you are not suggesting with forty years of hindsight that you are in a superior position to determine whether this is a case of sexual molestation to the doctors who did the autopsy or to the Chief of Detectives, who investigated the case, are you?"

"Objection, your Honor. Counsel is not offering that as substantive evidence."

"Sustained," Judge Toomin responded.

"No further questions," Stone told the judge.

Judge Toomin looked at Cassidy and asked if there was anything further that the State wanted to ask of the witness.

"No," Cassidy answered.

Judge Toomin turned and directed his attention to Dr. Donoghue, "Thank you doctor. You may step down."

The medical examiner stepped down from the witness stand as

the judge addressed the jury and informed them that the proceedings would break for lunch and resume in an hour.

The trial resumed that afternoon with the State presenting another witness who would tell of working with Kenneth Hansen at the Sky High Stables in 1974.

Williamson told the jury that Hansen had told him that he had gotten to know Silas Jayne in the 1950s. The witness said Hansen told him he had worked at the Idle Hour Stables and that Silas Jayne owned the stables.

He also told the jury that Hansen had spoken to him about how he liked to have sex with young boys.

On his cross-examination of the witness, Stone brought out the fact that in 1955, Williamson had not been born; that he first came to Chicago in 1970; and that he never saw Hansen pick up any hitchhikers.

"And I don't say this to embarrass you, but I believe it is your position that at some point when you were a teenager Mr. Hansen made an advance to you?"

"That's correct."

"And you said no?"

"That's correct."

"Did he fire you?"

"No."

"Did he dismiss you, send you packing?"

"No."

"Obviously, he didn't kill you?"

"No."

"Did he punish you in any way?"

"No."

"He asked, you said no?"

"That's right."

"End of conversation?"

"It wasn't a conversation."

"End of act?"

"Right."

On re-direct examination, Quinn also asked the witness about the incident.

"This advance that counsel brought up. Hansen crawled into bed with you when you slept over, is that right?"

"That's right."

"And you were eighteen at the time, is that right?"

"Yes."

"These other young boys Ken Hansen told you about that he liked to have sex with, were they as old as eighteen?"

"No."

"Were they younger than you?"

"Yes."

"Were they all younger than you?"

"Yes."

"Nothing further."

The witness was excused and now the State prepared to present its next witness, William "Red" Wemette.

Wemette was the first person Cassidy and Quinn interviewed in connection with the Peterson-Schuessler case. In 1993, the Federal Bureau of Alcohol, Tobacco, and Firearms (ATF) received information from one of its informants about the Peterson-Schuessler murders and shared this information with the Cook County State's Attorneys Office.

Cassidy and Quinn met with ATF Special Agents Jim Delorto, Jim Grady, and John Rotunno at a restaurant on the south side of Chicago. After the agents gave the two prosecutors details of what they had learned from their informant, Quinn and Cassidy became convinced they could successfully prosecute the prime suspect, even after more than forty years had passed since the crimes had been committed.

Wemette had worked as a bartender before becoming involved in the pornography business in the "Old Town" neighborhood of Chicago. Eventually, he became an informant for the government's case against an individual who was identified by the government as an associate of organized crime figures. As part of his expenses in the pornography business, Wemette had to pay a "street tax" levied on him by organized crime, which would allow him to stay in business.

Wemette was wired and videotapes were made of his monthly payments. The tapes and Wemette's testimony were then used in the prosecution of Frank John Schweihs by the federal government.

The prosecutors knew of Wemette's background, the fact that he had been a government informant for nearly twenty years, and was now in the Federal Witness Protection Program.

Cassidy began his direct examination of Wemette by asking the witness how he first met Kenneth Hansen.

Wemette told the jury that when he was nineteen, he visited the Y.A.K. Club in south suburban Frankfort, Illinois. There he was introduced to Ken Hansen and his brother, Kurt. A short time later, Wemette said, he met Hansen at the Sky High Stables where Hansen showed him the property and asked if he liked horses.

Eventually, Wemette began to work at the stables. He testified that he would also drive Hansen around since Hansen did not have a driver's license. On occasion, he said, Hansen would ask him to stop to pick up young, male hitchhikers who were between 12 and 16 years of age.

In the summer of 1968, Wemette said, he had a conversation with Hansen in the kitchen of Hansen's house trailer located on the property of Sky High Stables.

"Prior to the conversation I'm referring to, what had you and Mr. Hansen been doing?" Cassidy asked the witness.

"Drinking alcoholic beverages, Scotch. We were drinking Scotch."

"Were you intoxicated?"

"No, not at that time."

"What, if anything, did Mr. Hansen say to you?"

Over the objection of Stone, Wemette continued his testimony.

"He told me about a famous case, the Peterson-Schuessler boys."

"Before you proceed with the conversation any further, Mr. Wemette, let me ask you this: did Mr. Hansen at a later date also have a conversation with you in regard to this famous case, the Peterson-Schuessler boys?"

"Quite a few times."

"And approximately how many times?"

"Approximately a dozen."

"Was anyone else ever present for these conversations you had?"

"No."

"In regard to these conversations, during which conversations did Mr. Hansen speak most about the boys?"

"The initial conversation stands out in my mind most...He said that it was a very famous case and it was in the headlines and he almost made headlines himself and he indicated to me, he says, I came that close to getting caught."

Wemette placed two of his fingers a half-inch apart.

"During the first conversation you had with Mr. Hansen, though, did he say anything else with regard to the Peterson-Schuessler boys, the very famous case?"

"Yes."

"What else did he say?"

"He said he strangled the boys."

"Did he say how this happened?"

"He said he picked them up hitchhiking."

"Did he say where he took them?"

"To a barn on the north side of Chicago called the Idle Hour Stables."

"Besides...what else did he say in that conversation?"

"He said...I believe at that conversation he said he asked his brother for assistance, that his brother was there and he asked him to help him."

"Did he say, if anything, what his brother did?"

"I believe he said his brother injured one of the persons with a blunt instrument of some type."

Wemette then testified as to another conversation he had with Kenneth Hansen several weeks later, again at the Sky High Stables.

"He told me that he picked the boys up, and one boy, the youngest boy, he had taken into a separate room, and the two older boys were on a horse or a pony, I'm not sure which, and he sent them riding in an arena, or whatever, and the other boy, he had sexual relations with, oral sex, he performed oral sex on the younger boy...and then he told me that he sent the younger boy back and the other boy came back, the middle boy came back and he went with him and the older and younger boy interrupted them while they were...that the older boy and the younger boy...the younger boy had told the older boy what had happened and said, "come on, let's get my brother out of here...let's go, let's call our parents, let's call the police..."

"Did he say what happened then?"

"He said there was a scramble, kind of a scramble-type situation and he asked for assistance from his brother to help him."

Cassidy asked if there were any other conversations regarding what had happened to the boys, and Wemette answered that there were.

"He told me that his brother botched the job and when he disposed of the bodies that there was a piece of evidence left behind that could connect him to the murder. He seemed to be plagued with that, of getting caught."

"Did he tell you if he did anything to protect himself from being caught?"

"Yes, he did. He told me he moved to the south side of Chicago and low-balled himself, just tried to stay mediocre where he wouldn't be noticed."

"Did he tell you anything with regard to the Idle Hour Barn itself?"

"Yes, he told me it was burned, somebody burned it for him."

"And did he say why?"

"The case was heating up in the newspapers. He asked me a lot about the case and asked did I know anything about it and I said no."

"Did he ever tell you if anyone else was involved besides him and his brother, Kurt, Mr. Wemette?"

"He mentioned a third party that might be a forest preserve...he said it was a forest preserve employee, possibly a ranger."

"No further questions your Honor," Cassidy said.

Stone began his cross-examination of William Wemette.

"Mr. Wemette, I couldn't help but notice that there were two people that accompanied you into court. Do you know who they are?"

"Which two?" Wemette asked. "Would you point them out to me, please," he said.

Stone gestured with his hand to the people sitting in the row behind him.

"The young lady that walked in with you and the gentleman that's sitting behind me."

"Yes, they are part of the SRT unit for ATF...Special Response Team."

"And they're from the Federal Bureau of Alcohol, Tobacco, and Firearms?"

"Yes."

Wemette told the jury that he had been a cooperating government witness since 1971 and had been paid more than $14,500 from June 1993 by the government, and that he had been an informant for the FBI from 1971 to 1989. He estimated that since going to work as a "mole" for the FBI until providing his testimony in the present case he had been paid $25,000.

During his work as an informant for the ATF, Wemette testified, he had told Agent Rotunno about the conversation he had with Hansen.

"Did you ever write down in a diary or a book or a piece of paper anywhere the substance of any of those conversations?" Stone asked, referring to Wemette's talks with Hansen.

"No," Wemette replied.

"Well, after you had the conversation in 1968 where somebody tells you that they had committed a murder, did you pick up the phone and call the police?"

"No."

"Did you call the Cook County State's Attorneys Office?"

"No."

Stone continued to use his cross-examination to elicit from Wemette that in all the years he had worked as an informant he had not told any law enforcement officials about what he had been told by Hansen, until his conversation with the ATF.

Wemette also testified that at one time he had sought to obtain an easement for a strip of land on property owned by Kenneth Hansen's wife, Beverly. And that a later plan to open a restaurant and bar inside the clubroom of the stables owned by Beverly Hansen also fell through and that as a result Wemette felt resentful.

"Well it upset you enough so that you were upset with the Hansens, isn't that right?"

"No, I spoke to the boys after that, Mark and Danny, his sons, and Beverly," Wemette replied.

Stone continued his questioning, showing Wemette the sales contract between him and Beverly Hansen and began to question the witness about his real name. Wemette answered that he had changed his name from William Wemette to Robert R. Wemette, Jr. to adopt his father's name.

"Did you then change your name back to William Wemette?"

"No."

Stone paused for a moment, not certain of what the witness was saying or trying to avoid saying.

"Well, when you introduced yourself to the jury about an hour ago and swore to tell the truth, you told this jury your name is William Wemette, Stone said.

"That was my birth name," Wemette answered.

Stone briefly looked at his co-counsel, O'Donnell, as if he were going to ask O'Donnell something. Then he turned and faced the witness again.

"I'm sorry. I'm confused," Stone said. "What is your name as you sit here now?

"Objection, Judge," Cassidy said loudly as he sprang up from his seat.

"Overruled," Judge Toomin replied.

Cassidy remained standing and asked Judge Toomin for a sidebar. Both attorneys approached the bench.

He told Judge Toomin and Stone that Wemette went by another name and the name change was because of his prior testimony against members of organized crime. That was the reason for the presence of the people Stone had pointed to in the courtroom early in his cross-examination. Judge Toomin did not realize that Wemette went by a different name.

Stone offered to continue his questioning without asking what

Wemette's name was at present then resumed his cross-examination.

"Mr. Wemette, I don't care what your current name is. You have a name other than Wemette now," Stone continued.

"And that document…is a true and accurate copy of your contract with Beverly Hansen that bears your signature?"

"That's my signature, and it's Beverly's."

"Your witness," Stone said to Cassidy.

Cassidy confined his redirect to the fact that Wemette had testified one other time in 1989, and that the two agents who were now in the courtroom and had accompanied him to court did not know anything about the present case.

"No they don't. They just came here to protect me." Stone's re-cross was just as brief eliciting from Wemette that the two ATF agents present in the courtroom had nothing to do with the case or with Kenneth Hansen.

After Stone returned to his seat, the court told the jury that they would be in recess until Monday morning and cautioned them not to discuss the case over the weekend or to read, view, or listen to reports of the case in the media.

Monday
September 11, 1995

The trial resumed after the attorneys for the prosecution and defense met with Judge Toomin in the judge's chambers to discuss matters of witness testimony, and the State's intention to have their exhibits admitted into evidence when the State had finished presenting its last witnesses and rested its case against Kenneth Hansen.

Lt. John Farrell of the Chicago Police Department told how he and fellow officers from Area 5 detective headquarters arrested Hansen at his home on August 11, 1994 and transported him to ATF Headquarters in Chicago.

He told the jury that he and Agent Rotunno interviewed Hansen. In the interview, Hansen told them he picked up young boys who were hitchhiking and would have sex with them. Farrell also testified that he had told Hansen that Spry and Wemette were cooperating with the police on the case. Hansen, Farrell said, explained that he expected they would be cooperating against him because "I eventually spurned their sexual advances."

The next witness was Barbara Riley, the assistant state's attorney who interviewed Hansen while he was in custody at Area 5 Headquarters. Riley testified that after introducing herself to Hansen as an assistant state's attorney she informed Hansen of his rights.

Riley told the jury how Hansen recounted his background to her, his work at various stables, and that he described himself to her as bisexual. He admitted he knew Silas Jayne, but only on a business level. Hansen said he would occasionally sell a horse to Jayne, who would then sell it to one of his wealthier clients at a much higher price. Hansen, Riley testified, denied any knowledge about the Peterson-Schuessler slayings.

Riley was the State's last witness in their case, and after completing her testimony and being excused, Judge Toomin again met with the attorneys to discuss stipulations by both parties to allow certain evidence and exhibits to be entered into evidence. After the judge read the stipulations into the court record, Scott Cassidy informed the court that the State would rest.

Judge Toomin took the opportunity to inform the jury that before the defense would begin its case, court would be in recess until after lunch. The members of the jury returned to the jury room, and after the last of the jurors had entered the room the bailiff closed the door.

The four attorneys approached the bench and began to discuss and present their arguments concerning how the case would proceed.

Stone requested that the counts, involving the offenses of indecent liberties with a child be dismissed by a ruling for a directed verdict. Defense argued that no evidence had been presented of any such acts performed by the defendant on any of the three boys or that they had been sexually molested.

The court had to consider the law as it was written in 1955 concerning such crimes, rather than the law at the time of the trial. Under Chapter 38 of the Criminal Code Section 109, entitled "Sexual Crimes against Children Under Fifteen, Immoral and Improper or Indecent Liberties," the State had charged Hansen with "indecent liberties" involving the three boys.

Quinn read the pertinent sections of the statute to Judge Toomin.

"Any such person who shall take any such child or shall entice, allure, persuade any such child to any place, whatever, for the purpose either of taking any such immoral, improper or indecent liberties with such child with said intent…shall be imprisoned."

Quinn paused and looked up from the old volume containing the criminal statutes.

"Judge, the second he picked these kids up hitchhiking he's guilty under the statute as written at that time."

Stone argued that there was no evidence of the identity of the specific individual who was the subject of an alleged sex act; that the witnesses Wemette and Spry testified to two different versions of what they claimed were admissions by Hansen that he had killed the boys. And that the State had to prove there was a sex act committed and not just taken for some immoral purpose.

Judge Toomin denied the defense's motion for a directed verdict on the counts involving indecent liberties with a child.

Court reconvened with the Defense presenting its first witness in its case, AFT Agent John Rotunno. Rotunno's brief testimony consisted of telling the jury that one of the witnesses, Joe Plemmons, had told Rotunno that Plemmons had once caught the defendant having sex with young boys in a barn.

After a brief cross-examination by Quinn the witness was excused.

The attorneys again stipulated certain evidence, including official Department of Commerce Weather Bureau records for the weather conditions on October 16, 1955, and the registry of the Garland Building for October 16, 1955 reflecting the signature of Robert Peterson on line 20 of the registry.

After their discussions concerning the evidence to be admitted was concluded, O'Donnell stepped away from the bench.

"I'll be right back," he said to the judge and the state's attorneys.

Walking quickly to the door of the anteroom of the courtroom across from the jury, O'Donnell knocked and opened the door, but not completely. He motioned with his right hand to the person inside to come into the courtroom, then stood back and opened the door wide.

An elderly man in his late eighties cautiously walked out into the courtroom. Quickly and quietly closing the door of the anteroom, O'Donnell turned to the man standing next to him and gently took the man's arm as the pair slowly and deliberately walked toward the witness stand only a few feet away.

"Walk up to the chair," O'Donnell said softly to the man. "Remain standing and the Judge will swear you in," he said.

The elderly man cautiously approached the two-carpeted steps, leading to the witness chair. He hesitated a moment, appearing uncertain as to where he was to go once he negotiated the two steps.

One of the bailiffs approached and directed him to proceed up to the chair.

"Stand up there," the bailiff said, pointing in the direction of the witness chair.

Judge Toomin looked down at the witness still hesitating and standing to the right of him.

"Right up there," Judge Toomin said. "Step up, face this way."

The man slowly walked up the two steps and stood next to the witness chair and faced the judge.

"Please raise your right hand," the judge asked the witness. After swearing that the testimony he would give would be the truth, the man turned and glanced furtively for a second in the direction of those assembled in the courtroom, then looked back at Judge Toomin.

"Be seated, please. Keep your voice up as loud as you can, sir," the judge advised the witness.

O'Donnell waited until the man was comfortably seated.

"Will you state your name, please, sir and spell your last name for the record?"

"Frank M. Jayne, J-A-Y-N-E."

Jayne's voice was thin and weak and could hardly be heard by those sitting in the first row of the courtroom

"And will you keep your voice up loud enough so everyone in the courtroom can hear you, Frank, because I happen to be a little bit hard of hearing," O'Donnell asked.

"Yes. Well, I will try."

"And what is your address?"

"1098…" Jayne's voice trailed off as his eyes looked up to the ceiling, looking as if he were trying to remember.

"1098?" O'Donnell asked quickly.

"In Elgin, Illinois," Jayne said, his eyes focusing again on the defense attorney. "And the zip number?" he asked.

"Yes, if you know it," O'Donnell said.

"61123." Jayne responded, sounding pleased that he could remember the numbers. He smiled a bit, looking past O'Donnell and in the direction of the jurors.

"And Frank, how old are you?"

"74 going on 75. Oh, my…Nuts! I am 84," Jayne said and smiled at O'Donnell.

The sound of stifled laughter came from the rear of the courtroom.

"84?" O'Donnell said, ignoring the sound behind him.

"I was thinking…I was thinking of your age," Jayne said. "You mentioned it."

O'Donnell cleared his throat and pressed on.

"Principally what has been your business, profession, or occupation?"

"Farmer, horseman."

Jayne told the jury that he had been in the horse business as a trainer and seller of horses, including thoroughbreds and show horses. So were his brothers, he said. His brother Silas, Si, had operated the Idle Hour Stables, and they had been partners. He was familiar with some of the people who worked at the stables, he said, but Ken Hansen did not work there.

"No way," Jayne said.

"Why do you say no way?" O'Donnell asked.

"He wasn't that kind of a horseman. He had…"

"What kind of horseman was Mr. Hansen?"

Jayne responded that the horses they had were "high class" horses that they taught English riding and hunting and jumping, whereas Hansen had a livery business where people boarded their horses and rented horses by the hour.

He went on to tell how he first met Hansen in the early '60s. Jayne's son was selling hay to Hansen. Frank Jayne introduced his brother Silas to Hansen some time later when Hansen was looking to purchase a jumping horse.

O'Donnell asked the witness if he knew what security procedures were used at the Idle Hour Stables in the 1950s.

"Well, in the first place, we had a night watchman. And he slept all-day and patrolled around there at night. And he had dogs and good dogs." Jayne said that the watchman's job was to secure the premises. There were also four grooms living on the premises, Jayne said.

During cross-examination by Quinn, Jayne said that he knew of the Sky High stables that Hansen owned in Tinley Park, but didn't know when Hansen had purchased that stable. And that Si had sold the Happy Day Stables, located just south of the Idle Hour Stables, to their brother George Jayne in the early '50s. But he was certain that Hansen never worked at the Idle Hour Stables.

"He didn't have the expertise," Jayne said.

After some additional questioning Frank Jayne was excused. He slowly got up from the witness chair and teetered a bit as he approached the two steps leading down from the witness box. The bailiff who had helped him before guided him to the door leading to the anteroom, off the courtroom.

The defense proceeded with their case, questioning the next witness, Edwin Thomas, about his experience as a worker at Hansen's stables. Thomas had known Hansen since the late '50s when Thomas would visit the Broken H stable as a young boy, then worked at the stable with Roger Spry. Hansen fired Spry, Thomas said, and then Thomas took over the work at the stables.

Thomas also testified that he had known Joe Plemmons but had never known William Wemette during the time he worked at Hansen's stables.

At the conclusion of his direct examination of Thomas, Stone asked him about Roger Spry's reputation as a truthful person, since Thomas had known him from 1960 until the time Hansen fired him.

"What is his reputation?" Stone asked the witness.

"Very bad. Nobody trusted him. Nobody believes him. Nobody wants him around," Thomas responded.

Cassidy asked Thomas on cross-examination if he considered

himself good friends with Hansen.

"Yes"

"As a matter of fact, his lawyer is your lawyer, isn't that correct?" Cassidy asked.

"Yes."

"Mr. Art O'Donnell also represents you does he not?"

"Yes, he does."

"And you currently have a civil matter going, a law suit, do you not?"

"And Mr. O'Donnell is your attorney in that suit?"

"Yes."

The witness proceeded to tell the jury about how he lived at the stables run by Ken Hansen and his wife, how he met and spent time with Hansen's two sons, how Thomas eventually married and then divorced. He had never seen the defendant pick up boys hitchhiking, he said. Neither had he ever seen Robert Stitt, one of the witnesses in the trial who also worked and lived at the stables, pick up hitchhikers.

Thomas also said he had seen Joe Plemmons around the stables, but only for a few minutes and then Plemmons would leave.

When asked about William Wemette, Thomas testified that he had heard his name but could not recall if he had ever met him.

On his re-direct examination of the witness, O'Donnell asked Thomas if Hansen ever told Thomas he knew about the Peterson and Schuessler boys.

"Never." Thomas responded in a firm voice.

Cassidy and Quinn stood before the judge's bench, waiting for the judge to formally ask the defendant whether it was Hansen's decision not to take the witness stand.

After carefully informing the defendant that he had the right to testify or not testify on his own behalf, Judge Toomin asked Hansen if he understood what the judge had explained to him.

"Yes, sir," Hansen responded in a quiet and subdued voice.

"Nobody has promised you anything to cause you to make that decision?" the judge asked. Judge Toomin leaned forward, in order to better hear the defendant.

"No, sir," Hansen replied.

"Are you doing this of your own free will while conferring with your counsel?" Judge Toomin asked.

"Yes, sir."

Satisfied that the defendant had understood his rights and that he had the right not to testify as a witness in his own defense, Judge Toomin sat back in his chair.

"That matter has been resolved. You may be seated," the judge said to the defendant.

"I understand the Defense has further evidence at this time," the judge said. His voice was louder than usual, and emphasized his desire to keep things moving.

O'Donnell quickly rose to his feet, letting the judge know that he had gotten the message and wasn't going to be wasting time.

"Defense would call Mark Hansen."

Mark Hansen strode confidently to the witness stand and was sworn in. He was the younger of Kenneth Hansen's sons and had been a vociferous defender of his father in the months before the trail. In interviews given to the press concerning his father, he expressed his incredulity of the charges.

He told the jury that he currently was the owner of a horse stable and had been born in suburban Willow Springs, Illinois. He recalled the physical structures and location of the Bro-Ken H Stable that his father had owned and said that he remembered Roger Spry as one of the workers at the stables years ago. Roger Spry had also worked at the High Hopes Stables before Hansen had purchased the Bro-ken H, and then had purchased the Sky High Stables in Tinley Park, Illinois.

Roger Spry, he said, had never made any complaints to him about his father making sexual overtures to him.

He did state that he recalled that his father had occasionally picked up hitchhikers and brought them to the stables to work for him. He told the jury that when he was in his late teens, he had discovered that his father was homosexual. But, he said, that had never interfered with his relationship with his father.

After O'Donnell completed his brief direct examination of Mark Hansen, Judge Toomin allowed the State to begin its cross-examination of the witness.

"No questions, "Cassidy said.

The witness was excused and the attorneys for the State and the defense proceeded to enter testimony into the record by means of stipulation. Stipulation to facts is often used where there is no dispute between the parties concerning facts or testimony on an issue. It is also used to avoid unnecessary delay in the proceedings, where the time and expense of bringing in a particular witness or proof of the facts can be avoided by having both parties come to an agreement concerning the validity and accuracy of the facts or testimony presented.

In this case, the president of the management company of the Garland Building would have been called to testify that in fact there was a men's washroom on the 9th floor of that building.

The next stipulation was the testimony of Malcolm Peterson.

Both the defense and the prosecution agreed to the entry into evidence of his testimony by stipulation. The questions entered were those asked and answered by Mr. Peterson on October 30, 1955 at his home.

During the reading of the testimony, the courtroom was silent except for the strong, deep voice of Stone who read the stipulated testimony into the court record with an even tone in his voice and devoid of any emotion.

He paused once he had finished and turned to look at his opponent.

"So stipulated?" he asked.

"So stipulated," Cassidy replied.

Judge Toomin then asked to see the attorneys for a sidebar and a discussion was held off the record. After conferring for a few minutes, the attorneys walked back to their seats and the judge addressed the jury.

"Ladies and gentlemen, will you step into the jury room for a few minutes."

The jury rose to their feet. A few of them looked as if they had become teary-eyed during the reading of Peterson's testimony. At the point in his testimony, where he told of kissing his son goodbye and watching as the three friends walked down the sidewalk and away from their home, several members of the public seated in the front rows were visibly moved and wiped their eyes with their hands.

The judge waited until the last juror entered the jury room then signaled one of the court bailiff's to the bench.

"Bring in Mr. Hyme, the juror that has the funeral tomorrow," he instructed the bailiff.

After a few moments, the juror appeared and told the judge that he expected that he would be back in court at 12:30 or 1:00 p.m. the next day. The judge and the attorneys then discussed the trial's schedule for the next day, and Judge Toomin informed them that he would order the jury to return the next day at 12:00 noon.

The jury was then brought out of the jury room and Judge Toomin advised them of the schedule, including the fact that it looked as if they would be hearing the conclusion of the case the next day. He then stated again that they should not discuss the case among themselves or anyone else, and that should there be any mention of the case in the media, they were to turn the page, channel, or station and not listen, view, or read anything about the case. Judge Toomin announced that court was adjourned.

Wednesday
September 13, 1995

After resuming the proceedings and informing the jury that concluding evidence and final arguments and summations of law would be presented, Judge Toomin turned his attention to Jed Stone and Art O'Donnell.

"At this time, Mr. Stone, Mr. O'Donnell, I understand you have further evidence."

"Yes," O'Donnell said as he stood to address the court. "Defense will call Barbara Ashbaugh."

Barbara Ashbaugh testified that in 1955, she worked at the Idle Hour Stable, teaching horseback riding seven days a week, and worked there until it was sold in 1966. She testified that she had known Ken Hansen since 1946 when they were neighbors on Winnemac Street in Chicago. During her testimony she said that she did not remember seeing Ken Hansen at the Idle Hour Stables at all.

She did remember that there were gates, which were locked at night and that there was a night watchman on the property.

"Was he there most of the time that you were there?"

"Yes."

"The whole eleven years?"

"Yes. He would, every now and then he would, go into the city and be gone for three or four days, but, you know, he'd take a few days off."

"In addition to John, the fencing, and the locked gate, were there any people that slept on the property?"

"The barn help slept there, and there was a family that lived over the back barn and then Ralph Fleming and his wife lived there."

On cross-examination, Quinn asked if there was a fire at one of the back barns in May 1956, and she pointed to an aerial photograph of the property taken in April 1955 indicating where the barn had been. She also explained that the barn area contained the tack room and that the tack room contained stalls, leather strips and strapping used for the harnesses of horses.

Daniel Strong was the next witness for the defense, testifying that he had met Ken Hansen in Korea in 1953. He said he and Hansen were part of a unit that shared a squad tent where ten or twelve soldiers would sleep on cots.

Ken Hansen, Strong testified, never made any sexual advance toward him in the time he had known him in Korea.

Strong testified that in 1955, Ken Hansen and Hansen's wife visited Strong at his parents' home in Woodsboro, Texas. O'Donnell showed the witness several photographs depicting Strong, Ken and Beverly Hansen standing in front of Strong's parents' house and a picture of the Hansens and Strong taken on the beach at Bocacheca near Brownsville, Texas. He believed the pictures were taken in October of 1955.

After the photographs were entered into evidence, the defense rested.

Now the State was allowed to present its case in rebuttal of the defense.

The first witness presented by the State in rebuttal was Laura Schwarz. She testified that Ken Hansen had been married to her cousin Beverly Carlson Hanson, and in August 1955, she had been staying with the Hansens at their apartment on Winnemac Avenue in Chicago. The State intended that the evidence provided by this witness would show that the Hansens were residing on Winnemac Avenue, on the north side of Chicago, in the late summer of 1955 and not on the far south side as the defense contended.

The defense had attempted to show that the Hansens had purchased their stable on the far south side of Chicago in June of 1955.

On cross-examination by Stone, Schwarz testified that after Labor Day, 1955, Beverly Hansen did not live at the Bro-KEN - H Stables on the far south side.

The next witness for the State's rebuttal was Robert Milliken. Milliken testified that Edwin Thomas had picked him up hitchhiking when he was fifteen and took him to the Camelot Stables in Tinley Park, IL. There he met Ken Hansen. Sometime thereafter Milliken had sexual relations with Hansen and later told Edwin Thomas about the relationship with Hansen.

The State presented another witness, Bill Corwin, who testified that he had worked for George Jayne in the late '40s at Sportsman's Stables in Morton Grove, Illinois, not far from Park Ridge. He also said he came to know Silas Jayne from the late 1940's until Silas Jayne's death, and it was through Silas Jayne that Corwin knew Ken Hansen.

Corwin stated that he met Hansen at the Happy Day Stables, where Corwin worked for George Jayne, and that Corwin saw Hansen on occasion with Silas Jayne and George Jayne at horse shows.

Finally, Pat Quinn called Carvil Lee Miller to the stand. Miller testified that in 1950 he worked at the Happy Day Stables for George Jayne and has been in the horse business ever since. He met Hansen at Happy Day Stables in 1955 and testified that Hansen would "help around a lot" at the Happy Day Stables.

"And what would Ken Hansen do specifically, sir? Did Ken Hansen haul horses from Happy Days?" Quinn asked the witness.

"From...well, he hauled horses all over. He'd haul them from Happy Day to Idle Hour, Idle Hour back."

"And the Idle Hour was owned by Silas Jayne, is that right?"

"Yes."

"Nothing further," Quinn said.

After a brief cross-examination by Jed Stone and re-direct by Quinn, the State rested its rebuttal

"With that, your Honor, the People rest."

"Very well," Judge Toomin said, turning in his chair so that he would face the jury.

"Ladies and gentlemen, the evidence has now been completed by both sides, and we will be moving into the final stage of the trial, the final arguments followed by the instructions of law. As I may have explained to you last week, the final arguments will be presented in the following manner. The State has the opportunity to address you first followed by defense, and the State has the opportunity to speak to you last inasmuch as they do have the burden of proof in all criminal cases."

Turning again in his chair to face the packed courtroom, Judge Toomin looked in the direction of Assistant State's Attorney Patrick Quinn.

"You may proceed."

"Thank you, your Honor."

Quinn rose from his chair and calmly walked to a point midway between the table where his co-counsel remained seated and the judge's bench. He stopped and turned briefly in the direction of the table where defense counsel had leaned back in their chairs awaiting the State's closing argument.

"Defense counsel," Quinn said in the measured tone of politeness. He looked at O'Donnell and Stone then nodded in their direction. He could see Kenneth Hansen, seated next to his defense attorneys; his eyes were fixed on an undefined point across the room in a purposeful attempt to avoid making eye contact.

The assistant state's attorney turned and looked in the direction of his co-counsel, Scott Cassidy.

"Scott," Quinn said, acknowledging the dedication and immense effort his partner had put into the investigation and preparation of the case.

And finally, turning and facing the jury, he addressed the men and women who would decide the case.

"Ladies and gentlemen," he said. He paused for a moment then began his closing argument.

"Last Wednesday morning, I stood in front of you and told you what I believed the evidence would show. You have now seen that everything, everything I told you we would show you we have shown you. It was all true. Let's take a short look, though, and see what has not been true. Let's take a look at the defense opening statement in this case.

"Counsel told you in his opening statement that I had told you in my opening statement that this case was not about pedophilia. That was wrong. That was not true. I told you it was all about child molestation. That's what this case is all about. Right from the get go what they said was not true.

"Defense counsel has a theory about this. Robert Peterson went to the Garland Building to meet some phantom, some bad guy and continues on in his opening statement telling you about this phantom bad guy that must have done this horrible crime..."

In addition to this theory, Quinn said the defense wanted the jury to believe that the case revolved around the falsehoods of a federal agency; that the agents of the ATF conspired with witnesses to lie to them as a result of the bad press the ATF had received because of the Waco incident.

Quinn brought the jury through brief summaries of the witnesses, Ernie Niewiadomski and Ralph Helm.

The defendant's Army records, school records, the testimony of Laura Schwarz, and the defendant's own admission, Quinn said, showed that the defendant lived on Winnemac Avenue on the north side of the city in October of 1955.

"And if he wanted to go to the Idle Hour Stables from North Winnemac, the street that goes through two blocks south is Lawrence Avenue, and you would pass by Lawrence and Milwaukee Avenue...

"That is what this defendant told the people. He told Herb Hollatz that's what he did, he told Red Wemette that is what he did, he told Roger Spry that is what he did," that he picked these three kids up hitchhiking. He told two of those three that he took them to the stable where he subsequently sexually assaulted and murdered them."

Quinn summarized the testimony of the neighbor on Peterson Avenue, Park Ridge, IL, who heard a young voice scream, a child's voice. She remembered that scream, Quinn told the jury, because she had a great deal of experience in hearing screams having been an ambulance driver in London during the "blitz." And that after the first scream she heard another scream, and that both had come from the direction of the Idle Hour Stables.

He stated that the witnesses presented by the State showed that in fact Kenneth Hansen was working at the Idle Hour Stables in 1955, that he worked for Silas Jayne who owned the stables, and that the defendant had admitted picking up and killing the Peterson and Schuessler boys.

Quinn pointed to the People's exhibits numbers 17 and 23, black and white photographs taken by the police photographer who was one of the first to arrive at the scene, showing the bodies of the boys laying in a tangled heap in a ditch in Robinson's Woods. And he recounted the other testimony and evidence the jury had seen and heard throughout the trial. With each summary of the testimony of the witnesses and the evidence presented in the trial, Quinn would change the location from which he addressed the jury.

At times, he was at the very front of the jury box, his gestures measured and precise to emphasize the important points of testimony.

When he referred to the photographs showing the bodies of the boys, he would approach them slowly and stand next to each one as he described what Dr. Donoghue had testified to concerning the results of the autopsies.

Finally, Quinn reached the end of his closing argument. He returned to his place directly in front of the jurors.

"Ladies and gentlemen," he said as he lowered his voice, "after forty years the families of these victims and this whole community have a right to closure, to some sense of closure on this case.... This case and these children need to be put to rest. And, ladies and gentlemen, you can do that by finding this defendant guilty. But not just to put things to rest, you should do that because this defendant did it, because you know he did it from all the evidence you heard from that stand, again only from that stand.

"Ken Hansen said he did it because he did do it. Convict him."

Now it was the defense's turn to present its arguments.

"This case," Stone began, "is a mystery. It's made no clearer today than it was in October of 1955. Forty-one thousand people interviewed, attempts to retrace the boys' steps, combing of the forest preserve and the fields with police officers arm-to-arm looking for clues and now after seven days of trial and forty years, the deaths of Anton and John Schuessler and Robert Peterson are still shrouded in mystery."

Stone pointed out that the pathologists who performed the autopsies, Drs. Kearns and Hirsch, were dead. So were Beverly Hansen, Dep. Coroner Harry Glos, Silas Jayne, Kurt Hansen, and many of the police officers who investigated the case.

"Mr. Quinn asked for closure because the families of these boys want closure because society wants closure and those words scare me greatly because we are not here about closure. We're here for a much more narrow, but nonetheless extremely important, purpose. Did these gentlemen prove their case beyond a reasonable doubt? And if we substitute the desire for closure for the requirements of the law, we have done a grave injustice. This is not and cannot be about our personal desires to close the file. It can't be about that. It is, as the Court will instruct you as I submit to you, promised it would be, about whether or not Mr. Quinn and Mr. Cassidy have proven their case beyond a reasonable doubt."

Stone presented the defense's theory and the evidence, which he argued supported the defense. Hansen was on a belated honeymoon in Texas in October of 1955, he said.

As to the State's witnesses, Stone was blunt.

"What do you think about a person who claims to know about the murder of three children and holds that information back for twenty years, in one case for forty years? What do you think about such a person? Let's take a look at who these people are and see why, when the State rests their case on their believability, the State has to lose."

He described Roger Spry as "an admitted thief, a liar, a horse and saddle thief, and an arsonist" who was looking at three to seven years in the state prison.

Stone told the jury that the testimony of Herb Hollatz didn't make any sense. Although Hollatz was twenty-five years old at the time, and his father a police officer, Hollatz did not tell anyone of the admission of the defendant when Hansen said he killed "those boys everybody is looking for."

"According to Hollatz...Kenny looks up at him and says 'can I trust you, will you keep it a secret'...Does that ring true?...Does it make any sense that this is what happened and that his reaction was not to tell his father, who is a police officer, 'I know who killed the Schuessler and Peterson boys?'

"What about Plemmons, Joe Plemmons?" Stone asked the jury. "Is there anyone here who doubts that Joe Plemmons is a conman? Is there anyone here who doubts that that glib man who sat in front of you is a liar and finds it easy to lie to you?

"What about Red Wemette, the FBI mole? From 1971 to 1993 he's working for the FBI. He's in nearly daily contact with law enforcement.... He, like every other witness in this case, amazingly waits until the mid-1990s to come up with a story they sat on for twenty years. It's unworthy of belief.

"One after another after another, the witnesses in this case have not talked about murder, they have talked about picking up hitchhikers, not in 1955 but in the 1970s, twenty years after the murders.

"Now why would the State give you that information if not to try and inflame your prejudices, if not to try and blind you to the lack of evidence that they got in this case. You cannot convict a man of murder of a 1955 act with the suggestion that in 1970 he picked up a hitchhiker or worse, that someone else picked up a hitchhiker and that Ken and that boy may have engaged in an act of homosexual lust. You just can't say that that's evidence that in October of 1955 there was a murder."

Stone asked the jury to consider the Idle Hour Stables as it was in

1955, with a watchman on duty, grooms living on the grounds, and a family living on the premises.

Reaching the end of his argument, Stone stood closer to the jury.

"Ladies and gentlemen, these are the last words I get to speak on behalf of Ken. I sit down, and Mr. Cassidy gets to come up and talk to you, and then the Court will instruct you as to the law…

"This case began forty years ago as a mystery. It remains enshrouded a mystery today. And the People will try as hard as they want with the likes of Mr. Spry and Mr. Plemmons and Mr. Wemette, but they cannot unshroud the mystery. Thank you."

Judge Toomin waited until Stone had returned to his place at the defense table then looked at the jury.

"Anybody need a recess, folks?" he asked, allowing a few jurors to shake their heads in agreement. Judge Toomin understood. "All right, why don't you step back in the jury room for a few minutes, please?" He then ordered a brief recess.

During the recess, the prosecutors prepared their rebuttal closing argument. Cassidy would make the argument for the State, and he carefully reviewed the notes he had been taking during Stone's closing argument.

Judge Toomin ordered the jury back into the courtroom.

Cassidy pointed out that the jurors had promised to weigh the facts and decide the case based on the evidence and the law; that they must follow the law; and weigh the credibility of the witnesses when deciding what to believe. And he referred to the photographs the jury had been shown of the bodies of the boys in the ditch, the photographs taken during the autopsies of the boys showing their injuries.

"I'm about to finish, ladies and gentlemen, and I will not use those photographs. I will use this one."

Cassidy pointed to the enlargement of three individual photographs placed next to each other of Anton and John Schuessler and Robert Peterson. The photographs showed the smiling faces of three boys. They were the pictures given to us during the two-day search for the boys. The same photos that were later to be shown under bold headlines of the news that the bodies had been found.

"The boys have waited too long for today for it not to be done in any way but by law, so I will not try to prejudice you at the end with those photographs. No, I will not. They would not like that. And they have waited too long.

"Those boys were trailblazers of sorts…trailblazers in a sad sort of way. The path that they took, they did not choose. It was chosen by the man behind me; they had no choice but to follow that path. And at that time, if you have any children that followed that path before, but they have accepted it and they're smiling now, like they do in that photograph, and they welcome others, welcomed where they're at now similarly situated as them, those who have followed, taken from this world at a very young age, taken by no reason of their own, and they said, each of them, be patient, be patient, your time will come on that unjust world you left, you will receive justice.

"Justice is due them today. That is what they seek…justice, simple justice. And the justice they seek is in your hands.

"On behalf of Tony, Bobby, and John…thanks."

Scott Cassidy walked to the prosecution table and sat down. Both he and Pat Quinn sat quietly and looked at Judge Toomin as he began to address the jury and read the jury instructions.

"Members of the jury, the evidence and arguments in this case have been completed, and I will now instruct you as to the law…"

Twenty-four jury instructions were read to the jury. Such instructions can become monotonous and jurors have been known to let their minds wander as the judge reads the instructions to them.

In this case, however, the jurors listened intently to Judge Toomin as he read each instruction.

"Murder is the unlawful killing of a human being with malice aforethought, either expressed or implied," Judge Toomin continued. His voice echoed in the large, quiet courtroom.

After he had finished reading the instructions to the jury, Judge Toomin dismissed the alternate jurors and informed the jury that they would receive the packet of instructions for reference during their deliberations. They would also receive, he told them, all of the exhibits, which the Court received into evidence.

"The jury may retire," Judge Toomin concluded.

The men and women of the jury rose from their seats, almost in unison, and filed out of the jury box and into the jury room. It was 5:45 p.m.

September 13, 1995
7:30 p.m.

"All right," Judge Toomin said as he looked out at the courtroom, now filled with prosecutors and defense attorneys who, hearing that the case had gone to the jury, had come to the courtroom at the end of their workday.

"The court is assembled," the judge continued. "The jury indicated they had reached a verdict at about 7:20 p.m." Turning to his left, Judge Toomin spoke to the bailiff.

"And bring in the jury, please, Miss Murphy."

"Yes, your Honor," the bailiff responded.

She walked to the jury room, knocked on the door with three quick raps then opened the door and entered. A few moments later, the first jurors began to file out of the room and walk into the jury box.

Judge Toomin waited until the last jurors had taken their seats before addressing the foreman.

"Mr. Finkle, you are the foreperson?"

"Yes, sir," the man replied. He rose to his feet, holding several folded sheets of paper in front of him.

"Have you reached verdicts?"

"Yes."

"Would you give your papers to Deputy Murphy, please."

The man held out the folded papers to the Deputy, who took several steps from her station, retrieved it from the foreperson and handed it to the judge.

Judge Toomin unfolded the paper and scanned the page.

"Let the record reflect the Court has examined the verdict forms and finds them to be in proper order. I'll tender them to the clerk to read to the court as assembled."

The slight crinkling sound of the shuffling of papers and movements of those assembled in the courtroom came to an abrupt stop. The cavernous room was absolutely quiet.

Judge Toomin handed the verdict forms to the clerk who had been standing to his left in the jury box. The clerk took the papers from the judge and took a short step closer to the front of the witness stand as she held the papers in front of her and began to read the verdicts.

"We, the Jury, find the defendant, Kenneth Hansen, Guilty of Murder of Anton Schuessler Jr.

"We, the Jury, find the defendant, Kenneth Hansen, Guilty of Murder of Robert Peterson."

"We, the Jury, find the defendant, Kenneth Hansen, Guilty of Murder of John Schuessler."

O'Donnell then asked that the jury be polled, a procedure whereby each individual juror is asked "Was this then and is this now your verdict?"

After each juror answered affirmatively, Judge Toomin directed the clerk to enter judgment on the verdicts. He then informed the jurors that the proceedings were concluded and that they were dismissed. He extended his thanks and appreciation to the jurors for their service and asked that they meet with him for a few minutes in the jury room.

In some high profile cases, judges often give the jurors the opportunity to exit the courtroom by another entrance, allowing them to avoid questions by the media.

After a few minutes, Judge Toomin re-entered the courtroom and told the attorneys that a pre-sentence investigation of the defendant would be required, and also set the date for post-trial motions for October 20, 1995.

Kenneth Hansen was sentenced to 300 years in prison, but post-trial motions remained to be heard, and the inevitable process of appeal was only beginning.

May 12, 2000

In a surprising turn of events on May 12, 2000, the Illinois Appellate Court after a split decision agreed with the defendant Kenneth Hansen, then age sixty-seven. They reversed the convictions and a new trial was ordered. The courts felt Judge Toomin erroneously allowed testimony that had prejudiced the jury. The most important, they claimed, was Judge Toomin's ruling concerning evidence of Hansen's pattern of picking up underage boys and molesting them.

Justice Thomas E. Hoffman writing for the majority rejected the prosecutor's attempts to establish a motive for their contention that Hansen murdered the boys at the Idle Hour Stable on October 16, 1955. Specifically the Justices objected to the introduction of testimony from witnesses who said that Hansen frequently picked up young male hitchhikers and took them back to the stable for sex.

Hoffman wrote that most of the evidence of Hansen's sexual activities "pertains to incidents which occurred well after the victims' murders" therefore, the Judge continued, Hansen can hardly be said to have been motivated to kill the victims in 1955 to prevent the discovery of acts of pedophilia he committed in the 1960s and 1970s. Additionally, the Justice said the lower court erred in allowing into testimony portions of statements of key witnesses who recounted Hansen's sexual activities.

"We cannot say that the evidence that the defendant sexually assaulted innumerable young boys over a period of twenty years did not influence the outcome of this trial," Hoffman wrote. But in a dissent Justice Shelvin Louise Hall argued that the crimes evidence was admissible because it showed Hansen's pattern of assaulting minors. More significant, Judge Hall wrote is the "strong evidence" in the case, which includes Hansen's admission to four witnesses that he killed the boys. "That," Hall wrote, "renders harmless any error that may have occurred in admitting the evidence about Hansen's sexual activities."

Hansen who remained at Pontiac Correctional Center was told of the decision by his new attorney Leonard Goodman, who stated that they were thrilled and that Hansen was "speechless," just choked up with emotion.

The impact was devastating when Cassidy heard that Hansen's appellate court decision was overturned.

Judge Mary Ellen Coghlan, a former Assistant Cook County Public Defender and Assistant Illinois Attorney General, was assigned the case. The prosecution would be handled once again by

Scott Cassidy. Besides Cassidy, the prosecution consisted of attorneys Thomas Biesty, Linas Kelecius, and Jennifer Coleman. Hansen's new defense team included attorneys Leonard Goodman and Steven Weinberg. It wasn't long after the case was assigned to Judge Coghlan that a court date was set for May 21, 2001.

The trial was put off indefinitely when Cassidy announced the Cook County State's Attorneys office was appealing Judge Coghlan's ruling that the Carter brothers could not testify. Judge Coghlan ruled the testimony was inadmissible hearsay. The State was also hit like a tropical cyclone when Judge Coghlan informed the prosecution that the testimony of Joyce Mauer Saxon was admissible.

Joyce Mauer Saxon had come forward to say that her ex-husband Jack Reiling, now deceased, an ex-con with a history of alcoholism and violence confessed the murders of the Peterson-Schuessler brothers to her in 1956. Ms. Saxon had presented her testimony at an earlier trial and it was found to be inconsistent and contradictory.

Given these new rulings, Cassidy stated it could take a year to complete the appeal process. This did not set well with Hansen's lawyers who expressed their opinion by stating that Hansen, now sixty-seven years of age, had a severe heart attack in prison in December 1999 and had emergency triple heart bypass surgery and that he was in poor health and could die in prison while waiting for the ruling. However, Hansen was not released from prison; he was ordered held in custody on a three million dollar bond.

After using the appeals process wisely, the prosecution was ready for the second trial.

August 9, 2002
9:15 a.m.
Cook County Criminal Court

I arrived at that big, dark gray building at 26th Street and California Avenue, called the Cook County Criminal Courts Building. Sadly, I was quite familiar with this building. Working homicide you spend half your life there testifying at grand jury hearings and murder trials.

This would be the second time in seven years I appeared at

Kenneth Hansen's trial. I immediately went to room 304 where jury selection was to begin. At 10:35 a.m., Judge Coghlan arrived and promptly requested a transfer to room 506, to accommodate the crowd. I was able to secure a seat in the front row next to the jury box and at the back of the prosecutor's table. The defense table faced the juror's box.

Judge Coghlan took the bench. At 11:20 a.m., Kenneth Hansen, now age sixty-nine, slowly walked into the courtroom with his attorneys Leonard Goodman and Steven Weinberg. He looked like "Professor Backwards," leaning heavily on a cane with his left hand as he headed for his seat at the defendant's table. His suit looked like it came off the rack at "Smokey Joe's." His shirt was open without a tie. His face was unshaven, and his brown, horn-rimmed glasses sat awkwardly on his face.

The clerk brought in the prospective jurors to be seated, and they were sworn in unison, to answer all questions truthfully "in the case of the People of the state of Illinois versus Kenneth Hansen."

Hansen was named in a six-count indictment: three for murder and three for indecent liberties with a child during the commission of a crime. The Judge immediately began asking a number of questions of all the prospective jurors and planned to move on to individual queries later in the proceedings. After a full day of questioning, twelve were selected: eight men and four women. Four alternates were also chosen. The twelve jurors and four alternates stood to be sworn, then the judge adjourned the trial until the following Monday

Monday
August 12, 2002
10:30 a.m.

Judge Coghlan took the bench at 10:30 a.m. It was brought to her attention that a juror had failed to show up. A mild interruption occurred as she ordered a short recess. Immediately, an alternate juror was sworn in.

I took my seat in the front row. At 11:20 a.m., Kenneth Hansen hobbled into court once again with his cane and wearing the same clothing. Today, he had a tie around his neck. As he walked pass the jurors, he greeted them with a sarcastic "Good morning. Thank you for being here." While looking pale and nervous, he took a seat between his lawyers at the counsel table.

Judge Coghlan adjourned opening statements from both the prosecution and defense until after the lunch break. Promptly at 1:00 p.m., the trial resumed, and Judge Coghlan identified herself then asked counsel to please identify themselves. The State went first.

"Scott Cassidy. Good afternoon ladies and gentlemen."

"Thomas Biesty. Good afternoon ladies and gentlemen."

"Linas Kelecius. Good afternoon ladies and gentlemen."

"Jennifer Coleman. Good afternoon ladies and gentlemen."

Then counsel for Kenneth Hansen stood to identify themselves.

"Leonard Goodman. Good afternoon ladies and gentleman."

"Steven Weinberg. Good afternoon ladies and gentlemen."

The state opened its case as Assistant State's Attorney Linas Kelecius told the jurors what this case is about: murder and child molestation.

I looked across the room directly at Hansen who seemed to be upset with the remarks Kelecius was making. He began to shift nervously in his chair and shake his head like a swivel. Kelecius hammered away and painted Hansen as a person who wanted to live out a "sick sexual fantasy." For a brief moment, the jurors got a look at the real Kenneth Hansen.

During the defense's opening statement, Steven Weinberg ridiculed the State's case by telling the jury it was built on seasoned criminals, con artists, arsonists, pornographers, and government paid informants. He also told the jury the state would not be able to present any evidence directly linking Hansen to the murders.

The state's first witness was Hetty Salerno. She was now seventy-nine years old and living in Arizona. She testified once again that there wasn't any doubt that she heard screams for help coming from the Idle Hour Stables on the night of October 16, 1955, between the hours of 9:00 and 10:00 p.m. On cross-examination, Weinberg was quick to take advantage of Mrs. Salerno's age and her recollection of the questions asked to which she answered no.

But the one answer Weinberg could not erase from her memory

was the screams she heard coming from the stables, she stood courageously on that answer without doubt.

The state's second witness was Ernest Niewiadomski, now sixty-four years old. As he testified in the first trial, he was a student at Gordon Tech High School in Chicago, Illinois at the time of the murders. He told the jurors he met Tony and John Schuessler in the neighborhood, they lived across the alley from him. They would play scrub baseball games and some football on occasion in the neighborhood streets. Niewiadomski then told the jury he met John and Tony and their friend Robert Peterson at the Monte Cristo Bowling Alley somewhere around 7:30 p.m. on October 16, 1955. Niewiadomski talked to the Schuessler brothers, who said they had just come from viewing a movie downtown called, "The African Lion." When asked by Niewiadomski if they were going to bowl, John and Tony stated they didn't have any money.

On cross-examination Weinberg raised his voice occasionally for emphasis because he didn't have much to work with and was trying to create doubt due to memory lapses. He stopped just short of accusing Niewiadomski of fabricating his testimony.

As I sat listening to the testimony, my thoughts took me back to February 1958 when Ernest Niewiadomski was a member of the United States Marine Corp. stationed at MCAS in El Toro, California. Niewiadomski returned home on furlough and was asked by Lt. Morris to consent to a polygraph test. Obviously, Weinberg and Goodman didn't do their homework because they would have known Niewiadomski had taken a polygraph at a well-known laboratory in Chicago. Based on his responses, it was the opinion of the examiner that he was telling the truth on all questions asked.

The third witness for the State was William "Red" Wemette, fifty-three years old. Wemette stated he was only nineteen years old when he first met Hansen in the late 1960's and started having sex with him. He referred to Hansen as a former lover. There wasn't much Wemette could testify to that he hadn't in the first trial.

On cross-examination Goodman raised the issue of Wemette being paid more than fourteen thousand dollars by the government and a long-time Federal informer. Goodman also questioned why

Wemette had not mentioned the triple homicide to the FBI for more than twenty years.

He told Goodman this was a State murder case, not a Federal crime, so he didn't think they would listen or take any interest in what he had to say. Wemette closed his testimony by stating that when Kurt Hansen introduced him to his brother, Ken, he said: "I wanted a brother and got two sisters." With the end of cross-examination of Wemette by the defense, Judge Coghlan adjourned trial for the day.

August 13, 2002
Court Room 604
10:45 a.m.

I took my usual front row seat. Hansen appeared in court with his attorneys, again wearing the same clothing.

The first witness of the day for the State was Chief Cook County Medical Examiner, Dr. Edmund Donoghue. It wasn't a repetition of testimony from the first trial. This exchange reviewed more graphic and explicit details of coroner's forensic examinations. Donoghue testified that Anton Schuessler's cause of death was asphyxiation by manual strangulation, by someone's hands with external force applied to his neck. His brother John's cause of death was strangulation. Robert Peterson's cause of death was strangulation by ligature. There were multiple cuts and tears on the left side of the scalp caused by some sort of three-pronged instrument. Dr. Donoghue further testified that additional information was discovered following the exhumation of the three bodies. After examination of the tissue samples, finely divided soil known as diatomaceous soil and microscopic pieces of bone meal were found.

Weinberg during his cross-examination sought to cast doubt on the doctor's qualifications, whose medical background and training in the field of forensic pathology is untouchable.

One of the first questions asked was about digested food in the stomachs of Tony and John Schuessler. Weinberg was very concerned if Dr. Donoghue had formed an opinion as a medical examiner on a time of death by examining the contents in the brother's stomachs. Without hesitation he stated: "No." Weinberg then questioned whether the boys' bodies bore any evidence of hay?

"No, I didn't find any evidence of hay, oats, barley or horse feed," replied Dr. Donoghue.

Weinberg stated he was finished with this witness.

The next State's witness was Ralph Helm, age sixty-two. Between 8:45 p.m. and 9:00 p.m., he saw a boy, whom he later identified as Tony Schuessler, hitchhiking on the street with two boys dressed in "sports jackets" standing nearby.

At the conclusion for Helm's testimony, a brief recess was called.

2:10 p.m.

The State's next witness was Roger Spry, now age fifty-three. Spry stated that he had been on his own since the age of eleven. In 1960, he moved in with the Hansen family at the Bro-Ken-H Stables. Soon after that Hansen began climbing in bed with him. He further testified that Hansen molested him for years.

Spry further stated that when he was about fifteen years old, Hansen told him that he once picked up three boys, taking them to a barn, and was having sex with the younger boys, when the older boy appeared and threatened to report what Hansen had done. Hansen told Spry that he grabbed the older boy's throat and accidentally choked him to death, leaving Hansen no choice. It would be either them or me, so he killed the other two boys. Spry also testified that one day he was caught pocketing money from riders at the stable and Hansen told Spry, "You're going to end up just like that Peterson boy," if he did it again.

On cross-examination, Goodman repeatedly attempted to portray Spry as a convicted arsonist and alleged he fabricated this fairy-tale story, instead of facing several years in prison.

"Mr. Spry, for your testimony in this case you agreed with the government, that your arson charge would be dismissed, or reduced, or you would get a sentence of probation, which was eighteen months, in exchange for your testimony."

"Yes," Spry replied.

"Thank you," responded Goodman sarcastically.

Goodman told the jurors that Roger Spry couldn't face prison, so the next best thing was "let's make a deal."

August 14, 2002
Court Room 604
11:25 a.m.

The State began the day's proceeding by stating that film footage of the crime screen would be shown. Freelance photographer Dr. Richard Ritt had shot the film.

Goodman jumped from his seat and objected bitterly that it would be inflammatory and prejudicial if the jury were shown this videotape. Judge Coghlan made a swift ruling that the tape was admissible.

Ritt took the stand to explain how the film had come about. On October 18, 1955, he received a call from manager Fred Gesize of WGN-TV and was told he should rush to the crime scene at Robinson's Woods and film what he could.

The tape, which was not played at the first Hansen trial in 1995, showed the road leading to Robinson's Woods in the Che-Che-Pin-Qua forest preserve. It also showed the nude and battered bodies of the boys lying in the shallow ditch at the edge of the parking lot.

This evidence was among the most disturbing aspects of the trial for the jurors. Some grimaced, while others squinted their eyes. A few cried, visibly shaken from emotional distress. From my front row seat, I could also scrutinize Hansen's demeanor. He became restless and nervous in his seat. His face became distorted from his expressions.

The State's next witness was Herbert Hollatz, regarded as their strongest. State's Attorney Biesty led Hollatz through his testimony. He left home at the age of twenty-one and met Kenneth Hansen at the Park Ridge Stables. Hollatz then went to work for Hansen at the stables sometime around October 1955. Within one week, Hansen had performed oral sex on Hollatz. It was during this sexual rendezvous that Hansen confided in Hollatz, asking him if he could keep a promise. Hansen then told Hollatz, "I just killed three boys" about a week ago. Ironically, the sad part of Hollatz's testimony was that his father was a Chicago police officer. Judge Coghlan then called for a recess.

4:00 p.m.

Joe Plemmons, now age fifty-four, was the last of the big four State's witnesses that included Wemette, Spry, and Hollatz. The State didn't want repetition at this trial so the witness was asked a limited number of questions.

Plemmons testified that he began his acquaintance with Hansen in 1972 when he leased part of the Sky High Stables. They became good friends during that time.

Plemmons further testified that, in May 1972, Hansen told him his brother, Kurt, "held the boys over his head like a club." Also according to Plemmons, sometime in 1976, he and Hansen had a conversation during which Hansen commented: "It was either those boys or me" because "in 1955 you couldn't be gay." On another occasion in 1988, Plemmons testified that he brought up the subject of the murders, and Hansen confided that he worried about being caught some day. In an unforeseen answer Plemmons testified he came forward with the information relating to Hansen in November 1994, because he believed that Hansen lied to him about the death of Hanson's wife, Beverly.

Goodman quickly requested the jury be escorted from the courtroom then moved for a mistrial. This would be the second time during the trial he requested one. The defense implied that with Plemmons' unforeseen answer to Beverly Hansen's death, Goodman felt the jury would think Hansen was responsible. Judge Coghlan again denied his motion.

On cross-examination, Goodman hammered away at Plemmons' criminal record.

"A federal judge found you guilty of lying. So you are a convicted liar?"

"Yes."

"Now you have already told us you are a liar. Lying with the intent to actually deceive people." Goodman shot one question after another.

"Have you been known by several aliases?"

"Yes."

"Was it to conceal the fact that you're called Joe Plemmons? Or hide from the law? That's why you used multiple names while in the State of California, Pennsylvania and Wisconsin. You acquired about one hundred thousand dollars from the State of California by fraud didn't you?"

"Yes."

"You also used an alias name in Pennsylvania to obtain a horse business license."

"Yes."

Goodman looked at the jurors and said, "We have a man who lived his entire life with a pattern of defrauding people with lies."

Following Plemmons' testimony, the State rested. Judge Coghlan adjourned court at 5:45 p.m.

August 15, 2002
Courtroom 604
11:55 a.m.

The Deputy Sheriffs brought the jury in. Judge Coghlan asked the jurors to "be seated please, ladies and gentlemen." Hansen then entered the courtroom wearing the same clothing he had worn the day before. He immediately removed his horn-rimmed glasses. Squinting intensely, he looked around curiously then started smiling. His youngest son, Mark Hansen, was sitting in the back row of the courtroom. Hansen took his seat between his defense attorneys, Goodman and Weinberg.

The defense presented three witnesses who stated that Hansen never worked at the Idle Hour Stables during the relevant time period. Frank Jayne, now age ninety-one, did not appear in court. Both counsel stipulated his testimony from the first trial and Goodman read the stipulation into the record. He would testify that from 1950 to 1961 his brother, Silas, owned the Idle Hour Stables and that Hansen did not work there.

Barbara Ashbaugh was the defense's second witness. She testified that she was riding for Silas Jayne at the Idle Hour Stables during 1955 and 1959.

"Is that Silas Jayne?"

"Yes."

She stated Ken Hansen never worked there and that she lived next door to him in 1953 before he left for the military.

The third defense witness to testify was the charming and attractive Dorothy Jayne, widow of the once ruthless and notorious horseman Silas Jayne.

"Did you ever see Ken Hansen at the Idle Hour Stables in the 1950s?"

"No"

She further testified that she was the top rider at the Idle Hour Stables owned by Silas Jayne.

"I saw Hansen a number of times at various horse shows to recognize him."

On cross-examination, Assistant State's Attorney Jennifer Coleman attempted to cast doubt on Jayne's story by pointing out that Jayne did not testify on Hansen's behalf in 1995 when she knew he was on trial. Jayne further testified that she was in Kansas City, Kansas at a horse show when the murders occurred.

A key witness for the defense was Dr. Shaku Teas. Qualified as an expert in forensic pathology, she was a former Cook County medical examiner, who once worked with Dr. Donoghue. Weinberg guided Dr. Teas gingerly through her testimony.

Dr. Teas testified, after reviewing the autopsy report, that in her professional opinion the deaths of John and Tony Schuessler occurred within two to three hours after they ingested their last meal of soup containing macaroni and vegetables, according to the parents' testimony from the inquest in 1955 that was at approximately 1:30 p.m. This meant John and Tony had to have been killed by 4:30 p.m. on October 16, 1955. Her finding was based on the rate of digestion of a food material such as pasta. It is expected that the stomach of a healthy young boy would empty of such a soft carbohydrate within three hours.

Dr. Teas stated: "After reviewing everything from the autopsy, it is my opinion that a time of death at about 9:30 p.m. on October 16, 1955 would be inconsistent."

On cross-examination of Dr. Teas, Kelecius zeroed in like a

guided missile and hammered the witness for over two-and-half hours.

"Dr. Teas, did you read over the transcript of the Coroner's inquest held on October 19, 1955?"

"Yes."

"So Dr. Tea, what you're telling this jury, you're ignoring the eyewitness testimony of Earnest Niewiadomski, who knew the three boys and spoke with them at the Monte Cristo bowling alley between the hours of 7:30 p.m. and 7:45 p.m. on October 16,1955."

Dr. Teas did not respond.

"Then Dr. Teas according to you he was talking to three ghosts?" Kelecius assailed.

Over and over he asked, "Doesn't that cast doubt on your opinion?"

Dr. Teas told the jury that she relied on science rather than testimony. "I am looking at scientific evidence that is there," Teas said.

Court was adjourned.

August 16, 2002
2:35 p.m.

The prosecutors then recalled Dr. Donoghue to the stand to rebut the testimony of Dr. Teas. He told the jury that several factors had to be considered. One, the macaroni found in Tony and John's stomachs during the autopsy may not have been fully digested because the pasta was in a soup and therefore not chewed.

Secondly, he stated that the digestive process may have been slowed by the excitement they felt about making the trip to a downtown movie theater and being upset by the Walt Disney movie they viewed.

Before the defense concluded its rebuttal, Goodman announced that Kenneth Hansen would not testify.

The prosecution and defense rested their case.

August 19, 2002
10:00 a.m.

Prosecutor Thomas Biesty began the trial's endgame by deflating Leonard Goodman and Steve Weinberg's airy arguments. Biesty came very well prepared.

Biesty opened his closing arguments by accusing Hansen of

preying on unsuspecting friends. Biesty focused strongly on the States four key witnesses and reminded the jurors that the case was built around them: Joe Plemmons, Roger Spry, Herb Hollatz and William "Red" Wemette. You heard each and every one of them testify. The defense called them the "sleazy four" witnesses, but three of the four testified that Hansen was a former lover and admitted the killings of the boys to them on various occasions over the years. Biesty called Hansen "void of human emotion." Looking at the jury, Biesty said "I wouldn't call them sleazy; I call them courageous" for coming and helping to expose this man Hansen. He said these men had no other reason to come forward and embarrass themselves, than to portray the truth. "Today Tony, Bobby and John are gone, but their killer sits right here awaiting justice," he said. "Thank you."

Goodman then tried to persuade the jurors that Kenneth Hansen was innocent.

He opened his summation by telling the jury that the State had failed to provide any evidence directly linking Hansen to the murders. "Their case," he cautioned, "relied solely on accounts given by informants."

Then Goodman criticized Cassidy for telling the jury that Hansen must be guilty, because he did not put up a strong defense. He didn't hold back his animosity as he called Cassidy a "high-jacker," who tried to get the jury's sympathy by telling the jurors to send a message of hope to the families of all murdered children, whose cases are as yet unsolved, by finding Hansen guilty. Goodman also made it clear that he had nothing but contempt for the State's witnesses. "Please don't be taken in by the prosecution," he demanded. "You heard them call the group courageous. Well, they are nothing more than four liars and conmen."

Goodman made no effort to mention the testimony of Dr. Teas. He may have felt that the jury would discount some or all of it.

Cassidy's closing arguments were emotional and somewhat brief; but first, he wanted to clear the smoke from the air.

Using the visitor's log from the Garland Building, evidence earlier stipulated, Cassidy made it clear the boys were alive at 6:00 p.m. on Sunday, October 16, 1955. He wanted to be sure Dr. Teas' testimony had left no question as to the probable time of death in jury's mind. He also wanted to illustrate how far the defense was willing to distort the evidence to create reasonable doubt.

Cassidy continued his argument by telling the jurors that this case is truly about justice. It is about excellent police work, it is about people coming to court and testifying to matters that occurred forty-seven years ago. It is about twelve good men and women, ordinary people who live among us, who listened attentively to the evidence and rendered their verdict based upon the facts and the law.

Your verdict will give a measure of relief and comfort to hundreds of thousands of Chicagoans who will never forget that day, that day forty-seven years ago. Cassidy ended his argument where it all began.

"It began forty-seven years ago. At that time, three young boys accepted a ride from a man who promised them the childhood joy of being able to ride a horse. The upper left-hand corner is a photograph of Tony Schuessler, the innocent one. That is how he looked when he first met Kenneth Hansen. The photograph next to Tony is John and that is how he looked before he met Kenneth Hansen. The remaining photograph, as you know, is Bobby Peterson.

"This is a picture of life. Bobby is the courageous one. His screams would be heard forty-seven years later through the testimony of Hetty Salerno. We know he fought the good fight. Perhaps he made it outside of the barn and into the fields. For some moments, he escaped evilness and death.

"This is one of death. The photograph to the far left shows Tony, Bobby, and John. This is how Kenneth Hansen left them, lying beaten to death, naked in a dirt field.

"Tony, Bobby and John are all gone, and now their killer awaits your justice, the justice by law.

"Today is their day; justice awaits them. I say to John, Bobby and Tony today is your day. Thank you."

At 2:15 p.m., Judge Coghlan gave the jury their instructions. Quietly, she said: "Now then, you may retire to the jury room for your deliberations." The eight men and four women arrayed in two rows in the jury box rose like a graduating class and filed softly out to begin their deliberations.

It was 5:20 p.m. by my wristwatch when an unsigned note was passed with a five-word message: "We have reached a verdict." Attorneys, court-aids, reporters, and spectators rushed into the fifth floor courtroom.

Soon after, the jury filed into the courtroom, somber faced. Not one looked at Kenneth Hansen, sitting at his counsel's table.

Judge Coghlan walked slowly to the bench.

"Has the jury reached a verdict."

"Yes," responded the jury foreman.

The courtroom was hushed and tense.

Neither Goodman and Weinberg nor Hansen seemed surprised as they heard the word: "Guilty."

This would be the second time in seven years a jury would find Kenneth Hansen guilty of the murders of Robert Peterson and the Schuessler brothers, John and Anton.

Hansen's sentencing hearing was set, and court was adjourned.

October 1, 2002

For the final time, I appeared at the sentencing of Kenneth Hansen. The small glass-enclosed courtroom was filled with family members and reporters. I sat next to Mark Hansen.

The prosecution called a number of witnesses during the hearings. Karen Kujawa, daughter in-law of Eleanor Schuessler-Kujawa, took the stand and read a victim's impact statement written by Eleanor Schuessler-Kujawa's sister, Beatrice Blane, who was too ill to attend. In the letter, Blane wrote, "My nephews died at the hands of an animal." She further stated that Hansen put fear into the family that continues to this day. She wrote that her sister, who died in 1986, went to her grave crying out for justice. When Karen Kujawa reached the end of the letter, Hansen got up from his chair and blurted out, "I didn't do it."

Goodman called his sole witness, Mark Hansen, to the stand to testify on behalf of his father. Goodman left the courtroom area and walked into the audience where Mark was sitting, and asked if he wished to make a statement. He refused to take the stand.

Hansen stood between his attorneys at counsel's table wearing a tan jail uniform. He tried to persuade the judge of his innocence before sentencing. The judge was not swayed by his appeal.

Judge Coghlan called the slaying of the boys a "horrific crime" that haunted Chicago for nearly five decades. She stated there is nothing the court can ever do to bring them back. But, she stressed, she had the power to ensure that Hansen never has the opportunity to prey on young children for the rest of his life. With that, Hansen was sentenced to concurrent prison terms of not less than 200 years and not more than 300 years for the death of each boy.

Goodman began working on an appeal immediately. On August 25, 2004, the Appellate Court of Illinois, First District, Third Division affirmed Hansen's conviction.

Finally, Kenneth Hansen will never prey on young boys again.

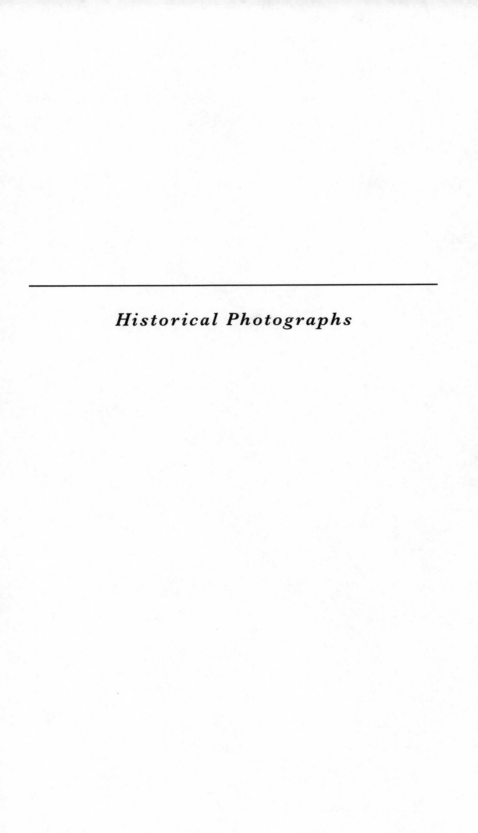

Historical Photographs

The bulletin written by Detective James Jack and issued by the Chicago Police Department after the boys were found slain. Photo courtesy of the Chicago Police Department.

The advertisement for the movie The African Lion.

The crime scene on October 18, 1955. Law enforcement officers are just beginning to arrive at the scene. Copyright 1955 by Hammill Studios, Inc. Reprinted with permission.

The entrance to the parking lot in Robinson's Woods were the boys bodies were found. Copyright 1955 by Hammill Studios, Inc. Reprinted with permission.

Malcolm Peterson and Anton Schuessler, Sr. during the inquest into the deaths of their sons. As published in the Chicago Sun-Times on October 19, 1955. Photo by Bob Kotalik. Copyright 1955 by Chicago Sun-Times, Inc. Reprinted with permission.

The Loop Theater where the boys went to see the African Lion. Photo courtesy of the Chicago Police Department.

Anton Schuessler, Sr. collapses at the Cook County Morgue after viewing the bodies of his sons. As published in the Chicago Sun-Times on October 18, 1955. Photo by Larry Nocerino. Copyright 1955 by Chicago Sun-Times, Inc. Reprinted with permission.

The burial service for Robert Peterson. As published in the Chicago Daily News on October 21, 1955. Copyright 1955 by Chicago Sun-Times, Inc. Reprinted with permission.

The casket of Anton Schuessler, Sr. is laid to rest next to his sons in St. Joseph's Cemetery. As published in the Chicago Daily News on November 15, 1955. Photo by Robert Stiewe. Copyright 1955 by Chicago Sun-Times, Inc. Reprinted with permission.

Left to right: Det. Frank Schulze, Det. Fred Koeppe, Malcolm Peterson, and Det. James Jack look for clues in ditch where boys were found. As published in the Chicago Sun-Times on October 21, 1955. Photo by Larson. Copyright 1955 by Chicago Sun-Times, Inc. Reprinted with permission.

Mr. and Mrs. Schuessler at home after the boys were found. As published in the Chicago Sun-Times on October 19, 1955. Photo by Merrill Palmer. Copyright 1955 by Chicago Sun-Times, Inc. Reprinted with permission.

Detectives Fred Koeppe and Frank Czech

Sergeant Michael Spiotto

Sergeant George Murphy

Captain Russell Corcoran

Detective James Jack

Ralph Helm with James Jack.

Detectives James Jack and Frank Czech at Midway Airport.

The front of the Monte Cristo Bowling Alley where the boys were seen by Ernest Niewiadomski.

The rear of the Monte Cristo Bowling Alley.

An aerial view of the location of the Idle Hour Stables. Photo Courtesy of the Cook County State's Attorneys Office.

The shoulder-to-shoulder search of the area surrounding Robinson's Woods. Photo Courtesy of the Cook County State's Attorneys Office.

The Gale Street Police Station.

The Farnsworth School.

Kenneth Hansen with an unidentified friend during the 1950s. Photo Courtesy of the Cook County State's Attorneys Office.

Kenneth Hansen with his wife Beverly Hansen during the 1950s. Photo Courtesy of the Cook County State's Attorneys Office.

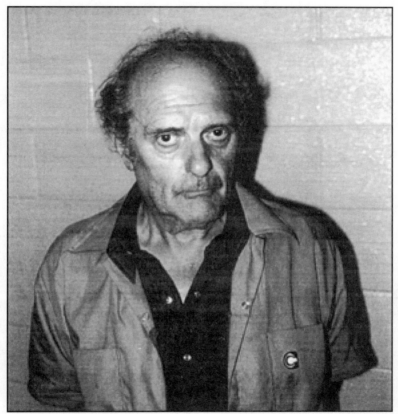

Kenneth Hansen as he looked around 1995. Photo Courtesy of the Cook County State's Attorneys Office.

Jury Interviews

August 30, 2002
12:10 p.m

The jurors who convicted Kenneth Hansen of murder were "one vote away from conviction on the first ballot." The eight men and four women refused to hold a post-verdict press conference. Most rushed out of the Criminal Courts Building avoiding news media, before hurrying back to their homes.

I was very fortunate to have a personal interview with two of the jurors who described their own reaction to certain testimony. This was a one-on-one, "Question and Answer," session that took place several days after the trial.

My first interview was with Mario Cabillero, age twenty, a student at a north suburban college.

Q. What were your thoughts when Judge Mary Ellen Coghlan read the charges?

A. I felt this was a serious case and nothing to joke at. I was surprised that they picked me, being so young.

Q. Was it a male or female juror who voted not guilty on the first eleven to one secret ballot?

A. I don't know. We didn't sign the ballot.

Q. What evidence did you review to vote guilty on the second ballot?

A. There were discussions but nothing earth-shattering. We just didn't walk in and agree. There were some discussions over certain points. We reviewed the birth certificates of Hansen's two children to see where he was living at the time, reviewed pictures of the Idle Hour Stables, also the area where the kids were found. We didn't believe the doctor, the forensic pathologist for the defense, Dr. Shaker Teas. She challenged the time the boys died then left out all the eyewitnesses. We had some help; there was a biology teacher from a high school who was on the jury with us.

Q. Did you believe the "sleazy four" as the defense called them: Joe Plemmons, Roger Spry, Herb Hollatz and William "Red" Wemette?

A. There were some questions about a few of them, I tried to create a picture caricature about them, such as what type of life they were living. All the men didn't have any connection with each other, so why would they come in to lie. Most of them had homosexual pasts, that didn't matter.

Q. Was Dr. Shaker Teas a big factor in making your decision?

A. Yes, her testimony was questionable, she had no supporting details on anything. The prosecution did a good job. They went step-by-step and laid a foundation for us to understand. The state's eyewitness, Niewiadomski, put the boys at the bowling alley at about 7:30 p.m.

Q. What was your reaction when you saw the pictures of the three boys' battered and nude bodies lying in a ditch in the woods?

A. They were very disturbing pictures. It was a real shame how they died. They needed justice.

Q. What, if any, holes did you find in Hansen's defense?

A. One reason, he didn't have a good alibi. Secondly, he just sat there between his attorneys at the table with no expression whatsoever on his face, or when the pictures of the boys were shown to the whole court, he was "ice cold."

Q. Was your mind made up before closing arguments or after, for your guilty ballot?

A. What put the nail in the coffin was after the closing arguments, the defense didn't have anything to say. The state hit a home run from the start. There wasn't any doubt in my mind in the verdict on this trial.

Q. What did you think of Kenneth Hansen's demeanor?

A. His cold attitude and his refusal to testify didn't help him.

Q. Mario, that ends our interview. Is there anything you would like to add as a juror to one of the most gruesome, hideous, and senseless crimes in four decades in the City of Chicago?

A. On a personal note, it was a real experience to be chosen for this case. It's something that will stick in my mind forever. It's something I can tell my grandchildren.

Q. What did you feel about the verdict you rendered?

A. Justice was served by what will come after. Mr. Hansen should get what he deserves.

September 16, 2002
7:00 p.m.

My second interview was with Robert Ownes, age fifty-two, who lives in the northern suburbs, working for a company in the shipping and receiving department.

Q. What were your thoughts when Judge Mary Ellen Coughlan read the charges?

A. "Gee" this is a capitol offense. It's going to be a long trial.

Q. What evidence did you review to vote guilty on the second ballot?

A. The foreman read his notes, then went to the person to his right, if that juror agreed and had nothing to add with this witness they would go down the line until all twelve reviewed each one of them. The foreman would then ask all the jurors if they had any questions of the witnesses.

Q. Did you believe the "sleazy four" as the defense called them, Joe Plemmons, Roger Spry, Herb Hollatz and William "Red" Wemette?

A. As the trial went on, and as I listened to the four of them, and everything in-between, by the time I went to vote I felt all of them were telling the truth. Each piece fit and added more and more evidence against Hansen. To me it was overwhelming.

Q. Was Dr. Teas a big factor in making your decision?

A. She was not believable. The defense talked about stomach content, which was not a factor because of what Dr. Donoghue said. And there were several eyewitnesses.

Q. What was your reaction when you saw the pictures of the three boys' battered, nude bodies lying in a ditch in the woods?

A. It was painful and nauseating to see the boys. You wonder about the pain they suffered before they were killed. Also, they were strangled for no reason because they didn't want to have sex with someone.

Q. Was your mind made up before closing arguments or after, for your guilty ballot?

A. No, we all kind of made up our minds as we heard day-to-day evidence. By the time the entire case ended and it was in the jurors hands to decide, my mind was made up.

Q. What holes did you find in Hansen's defense?

A. The defense didn't let us know a reason about Hansen's whereabouts the days before and after the murders. I was also upset with the defense when they spent three hours talking about stomach contents. I think they were trying to shed doubt about when the boys died, which was ridiculous.

Q. What did you think of Kenneth Hansen's demeanor?

A. It seems to me he only sat at that table looking straight ahead, took some notes. He acted like it was better sitting in Court than in a cell.

Q. Bob, that ends our interview. Is there anything you would like to add as a juror to one of the most gruesome, hideous and senseless crimes in four decades in the City of Chicago?

A. I believe that justice was finally served. It took four scumbags against one scumbag to get the story out. I believe all four men feel better about themselves today, now that they put Hansen where he belongs. I'm really glad I was part of this jury to have justice served.

Both jurors were high in their praise for the prosecution, and agreed that they "put on a heckuva of a good closing argument."

Character Summaries

Mr. Malcolm Peterson, father of Robert Peterson, resides in suburban Chicago. He did not testify at either the 1995 or 2002 trial of Kenneth Hansen, but testimony from his appearance at the 1955 Coroner's inquest was stipulated by the state and defense for use at trial.

Mrs. Dorothy Peterson, mother of Robert Peterson, resides in suburban Chicago.

Mrs. Eleanor Schuessler, mother of John and Anton, Jr., married Valentine Kujawa six months after the death of her two sons and the subsequent death of her husband. She died in 1986 and is buried next to her sons and first husband, Anton, Sr.

Mr. Anton Schuessler, Sr., father of John and Anton, Jr., passed away at age 42, twenty-six days after his sons were found murdered. On November 11, 1955, he had a heart attack while being given "Electrical Shock Treatment" for depression. He died at Forest Sanitarium and Rest Home in Des Plaines, IL.

Detective Frank Czech was my partner for several years and dear friend. He worked as a detective at Gale Street until he retired from the Department in 1960. Sadly, Frank died shortly after his retirement in 1961.

Sergeant Detective George Murphy, Sr. was supervising detective of the 33rd District. He formed and directed the initial investigating team assigned the task of finding the boys. He continued to work at the Gale Street station, which was later re-named the 16th District, as a Detective Sergeant for 37 years. Murphy died in April 1996 at Holy Family Health Center in Des Plaines, IL at the age of 91. He was my mentor.

Captain Russell Corcoran, former Commander of the 33rd Police District and part of the team spearheading the investigation for the search of the boys killers. A 30-year veteran of the Police Department, he died at the age of 67 in 1977.

Captain Patrick J. Deeley, Lieutenant Commander of the special investigation unit in 1955, he led the investigation into the deaths of the boys. After forty years of service to the Department, he retired in 1970. He became an investigator in the Mayor's office until his death at the age of 69 in 1976.

Captain Michael A. Spiotto was assigned to the special investigating unit and commanded thirty detectives during the Peterson-Schuessler murder case. Later, he took full command of the unit. He impressed his supervisors with his great investigative ability, reaching the rank of Captain in 1962. In 1966, he became deputy Chief in the detective division. He was promoted to first deputy superintendent of police in 1977 and remained in that role until he retired after a 35-year career. He died at the age of 89 on January 30, 2004 of heart failure.

Captain William J. Duffy was assigned to the 33rd District as a detective in 1955, working on the Peterson and Schuessler case. In the 1960s, he became a captain assigned to direct the Chicago Police Department's Intelligence Division, known as "Scotland Yard." He served as Deputy Police Superintendent of the Chicago Police Department from 1979 to 1988, when he retired. He died in 1991 at the age of 69.

Detective Fred Koeppe continued to work as a District Detective at the Gale Street station. He has since passed away.

Detective Frank Schulze continued to work as a District Detective at the Gale Street station. He has since passed away.

Commissioner Timothy J. O'Connor was appointed Police Commissioner in 1950 at the age of 47, the youngest man ever named to the post. After ten years, in 1960, he reverted his civil service rank of Captain and was assigned to the crime laboratory then promoted to assistant deputy superintendent until his retirement. In 1967, O'Connor died at the age of 65.

Joseph D. Lohman was Sheriff of Cook County from 1954

to 1958. He later became Illinois State Treasurer from 1959 - 1961. After suffering a heart attack, Lohman died in 1968 at the age of 58.

Lieutenant Detective John "Jack" Killackey was one of the detectives assigned to the special investigation unit in 1955. He became Lt. Commander of Area Four Homicide in the 1960s and later retired from the Chicago Police Department. He currently resides in the Chicago north suburban area.

Lieutenant John R. Konen, was a sergeant at Police Headquarters assigned to the special investigation unit in 1955. In 1960, he was promoted to lieutenant. Lt. Konen often expressed what I and many others in the SIU felt, "This case haunted him." Lt. Konen died in December 2004 at the age of 92.

Mr. Walter McCarron was the coroner of Cook County from 1952 - 1960. He conducted the Coroner's Inquest into the deaths of the Peterson and Schuessler boys. He died in 1991 at the age of 85.

Dr. Jerry Kearns, Chief Pathologist for Cook County Coroner's office from 1931-1956. Dr. Kearns performed the autopsies on the boys and provided expert evidence on the causes of death. He died in 1982.

Harry J. Glos was Chief Investigator of the Cook County Coroner's office for five years. Later he became the Chief of Police of North Lake, IL. He died at the age of 80 in May 1994.

John Gutkneckt was State's Attorney from 1952 to 1956. He was very influential in making two important decisions in the case. The first was to request polygraph tests for both Mr. and Mrs. Schuessler and Mr. and Mrs. Peterson. The second was to exhume the bodies of the boys. Gutkneckt died in 1972 at the age of 82.

Art Petacque started as a copy boy at the Chicago Sun in 1942, then worked with the Chicago Sun-Times from 1947 until his retirement in 1991. He was a legendary mob and crime reporter and dear friend of mine, dating back to 1955. In 1974, he shared a Pulitzer Prize with Hugh Hough, also with the Sun-Times. He also won an Emmy in 1984 while reporting for ABC TV in Chicago. Petacque died in June 2001 at the age of 76.

Dr. Edmund Donoghue began serving as Chief Medical Examiner for Cook County in 1977 and continues in that capacity to this day. He testified at both the 1995 and 2002 trials of Kenneth Hansen. His is currently the director of residency training at Stroger Hospital (formerly Cook County Hospital).

Judge Patrick Quinn served as prosecuting attorney during the 1995 murder trial of Kenneth Hansen. He continued to work for the State's Attorney until his election as Justice of the Illinois Appellate Court, where he continues to serve.

Assistant State's Attorney Scott Cassidy served as prosecuting attorney during the 1995 trial as well as the 2002 trial. He continues to work as a supervisor in the criminal division of the State's Attorneys office.

Attorney Jed Stone served as defense attorney during the 1995 trial. He continues to practice as a criminal defense attorney in Chicago.

Attorney Arthur O'Donnell served as defense attorney during the 1995 trial. After a long and successful career as a criminal defense attorney, O'Donnell died in August 2000 of leukemia at the age of 76 in his home in Conrad, California.

Judge Michael Toomin presided over the trial in 1995. He continues to hear criminal cases at the Cook County Criminal Court at 26th and California in Chicago.

Judge Mary Ellen Coghlan presided over the trial in 2002. She continues to hear criminal cases at the Cook County Criminal Court at 26th and California in Chicago.

Attorney Leonard C. Goodman served as defense attorney during the re-trial in 2002. He continues to practice as a criminal defense attorney in the Chicago area.

Attorney Steven J. Weinberg served as defense attorney during the re-trial in 2002. He continues to practice as a criminal defense attorney in the Chicago area.

State's Witness Ernest J. Niewiadomski was a schoolboy acquaintance of John and Anton Schuessler. He testified as a state's witness at both the 1995 and 2002 trials. He owns a restaurant and lives in the Chicago area.

State's Witness Ralph J. Helm was the last known person to see the boys alive. At the time of the murders, he was a student in high school walking his girlfriend home from the movies. He testified as a state witness in the 1995 and 2002 trials that he had seen the boys hitchhiking on the night they disappeared. Helms is now a police investigator for the Metropolitan Water Reclamation District of Greater Chicago. He lives in the western suburbs with his family.

State's Witness Hetty Salerno was a prosecution witness during the 1995 and 2002 trials. She currently lives in Arizona.

State's Witness William "Red" Wemette was a witness for the state during the 1995 and 2002 trials. Wemette worked as an FBI informant.

State's Witness Roger Spry was a witness for the state during the 1995 and 2002 trials. He lived on and off with Kenneth Hansen for 20 years. He is currently 53 years old.

State's Witness Joe Plemmons was a witness for the state during the 1995 and 2002 trials. He is currently 53 years old. He is still in the horse business.

State's Witness Herbert Hollatz was a witness for the state during the 1995 and 2002 trials. He became friends with Hansen in 1952 and met him again in 1955. Hansen confided in Hollatz that he had killed the boys one week after the murder. He currently lives in the western part of the United States.

Silas Jayne was the owner of the Idle Hour Stables. He was convicted of conspiring to have his brother, George Jayne, killed and served six years in prison. He was paroled in May 1979 and died from leukemia at the age of 80 in July 1987.

Kenneth Hansen was convicted in September 1995 of the murders of Robert Peterson and John and Anton Schuessler, Jr. He was sentenced to 200-300 years in Pontiac State Prison. In 2000, the Illinois Appellate Court overturned his conviction and ordered a new trial. Hansen was re-tried and convicted again in August 2002 and sentenced to 200-300 years in prison. He is serving his term in Pontiac State Prison.

I wasn't even born on the night Robert, John, and Anton lost their lives. Nor was I in Chicago when the sensational trials of Kenneth Hansen occurred. I learned the story of the Peterson-Schuessler murders by chance. A business acquaintance contacted me saying that she had just read 100 pages of a very heartbreaking memoir. She explained that it was written by a former police detective, and he was seeking guidance to get his book published. I have to say that from the first time I spoke with Mr. Jack, and heard his incredible story, I knew I had to publish it.

Each day, we hear stories of children being preyed on by monsters who do not seem to understand the boundaries of normal sexual behavior. More than fifty years ago, we were sent a warning. As State's Attorney Scott Cassidy said in his trial summation in 1995, "Those boys were trailblazers of sorts...trailblazers in a sad sort of way. The path that they took, they did not choose." Yet, that path gave us a glimpse of the problem we were facing. And it was our duty to act on that knowledge and learn from this heinous crime. Instead, we did nothing. With each passing year, the problem of pedophilia grows in magnitude. Now, with the aid of technology, all children are at risk. Isn't it time we stopped turning a blind eye and thinking, "this will never happen to my children," and find better ways to protect all children.

During the funeral for John and Anton Schuessler, the Archbishop of Chicago, Cardinal Francis Stritch, sent a note saying: "I beg almighty God and pray that out of this tragedy will come a better public consensus for the protection of our youth." Isn't it time we answered his prayer?

Franchee D. Harmon
Editor-in-Chief

About 8:55 p.m. on Sunday October 16, 1955, while hitchhiking a ride home in the rain, Robert, John, and Anton walked into a trap from which they were unable to extricate themselves. We ask ourselves the question over and over why intelligent children find themselves in situations of harm. But really the answer to that is not hard to understand, because they did exactly what you or I might have done at that age under those circumstances. They completely trusted a friendly, young man who offered them a ride in the rain. He baited the trap and then snapped it shut. They took that fateful ride with that "animal" Hansen to the Idle Hour Stables. This sexual predator then strangled to death all three boys. No one can replace the lives lost; the families will grieve forever. The boys never experienced high school proms or college, took the vows "I do" or had children. Instead Robert, John, and Anton will remain forever young in our hearts. My hope is that this story helps prevent other children from falling prey to such animals.

James A. Jack

Acknowledgements

How do you say "thank you" to so many who have helped so much? Each of your contributions has been indispensable, and I am sincerely grateful for your help. I did my best to include everyone who assisted in making my book work, and I sincerely regret if I omitted anyone.

I would like to begin by saying this book would not have been possible without the contribution from members of the Chicago Police Department, County, State, and Federal law enforcement agencies throughout the U.S.

I wish to extend my gratitude to the greatest group of Chicago Police officers assembled—the Special Investigating Unit (SIU) task force: Jack (John) Killackey, John Neurauter, Michael Spiotto, Pat Deeley, Russell Corcoran, Joe Morris, Tom Mulvey, James McMahon, Bill Duffy, Michael Delaney, John Konen, Fred Koeppe, Frank Schulze, Valentine Ridge, John Sarnowski, Ed Kacinski, James Wuff, James Fitzgerald, John Hartigan, Pat Groark, Walter McTigue, Al O'Neil, Jimmy Lanners, Alice McCarthy, Antoinette (Toni) Quinn, George Lundt, Jim Kelly, Mike Ricci, Charles Rizzo, George Murphy, and my partner, mentor, and best friend Frank Czech.

I also wish to acknowledge many, many other colleagues especially the Chicago Crime Detection Laboratory for their assistance at the "drop-of-a-dime:" Director Lt. John Ascher, polygraph examiners—Walter Gehr, Edward Walsh and James Doheny. I thank you.

Special thanks to my editor/publisher Franchee Harmon and assistants Mary Runkle and Derrick Hill at HPH Publishing for their continued support, respect and faith in my project. I'm lucky to have her guidance, advice, editorial ideas, and support. Furthermore, she is a pleasure to work with.

I will forever by grateful to my doctors, David Guthman, Edward Pinsel, Steven Leibach, Rollo Nesset and Scott Glazer. Thank you for many kindnesses. Also, I would like to thank your wonderful assistants: Sue and Nina.

I would like to thank Sandra Sugg, Danielle Lendino, and Scherron Johnson for their transcription services. Thanks Marilyn

Kramer for your meticulous editing.

My heartfelt thanks to all of my friends of the news media in newspaper, radio and television: Bob Herguth and Rummana Hussain, Chicago Sun-Times; Trina Higgins, manager, Public Information Bureau and Ron Theel—who have the best photo library around—Chicago Sun-Times; Steve Miller, WBBM news reporter; Carlos Sadovi, Chicago Tribune; also my dear departed friend Art Petacque, Chicago Sun-Times; Edmund Rooney and Buddy McHugh, Chicago Daily News; Anne Lunde, managing editor, and Alan Schmidt, Pioneer Press; and Mike West, Kurtis Production LTD.

I owe more thanks to Gary and Phil O'Brill, Rich, Mike and Ken Stobart, and last but certainly not least, I must acknowledge Christine Arendarczyk of K& M Printing Company.

I wish to thank all the wonderful people who agreed to speak with me informally—jurors in the second trial—Bob Ownes and Mario Caballero. Peter Cirelli of Barrington Feed, thanks for the information you supplied for my project. Dick Kuna, I really needed your knowledge. Edward Dubowski, Fire Chief for the city of Park Ridge, thanks for your help. John Dineen, Chicago Police Department, Fraternal Order of Police Past President, I won't forget your help. My deep gratitude to my friend Dave Gilbert, President Clear Blue, and many thanks Steve Crews.

James McGuire thanks for your photography.

I am particularly grateful for assistance and research provided by Barbara Royce and Barbara Wiedlin of the Palatine Library.

To Jeff Lewis and Becky Jackson who made the book happen. Your computer genius along with your exceptional knowledge and the long hours you committed to this project can be found on each of its pages.

My acknowledgement would not be complete without a special show of gratitude to my legal team of John Doherty and Mike Goldstein. Thank you for everything.

A special thanks to my favorite restaurants and their owners: Lorenzo and Rose at Nanna's Cucina Deli; Ann and Patti at Pomigliano Italian Meals; and I could not forget Peter O'Brien at

O'Brien's Restaurant.

My special thanks to Raymond Benson for your relentless help and advice.

I will forever to grateful to you, Scott Cassidy, Thomas Biesty, Linos Kelecius, and Jennifer Coleman from the Cook County State's Attorneys office—who prosecuted the second trial. They were at their best while giving their summation. I am also indebted to Pat Quinn who, along with Scott Cassidy, led the prosecution for the State's Attorneys office during the first trial. They pounded away at the facts. You guys are the greatest.

I wish to extend my gratitude to both judges, Michael Toomin and Mary Ellen Coghlan of the Cook County Circuit Court, for their professionalism during trials one and two.

Finally, I owe my greatest debt of gratitude to my family from bottom to top for tolerating me and the stress of doing this book. You were always there no matter what. Without your support, faith, and confidence, throughout the years, I couldn't have completed the project.

Index